Family Economic Behavior:
Problems and Prospects

Contributors

Gwen J. Bymers, Ph.D.
Chairman, Department of Consumer Economics and Public Policy
New York State College of Human Ecology
Cornell University

Richard A. Easterlin, Ph.D.
Professor of Economics
University of Pennsylvania

Marcus Felson
Doctoral Candidate
Department of Sociology
University of Michigan

Robert Ferber, Ph.D.
Professor of Economics;
Director of Survey Research Laboratory
University of Illinois

Reuben Hill, Ph.D.
Professor of Sociology;
Program Director
Minnesota Family Study Center
University of Minnesota

Allen C. Kelley, Ph.D.
Professor of Economics
Duke University

David M. Klein
Graduate Student
Department of Sociology
University of Minnesota;
Research Assistant
Minnesota Family Study Center

E. Scott Maynes, Ph.D.
Professor of Economics
University of Minnesota

Martin Pfaff, Ph.D.
Professor of Economics
Wayne State University; and
University of Augsburg

A. Marshall Puckett
Economist;
Assistant Vice President
Research and Statistics Function
Federal Reserve Bank of New York

Francis H. Schott, Ph.D.
Vice President and Economist
The Equitable Life Assurance Society of the United States;
Adjunct Professor of Economics,
Baruch College
City University of New York

Robert A. Scott, Ph.D.
Associate Professor of Sociology
Princeton University

David R. Segal, Ph.D.
Associate Professor of Sociology
University of Michigan

Eleanor Bernert Sheldon, Ph.D.
President
Social Science Research Council
New York. New York

Arnold R. Shore, Ph.D.
Research Coordinator
Negative Income Tax Experiment
MATHEMATICA, Inc.

Burkhard Strumpel, Ph.D.
Program Director
Institute for Social Research;
Associate Professor of Economics
University of Michigan

Helen M. Thal, Ed.D.
Director, Education Services
Institute of Life Insurance

FAMILY ECONOMIC BEHAVIOR

Problems and Prospects

edited by

Eleanor Bernert Sheldon

From a conference on Social Structure, Family Life Styles, and Economic Behavior, sponsored by the Institute of Life Insurance at Williamsburg, Virginia
January 1972

J. B. Lippincott Company

Philadelphia   Toronto

Copyright © 1973 by J. B. Lippincott Company
This book is fully protected by copyright and, with the exception of brief excerpts for review, no part of it may be reproduced in any form by print, photoprint, microfilm, or any other means without written permission from the publisher.
ISBN 0-397-59058-X
Library of Congress Catalog Card Number 73-10458
SP-B
Printed in the United States of America
1 3 4 2

Library of Congress Cataloging in Publication Data
Main entry under title:

Family economic behavior.

"From a conference on social structure, family life styles, and economic behavior, sponsored by the Institute of Life Insurance at Williamsburg, Virginia, January 1972."

Includes bibliographies.

1. Sheldon, Eleanor Harriet (Bernert) 1920– ed. II. Institute of Life Insurance, New York.
HC110.C6F3   301.5'1   73-10458
ISBN 0-397-59058-X

For
Margaret Jarman Hagood
1907-1963

Foreword

The life- and health insurance business, perhaps to an extent greater than other industries, has a stake in the stability of the family as an economic and social institution. No other service or product serves the individual family in quite the same way as does the life insurance contract. The financial services offered by life insurance companies play a significant role in maintaining the family at critical times.

The Institute of Life Insurance is charged with two responsibilities:

1. To communicate to the nation's families basic information about the life insurance business and its services
2. To communicate to the business data that accurately measures attitudes and opinions prevalent in the society and having a bearing on life insurance company practices and services

In carrying out these responsibilities, the Institute staff is a heavy user of research as well as a supplier of data related to social and economic issues, to family behavior, and to consumer needs and demands.

Over the years, as we searched for information about families and their economic behavior, we were frequently led back to the Consumer Behavior Studies of the 1950s. With *Household Decision-Making,* edited by Nelson N. Foote and published in 1961, that series ended, and by the end of the decade there existed a paucity of scholarly research related to the economics of the family. This led us to explore the problem with scholars and researchers throughout the country, and it was suggested that it might be appropriate for the Institute of Life Insurance to bring together research scholars from several disciplines in an attempt to stimulate new research and open new ways of communicating what was already known. It was our hope that studies in family economic behavior might ultimately find a logical place in the literature of the family.

The Institute's response to this general idea emerged gradually. First, we organized the Family Economics Studies Program as an in-house activity. It became apparent that we needed to be in close communication with the university community, and this could be facilitated only if we had a consultant well respected by his professional colleagues and at the same time sympathetic to our aims and purposes. We needed one conversant in economics and sociology and whose own scholarly research was recognized and highly regarded. Thus, we invited Albert I. Hermalin, research associate of the Population Studies Center at the University of Michigan and an assistant professor of sociology there, to join us as consultant and adviser. Dr. Hermalin formerly had been on the Institute staff as associate director of statistics and research.

Finally, the Family Economics Studies Program focused on a conference, and Williamsburg was the result.

At the time the program was evolving, the planners identified four objectives:

1. To contribute to an improved theoretical framework for studying the economic and related behavior of families
2. To point up areas of needed research
3. To provide examples of stimulating studies
4. To demonstrate the dimensions of the field and imaginative approaches for studying it

We knew at the outset that one conference couldn't deal with all the issues that relate to economic behavior in the 1970s, but we hoped that the Williamsburg Conference would be a firm beginning. During the 18 months of planning we gained confidence and were encouraged by the group of scholars who agreed to take part in the project. We were encouraged also by the interest expressed by many in the academic community as word of our project reached them.

The planners set about identifying scholars then engaged in research who, it was believed, would help achieve the four objectives. The first step, it seemed, was to commission a paper to review the state of the art, so to speak, to create a setting within which the conference could be structured. Professor Robert Ferber accepted this assignment. Prevalent attitudes and forces in society suggested themes to be dealt with in their relation to the economic functioning of the family: decisions in family size, social stratification, pressures for welfare reform, and consumerism. Finally, we decided it would be useful to look at family economic behavior from the viewpoint of subjective attitudes and values concerning life-styles, and from the more detached vantage of the financial institution.

It is not for us to say whether the four objectives have been achieved. The contribution of Reuben Hill and David M. Klein, however, is a comprehensive summary of the conference, bringing into focus the theoretical and research implications of the papers presented and the discussions that followed.

The Family Economics Studies Program, the Williamsburg Conference, and this volume would not have been possible without the support and interest of leaders in the life insurance business as expressed through the action of the Board of Directors of the Institute of Life Insurance and the creative and imaginative leadership of its president, Blake T. Newton, Jr. We wish to acknowledge also the extraordinary counsel of Albert Hermalin, who helped to forge the conference; the supportive assistance of Reuben Hill; and the scholarly excellence of Eleanor Bernert Sheldon, who joined us as participant and later as editor. Speaking for myself, I must thank William E. Kingsley and Robert A. Driscoll, my Institute colleagues, whose management skills and other talents helped further this effort. I also thank Anne M. Daly, who was the Institute person responsible for the production of the manuscript.

The Williamsburg Conference made apparent, as Reuben Hill says, that communication across the disciplines is easier to discuss than to accomplish. We believe it is worth the continuing effort, and we are pleased to have made the first step.

Helen M. Thal, Director
Education Services
Institute of Life Insurance

Preface

For longer than we would like to contemplate, social scientists, among others, have sought to understand family economic behavior. Explanatory theories and research have ranged from a concern with more strictly economic variables (e.g., family income) to models of household decision-making (e.g., family-life cycle) and social-psychological propensities to consume and to save (e.g., motivations, expectations, values). Usually affiliated with each theory is a distinct disciplinary approach: that of the economist, or the sociologist, or the psychologist. For the past 15 or 20 years there have been self-conscious, though intermittent, efforts to fuse disciplinary lines and bodies of knowledge and thereby to develop more appropriate frameworks in examining the variance in earning, consumption, and savings behavior [1]. This volume is another effort to extend the range of such cross-disciplinary considerations.

In their opening statement, Hill and Klein emphasize that this assemblage of persons, papers and discussions did little to further interdisciplinary communication, though their concluding chapter suggests a theoretical synthesis and research agenda. This latter statement, in and of itself, contributes to the long-term effort for a more comprehensive approach to studying family economic behavior.

Plan of the volume

In concert, the papers and discussions that comprise this volume address the complex problem of how and why families earn, spend, and save. The dynamics of family economic behavior (Ferber), the relation of family size to family economic behavior (Easterlin), social stratification and family economic behavior (Segal and Felson), life-styles and values (Strumpel), guaranteed income, work response, and family composition (Shore and Scott), consumerism (Maynes), and financial management (Schott) exemplify the breadth and multidimensionality of the simply stated problem.

The threads loosely linking these dimensions are provided by Hill and Klein who introduce the reader to each major paper and discussion. They present an outline of the theory-relevant purposes and stated or inferred empirical generalizations for each section. In anticipation of these Hill-Klein contributions, we include here their scheme relating the theoretical and empirical summarizations.

> We distinguish three types of theoretical enterprise. *Description* refers to the specification and clarification of concepts and the identification of antecedent variables and consequences. *Explanation* refers to the specification of the causal relationships among concepts or variables, and may take either of two forms. *Historical explanation* refers to the linking of time- and space-bound antecedents of particular events to statements about those events. *Deductive explanation* refers to the linking of observations to abstract statements in the form of recurring probabilities or general laws. Description, historical explanation, and deductive explanation can be viewed as sequential steps or stages in theory building. The systematic theorist identifies or constructs his parameters, observes empirical phenomena, and tests relationships among them or adapts the observations and tests of other scientists, and fits his data into an abstract and logic-deductive system. (We readily admit that stating it this way oversimplifies the theory generation and verification process. Here we interpret "fitting the data" loosely so that it incorporates both *a priori* and inductively formulated theories.) In our own field, family sociology, it is often lamented that the development of theory is stalled at the first or second stage.
>
> We also make distinctions among the modes of expression that theories utilize. Perhaps the most common is conventional language, which is simply the normal prose style of verbalization. In contrast is the formalized language of symbolic logic or mathematics. There are several alternative formal modes of expression. Examples include mathematical models with structural equations, the axiomatic format, conceptual models employing causal diagrams or linear graphs, taxonomic tables, and property-space matrices. In practice these communication devices are not mutually exclusive.
>
> Within the social sciences there is a strong movement to transform the conventional language of theory into the more sophisticated kinds of formalized language. The exponents of this movement usually argue that the long-standing problems of vagueness and ambiguity inherent in conventional language can thereby be overcome. The limits of the utility of this proposal are subject to controversy, however, and each alternative mode of formalized expression has its advocates as well. It seems fair to conclude that economics is "ahead" of her sister disciplines in the adoption of mathematical models.
>
> The question we address is, "Which type of theoretical enterprise is undertaken by each of the major presentations at the conference, and which modes of expression are used?" Although some formalized modes of expression are often used as visual aids for presenting data, we wish to examine here only their use as theory systematization devices. In addition we will attempt to identify the dependent and independent variables employed and will construct empirical generalizations (symbolized "EG") that summarize the research findings reported.
>
> Many additional, more specific propositions and hypotheses will no doubt come to the reader's attention as he surveys the papers. Our hope is that a large majority of these concrete statements can be derived deductively

from our higher-order empirical generalizations. By concentrating on *empirical* generalizations, we hope to cover the context and content of theory beyond the basic underlying assumptions. In any case, responsibility for the empirical generalizations is our own, including any errors of commission or omission.

As I am a demographic-sociologist, not a family sociologist, nor an economist, nor a psychologist, my role in the planning, conduct and production of this conference volume has been peripheral. From the periphery, however, I have been exposed to the ferment and intellectual excitement of the contributing scholars and bodies of knowledge and understandings that promise to transcend the current disparateness in the field, "family economic behavior." It has been an instructive experience.

I am particularly grateful to Reuben Hill and his associate, David Klein, for a first-rate education in family sociology and for performing the editor's task of integrating the conference materials and culling from them a theoretical synthesis and research agenda. I am indebted to Dr. Helen Thal and the Institute of Life Insurance for initiating and sponsoring the conference and for inviting me to participate. If credit is to be granted for the success of the endeavor it belongs to Reuben Hill and Albert Hermalin. Responsibility for the shortcomings of the volume is mine.

Eleanor Bernert Sheldon
President
Social Science Research Council

1. Foote, Nelson N., (ed.) *Household Decision Making.* New York: New York University Press, 1961.

Contents

1 Understanding Family Consumption: Common Ground for Integrating Uncommon Disciplinary Perspectives · *Reuben Hill and David Klein* 1

2 Family Decision Making and Economic Behavior: A Review
Introduction · *Reuben Hill and David Klein* 25
Family Decision Making and Economic Behavior: A Review · *Robert Ferber* 29

3 Economic Life-Styles, Values, and Subjective Welfare—An Empirical Approach
Introduction · *Reuben Hill and David Klein* 65
Economic Life-Styles, Values, and Subjective Welfare—An Empirical Approach ·
Burkhard Strumpel 69
A Response · *Martin Pfaff* 126

4 Social Stratification and Family Economic Behavior
Introduction · *Reuben Hill and David Klein* 141
Social Stratification and Family Economic Behavior · *David R. Segal and Marcus Felson* 143

5 Relative Economic Status and the American Fertility Swing
Introduction · *Reuben Hill and David Klein* 167
Relative Economic Status and the American Fertility Swing
Richard A. Easterlin 170
A Response · *Allen C. Kelley* 224

6 Work Response and Family Composition Changes in a Negative Income Tax Experiment: Preliminary Mid-Experiment Results
Introduction · *Reuben Hill and David Klein* 231
Work Response and Family Composition Changes in a Negative Income Tax Experiment: Preliminary Mid-Experiment Results · *Arnold R. Shore, Robert A. Scott* 233

7 Consumerism: Origin and Research Implications
   Introduction · *Reuben Hill and David Klein* 267
   Consumerism: Origin and Research Implications ·
   E. Scott Maynes 270
   A Response · *Gwen J. Bymers* 295

8 Consumer Financial Management and Financial Institution Response—A Two-Decade Perspective
   Introduction · *Reuben Hill and David Klein* 307
   Consumer Financial Management and Financial Institution Response—A Two-Decade Perspective ·
   Francis H. Schott 311
   A Response · *A. Marshall Puckett* 363

9 Toward a Research Agenda and Theoretical Synthesis ·
   Reuben Hill and David Klein 371

   List of Attendance 405

   Index 413

1

Understanding Family Consumption:

COMMON GROUND FOR INTEGRATING
UNCOMMON DISCIPLINARY PERSPECTIVES

Understanding Family Consumption: Common Ground for Integrating Uncommon Disciplinary Perspectives

By Reuben Hill and David M. Klein

The Williamsburg Conference was a disturbing, disconcerting, disillusioning, but intellectually challenging happening. Participants at the conference belonged to different disciplines in the social sciences. These participants supported their own individual disciplines, and had few overlapping interests and different imputations of meanings for concepts describing these interests. There is as yet no common interdisciplinary vocabulary of concepts about the issues of family consumption.

Interdisciplinary seminars on issues of family consumption should probably be held more frequently than once a decade, if only to end the complacency of the different members and to reduce their insulation from one another. We need to begin the work of building interdisciplinary concepts to improve our communication. A major task of this first section of *Family Economic Behavior: Problems and Prospects* is to render visible some of the failure of communication, the dissonance, and challenge which occurred as the members of the conference discussed their differing attitudes about crucial issues of family consumption.

In preparing our overview, and also Section 9, "Toward a Research Agenda," we had available the seven conference papers and various critiques by discussants, detailed notes of rapporteurs for each session, written commentaries of participants who took the floor, and transcripts of exchanges among conferees after each presentation.

From these sources we have attempted to identify the theoretical and methodological issues treated as well as the issues not yet researched but rendered salient by several participants. We have tried to present the diverse and common universes of discourse among disciplines, including the basic assumptions about the nature of man and the family as passive reactors or as style makers and initiators, and we have indicated some of the conceptual problems interfering with communication among the disciplines represented at the conference. We have sought to identify the several key phenomena (dependent variables) which are to be explained by the disciplines and have noted some shifts as to what is *determinant* and *consequent* from discipline to discipline.

We have examined several different theoretical models advanced by participants to encompass the wide range of phenomena in interaction within the scope of the conference theme: social structure, family life styles, and economic behavior. And finally, both here and in Section 9, we have pointed out and grouped several dozen research ideas highlighting needed research to increase understanding of consumption. These are the diverse materials from which we endeavored to construct an overview, if not an integration, of family consumption in the 1970s.

The authors of this section are not without conceptual preferences for viewing the consumption process. We are family sociologists whose basic training has been in sociology and social psychology. The family is our preferred point of reference for viewing the major social processes of the society and the economy. We think research and theory on consumer behavior made a significant advance when it disaggregated macrodata from the level of the economy to the level of the family, and that consumer theory took a step forward when, as James Morgan suggests, it substituted for bachelor economics a family theory of consumption. We see the family as the optimum unit of study precisely because (1) the family is the accumulating unit, the inventory of acquisitions over time being a nuclear family inventory; (2) the nuclear family is the decision-making unit in asset accumulation and consumption; (3) the nuclear family is more accessible for study than its competitors and more easily definable for purposes of study than is the household, which may include lodgers who have little part in family acquisitions.

The Interdisciplinary Challenge in Social Science

In sponsoring this symposium, the Institute of Life Insurance clothed its objectives in a forward-reaching perspective. Its staff envisioned that the exchange of ideas would point to research topics and research strategies deserving further attention and having applications in the real world of managing family resources. Within this framework it seems less important that the ideas exchanged be evaluated as facts or scientific laws, and more important that they be interpreted as stimuli for generating further work. With this in mind we wish first to describe the conference itself.

Composition of the Conference

Table 1 provides a frequency distribution of the professional affiliations of the conferees. It indicates that virtually two-thirds were directly affiliated with institutions of higher learning, and they were representatives of disciplines with a natural interest in family-consumption behavior. In addition to this concentration in academia, another noticeable characteristic of the composition of the conference is the wide range of representation by organizations that have an "applied" orientation. Given this particular distribution of attendees and a knowledge of the intended purposes of the conference, one might estimate the expectations of the audience as well as the directions the conference might take.

TABLE 1. PRIMARY PROFESSIONAL AFFILIATIONS OF CONFEREES

Professional Area	Number	Per Cent
College or University Staff		
Home Economics and Family Economics Management	33	27.7
Sociology	18	15.1
Economics and Consumer Economics	12	10.1
Family Studies, Family Social Science, Child Development, and Family Relations	7	5.9
Psychology and Social Psychology	4	3.4
Business Administration	2	1.7
College Administration	2	1.7
Public and International Relations	1	0.8
Total College or University Staff	79	66.4
Life Insurance Organizations (includes social scientists in research, education, information, and public relations divisions)	13	10.9
Foundations and Research Centers	8	6.7
Family and Consumer Service Agencies	7	5.9
Government (all levels)	6	5.0
Church Organizations	3	2.5
Federal Reserve Banks (research function)	1	0.8
Other	2	1.7
Total	119	99.9

Note: Since Table 1 is based on employment data, it does not necessarily reflect the academic training of attendees, especially those employed outside colleges and universities.

By way of comparison, Table 2 indicates the primary affiliations of the major participants. Authors and presenters of papers, formal discussants, and rapporteurs are included as major discussants. The rapporteur for each session was charged with the responsibility of identifying and recording the communication problems and interdisciplinary challenges initiated from the floor. Although their voices were not necessarily heard by the conference audience, the rapporteurs' summaries and perspectives are included in this overview. Table 2 also gives a rough approximation of the

TABLE 2. PRIMARY PROFESSIONAL AFFILIATION OF MAJOR PARTICIPANTS

Professional Affiliation	Participation Roles			
	Authors of Papers	Assigned Discussants	Rapporteurs	Totals
Economics	5	5	2	12
Sociology	5	1	3	9[a]
Psychology and Social Psychology	0	1	2	3
Totals	10	7	7	24

[a] One sociologist served both as co-author of a presentation and as rapporteur for another presentation; he is counted twice.

Note: Six participants identified by professional area in Table 1 are categorized here by the discipline in which they have received their highest training. Four are employed by life insurance organizations, one by a research foundation, and one by a federal reserve bank. Three of these six are listed as economists, one as a sociologist, and two as psychologists or social psychologists. According to the categories listed in Table 1, 17 of the 24 major participants are academic economists or sociologists.

comparative inputs to the conference made by the various social sciences.

Admittedly deficient in several respects, Table 2 does not measure the quality of contributions made by the disciplines represented. It does not identify the affiliations of the originators of the many stimulating comments and questions during the open discussions. In a real sense they should be characterized as major participants as well.[1] Finally, Table 2 fails to capture the many informal conversations that took place outside the conference hall, some of which must surely qualify as pertinent and thought provoking. In sum, it seems clear that economists and sociologists emerge as the most active group of participants, respectively, with a small minority representation provided by psychologists and social psychologists.

While other inferences might be drawn from an examination of Tables 1 and 2, our purpose is to demonstrate that the flavor and direction of this or any other interdisciplinary symposium in part depends on the particular combination of talents and resources assembled. The Williamsburg Conference drew on a pool of widely ranging interest groups for its attendees and brought to the rostrum professionals possessing distinctive lenses from which to view the world of the consumer. Any evaluation of the communication process displayed here should be interpreted within this context.

Communicating Across and Within Disciplines

Jagdish Sheth, a University of Illinois consumer psychologist, suggests that family members may bring different "cognitive worlds" to bear on the consumer decision-making process. Is this assertion equally plausible with respect to the "family" of social scientists? When economists, sociologists, psychologists, and other social scientists sit at the same conference table, their differing vantage points (or differing family roles, to carry the analogy further) appear to engender communication problems.

To take a different tack, Scott Maynes in his presentation suggested that misinformation in the marketplace is in part a function of the specialization of seller functions. Since social scientists are both consumers and sellers of ideas, the Maynes analogy may be heuristically appropriate for understanding the barriers to communication across disciplines.

We wish to focus the remainder of this section on the failure of communication as it arises from two sources:

1. Conceptual traditions. Failure of communication may occur because concepts are not explicity defined, because one label is attached to more than one definition, or because more than one label is attached to a single definition.
2. Underlying assumptions. Failure of communication may occur because basic assumptions are not explicitly expressed, or when expressed are so contradictory to the receiver's basic assumptions that they are handled with typical techniques for resolving the dissonance.

We will examine, in turn, the most critical conceptual and assumptive communication problems that emerged during the symposium.

Confrontations Generated by Differences in Concepts

1. *What are the conceptual boundaries of consumer behavior?*—Robert Ferber suggested that consumer behavior includes the actions that consumers take. He offered a useful taxonomy of financial behavior that includes money management, spending behavior, saving behavior, and asset management. To what extent are these financial behaviors consumer behaviors? Is a decision to save also a decision to consume or not to consume? Furthermore, to what extent can nonfinancial decisions and actions be considered consumer behavior?

Fertility may restrict consumption alternatives and be associated with relative economic status, as Richard Easterlin suggested, but is reproductive behavior a consumption act? Do we purchase our children in the same sense that we purchase other goods and services? Perhaps we only take out a long-term renewable lease on our progeny. We might profit here by reinventing the familiar distinction between consumption and production. In any case, it seems clear that the conference moved beyond the traditional limits of consumption at the points where subjective welfare (Strumpel), fertility (Easterlin), and work incentive (Shore-Scott) became the topics of attention.

On other occasions the conference concentrated on issues that can be reasonably considered subcategories of consumer behavior. A question might be raised, for example, about the relationship between consumer behavior or consumership and the ideology of consumer welfare or consumerism. Scott Maynes emphasized the rational process of looking for and demanding the highest quality product at the single lowest price. Gwen Bymers preferred to define consumerism in terms of the rising level of expectations and public awareness about problems and issues in the public sector of the economy, and she thought this definition makes one less pessimistic about the effectiveness of consumer markets. Francis Schott viewed consumerism as rational adjustment to available choices and saw consumers putting pressure on the economic system if it does not respond.

To the extent that consumption is a process, what phases of the process have been identified? Generally speaking, the conferees highlighted decision making, the purchase and consumption acts, and evaluative responses in terms of satisfaction or dissatisfaction as the crucial phases. There was much concern that we know too little about the end points of this process. More will be said about this concern later. At this point it is sufficient to notice that the rigor of conceptual clarity demands that each phase be distinguished insofar as it is thought to be a useful conceptual tool.

The responsibility for clarifying the boundaries and dimensions of consumption does not fall on any one discipline, of course, but it does seem clear from the widely ranging presentations at this conference that there is as yet no unified conceptual framework from which to view the phenomena to be explained.

2. *What is the appropriate behaving unit for examining consumption?* —This remains a key issue on which disciplines are divided. Quite naturally, the psychologist tends to see the individual as the appropriate unit of analysis for studying human behavior. Elizabeth Douvan offered the stimulating suggestion that distinctive personality types might exist with respect to style of economic response. The importance of the family as a socialization agent in this context was dutifully recognized. In contrast, the economist and the demographer have traditionally approached the behaving unit from the aggregate level, seeking to differentiate consumption patterns by fairly broad socioeconomic categories. A noticeable exception might be the consumer advocate-economist, exemplified by Maynes, who appeared to be more concerned with individual choice and individual welfare than his macroeconomist colleagues. The sociologist, also distinctly, occupies an even less homogeneous position on this matter than most of his social science siblings, ranging from one extreme to the other of the macro-microanalytic continuum. At this symposium the voice of the family sociologist was often heard, and since this is our own perspective, we prefer to see the family unit as the deciding, behaving, and evaluating unit.

The behaving units for the seven major presentations can be summarized briefly as follows:

Behaving Unit

Ferber	family (internal dynamics of)
Strumpel	household (head of; by socioeconomic category)
Segal-Felson	household (head of; by socioeconomic category)
Easterlin	young adult (relative economic status of male, fertility of female; aggregated)
Shore-Scott	family
Maynes	individual
Schott	household (aggregated)

The behaving unit presents a potential communication problem when work at one level is translated into insights at another level. When a researcher reports his findings, his audience must not only know whether the consumer studied is the individual, the household, the family, or some other unit, but the listener or reader must also be able to correlate the implications from the unit studied to the unit of his own preference. We are not suggesting, then, that one particular behaving unit is better for all purposes than any other unit, but that a need exists for the conceptual apparatus that would permit us to bridge the various levels [2][9].

3. *What is the relevance of the concept of "time" for consumer behavior analysis?*—Perhaps no other single concept so tenaciously occupied the attention of the conferees as the concept of "time." It was repeatedly emphasized by many that our understanding of family consumption can not go very far until time-series data have been accumulated. It was not always clear, however, what such data would be expected to provide. Repeated measures of crucial variables with successive cohorts might be useful for establishing historical trends. Equally important, however, might be the measurement of *developmental time*. Ferber and Guy Orcutt appeared to have had this latter approach in mind when they alerted the conference to the utility of panel studies, which of course involve repeated measures for the same cohort. In the context of the family, developmental time can be broken into meaningful categories by "stages of the family life cycle" which have already received extended treatment in the sociological literature of the family [3, 4].

Apart from the methodological uses of "time," there are several other useful ways in which it can be conceptualized. A sampler of these from the conference is provided below.

Time sequences: We need to understand better the stages of the decision-making process, the conditions under which steps such as preplanning or plan-fulfillment are left out, and the conditions under which steps are reversed so that consumer choices precede the rationalizations for them (Ferber, Foote).

Time horizons: We need to distinguish between long-term and short-term goals and expectations (Juster, Nayar). The long-term effects of a negative tax experiment are crucial for policy evaluation (Felson, Morgan, Moss). The future orientations of our respondents are crucial for assessing financial decisions (Ferber), differences of life-style (Segal-Felson), and patterns of asset management (Schott). Future orientation is only one aspect of fate-control (Strumpel).

Time duration: Time can be conceptualized as duration (Bymers). Learned habit patterns may contribute to inertia or resistance to rational change (Morgan, Ferber), or to lagging adjustment to new opportunities (Katona, Puckett).

Time resources: Time can be conceptualized as a resource, but only if it is available and valuable (Maynes, Bymers). Time past, to the extent that it bears relevant experiences, can be a resource for current consumer behavior (implicit in all major presentations).

Time costs: There are pragmatic limits on the allocation of time (Juster). There is a time drain in the mere maintenance of durables and utilization of nondurables and services (Lindsay), which may vary inversely with social class (Ferber). The value of time is increasing relative to its availability so that the expenditure of a unit of time is becoming more costly (Segal). The information search involved in selecting products for purchase is an expenditure (Maynes). Time is a constraint in the sense that there are limits on one's ability to predict the future (Pfaff).

Many of these theoretical uses of "time" have strong implications that go beyond the criterion of conceptual clarity for purposes of communication. Some of the comments suggested assumptions, others were almost testable hypotheses. Our hope is that by debating and explicating its various dimensions, this conference has helped develop the backdrop for future work which must cope with the concept of "time."

4. *What dispositional constructs are useful for analyzing consumer behavior?*—One of the outstanding features or themes of the conference was its repeated imputation of what we will call dispositional constructs. We take a dispositional construct generically to mean a tendency to act or an intervening variable that is a mental state or that contributes directly to a mental state [3] [6, 8].

The dispositional constructs which received the bulk of attention at the conference were achievement motivation, aspirations, attitudes, expectations, felt needs, goals, interests, perceptions, preferences, self-esteem, tastes, values, and wants. For the most part these constructs are linguistic tools of the psychologist. From the standpoint of communication, the conferees were able to recognize these dispositional constructs as important for explaining consumer behavior, but were less successful in explicitly defining and interrelating them. The one notable exception was Burkhard Strumpel, who offered definitions of values and aspirations and made them operational in his study.

The conferees seemed to share a sense of frustration over the meaning and utility of these various concepts. Norman Ryder, for example, saw a tendency for economists to employ "tastes" as a "grand residual." Gordon Bivens suggested that we need to involve others, especially philosophers, in the study of values and formation of values. We would add that psychologists can also aid significantly in sharpening our concepts in this general area.

5. *What are the appropriate contextual social categories for analyzing the constraints on consumer behavior?*—Social categories are useful for classifying the social placement of respondents and for comparing behavioral outcomes among groups. Even within the discipline of sociology, however, there is little consensus about which set of categories is most appropriate or which indicators are most adequate for capturing those categories. It is not surprising, therefore, that the conference produced a confrontation in this conceptual area.

In the presentations there was heavy reliance on the more traditional indicators of socioeconomic status: income, education, occupation, and ethnic origin. Other social categories were less frequently employed, such as age, duration of marriage, and gender, and they apppeared useful particularly with respect to decision-making processes. Bymers, reacting to Strumpel's presentation, was quick to caution that we need to consider categories besides income and occupation when we place families in social context. Douvan warned that there are "many routes to honor," suggesting the importance of subjective aspects in the amorphous variable of social status. By turning to the role of reference groups and identification of social class at several points, the conference became sensitized to the complex nature of social placement.

Even if nothing else was accomplished in this area, it can be said with certainty that conferees came away assured that measures of levels of living must go beyond inventories of durable products or income levels to have much construct validity. Our unfinished business is even more imposing with respect to the concept of family life-style. Although life-style was a rallying point for the conference, we have only begun to explore its meaning, let alone its significance, for the study of family consumption.

One of the more interesting developments that emerged from the conference was the treatment of social placement in terms of "relativity." Because of the divergent contexts to which this approach was applied, it is worthwhile to summarize these concepts.

Relative achievement (Strumpel)—the relationship between accomplishments and aspirations.

Relative deprivation (Segal-Felson)—the relationship between the level of affluence of one social group (e.g., a family) and the level of affluence of another social group (e.g., some neighborhood reference group).

Relative economic status (Easterlin)—the relationship between the experiences of sons and fathers on the labor market.

Relative performance (Puckett)—the relationship between the performance (in terms of returns or asset accumulation) of savings or investment markets and the expectations of performance by the saver or investor.

By inspecting these concepts of relativity, it should be apparent they vary in degree of generality and level of abstraction and are not exactly interchangeable. Relative achievement and relative performance clearly use dispositional constructs as criteria, while relative deprivation and relative economic status use more behavioral criteria. All four constructs share, however, the feature of expected discrepancy in value between the central variable and its criterion. Without these discrepancies the concepts might become uninteresting. More work is required to clarify the concepts, to invent similar ones where they appear to be useful, and to examine the scalar qualities of measurement of relativity.[4]

6. *Welfare: A crucial concept for understanding family consumption?* —Welfare means many things to many people. According to Webster's dictionary it refers to a "condition of health, happiness, and prosperity; well-being." To the politician and the layman welfare may conjure up a picture of the socialist state, a bureaucratic system of doles to extortionists, or a humanitarian social policy. During the conference, the concept of welfare followed a particular chronological development through a succession of exchanges. Below, we reconstruct the highlights of this chronology and discuss its implications.

Although he did not introduce the concept of welfare, Ferber identified satisfaction with decisions and purchases as a step in the consumption process. Orcutt, in his discussion, raised the question rhetorically as to how role allocation might affect the well-being of families. During the informal discussion period, it became clear that the scope of the construct "satisfaction" was subject to debate. Martin Pfaff and James Morgan suggested that noncontingent transfers and philanthropy, in addition to fair exchanges, are important objects of study. Marc Felson introduced the utility maximization notion familiar to economists and suggested that it includes nonmaterial goals and uncompensated service to others. Because of the role of perception and nonmaterial aspects of satisfaction, Felson asserted that families probably attempt to maximize their "subjective utility." Although approached obtusely, the conference was sensitized to the potential consequences of consumption for consumers and to the complex nature of "welfare" without having that term as an anchor point.

Strumpel added appreciably to the texture of this exchange by introducing the concept "subjective welfare," and demonstrating to what extent it departed from "welfare" as used in "welfare economics." Although not explicitly defined, it was differentiated from the command of material resources and essentially equated with satisfaction in terms of "subjective measures of quality of life or economic welfare." This avowed psychological approach to welfare is appropriate, Strumpel said, because "Welfare is in the eye of the beholder."

Strumpel proceeded to discuss his own study, which affects satisfaction in terms of the *self* reports of subjects (male heads of households) about their satisfaction with income, standard of living, job, education, and changes in prospective income and standard of living. It is clear that Strumpel was concerned with welfare in terms of an over-all economic style of life. We might be tempted to conceptualize satisafaction with life-style as more encompassing than, but inclusive of, satisfaction with consumption decisions and behaviors. It is not clear, however, that this temptation is warranted, in as much as Strumpel did not include the kinds of financial behaviors in his study that Ferber had earlier discussed. It appears, then, that the study of satisfaction is itself dependent on the conceptual boundaries accepted with respect to consumption. This is the case because one must always answer the question, "satisfied with what?" The "what" is different for Ferber and Strumpel, and this situation leaves us with a conceptual void at the point where the two approaches might be linked.

In his formal discussion of Strumpel's paper, Pfaff reiterated the altruistic perspective of "grants economics" for which he and Kenneth E. Boulding are leading spokesmen. Utility maximization may best be understood, he said, in terms of "positive utility interdependence," which operates from the assumption that "the better off others are, the better we feel." Since the "others" in this approach are said to be significant others or reference groups, one person's welfare ought to be positively related to the welfare of other members of the reference group. An implication of this position that neither Pfaff nor Strumpel explored relates to the subjective welfare of family members. If male heads of families exhibit certain satisfaction patterns, what can be said of the satisfaction patterns of wives and children?

Arnold Shore and Robert Scott added a new dimension to the conceptualization of welfare by presenting findings from an experiment that was apparently designed to stabilize welfare and that has the potential of supplanting part or all of our existing national welfare policy. That man does not necessarily maximize utility in the strict material sense was reinforced by their findings, which showed a less than optimal exploitation of economic opportunities by experimental subjects. Shore and Scott appear, however, to have been operating from the more conventional conceptualization of welfare in objective terms. Recognizing this perspective, Felson and Maynes expressed an eager interest in finding out what the subjects themselves think of the experimental tax plan and what their values are.

Maynes' approach to welfare departed from yet another perspective. As we mentioned earlier, Maynes saw consumerism as the ideology of consumer welfare. Thus, grievances about price-quality characteristics might be viewed as indicators of consumer dissatisfaction. Bymers warned that grievances probably are not perfect indicators because consumers may not always make their dissatisfactions public, but may instead willingly absorb costs for product failure, for example. The problem of weighting desired product characteristics was raised by Morgan and Thomas Juster, and Maynes sympathized with their concern. In effect, he acknowledged that no matter how much objective price-quality information sellers provide about their products, the consumer will subjectively weigh these characteristics.

To a large extent confusion over the concept of welfare remains unresolved. There is a question about whether or not it is equivalent to satisfaction and/or utility, two other concepts frequently verbalized at the conference. There is a question about whose point of view really matters when using the welfare concept: that of the individual, the researcher, the nation, some interest group, or the family. There is, furthermore, a question about whether either objective or subjective measures of welfare alone are necessary or sufficient.

In separate postconference correspondence, Felson expressed his discomfort with the way this conceptual area had been treated. He suggested that, despite the labeling of economists as advocates of Economic Man, the modern economist no longer clings to an economic reductionism that fails to take nonmaterial goals and values into account. He then proposed that satisfaction is a more general term than utility, and that it more properly reflects the wide-ranging concerns of contemporary economists. If in the distant past welfare was the political scientist's favored concept, utility the economist's, and satisfaction the social psychologist's, these distinctions no longer appear to be holding.

Having examined the conceptually related communication problems at the conference, we turn to communication problems that center around the expressed or implied core assumptions of the various participants.

Communication Problems Generated by Assumptions

Many of the assumptions expressed at the conference relate in one way or another to the fundamental postulate of the rationality of man. One may either espouse this postulate or a corollary, or else deny this position while offering an alternative view. Assumptions of this sort are problematic for communication, we believe, because they are so paradigmatic[5] [7, pp. 174–187]. When we take them for granted in the most casual way, we are likely to be unprepared for the consequences they might have for our audience, the members of which may not all be part of the same scientific community, to say nothing of the consequences they have for our subject matters and our theories about them.

The assumption that man is rational implies that man is essentially a problem-solver, and that problem-solving is a logical process. Joan Aldous identified the phases of this assumed process following John Dewey [1]:

1. "Identification and definition of the problem"
2. "Collection of information relevant to the problem"
3. "Producing alternatives for action"
4. "Choice of a course of action from among the alternatives"
5. "Taking action"
6. "Evaluation of the consequences of the action"

Among the corollaries of the rationality postulate are that man has the resources and skills required to make rational choices, that a solution for a problem exists, and that man is goal-oriented, the goal being a maximally effective solution.

It is not surprising that the social sciences should adopt a model of man that rests on rational, planned, goal-oriented, and deliberate action. After all, that is also the image that the scientist has of himself. The scientist as puzzle-solver or detective is a characterization that conforms with the predominant methodological ethic in science. In order to choose among alternatives for action, the scientist generates and tests hypotheses, ideally with the rigor of a carefully controlled experiment. Neither is it surprising that the postulate of the rationality of man should be extended to the rationality of groups, including the family. This borrowed assumption indicates the compelling nature of the metaphor in scientific discourse [10].

When the rationality postulate is overlaid upon the study of economic behavior, a particular outcome is likely to emerge. Problems, goals, and means to those goals can be seen as economic problems, economic goals, and economic means. The rational-economic man reacts to the objective, external stimuli in his environment and acts in pursuit of the goal of maximum economic welfare. It is in the shadow of this rationality postulate that much of the confrontation occurred during the conference.

The picture that emerged from Ferber's presentation is that the family is isomorphic with a planning committee. A family goes through a series of rational steps to maximize its material returns through spending and saving. Perry Nayar challenged this rational-economic perspective and suggested that attention to the power relations within the family would help give a more dynamic texture to the decision-making process. Even Nayar, however, accepted the notion that power depends on resources, among which are income and information. What he added is that these resources are not evenly distributed at some optimally high level and that, in any case, such resources are channeled through the perceptual filters of family members.

It should be cautioned that the view of the family as a planning committee is not necessarily one to which Ferber himself is committed. The work that he reviewed is largely responsible for this perspective on the family, but Ferber also alerted us to the potential for impulsive buying, for example. He also began his presentation by commenting that the determinants of consumer behavior go beyond the desire to maximize consumer utility and include "goals and expectations, demographic characteristics, social structure, and the norms and values of society." His major theme might, in fact, be seen as an attempt to broaden our horizon beyond the explanation of rational economic behavior. Later, in our discussion of research implications, we introduce an alternative view of the family as a decision-making group which starts from a very different set of assumptions.

The presentations by Maynes, Easterlin, and Shore-Scott also appear to be based on the rationality postulate. Maynes argued in effect that the major reason that consumers do not select products rationally is that the necessary price-quality information is not always available. Although recognizing that all the evidence is not yet in, Maynes appeared to be willing for the present to cling to what he called "the rationality model of consumer choice." Bymers reacted by focusing on the inhibiting factors involved in processing and using available information, a notion which Maynes mentioned but did not explore. Jacob Jacoby added that the amount of information available is not linearly related to the perfection of the consumer market. There is a point of sensory overload when too much information is dysfunctional and dissatisfying.

Easterlin appeared to invoke the rationality postulate to conclude that fertility patterns are largely governed by the comparative labor-market experiences of fathers and sons. This is necessarily so because the aggregate data he used do not capture the experiences of actual father-son pairs, a point that Ryder noted during the discussion period. Furthermore, although the visual correlations that Easterlin found are intriguing and suggestive, they do not tell us if sons actually compare their economic prospects with their fathers' experiences and make choices on the basis of such comparisons. The explanation for these ecological correlations rested, then, on the inference that reproductive behavior is a planned or at least conditioned event undertaken by rational-economic man. Interestingly, Easterlin did not ask whether the rationality postulate applies equally to woman as it does to man. The female's role in reproductive decisions was not explored. Nevertheless, Easterlin did show some sensitivity to these issues in the part of his paper dealing with research implications.

Felson, in his rapporteur notes, made a valiant attempt to explicate core assumptions that he found hidden in the Shore-Scott presentation. Included among these assumptions were the following:

1. Man pursues material gain, rationally, with full knowledge, in the short run and with the short run in mind.
2. This leads to greater amounts of work incentive.
3. This work incentive leads to more work actually being done.

It is the first assumption, a compound one, that concerns us here. Felson wondered whether poor people have the sophistication necessary to maximize their material gains. Maynes added that lack of information might handicap the efficiency of the labor market just as he reported that it hampers the consumer market. Morgan and Milton Moss wondered whether long-range planning might also affect decisions bearing directly on striving for the immediate goal.

Central to the assertions and counter-assertions about rationality is the notion that individuals and families mobilize available resources to solve their problems. Making the statement in this way is important, for it differs from the stronger assertion that man *possesses* the required resources. Thus, when Maynes drew our attention to the apparent fact that the consumer cannot act in an optimally rational manner without the necessary information available, he was still able to maintain that man actively searches for the information that will enable the most rational choice possible.

Schott provided an apt example that tends toward the stronger position. The thrust of his argument was that investment patterns reflect an increased sophistication of the general public. For reasons apparently associated with increased education levels and increased disposable income levels, consumers are more capable today of "intermediating" and "disintermediating" to maximize their investment returns. Clearly, not everyone has all the required resources to make a rational investment decision, but apparently some investors possess the requisites. Much of the reaction to Schott's paper was speculation about what characteristics differentiate

18 · *Understanding Family Consumption*

"haves" from "have nots" and about ways for learning more about such differences.

Marshall Puckett's formal discussion of Schott's paper introduced the notion of an expectation-performance discrepancy. One of the interesting uses of this discrepancy notion that was not explicitly suggested during the conference is that it might serve as an indicator of *un*sophistication. Because of delayed learning, conditioned by the shock of depression, for example, investors do not act in the expected optimally rational manner. George Katona, in postconference correspondence, raised some additional points. He referred to studies at Michigan which showed that even well-educated persons buy and sell stocks with only limited information. He also re-emphasized the importance of values as determinants of consumer behavior. Supporting Strumpel's findings, Katona suggested that the premium on security may partially explain why some families continue to save in depository accounts during periods when the stock market is providing higher rates of return. In addition, Katona warned that by aggregating his data, Schott could not pinpoint the socioeconomic segments that contain the most and least resourceful investors.

Certainly one of the reasons why the resourceful-rational man is attractive to the social sciences is because findings thus far gathered have been largely based on middle- and upper-middle-class samples. This is the case in the studies Ferber reported and may be why the family emerges as a highly literate, account-keeping, forward-planning, sophisticated unit of consumption. The same can be said about the research reported at the conference that was based on aggregate data. In these studies we were apt to get a picture of the "ideal-typical" family, but little idea of the range in family behavior. For this reason, Strumpel's cross-tabulation of values by occupational group and Shore-Scott's poverty level sample represented important models for the design of future research.

If man is a goal-striving individual, what kinds of goals are compatible with rational conduct? Maynes suggested that a search for information will only be undertaken as long as its perceived potential benefits are at least as great as its perceived costs. In an earlier discussion of welfare, we raised some of the conceptual issues associated with this question. The *hedonistic principle,* which suggests that maximization of utility in its most competitive sense is the driving force in man's economic behavior, was one alternative view. When this was seen as a variant of strict materialism, even the economists at the conference were quick to disclaim it. But when seen as a diffuse psychological process, it became less noxious.

Another attractive alternative was suggested by the *reciprocity principle* to the effect that the most rational goal is a fair exchange. From the hedonistic perspective reciprocity represents the lower limit of rationality, as was evident in the Maynes' example above. In contrast, the reciprocity principle views the family and its environment interacting most effectively on the basis of a *quid pro quo*. The consumer wants his money's worth, and Maynes could advocate that advertising expenditures be balanced to help redress buyer-seller injustice.

A third variant of postulated goals was suggested by the *altruistic principle*. Following this line of reasoning, Pfaff and Morgan suggested that philanthropic grants or transfers characterize much of the economic activity of families. We would expect, for example, older generations of kin to provide aid and assistance to their offspring on a noncontingent basis, perhaps with the intent or hope that such aid would be passed on to successive generations and thereby partially insuring the status of the family lineage [6] [3]. Whether this is an entirely altruistic motive is subject to debate.

There is undoubtedly room in the rationality postulate for more than one of the above three principles to operate. What remains undetermined are the conditions and causal linkages through which each is empirically demonstrable. Part of the semantics of confrontation evidenced revolves around the reification of assumptions and supposed inadmissability of conditional alternatives.

One final area of confrontation will now be discussed. This is the methodological assumption that subjective or, alternatively, objective measures of variables are most appropriate for analysis of family consumption. During the discussion of the Segal-Felson paper, a lively debate ensued around this issue. Douvan, a psychologist, suggested that economists had been spoiled by their "neat quantitative models." She saw such subjective variables as psychological satisfaction, quality of life, class identification, the sense of honor or status, and self-esteem as more profitable variables to explore. Interestingly, she pointed to an economist, Strumpel, and his work as exemplary of the direction she was proposing.

The discussion then centered around the content validity of the Segal-Felson consumption and credit mobilization indices as measures of "quality of material life style." Marguerite Burke thought current inventories and outlays for durables, semidurables, nondurables, and services were also relevant. Juster, Douvan, Eleanor Sheldon, and Beatrice Paolucci raised similar questions later about Schott's definition of assets and about the conference generally to the effect that "human capital assets" had largely been ignored. The role of the wife-mother in economic socialization, expressive family integration, and the development of social skills was an additional factor mentioned by these conferees as a possible source of human resources. Maynes, Douvan, Hy Rodman, and David Segal continued the discussion of the relative merit and feasibility of measuring what Segal called "elusive" and what we earlier labeled "dispositional" constructs.

In correspondence after the conference Al Hermalin referred to this exchange as a battle over "conceptual models" to which the different disciplines have differing allegiances. When confronted, he surmised, the disciplines each fall into the "essentialism trap," resorting to description and explanation in terms and assumptions familiar to each. His own avowed bias was reflected in the conjecture that many of the subjective status variables would turn out to be highly correlated with the usual objective ones, and therefore add little to explanation. On the other hand, Segal did not see this modeling problem as one of gross oversimplification. Instead, he saw fairly complex models competing because they assumed either statistical interaction or additive relationships among similar sets of independent variables.

It has not always been possible to draw sharp lines between disciplines when discussing the context and content of communication problems. More than anything else, this probably reflects the fact that confrontations and misunderstandings frequently occurred as *intra*disciplinary skirmishes. Neither would we conclude that interdisciplinary confrontations are undesirable. The differing conceptual frameworks and substantive areas of interest represented by the social sciences give a breadth to this family of disciplines that would not otherwise be possible. What is desirable is that shared meanings be constructed to permit a linking of the insights of the various disciplines. Verbal confrontation adds vitality to an exchange, but confusion represents wasted energy. Finally, not all disputes reflect problems of communication. Some certainly are engendered by legitimate differences in scientific values and preferences. Criteria for assessing research findings, hypotheses thought worthy of formulation and testing, and the relationship between social science and social policy are the kinds of issues that conceptual clarity and explicit assumptions are not likely to resolve.

Expanding Horizons Through Multidisciplinary Perspectives

It would be misleading to try to force the argument that failure of communication dominated the symposium, for this clearly was not the case. Looking back over each of the areas of failure already identified, it is possible to extract these hopeful signs of disciplinary convergence in progress.

1. The conceptualization of consumer behavior is apparently expanding beyond its more traditional bounds of "buying and using up." With this expansion, the interests of sociologists, psychologists, and social psychologists are more readily absorbed. Marketing experts are now teaching their students that a comprehensive theory of consumer behavior will have to draw heavily on the insights of the behavioral sciences [5].

2. Although still largely dominated by sociologists at this conference, the view of the family as a unit of consumption is gaining ground so that it is approaching equality with alternative perspectives. Even the title of the conference helps bear this out.
3. With little dissent, there is an increased sensitivity to the importance of time, especially as it can be appropriately utilized in longitudinal studies.
4. The importance of dispositional constructs for the understanding of consumption is legion. Strumpel's "psychological economics" no longer should sound strange to the conferee or the reader. Stark rationality must be modified by at least some of these psychological variables, and psychologists turned to for expertise in handling the inherent difficulties of measurement.
5. The life-style and welfare variables are at least complex enough to permit and even demand contributions to their proper conceptualization from each of the social sciences.

It is fortunate indeed that the papers by Ferber and Strumpel were delivered early in the symposium. Each may be viewed as a horizon expander—Ferber's for placing consumption in a framework of social interaction, and Strumpel's for exploring the social-psychological antecedents of economic life-style. In addition, the discussion of the Maynes' paper repeatedly drew attention to the desirable co-operation among economists, sociologists, legal scholars, and philosophers to conceptualize and transform insights about the consumer market into policy-relevant proposals. As a final example, Douvan, a psychologist, suggested that economics has much to offer psychology in terms of our understanding of resource management and value optimization.

Notes

1. In a separate check of discussion transcripts, rapporteur notes, and other available materials, it was discovered that 54 per cent of the contributors to exchanges from the floor and postconference correspondence were academic economists and sociologists. These same groups, comprising only one-fourth of the conferees (see Table I), also accounted for 58 per cent of the total number of comments. These were the only professional groups that were clearly overrepresented in conference participation.

2. It should be noted that bridging macro- and microlevels of analysis is not only a conceptual problem, but also a methodological one. We have yet to discover, for example, an entirely satisfactory way of weighting and combining measures of individual behaviors into an index of family behavior. The issue has been sharpened and five alternatives suggested by Murray A. Straus, "Measuring Families," in Harold T. Christensen, ed., *Handbook of Marriage and the Family,* Chicago: Rand McNally, 1964, especially pp. 341–349.

3. It is interesting to note that psychology and sociology have traditionally differed markedly in their definitions of "intervening variable." In psychology interven-

ing variables are usually first-order abstractions of observable data, or operationally defined concepts that intervene between reality and hypothetical constructs. See Kenneth MacCorquodale and Paul E. Meehl, "On a Distinction Between Hypothetical Constructs and Intervening Variables," *Psychological Review* 55, 1948, pp. 95–107. In sociology intervening variables are usually intermediate links in a causal chain which may or may not be psychological variables. We are using the term "intervening" in the sociological sense here. Dispositional constructs, therefore, are viewed as only one of many possible kinds of intervening variables. For a psychological approach to this concept in a consumption context, see John A. Howard and Jagdish N. Sheth, *The Theory of Buyer Behavior*, New York: John Wiley and Sons, 1969, especially p. 17.

4. One might ask whether or not we are limited to ordinal measurement with this type of concept and how restrictive the requirement would be.

5. We have in mind the Kuhnian notion of a paradigm as "the constellation of group commitments." In this view, a particularly tenacious assumption such as "man is rational" is part of the "disciplinary matrix" shared by a scientific community. See Thomas S. Kuhn [7].

6. In large measure, this proposition is supported by the findings of a detailed study of consumership across three generations. See Reuben Hill [3].

References

1. Aldous, Joan, "A Framework for the Analysis of Family Problem Solving," in Joan Aldous, *et al.*, eds., *Family Problem Solving*, Chicago: Dryden Press, 1971, pp. 265–281.

2. Foote, Nelson N., *Household Decision Making: Consumer Behavior*, 4, New York: New York University Press, 1961.

3. Hill, Reuben, *Family Development in Three Generations*, Cambridge, Mass.: Schenkman, 1970.

4. ———, and Roy H. Rodgers, "The Developmental Approach," in Harold T. Christensen, ed., *Handbook of Marriage and the Family*, Chicago: Rand McNally, 1964. For important examples of conceptualization and research application.

5. Holloway, Robert J., *et al*, *Consumer Behavior: Contemporary Research in Action*, New York: Houghton Mifflin, 1969.

6. Howard, John A., and Jagdish N. Sheth, *The Theory of Buyer Behavior*, New York: John Wiley and Sons, 1969.

7. Kuhn, Thomas S., *The Structure of Scientific Revolutions*, ed. 2. Chicago: University of Chicago Press, 1970.

8. MacCorquodale, Kenneth, and Paul E. Meehl, "On a Distinction Between Hypothetical Constructs and Intervening Variables," *Psychological Review* 55, March, 1948 pp. 95–107.

9. Straus, Murray A., "Measuring Families," in Harold T. Christensen, ed., *Handbook of Marriage and the Family*, Chicago: Rand McNally, 1964, pp. 335–400.

10. Weick, Karl E., "Group Processes, Family Processes, and Problem Solving," in Joan Aldous, et al., eds., *Family Problem Solving*, Chicago: Dryden Press, 1971. For a discussion of this and other group metaphors.

2

*Family Decision Making
and
Economic Behavior*

A REVIEW

Introduction

In his paper "Family Decision Making and Economic Behavior," Robert Ferber presented a theoretical framework within which a literature review is provided. His purposes may be outlined as follows:

1. To identify the antecedents of consumer behavior (especially spending and saving behavior)
2. To provide a taxonomic description of consumer decisions
3. To describe the decision-making process as a series of steps involving the roles of different family members
4. To identify the causes of planned and impulsive decisions
5. To describe the role of reference groups and information-searching as inputs to consumer decisions
6. To identify the values and family structural characteristics associated with saving behavior

It seems evident that Ferber has defined his task as one of description rather than as an attempt to provide a systematic causal explanation. He put much effort into specifying the frequencies with which various decision-making patterns occur in the studies he reviewed.

Ferber's theoretical mode of expression was for the most part conventional. He employed fairly abstract conceptual models at two points to help summarize the relationships among concepts that his review led him to postulate. These conceptual models share the advantages and disadvantages of conceptual models generally. Because of their high level of abstraction, for example, it is not possible to specify the direction (positive or negative) or strength of relationship among the concepts of interest.

Dr. Guy H. Orcutt, of Yale, in his formal discussion of this paper, reorganized Ferber's models into a more dynamic presentation that accounts for feed-back processes. Essentially, he viewed exogenous variables (markets, governments, reference groups), combining with family status variables at Time $_1$ (assets, family structure, age, education, member roles, etc.) to affect the "operating characteristics" of the family (attitudes, resources, goals, characteristics of members, decisions, etc.) and thereby to produce changes in the values of the exogenous and family status variables at Time $_2$.

Comparing Ferber's Charts 1 and 2 (pages 31, and 55), one becomes sensitized to the problem of identifying the key dependent variable for his analysis. Chart 1 proposes that financial behaviors are the ultimate dependent variables, while Chart 2 terminates with financial decisions. Ferber himself, however, led us to believe that the congruence between decisions and subsequent actions is not always precise. In reviewing one study he observed that

> there is some indication that joint participation in the financial planning process was more likely to lead to sharing of knowledge on the family finances and, as a result, to the wife taking charge of the financial records.

Joint decisions, therefore, are not always predictive of joint task responsibilities.

It should be noted that Ferber's paper is not totally void of historical statements, and an analysis of one of them can be used to highlight the distinction between decisions and behaviors mentioned above. Ferber made the following assertion: "To the extent that impulse buying is increasing, family deliberation is likely to be decreasing." One alternative explanation might be that deliberation in the family decision-making process remains constant, but that sensitization to immediate needs changes the purchasing behavior of the purchasing agent more often than previously. In effect, the buyer violates previously reached decisions and may be faced with justifying his actions to members of the family later. Another interpretation of this historical trend might also be proposed. It is possible that as deliberation over impulsive choices decreases, deliberation over planned choices increases, so that total deliberation remains at least as high as it was previously. Obviously, these interpretations require further empirical testing.

Several other difficulties in Ferber's conceptual models deserve brief mention. Apparently in the interest of simplification, the process-nature of decision making succumbed. The important variable, information search, either became residual or was subsumed under the decision-making concept. Decisions, themselves, are not single acts but a complex set of acts involving, for example,

1. Whether or not to spend, save, or both
2. What product characteristics to seek out
3. How much of the available resources to allocate
4. When to engage in a particular financial behavior
5. Who will perform the financial behavior
6. Where or with whom to conduct the financial behavior

Ferber clearly recognized these dimensions but did not fit them into his conceptual models.

The reader should also notice that Chart 2 disregards nonfinancial decisions (e.g., the decision to have a baby) and their feed-back effects on family structure (e.g., increased family size). Chart 2 also appears to discount the attitudes of wives as inputs to family goals, which is curiously similar to a deficiency noted in Easterlin's underlying assumptions.

Finally, the feed-back from decisions to resources and the unique inputs of family developmental changes, while incorporated in Chart 1, were dropped for Chart 2. Perhaps the reason for the first deletion was associated with the concomitant removal of financial behaviors as dependent variables. The feed-back from decisions to resources is not direct and loses its meaning without financial behaviors postulated as intervening links.

This extended treatment of the shortcomings of Ferber's conceptual models has not been undertaken as a severe criticism of Ferber's theorizing, but rather to suggest how future modeling from similar data might be extended.

Below we list several *empirical generalizations*—which we have symbolized EG and numbered consecutively as they appear in the introductions—adduced from Ferber's presentation. Names in parentheses are provided in those cases where the primary contributors are discussants.

EG1. Joint financial decision making is characteristic of young, middle-class families, costly expenditures, satisfied marriages, families with high social network connectedness, families whose members have shared interest in or use of the product, and families where members have nearly equal resources to make the decision.

EG2. Wife-dominated financial decisions are characteristic of lower-income families, older families, rural families, and decisions for which the wife has special competence or interest.

EG3. Husband-dominated financial decisions are characteristic of higher-income families, and decisions for which the husband has special competence or interest.

EG4. Planned financial decisions and behaviors are characteristic of young, well-educated families with many financial obligations, families with a higher occupational status, first purchases, costly expenditures, important decisions, families with a strong future or security orientation, families with teenagers, and families with the expertise to make rational decisions.

EG5. Impulsive financial decisions and behaviors are characteristic of special occasions and opportunities that arouse needs, replacement purchases when satisfaction with an old product is high, and nondurable purchases.

EG6. Satisfaction with a financial decision of behavior is characteristic of decisions that involve consultation with outside sources of information, discussion within the family, and consideration of a range of alternative courses of action.

EG7. The extent of a search for information is positively associated with the expected gain relative to the cost of the information, with the cost of the purchase, and with young, better-educated, and higher-income families.

EG8. The use of reference groups as sources for information in financial decisions is characteristic of younger and better-educated families, socially conspicuous products, and family members with moderate self-confidence.

EG9. Role allocation in family financial decision making is determined in part by the culture-specific power resources and perceptions of family members (Nayar, Rodman).

One of the most obvious attributes of nearly all of the above statements is their complexity. They attempt to tie together the findings of several diverse studies. Attention is paid to the correlates of various decision-role patterns (EG1 through 3), planned versus impulsive choice patterns (EG4 and 5), satisfaction (EG6), and search for information (EG7 and 8). No assertions of causal attribution are made in the first eight empirical generalizations, nor are the individual or relative strengths of the associations proposed. We would not expect all of the suggested correlates within each statement to be independent of each other.

EG9 might serve as a partial explanation for the associations expressed in EG1 through 3. Thus, joint decision making would be expected to occur when resources are equal, while spouse-dominated decisions would be expected when that spouse controlled the majority of relevant resources. EG9 does not tell us how big a disparity in resources is sufficient for "disjoint" financial decision making, nor does it explain any of the other asserted associations, since the required antecedent conditions are not established. For example, it might have to be determined that wives control a disproportionate number of resources in rural families for a resource theory to be accepted as a satisfactory explanation of wife-dominated financial decisions in those families.

Although it might be possible to construct a logically sound deductive explanation of the observations Ferber discussed, the important point is that such a theoretical formulation has yet to be constructed, or at least it escaped the Williamsburg conferees.

Reuben Hill and David M. Klein

Family Decision Making and Economic Behavior
A Review

By Robert Ferber

Ever since its inception the avowed objective of economics has been maximization of consumer utility, or consumer welfare, subject to constraints on available resources. An early approach, still used in much mathematical model building, was to assume that the individual acted as an "economic man," maximizing his utility subject only to relative prices and to the constraint of his income or financial resources.

Although this approach is still very useful as a first approximation, particularly in mathematical model building, it has long since been recognized that individuals do not act on the basis of economic considerations alone, and that regardless of whether an individual's set of utilities can be considered as rational from an economic point of view, many different considerations intervene between the formation of these utilities and their realization in the marketplace. These considerations involve not only economic factors but also a host of additional factors that lead into subareas of many of the other social sciences, especially sociology, social psychology, and psychology. Conceptually, this development has been recognized by the increasing use of the term "consumer behavior," to denote the study of the actions that consumers take and of the determinants of these actions.

From a more concrete point of view, however, relatively little attention has been given to bringing together these various dimensions of consumer behavior within the framework of the family to provide more realistic explanations of economic behavior. This oversight constitutes a major gap in economic research, and is unfortunate for at least two reasons. One is that the economic actions of the family constitute a very large part of consumer behavior, for these actions encompass what families do in earning, spending, and saving (as well as the factors affecting decisions behind these actions). These decisions are motivated not only by economic variables but also by a host of additional factors, such as goals and expectations, demographic characteristics, social structure, and the norms and values of society. Hence, understanding these decisions involves the introduction of variables from many different fields.

The second reason is that in each of these different fields information has been accumulating on family economic behavior. These studies are frequently very narrow and restricted, and even more frequently do not receive any attention from economists, partly because they are not done by economists nor do they appear in economics publications. As will be shown in this paper, an appreciable amount of this type of information exists and needs to be brought together within a more general framework in the study of family economic behavior.

Another facet of this subject is the impact that family economic behavior itself may have on the political and social structure of our society. That such behavior does have an impact is unquestioned, but the awareness and the study of the nature of this impact are as yet only in the formative stages.

In line with the foregoing comments, it is the objective of this paper to review consumer financial behavior with particular reference to saving and spending within a broad decision-making framework. Hopefully, this broader framework will allow for many different types of variables to be taken into account and will also serve as a basis for reviewing and synthesizing what has been done on this general subject and for highlighting principal areas where additional research is needed.

I. A Decision-Making Framework

The approach taken in this paper is to consider the different types of decisions that enter into family saving and spending behavior, the manner in which they relate to each other, and what is known about each of these decisions from different disciplines. The broad interrelations are tied together by a simple framework which serves as the basis for synthesizing what is and is not known about each type of decision, rather than what has been studied of this subject in each discipline separately.

Reviews of the latter type have been undertaken periodically; they are very useful in themselves and also provide part of the material for this paper. This framework is not meant to substitute for the much more elaborate decision-making framework developed in other studies [44]. Its purpose is to provide some structure to this review of a particular class of economic decisions, and for this purpose a relatively simple framework seems sufficient.

The basis for the framework is segmentation of family economic decisions into two types—financial and nonfinancial. Financial decisions for the present purposes involve four principal types of decisions; namely, money management, saving decisions, spending decisions, and asset management (Chart 1). Nonfinancial decisions are most easily defined as including all other types of economic decisions. The focus of this paper is on

CHART 1. INTERRELATION OF SAVING AND SPENDING DECISIONS

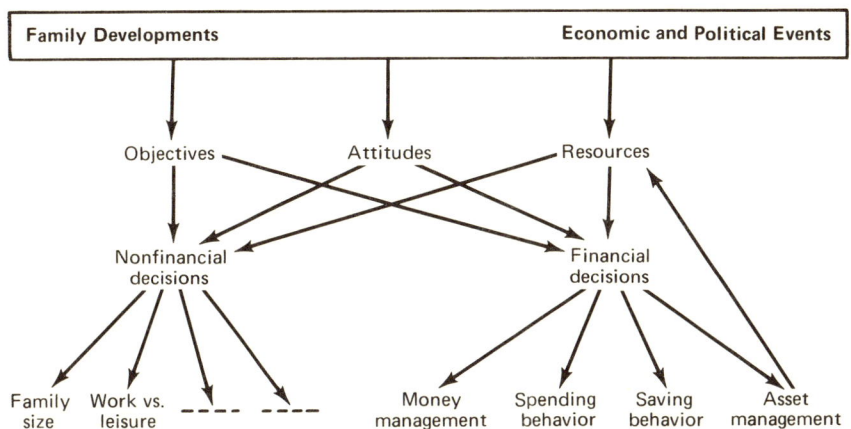

financial decisions; therefore it seems unnecessary to provide any further classification of nonfinancial decisions other than to point out that they cover a wide variety of decisions, including the option of whether or not to have children, choice between work and leisure, choice of an occupation, and the decision of where to live.[1]

Both financial and nonfinancial decisions are affected directly by the available financial resources of the family, by the objectives or goals of the family, and by the attitudes of the family members. Objectives and attitudes encompass many different facets. Thus, objectives encompass both the material and the nonmaterial goals of the family in the long run as well as in the short run, though from the point of view of this paper the material short-run goals are likely to be more influential than any other type. The concept of attitudes refers not only to the expectations and outlook of the different family members on economic and related events but also to their system of preferences and of value judgments among alternative types of economic behavior, particularly as between spending and saving.

It should also be noted that to a large extent this framework itself is dominated by a number of factors that are exogenous to it; in particular, economic and political events in the community in which the family resides and personal developments with the individual family members (such as births, deaths, marriages, accidents, job layoffs, etc.). As noted in Chart 1, these broader factors serve as a backdrop for our framework, which is essentially concerned with microbehavior.

Financial decisions

Before considering individual decisions made by the family in the financial area, it seems wise to take an overview and to consider some of the basic factors that underlie these decisions within the framework of the family. Such factors relate partly to the role of financial planning within the family and partly to the nature and extent of financial decisions. It should be stressed that financial planning and financial decision making are not the same thing, and though the former may involve the latter, very different sorts of events are involved. Paramount in both respects are the roles of husbands and wives, a subject on which a fair amount of information seems to be available in some not very widely publicized sources. Special attention has been given to the effect of working wives, as we shall see.

1. *Money management*—An arrangement within the family for the handling of money, payment of bills, budgeting, and keeping accounts is of value not only in itself but also for throwing light on the influence of different family members in financial decisions. In addition, the family member who performs such a caretaker role is likely to be a key source of information in seeking financial data about the family. Of additional interest is the question of the extent to which the financial caretaker in one sense is also the financial caretaker in another sense, and of the interrelationship between the financial caretaker role and other aspects of financial decisions.

2. *Spending behavior*—A multitude of decisions are encompassed under this heading, probably much more than any of the other decision categories used in this paper, because of the many forms and ways in which spending can take place. These decisions can be classified under two broad categories; namely, formation of the decisions and their execution. The act of forming a decision may, however, lead to a considerable amount of physical activity in addition to thinking and discussion, for this stage very likely will involve shopping around, looking at and testing different types of products (especially durable goods) and speaking to people who already have the product. For some products, these decisions will be routine and virtually automatic, as in the purchase of most types of groceries. For other types of products, such as houses, automobiles, and many large durable goods, a great deal of effort may be involved at this stage, and the decision itself may encompass many ramifications.

For the present purposes, it would seem desirable to subcategorize these types of decisions into two components—decisions relating to whether or not to buy the product, and decisions relating to characteristics of the product. Admittedly, in some instances these decisions will be made simultaneously, especially so for convenience products and routinely purchased items. In other cases, however, as with durable goods these decisions can be shown to be very distinct, as will be brought out in a later section of this paper.

It is recognized that decisions relating to the characteristics of the product may themselves have many facets, and that the manner in which the decision may be made for one product characteristic (say, brands) may be very different from the manner in which the decision will be made about another product characteristic (say, color of a car).

The execution of these decisions relates to the circumstances surrounding the physical act of making the purchase and the family members who participate in doing so. A number of interesting studies will be discussed under this heading.

It should also be noted that the spending behavior may lead to changes in the goals and objectives of the family, as noted in Chart 1. This is still another dynamic aspect of this framework.

3. *Saving behavior*—In many ways the central decision under this heading relates to the allocation of available financial resources for a given period between spending and saving, specifically what amount or proportion of these total resources should be allocated to saving and what proportion or amount to spending. For the present purposes, it seems more useful to consider "saving" and "spending" in dollar terms rather than in physical consumption as used in many analytical studies in economics. From the viewpoint of decision making, this definition appears dominant both in the minds of families and in the course of the studies undertaken on this subject.

As noted in Chart 1, in a very general sense the decision to save or to spend is influenced by the available financial resources, by the objectives of the family, and by the attitudes of the family members. Other factors are also undoubtedly relevant, though perhaps less important, such as family composition and personal economic circumstances. Such factors will be introduced in the course of the review of the literature.

Once a decision has been made to save, a number of other decisions have to be made regarding such matters as the forms in which to save, the specific institutions or securities, who will take the responsibility for saving, when it will be done, where it will be done, etc. These various decisions would seem to be separable into two major classes, one class relating to decisions about what should be done and the other to their execution, such as who will be in charge of the mechanics of actually performing the action.

It should also be noted that the various decisions about saving do not necessarily follow after the decision to save has been made. In fact, the decision to save may at times be made simultaneously with the form of saving, since availability of a particular saving opportunity (such as unusually high interest rates) may itself influence how much should be saved. There is little question, however, that these decisions concerning saving do affect the resources of the family, through asset management, and this is one of the major dynamic aspects of this framework.

4. *Asset management*—The management of the financial assets of a family involves decisions that should be studied separately. This is especially true if a family has any appreciable amount of assets, in which case this function may necessitate a great deal of expertise and specialization. In principle, these decisions could be classified in the same manner as those relating to spending and saving behavior, especially since some of them must necessarily be closely related to saving behavior. Nevertheless, the dearth of studies on decision making in this area suggests that such a classification is needless, and it is therefore not proposed at this time.

In the remainder of this paper this simple framework is used to bring together the principal studies of family financial decision making. The focus is on empirical studies of decision making, considering in turn what we know about each of the types of financial decisions shown in Chart 1. However, as a result of the dearth of material, the summary of family decision making on saving behavior and on asset management is combined under a single heading.

To offset the heavy emphasis on empirical studies, and partly to take advantage of this emphasis, a following section provides a more detailed framework for studying family financial decision making, based on the results brought together in the earlier parts of this paper.[5]

It should be stressed that throughout this paper the emphasis is on the roles of the different family members in influencing or in carrying out different types of financial decisions. In the course of this review, use will be made of the extensive literature on family role behavior, though it does not seem necessary, or useful, to review this literature here.

II. Financial Decisions

Despite its basic importance for the understanding of consumer financial behavior, the role of financial planning within the family—in the sense of explicit consideration of the allocation of expected financial resources between saving and spending—seems to have received very little attention in empirical work, and would seem to be a prime area for future research. This is all the more odd because from a normative point of view a great deal of attention has been given to this question, and virtually every text on home economics and on consumer home management discusses the desirability of a financial plan, its components, and its relation to family goals [56]. Hazel Kyrk inferred that family financial planning and budgeting are important among newly formed families and among families with a low income. As the expenditure pattern becomes more standardized and as income increases, financial planning and budgeting were asserted to be less frequent [56, pp. 323-24].

From an empirical point of view, attention has been given to the meaning and nature of financial security, which is best discussed in connection with the studies of saving behavior. Little attention, however, has been given to what types of families make financial plans and the nature of these plans. The studies that have been made are essentially in the home economics literature. They tend to focus on farm families and give very general information about financial planning only as part of a large study. Illustrative of these is a personal-interview study among 60 co-operating young rural couples (both husbands and wives) in New York. In this study, Wells reported widespread evidence of financial planning among these families, with the extent of planning becoming more complex as family income, assets, and financial obligations increased [80]. The exact nature of these financial plans was not discussed.

In another study, Honey and Smith noted that 58 per cent of students in home economics courses at Pennsylvania State University reported, again as part of a larger questionnaire, that their parents had a financial plan [42]. Again, they did not indicate the nature of these financial plans. Moreover, in view of the very special nature of this sample, there can be no basis for making any inferences regarding the extent of financial planning in the general population.

A much lower frequency of financial plans was reported indirectly in a study by Rayburn of the money-management practices of 4-H teenagers in two counties in Mississippi. In an interview with the mothers of these teenagers only 13 per cent replied, in response to a direct question, that their families had a "financial plan"; the term, however, did not seem to have been defined [71].

In yet another study, the existence of financial planning was reported among both middle- and lower-class families in Michigan, with the observation that housewives seemed to have more influence on the plan in the case of the lower-class families. The sample, however, was very small (only 50 families), and it is not clear what was meant by a financial plan [7].

That financial planning can play an important role in the economic welfare of the family was suggested by two other studies from home economics. In one case, Honey reported, in connection with a study of financial management by 426 farm families in Pennsylvania, that a major source of dissatisfaction was lack of a financial plan where one did not exist [40]. In the other case, Freeman and Due showed from a case study of two farm families over 23 years how the different goals of these families led to very different expenditure and saving patterns over the years [34].

In their pioneering study of family change conducted by interviewing members of three generations of the same families, Rueben Hill and his associates found that family recordkeeping, as well as budgeting and advance financial planning, have been increasing in frequency substantially over the generations [39]. For example, only 7 per cent of the grandparents, but 21 per cent of the parents and 26 per cent of the married children, reported preparing plans for distributing income. Similarly, 8 per cent of the grandparents, 21 per cent of the parents, and 24 per cent of the married children reported the use of procedures for estimating expenses and setting specific amounts aside. From a reverse point of view, 64 per cent of the grandparents, 36 per cent of the parents, and only 19 per cent of the married children did not know the meaning of the term budgeting.

In line with these replies, the proportion of married children having particular types of assets a given number of years after marriage was much higher than the corresponding proportion of parents, which in turn was much higher than the corresponding proportion of grandparents [39].

Family roles in financial decisions

In contrast to the role of financial planning, the role of different family members in making financial decisions has been investigated fairly extensively, principally by home economists and sociologists, in different ways and often with conflicting results.

In one of the more interesting studies, Schomaker, following a scheme originally advanced by Herbert Simon, classified the financial decision into five steps—problem recognition, observation and acquisition of information, deliberation, choice, and action [73]. Studying the role of 100 farmers and their wives at each of these stages, she found that financial problems were recognized half the time as a result of immediate necessity and most of the rest of the time as a result of a growing need. Usually the husband expressed recognition of financial problems. Information as a basis for solving the problem was sought from a variety of sources, but primarily from people outside of the family and from magazines. More than two-thirds of the families discussed the problem among themselves, and approximately three-fourths of this group considered two or more alternative solutions. Both these practices, as well as information seeking, were more frequent among younger and better-educated families.

The husband was reported to be the one who made the final decision nearly 60 per cent of the time, and jointly with the wife about one-third of the time, the latter percentage being higher for families with younger husbands. Age of husband and education, incidentally, were also prime determinants of the tendency of a family to follow the five-step decision-making process.

In a further analysis, it was found that satisfactory, as distinct from unsatisfactory, financial decisions were more likely to be characterized by more frequent consultation of sources of information and of people outside the family, more discussion of the problem within the family, and consideration of a larger number of alternative solutions [74].

On the other hand, explicit use of decision making was not found to be overly frequent in another study of farm families in New York state. In this study only one-third of the sample of farm families were found consciously to use various decision-making steps such as those outlined by Schomaker [23].

Like many other studies of this type, the sample was highly specialized, and was further restricted to couples where both the husband and wife were willing to co-operate, so that the results are best treated as hypotheses for future study.

A very different view of decision making was provided in one of the Detroit area studies, from which the authors, Blood and Wolfe, generalized, "The economic function of the family is therefore primarily the husband's function. Even when the wife works, the reasons why she works and the relative permanence of her work reflect his career. . . . Her job uniquely is to bear the children. . . ." [6]. This was one of the very few studies based on a broad probability-type sample, covering urban and suburban as well as farm families in the Detroit area.

A similar view was encountered in a factor analysis of replies obtained from husbands and wives in a more general study of their roles and relation to each other. In this study, Thorp found a factor that reflects the traditional division of influence, with the husband having the main responsibility for earning money and the wife for running the household and raising children [76]. However, the questions used in the study were very general and little attention was given to individual types of financial decisions.

Whether for this or other reasons, these views differed substantially from the findings of other studies (and would also not exactly make the authors popular among Women's Lib groups). Indeed, about the only supporting evidence was the finding of various home economics projects that the wife makes most of the household decisions; that is, decisions that pertain purely to household activities and to shopping. Of these types of decisions, 85 per cent were reported as made by the housewife alone [22].

On the other hand, Wilkening found that joint involvement in five types of farm and home financial decisions among 614 Wisconsin farmers and their wives characterized nearly 40 per cent of those with farm incomes under $6,000 and over $9,000, and half of those with incomes in the middle bracket [82]. Wilkening also found that the wife's involvement decreased as the farm was more commercialized and increased among families with more debt or where the wife was more socially active.

Further evidence that joint decision making is frequent among farm families was produced in a study by Honey, Britton, and Hotchkiss, who reported that their interviews with 252 rural Pennsylvania families indicated that wives and husbands generally followed the practice of talking over financial matters and making decisions together [41].

There is also some evidence that among younger families, at least, wives have substantial influence in financial decisions. Thus, in one study where undergraduate married couples were observed while they decided how to spend a hypothetical gift of $300, the most frequent occurrence (56 per cent of the time) was for both husband and wife to have about equal degrees of influence [52]. Although this is a somewhat artificial situation, it is especially interesting to note that, based on prior reports by the couples, the husbands generally had less influence than had been anticipated by either member.

As we shall see later, joint decision making characterizes many different aspects of family financial behavior, although it varies with the nature of the problem. It is a phenomenon of interest not just in a financial sense but has been studied in its broader aspects by family sociologists. Among other things, these studies seem to show rather conclusively that joint decision making is likely to be associated with satisfaction in marriage, especially when age and education of the couple are similar [27].

Money management decisions

To modify a framework suggested by Kyrk [56] there seem to be five alternatives in the allocation of the money-management function between husbands and wives: [2]

1. The husband doles out the funds to the wife as needed, and he usually pays the bills.
2. The husband gives the wife a regular allowance which she uses for specific purposes, and he uses the rest.
3. The wife receives the entire income by the husband's turning his pay over to her; she gives him an allowance and uses the rest.
4. The wife receives the entire income; she doles out funds to the husband as needed, and she usually pays the bills.
5. The husband and wife decide jointly at the start (or end) of every pay period how the money should be spent and each then assumes a specific task.

The first two alternatives represent a form of patriarchal system and the second two a form of matriarchal system.

The available evidence indicates that, as might be expected, the patriarchal system has dominated in the past, especially among older people. In a study in England, for example, Young found that wives generally did not know what their husbands earned [86]. Indeed, among people age 65 and over in a working class in East London, Townsend found that not only did few wives (7 of 45) know what their husbands earned, but "many did not think they had a right to know," [77]. The usual procedure among those families was that the wife had a preset allowance (with no excesses allowed!) and also had the responsibility of paying the bills. When the husband retired, however, or if he were overtaken by illness, Townsend noted that the wife then usually became the major financial influence and the procedure was modified so that each of them had a separate allowance.

For the United States, such evidence as is available suggests that decisions regarding money management are more likely to be made on a joint basis, while the accounting and recordkeeping are more likely to be looked after by the wife. Thus, in her study of 60 young rural couples in New York State, Wells found that responsibilities tend to be shared on a joint basis for families married fairly recently, and that these responsibilities tend to be shifted to individual members as the number of years married increased [80]. Similarly, the frequency of accountkeeping and budgeting tend to decline as the number of years married increased.

In another study of farm husbands and wives, this time in Wisconsin, Wilkening and Bharadwaj stated that "while the division of labor between farm and household was expected, the division of labor within the family area between husband and wife suggests that responsibility for family tasks follows the interest and availability of the spouses rather than following traditional role expectations that the women ought to be responsible for all household tasks" [83]. In particular, the investigators found that the wives tend to take a very active role in money management and generally look after keeping track of money, paying bills, and keeping farm records.

An interesting relationship between accountkeeping and budgeting was suggested by Wells in her study [80]. She noted that among families that budgeted, more wives than husbands kept account records; while among families that did not budget, account records were kept more often either by both husband and wife or by the husband only. Although the sample was very small (60 families), there was some indication that joint participation in the financial planning process is more likely to lead to sharing of knowledge about the family finances and, as a result, to the wife's taking charge of the financial records. At the same time, it should be noted that this sample was restricted to co-operative younger families in which both husband and wife were willing to be interviewed. In a broader coverage study made about the same time, for example, Morse found that only 51 per cent of a sample of 527 rural families in Kansas were keeping account records, the wives keeping these records in two-thirds of the families and the husbands in the rest [62].

Of three studies that provided information on money management in urban areas, two were conducted by the Survey Research Center of the University of Michigan and yielded roughly similar results. The questions related to money and bills, and the findings on which member of the couple has the main influence are as follows [[3] 74a, 85a].

Study	Husband	Joint	Wife.	Other
Detroit Area Study, 1955 (Sharp and Mott)	26%	34%	40%	—%
Nationwide, 1954 (Wolgast)	27	28	40	5
Peoria-Decatur, 1968 (Ferber and Nicosia)	36	29	34	1

In other words, the wife seemed to carry this responsibility most of the time, but in a substantial number of families the responsibility was either shared or looked after by the husband. Sharp and Mott also noted that the husband is likely to carry this responsibility more often and the wife less often among higher-income families. The Peoria-Decatur panel of young married couples, however, suggested that husbands generally carry a larger share of this burden than wives. Whether this difference is due to the nature of the sample, location, or different time period can not be ascertained.

A somewhat broader approach to the question of husband-wife influence on money management was taken in a study by the Life Insurance Agency Management Association. By means of a mail survey to 2,000 husband-wife families (who were members of an established mail panel) in which the husbands were under 45 years of age, it sought among other things to ascertain who was the "financial officer" in the family [59]. This determination was based on responses to four questions; namely, who keeps the budget if the family has one, who is responsible for bills and expenses, who makes out most of the checks if the family has a checking account, and who is most likely to know the family's income and asset position.

Based on these responses, the wife was judged to be the financial officer in about 4 in every 10 of these families, the husband in one of every four families, and husband and wife together in about one-third of the families. Wives were especially predominant in the writing of checks, keeping of budgets, and being responsible for financial records. They were more likely to be the financial officer if they had full- or part-time jobs, if the husband's education was below college level, and if the husband was in a laboring occupation. To what extent the results might have been influenced by panel effects is not clear.

The extent to which other family members participate in these tasks is hardly noted in the literature. Indeed, the focus of virtually all these other studies was such as to exclude the possibility of obtaining such information. Of the studies cited in this section, only Wolgast apparently left provision for other family members to have influence on various decisions, and she found, in fact, that in 5 per cent of the families members other than the wife or the husband were responsible for keeping track of money and paying bills. An interesting corroboration of this percentage was provided by the study of Honey and Smith, based on reports obtained from home economics students, in which 5 per cent of these students reported that they had kept expense records for the family while at home [42].

Spending decisions

In accordance with the outline presented earlier for this section, attention will be given first to family roles in decisions relating to the purchase of products, primarily to husband-wife roles, and second to family roles in decisions related to product attributes, particularly to the brand. It should be stressed that this section makes no pretense at covering the extensive literature, mainly from marketing and home economics, dealing with the determinants of buyer behavior and the means of forecasting such behavior. Besides being outside the scope of this paper, that literature has been reviewed in a number of other sources [10]. Variables from these more general reviews are brought in when they relate to family decision making in regard to spending behavior.

1. *Marital roles*—At least two general hypotheses have been advanced to explain the role of husband and wife in influencing spending in different families. Bott suggested that the extent to which families do things jointly, such as spending money, depends on the "connectedness" of their social network; that is, whether husband and wife have the same friends and interests [8]. Connectedness is said to be more prevalent if the family has low mobility, lives in a fairly homogeneous neighborhood, and the husband is in the working (blue-collar) class.

Taking a somewhat different approach, Komarovsky advanced the idea, based on examination of various empirical studies, that "there is greater autonomy with regard to expenditures at the bottom and at the top of the socioeconomic hierarchy than among the middle classes" [54]. The studies she examined tend to support the fact that the wife in the lower socioeconomic classes seems to have greater influence in decision making relating to expenditures. In addition, in all social classes she found a higher rate of joint decision making on spending among young couples.

A roughly similar point of view was taken by Barton. He argued that, according to marketing research observations, housewives 45 years of age and over tend to have accumulated sufficient experience so that they can act essentially as professional purchasing agents for the family, even with regard to men's clothes and furnishings; and they know the needs of their family well enough so that consultation is much less likely to be needed [2].

The empirical studies of these questions have taken many different forms and, not surprisingly, yield results that are not always compatible. In one of the earlier studies of this subject, based on the replies of marketing students in seven universities about their parents' behavior, Converse and Crawford estimated the per cent of purchases made by various family members as well as the per cent of purchases influenced by women, men, and children, according to category of the products [15]. They found that men make most purchases of their own clothing and toilet articles, hardware, cars, and gas and oil; women, of their own clothing and children's clothing and of home furnishings; while children are important only with regard to their own clothing purchases. They also found that joint purchases are in the majority only for furniture, and that joint shopping and joint influence tend to be lower among low-income families.

Another study based on interviews with parents corroborated some of the Converse and Crawford findings in that purchases of furniture and household equipment were planned on a joint basis approximately 75 per cent of the time, and that children usually participated with the parents only in buying their own clothing [79]. In her study, however, Wolgast noted that joint decisions on the purchase of household goods were reported only 54 per cent of the time, while Sharp and Mott reported joint decisions on a major item, such as the selection of a house or an apartment, only 58 per cent of the time. It will be recalled, however, that the data in the latter study were obtained from the wife in every case.

On the basis of these various studies, one may infer that a tendency toward increased joint decision making with regard to purchases is likely to characterize younger families, those families in which the husband and wife have been married a short time, middle-class families, and also those purchases where a substantial outlay relative to family income may be involved. In addition, Granbois hypothesized that joint participation in the process of deciding purchases "will vary directly with the degree in which they (family members) directly engage in use of the product" and is more likely "the more nearly equal the contribution of resources such as income, education, and social participation by husbands and wives . . ." [37, pp. 196–7].

Perhaps the single purchase decision studied most often with regard to husband-wife roles is the auto purchase, and here too the findings were somewhat different. In her study, Wolgast reported that the timing of the car purchase was set by the husband in more than half the families, and jointly in another 28 per cent of the cases. Sharp and Mott reported that in the purchase of the family car the husband had the greater influence 70 per cent of the time and that the decision was made jointly 25 per cent of the time, with the dominance of the husband becoming more frequent as income rose.

On the other hand, Davis, in a study of 211 French-speaking Catholic families in and around Quebec City, found that the relative influence in seven different types of auto-purchase decisions (such as when, where, how much, make, etc.) varied substantially within the family, with the main influence being exerted either by the husband or by the husband and wife together [19].

A similar finding was reported by Jaffe and Senft. On the basis of a study of 10 different products conducted by personal interviews with one or more members of 300 middle-income households in Hartford, Cleveland, and Seattle, they found that husband-wife roles vary substantially depending partly on the product and partly on the stage in the consumption process. The stages in the consumption process used were information gathering, latent (initiator) stage, purchase, use, and consolidation. [45]. They also found, as had Converse and Crawford, that the husband is more important than originally thought in the selection and the purchase of many of these products.

Two other very different studies tended to support the hypothesis that husband and wife roles vary substantially with the particular type of decision, and that many different decisions may underlie a particular purchase. In one such case, Cahalan reported on a study conducted first by interviewing husbands and wives together to obtain facts on purchases, and later by interviewing them separately for their opinions. While the wife was more influential in deciding whether to *consider* buying major appliances and in *thinking* about spending money, the husband seemed to be more influential in the purchase *decision* and in whether to *consider* buying a new car [13]. He also found that husbands in high-status families tend to be more frequently dominant in these decisions than husbands in low-status families.

In the other study, which relates to 12 different aspects of car and furniture purchase decisions of 100 families in Chicago suburbs, Davis found that the decision roles in the purchase of a car are not related to decision roles in the purchase of furniture [20]. Moreover, for the same family,

Davis advanced the rather surprising hypothesis that the relative influence in "product selection" (model, make, color) is unrelated to the relative influence of that member in "allocation" or "scheduling" (how much or when to buy).

This result may not be too surprising in view of the growing literature in the area of consumer marketing to the effect that people who are opinion leaders in one sense are not necessarily opinion leaders in another sense [53]. This is so even though it also seems to be true that opinion leaders in accepting innovations relating to household goods are more likely to be younger people, well educated, married and having children, and with higher incomes [63]. The fact remains that people who tend to take the initiative and tend to be innovative with regard to one aspect of purchase behavior may not be equally aggressive in other aspects.

2. *Impulse purchases*—To the extent that products are bought without any prior plan, or on "impulse," family decision making is likely to be at a minimum. Hence, although this subject is on the periphery of the present paper, it is nevertheless relevant and deserves some consideration here.

A study of these types of purchases can be considered in two respects; first, with regard to the frequency with which purchases are made that are "unplanned;" and second, with regard to those goods bought on "impulse." In the former case, the purchase possibility may have been discussed within the family and may have been considered by the purchaser but not in any overt sense; in the latter case, the purchase was presumably not considered and was only consummated as the result of a special occasion or opportunity leading to the recognition of a need or the arousal of a latent desire.

Two earlier studies of this question found that impulse purchases were quite frequent even for major items. Thus, Katona and Mueller in analyzing data from a random sample of 1,000 United States families found that about one-quarter of the purchases of four major household durables were made with "almost a complete lack of deliberation" [50]. The primary reasons for these purchases were urgent need or a special deal. In the case of men's sport shirts, impulse buying seems to have been even more frequent.

In another study about the same time, based on panel data from 150 families in Decatur, Illinois, Ferber found that about one-fifth of the durable goods and clothing purchases made by the panel families were on impulse—unplanned and postponable [32]. Both studies indicated that purchase planning, and highly deliberate decision making, were most common among the better educated, the middle-income groups, younger families, and professional and managerial families.

That many purchases of durable goods were made without any particular plan and on the basis of need has also been demonstrated in a study of the Consumers Union membership by Juster [46]. Indeed, until the advent of subjective probabilities in the use of ascertaining purchase plans, the largest proportion of purchases of durable goods was accounted for by people who had not reported any plan [46, pp. 24–26.]. This does not mean that families were necessarily making these purchases without any discussions but rather that the survey techniques were not obtaining the most relevant information. Furthermore many purchases may have been made on the basis of immediate urgency, in which case family discussion might be minimal. Granbois suggested the hypothesis that "households are more apt to form purchase plans for goods that they do not already have than for goods they own but intend to replace whenever necessary" [37]. In other words, the replacement of goods already on hand is more likely to be left to need and urgency than to deliberate planning.

Satisfaction with a product is likely to be another variable serving to reduce family discussion and planning. In a recent study Newman and Staelin found that the most important variable in distinguishing between decision times in the purchase of a durable good was satisfaction with the old product [65]. Satisfied users took appreciably less time to make the decision, which also suggests that the amount of discussion within the family was less in those cases.

The amount of the purchase is also likely to affect family planning, small purchases tending to be made with a much shorter time horizon, and very likely with less discussion. Thus Pratt, in his study on the average length of the purchase planning period based on data from a General Electric panel, found the average planning period to vary from one week for small radios to 16 weeks for clothes driers [70]. In a similar study investigating the circumstances of the purchase of small electrical appliances, Udell found that the planning period for these appliances ranged from 22 per cent for one day to 83 per cent for a period of up to one month [78].

Studies of impulse purchases of nondurables have focused primarily on food products or items purchased in supermarkets. As one might expect, such impulse buying, in the sense of purchases not planned at the time of entry into the store, was found to be substantial. West, in a survey of about 5,000 Canadian shoppers, found that 37 per cent of their total purchases were not planned (not reported to the interviewer) when the shopper entered the store [81]. The Dupont Company, in a similar series of studies in the United States in 1945, 1949, 1954, and 1959, found the frequency of impulse purchases in supermarkets to be rising over time, from 38 per cent in 1945 to 51 per cent in 1959 [25]. At the same time, the per cent of items planned specifically in advance declined from 48 per cent in 1945 to 30 per cent in 1959.

These findings are in accord with the observed proliferation of items in supermarkets and the increase in efforts of marketing people to put items into racks or in a form where they are easily picked up on the spur of the moment. A more general interpretation of this phenomenon was provided by Stern, who argued that impulse buying may be rational behavior, giving the shopper a chance to adjust to deals and to merchandising opportunities found in the store [75]. He cited the factors affecting impulse buying as low price, marginal need for the item, mass distribution opportunities, self-service, mass advertising, prominent store display, short product life of many goods, small size or light weight, and ease of storage. To the extent that impulse buying is increasing, family deliberation is likely to be decreasing.

3. *Brand choice*—Of the huge marketing literature dealing with the determinants of brand choice, very little has been concerned with the roles of different family members in this choice. To many marketing people, brand choice is a matter of habit formation which, once established, is likely to continue almost indefinitely. Thus, in one very well-known marketing study, Kuehn noted that buying decisions are a learning process, with more search behavior taking place when there is more uncertainty about the product, and that the probability of buying the same brand on two consecutive purchases tends to increase as the interval between purchases decreases (at least for frozen orange juice) [55]. Other models took an even more sanguine view of brand choice determination, such as the Bernoulli process model (constant probabilities of brand choice), but even the more sophisticated Markov process models or the probability diffusion models treated the family as an entity [60].

If anything, the focus in marketing has been on newly formed households and on inducing them to try a product. Thus, ". . . younger housewives are easier to educate to an awareness of product and brand; it is easier to get across to the younger housewives the reasons why they should try or buy it; and younger housewives are less fixed in their buying habits and brand loyalty, and will be more inclined to *change* their buying pattern in response to advertising" [61].

The main focus on family decision making with regard to brand choice has been on automobiles. In one relatively early study, it was concluded that the husband decides what make of car to buy in 61 per cent of the families and the husband and wife together in 39 per cent [29]. George Brown cited two other studies supporting his assertion that the husband is the primary decision maker in new car purchases, giving data from a Starch study for *True* magazine and from a J. Walter Thompson panel indicating that in the decision about the model, the husband invariably decided either by himself or in conjunction with the wife. It might be noted that True magazine focuses entirely on a male audience, at least at the time that the study was made [11].

More recent studies suggested, however, that family interactions may well influence brand choice. Thus, Coulson found in a pilot study that wives' awareness of brand preferences of other family members varies greatly with the product class [16]. Awareness is highest when the brand name is clearly visible in use, such as for beer or cigarettes, and is less when the product is altered just prior to use.

In two other studies involving husband-wife interviews, Davis and Silk reported that housewives frequently buy the brands that the husbands request [21]. In one survey, more than half the housewives reported doing so for convenience products, while in another survey "the percentage of wives who reported that their husbands' brand comments were very important to them in making brand decisions ranged from 26 per cent for peanut butter to 98 per cent for dog food" [21]. Also of interest is their finding that the husbands in their interviews consistently underestimated the importance of their comments on brands to the wives.

4. *Influence of children*—The studies of Converse and Crawford and of Van Syckle have already been cited to the effect that children seem to influence only the purchase of their own clothing. The relatively few other studies on the influence of children on family spending decisions yielded similar results. Thus Brown in his study on automobile buying decisions reported that parents claim that their children, even the teenagers, have little influence on the make of car purchased. Rayburn [71] reported that 27 per cent of the mothers she interviewed said that their teenagers were consulted on family purchases, but further details were not obtained.

Perhaps even more surprising is a study by Berey and Pollay in which they ascertained cereal preferences of 48 children in an elementary school and compared them with the cereals that their mothers had purchased and were in the house. A negative correlation was found between the assertiveness of the child (based on teacher ratings) and the tendency of the mother to buy the preferred cereal [5]. The explanation advanced by the authors of this odd finding was that the mothers seemed to be more concerned with buying products that would contribute to the health of the child than with satisfying the child's whims. (The sample was from a middle- to upper-middle-income segment.)

On the other hand, an advertising research study by Munn, based on mail questionnaires to parents with small children, stated that 9 of 10 parents reported they were influenced by their children in the choice of specific branded products [64]. In addition, substantial proportions reported products being used in the home of the type advertised in children's television programs to which their children had apparently been exposed (based on the choice of the sampling frame). However, the nature of the study (a mail questionnaire), the lack of any control group, and the low rate of response (44 per cent) cast doubt on the significance of these findings.

Some attention has also been given to decision making by children, especially by teenagers. In one such study, Gibbs showed that teenager purchases of grooming, clothing, and recreation items in a Georgia high school were mostly planned, although many girls' grooming items were still purchased on the basis of impulse [36]. It does not seem necessary to delve into this literature here [see 14]. Especially pertinent, however, are the findings of one study that spending and saving habits of adolescent siblings show only low correlations with each other as well as with those of the other children and of the mothers [68].

5. *Role of reference groups and information*—Both the search for information and the use of reference groups are bound to influence substantially family decision making. An attempt is made in this subsection, therefore, to indicate some of the more pertinent studies in this area. Unlike other topics treated in this paper, extensive material is available on this subject and is summarized from different points of view in the general references listed [*42*]. For this purpose, it seems desirable to segment these studies into those dealing primarily with reference groups and those dealing primarily with the role of information.

(a) *Reference groups*—The role of reference groups in influencing consumer spending and saving behavior was brought out more than 20 years ago in two well-known and very different studies, by Katz and Lazarsfeld in sociology [51] and by Duesenberry in economics [24]. Katz and Lazarsfeld placed the main emphasis on the influence of friends and relatives regarding purchasing behavior while Duesenberry focused more on saving behavior. In the latter connection, virtually no other studies seem to have been made of the influence of reference groups on family saving behavior. One exception is that in her study, Schomaker reported that wide use was made of consultative sources in the financial decisions made by her sample families. In particular, people outside the family were consulted 88 per cent of the time, relatives 38 per cent of the time, and "specialists" 22 per cent of the time; all these proportions tended to be higher for younger families and for better-educated families [73]. Indeed, she reported that the main influence on the decisions seems to have been the information obtained from these reference groups.

On the spending side, the well-known study by Whyte seems to be confirmed in a number of other products and ways. In his study, it will be recalled, ownership of window air conditioners was highly clustered in Philadelphia in a manner to suggest that it was influenced by ownership of the same product by neighbors [85]. A very similar finding was obtained by Kurt Lewin in an experiment with changing the diets of housewives. He found that the housewives tended to be much more co-operative when diet changes were suggested in discussion groups than when the same changes were suggested in either lectures or in personal conversations [58].

In a somewhat later study, reference group influence was found to be high in housewives' brand selection when the product was socially conspicuous, such as beer or cigarettes, but such influence was found to be low when the product was not conspicuous [9]. Udell also reported in his study of small appliance purchases that the sample members reported discussion with friends, relatives, and neighbors as most influential in their decision to purchase [78].

Still another study in a very different field showed that in their choice of a physician and of medical services, newcomers to an area seemed to rely very heavily on friends, neighbors, or recent acquaintances in the same socioeconomic class, especially if the newcomers were younger families with children [30].

Perhaps one of the more striking instances of the use of a reference group is in a study by Bell, who found in interviews with buyers of new Chevrolets that many of them tended to use "purchase pals" in making their purchase [4]. In other words, many of these people, especially those who had neither very low self-confidence nor very high self-confidence with regard to car buying, would bring along a friend, neighbor, or relative to assist in making the car-purchase decision.

(b) *Role of information*—The extent to which information is sought, and its role in influencing purchasing behavior, has been studied extensively in the marketing literature, so much so that entire books have been devoted to the subject [17]. Referring to studies at Harvard, Cox suggested that "the nature and amount of risk will define consumer information needs." In terms of economics, Farley advanced the hypothesis that the amount of search for information is a function of the expected gain relative to the cost of obtaining the information [28]. Hence, he inferred that purchasers of large quantities of a particular product will search for more information to obtain lower prices, and that a more expensive item is itself likely to occasion more search for information.

A principal source of research on information is with regard to the acceptance of new products, and it is here that information can be shown to interact with the role of reference groups in family decision making. Perhaps the best manifestation of this relationship is the two-step flow hypothesis on acceptance of new products; namely, the initial flow of information from impersonal sources to opinion leaders, and the derived effect of opinion leaders' influencing their friends, neighbors, and acquaintances by means of word-of-mouth. This hypothesis was originally formulated in a voter study [57], and was substantiated in a later study by Johan Arndt in an experiment on acceptance of a new food product by married students [1].

Various other studies have indicated that information plays a key role in the adoption of new products [3]. In particular, these studies indicated that the use of the mass media seems to be especially high at the awareness stage, with personal influence being of very great importance in influencing the purchase decision. As might be expected, those who are most likely to seek information, and do so to the greatest extent, are younger people, better-educated people, and those with higher incomes [72]. Also, greater knowledge about one type of product seems to be associated with greater knowledge about another product, at least in the case of food and textiles [38], although more information does not necessarily lead to greater satisfaction in purchasing [66]. To what extent the same findings are valid for financial decisions remains to be investigated.

Saving and investment decisions

(a) *Saving goals*—A great deal has appeared in the economics and home economics literature about saving goals and reasons for saving. Reasons for saving were discussed by Keynes in his *General Theory,* and more recently by George Katona in some of his works [47]. The literature is at least as extensive in home economics, though the focus there seems to be primarily on the financial and saving goals of rural families. For a number of years during the 1950s and the early 1960s a co-operative study was undertaken among nine North Central states covering 2,000 rural families about the meaning and the nature of financial security, and about the factors affecting their security. This publication contains a list of the other studies undertaken as part of this work [84]. Indicative of the type of studies undertaken is one by Phelan and Ruef, where they reported that planning, protection, and saving are the three key values related to the investments of 93 rural Pennsylvania couples [69].

Similarly, in a study of Indiana farmers, Oberly concluded that the number and kinds of financial decisions and of family goals are influenced by family characteristics and are much more common in a conscious sense among younger families, among those better educated, among families at both extremes of the income scale, and especially among families in which the wife has a professional or a managerial job [67].

In still another study of this type, based on interviews with both husbands and wives in 65 families in New York State, approximately half urban and half rural, Crow found that families were mainly concerned with financial security in the sense of reserves for emergencies, adequate level of living, future security, and increase in the level of living. Saving was undertaken mostly for security, for steady return, and for the long run rather than for substantial or quick gains [18]. Indications of a relationship were noted among goals, concepts of financial security, and financial management practices, such as the tendency for those concerned with job security to be more oriented toward financial security and very strongly disinclined to venture into debt.

In their three-generation study, Reuben Hill and his associates reported that "in analyzing the reasons for saving given by respondents, the child generation offers family advancement, educational, and style of consumption type reasons much more than the other generations (56 per cent compared with 34 per cent for parents and 27 per cent for grandparents). The older generations are more likely to save for retirement and for emergencies" [39, p. 128]. The authors also noted that the younger generations were much more likely to be involved in self-imposed regular saving plans.

These findings are useful in explaining why people think they should save or whether they should save at all, and reflect in effect the end product of the family's decision making in this regard. They do not, however, explain how these decisions were made in the first place, or the roles of the different family members in defining these objectives. In other words, the dynamics of the process is yet another area for further study.

(b) *Saving and investment management*—The extensive work in economics on the determinants of saving and of asset holding [31] [4] has not been paralleled by much comparable work on family roles in saving or investment behavior. Hence, as noted previously, it seems best to combine what has been done under these two headings in this single subsection.

(c) *To save or to spend*—Decisions on the allocation of family income between saving and spending can be considered from two very different perspectives—the extent to which the family as a unit gives priority to saving and, with regard to family roles, which family members are involved in saving decisions.

At least two different approaches have been taken to investigate the priority of saving. One is what may be termed the "direct approach," whereby the family was asked how it allocates income between saving and spending and the priority given to saving relative to spending. This approach was exemplified in questions asked of the consumer decision panel of young married couples in Decatur and Peoria, Illinos, by Nicosia and Ferber. The results indicated, rather surprisingly, that half of the 312 couples were giving some priority to saving by following a definite plan for saving part of their income in advance of spending. One of every five couples indicated that it would give top priority to saving under almost any circumstances. Undoubtedly pertinent is the fact that these couples had been married only three to six months at the time these questions were asked.

The more indirect approach has been to impute saving priorities to the family on the basis of general information on the family's saving and spending habits, on its type of savings, and on its budgeting practices. From this type of information, inferences have been made about saving priorities. Thus, in his early work, Katona had stressed the distinction between contractual and discretionary saving, pointing out that certain types of saving by their very nature must receive top priority, because they have to be made every month (or every week), while other types of saving are more discretionary and hence are likely to have lower priority [48]. Katona noted, for example, that a monthly payment on a mortgage or a regular deduction from a paycheck for purchasing savings bonds must by definition have top priority because they are contractual in nature and are made as a matter of course.

Part of this saving may be unconscious in the sense that the family looks on it as a form of expenditure and, in the case of mortgage payments, may not even be aware of how much is being saved in the form of home equity. It is not unlikely that some families prefer to delude themselves that such payments are a form of expenditure, partly because they feel obligated to make the payments if they are regarded as an expenditure, and partly because in this way they can look forward to being pleasantly surprised when, say, the mortgage is fully paid and they realize they have undisputed equity in their own home.

Some families are essentially saving-oriented and give priority to saving regardless of their level of assets, as Katona has shown [48, Chapters 18–19]. Thus people who save in the form of pension plans are also more likely to save in other forms [49].

(d) *Family roles*—The roles of the different family members in making saving and investment decisions are largely a mystery. Some information on this question in a static sense is available from the "purchase influence" studies. In her study Wolgast found that "seeing that money gets saved" was a joint responsibility of husband and wife in 48 per cent of the sample families, of the wife in 27 per cent, and of the husband in 15 per cent. In their study, Sharp and Mott reported that the purchase of life insurance was looked after primarily by the husband in 43 per cent of the sample households, by both jointly in 42 per cent, and by the wives primarily in 15 per cent of the households, and that the frequency of dominance by the husband or by both jointly increased as income level rose.

From their panel data on young married couples, Ferber and Nicosia found that saving decisions are reported as being made overwhelmingly on a joint basis. Four-fifths of the couples reported this practice; the husbands only, in 14 per cent of the cases; the wives only, in 6 per cent. The very special nature of the sample—all being married 6 months or less—undoubtedly influenced these responses (though it is hard to imagine a similarly high proportion of joint decisions in a corresponding sample, say, 40 years earlier).

The fact remains, however, that these few studies and the general nature of the findings only serve to highlight the need for information on the dynamics of the family decision-making process with regard to saving and investment behavior.

(e) *Role of teenagers*—Rather surprisingly, the one family member who seems to have received some attention in the literature with regard to saving and investments is the teenager. Hence it would seem desirable to summarize briefly some of the findings for this group.

In his study of teenagers cited earlier, Cateora reported that his sample of teenagers placed great emphasis on saving. He found that the higher the social position of the family, the more concerned were teenagers with saving.

This finding seems to be borne out by other studies. In their study on the reports of college students about their parents, Honey and Smith noted that when these students were at home, more than four-fifths reported saving some money. (Also nearly two-thirds kept some form of expense records and nearly 40 per cent contributed to their own support.)

In another study of 610 "lower-class" teenagers in six Southern Illinois counties, Fults and Zunich found that 22 per cent saved on a regular basis [35]. In still another study in the same area, of 294 randomly selected 13–18 year-old teenagers in Southern Illinois high schools, 65 per cent were earning money in addition to getting an allowance, and virtually all of them were trying to save some money, the principal saving objectives being for education (64 per cent), for the future (26 per cent), or for a specific product or service (10 per cent) [87]. The principal forms of saving were savings and loan associations (44 per cent), banks (38 per cent), and government savings bonds (11 per cent).

It is also pertinent to mention in this section the study of the spending and saving patterns of adolescent siblings by Phelan and Schvanevaldt. They found very different attitudes toward saving on the part of the two siblings as well as between each of the siblings and their mothers, even though the spending and saving habits of the siblings seemed to be influenced by social class of the parents, by age of the child, and by amount of supervision received from the parents. Appreciable differences were also noted between siblings in their money-handling practices.

These studies would seem to suggest that despite the reputed spending tendencies of teenagers they are generally highly conscious of saving and undoubtedly develop saving and investment attitudes during these years that influence their behavior for the rest of their lives.

III. Conclusion: A Modified Framework

The studies summarized in the foregoing sections seem to indicate clearly that financial decision making within the family is influenced by a great many different factors, and that the strength of these factors varies not only with the characteristics of the family but also with the nature of the decision that has to be made. In view of the disparate nature of these influences it seems hardly necessary or desirable to conclude this paper with a summary of how each of these influences affect family financial decision making; in this respect the findings in the preceding sections speak for themselves. However, it would seem useful to indicate how the framework presented at the beginning of this book relating to the interrelation of financial and nonfinancial decisions (Chart 1) might be modified on the basis of these findings to focus on the general factors that appear to enter into financial decision making within the family. This would seem all the more desirable because the theoretical representations of family behavior presented to date attempt to focus either on general family behavior [26], on the relation between family behavior and other types of behavior [12], on the steps of the decision process [73], or on the various factors that appear to influence buyer behavior and their interrelations [43]. These other frameworks are extremely useful in themselves. The present framework is meant as a supplement rather than as a substitute, with the specific objective of focusing on family financial decisions and on the dynamics of the decision-making process within the family.

Such a modified framework is presented in Chart 2. The three rectangular boxes at the top of the diagram represent general exogenous forces influencing the financial position of the family and the attitudes of the different family members. Thus reference groups (including mass media and other printed materials) clearly influence the attitude of both husband and wife. (If one of these members is not present, the box for that person will be empty.) Also the characteristics of the individual family members obviously influence their attitudes; and some of their characteristics, such as occupation and employment status, influence the financial resources of the family. The third set of exogenous factors reflects primarily external economic events, the principal influence of which is on the family's financial resources.

The attitudes of husband and wife affect financial decisions not only directly but also through their interactions in the formation of family goals. At the same time, their attitudes, combined with the characteristics of the different family members, determine the structure of the family, which in turn will influence financial decisions, especially money management and spending decisions. In addition, financial resources obviously affect the

CHART 2. THE FACTORS ENTERING INTO FINANCIAL DECISIONS WITHIN THE FAMILY

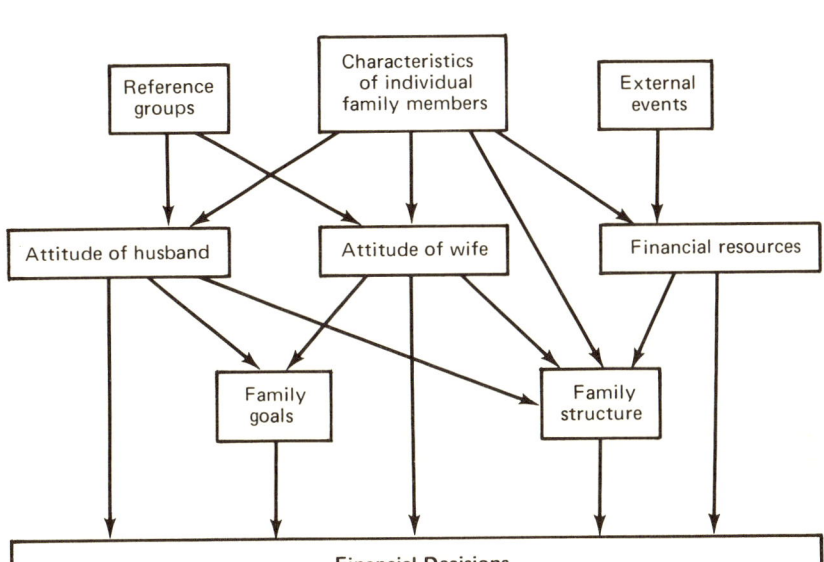

structure of the family, and influence financial decisions through this means as well as directly.

All of these activities and decisions take place over time, of course, with numerous lag relationships involved at different stages. The framework is, therefore, highly dynamic, though it is only when the relationships are specified more rigorously that the full extent of this phenomenon becomes clear.

No attempt has been made in this diagram to single out individual financial decisions or to highlight individual variables among the broad categories depicted, nor has any attempt been made to allow for the attitudes or preferences of family members other than the wife or husband. This is partly for the sake of simplicity and partly because for most types of financial decisions the attitudes of these other family members tend to be much less important than those of the husband or the wife, at least on the average. Nevertheless, it is hoped this framework will prove useful as a basis for future studies of family financial decisions and as a basis for further development of models of such decisions.

To be sure, one may question whether, from the point of view of developing better models of economic behavior, it makes much difference if much is known about the processes of family decisions. More concretely, does information about family decision processes enter into the construction of better models of consumer economic behavior? If the answer were no, an economist might well argue that we need not bother with these questions; that while they may be very interesting, they belong more to home economics and to sociology, say, than to economics or finance.

On a preliminary basis, however, such information would seem to be highly relevant. This was illustrated by a recent paper by Ferber and Nicosia on a model of asset accumulation by young married couples [33], based on data from the consumer panel of young married couples mentioned earlier. Very briefly, that model is composed of three submodels in a recursive chain, one submodel to explain consumer attitudes toward saving and their awareness of promotion of different forms of saving, another submodel to explain the amount saved in the current period and its allocation among different forms of saving, and the third submodel to explain the total wealth of the couple and its allocation by type of investment.

The empirical results, based entirely on the third of these submodels, indicated that there were sharp differences between husbands and wives in their priorities of allocating wealth and in their saving plans. Moreover, attitudinal variables and family characteristics affected the allocation of wealth differently according to whether it was the husband or the wife who made the decision. Although those equations did not include specific information on the type of decision-making processes within the family, these findings suggest rather strongly that information of this type can prove highly useful in the development of better economic models of consumer behavior, and probably other types of models as well. Clearly, therefore, more attention needs to be given to the twin problems of how to specify such models to make most effective use of this type of data, and how to get the data.

All the aforementioned activities and decisions take place over time, of course, with numerous lag relationships at different stages. The framework is therefore highly dynamic, though it is only when the relationships are specified more rigorously that the full extent of the phenomenon becomes clear.

Notes

1. Such decisions are not devoid of financial consequences either, and in this sense the distinction between financial and nonfinancial decisions is by no means as clear-cut as is implied by Chart 1. The distinction is pertinent only in the sense that the primary (and conscious) focus is on financial variables in decisions related to family economic behavior.

2. The entire focus on this subject in the literature seems to have been on hus-

band-wife relationships. The cases where there may be only one such member with children or other relatives present does not seem to have been considered and would seem to be another area for future study.

3. The first two studies have been published. The third comes from unpublished data from a consumer panel of newly married couples in Peroria and Decatur, Illinois. It should be noted that the Sharp and Mott question asked who had more influence rather than the Wolgast approach of asking who made the decision. The data on young married couples in Decatur and Peoria, Illinois, interviewed about every six months since the fall of 1968, relates to "who usually looks after paying bills?"

4. This article contains a summary of the extensive work in economics on the determinants of saving and of asset holding up to 1962.

5. For lack of space, an appendix on the methodology of decision-making studies has been omitted. Copies are available, however, from the author.

References

1. Arndt, Johan, "A Test of the Two-Step Flow in Diffusion of a New Product," *Journalism Quarterly* 45, Autumn 1968, pp. 457–465; reprinted in R. J. Holloway, R. A. Mittelstaedt, and M. Venkatesan, eds., *Consumer Behavior, Contemporary Research in Action*, Boston: Houghton Mifflin Company, 1971, pp. 235–246.

2. Barton, S. G., "The Life Cycle and Buying Patterns," in L. H. Clark, ed., *The Life Cycle and Consumer Behavior*, New York: New York University Press, 1955, pp. 53–57.

3. Beal, G. M., and E. M. Rogers, "Information Sources in the Adoption Process of New Fabrics," *Journal of Home Economics* 49, October 1957, pp. 630–634; R. G. Mason, "The Use of Information Sources in the Process of Adoption," *Rural Sociology* 29, March 1964, pp. 40–52.

4. Bell, G. D., "Self-Confidence, Persuasibility and Cognitive Dissonance Among Automobile Buyers," in D. F. Cox, *Risk-Taking and Information Handling in Consumer Behavior*, Boston: Graduate School of Business, Harvard University, 1967.

5. Berey, L. A., and R. W. Pollay, "The Influencing Role of the Child in Family Decision-Making," *Journal of Marketing Research* 5, February 1968, pp. 70–71.

6. Blood, R., and D. M. Wolfe, *Husbands and Wives and America: Dynamics of Married Life*, Glencoe, Illinois: Free Press, 1963, p. 114.

7. Bortel, D. G. van, and I. H. Gross, *Comparison of Home Management in Two Socioeconomic Groups*, Bulletin 240, East Lansing: Michigan State College Agriculture Experiment Station, 1952.

8. Bott, E., "Urban Families: Conjugal Roles and Social Networks," *Human Relations* 8, 1955, pp. 345–384.

9. Bourne, F. S., "Group Influence in Marketing and Public Relations," in Rensis Likert and S. P. Hayes, eds., *Some Applications of Behavioral Research*, Paris, France: UNESCO, 1957.

10. Britt, Steuart H., ed., *Consumer Behavior in Theory and Action*, New York: John Wiley & Sons, 1970; Johan Arndt, ed., *Insights into Consumer Behavior*, Boston: Allyn & Bacon, 1968; J. F. Engel, D. T. Kollat, and R. D. Blackwell, *Consumer Behavior*, New York: Holt, Rinehart & Winston, 1968; J. N. Sheth, "A Review of Buyer Behavior," *Management Science* 13, August 1967, pp. B718–B757; M. C. Burk, "Survey of Interpretations of Con-

sumer Behavior by Social Scientists in the Postwar Period," *Journal of Farm Economics* 49, February 1967, pp. 1–31; F. E. May, "Buyer Behavior: Some Research Findings," *Journal of Business* 38, October 1965, pp. 379–396.

11. Brown, G. H., "The Automobile Buying Decision Within the Family," in N. N. Foote, ed., *Household Decision-Making,* New York: New York University Press, 1961, pp. 193–199.

12. Burk, M. C., "An Integrated Approach to Consumer Behavior," *Journal of Home Economics* 59, March 1967, pp. 155–162.

13. Cahalan, Don, "Comments," in N. N. Foote, ed., *Household Decision-Making,* New York: New York University Press, 1961, pp. 225–228.

14. Cateora, R. R., *An Analysis of the Teenage Market,* Austin: University of Texas Bureau of Business Research, 1961.

15. Converse, P. D., and C. M. Crawford, "Family Buying: Who Does It? Who Influences It?" *Current Economic Comment* 11, November 1949, pp. 38–50.

16. Coulson, J. S., "Buying Decisions Within the Family and the Consumer-Brand Relationship," in J. W. Newman, ed., *On Knowing the Consumer,* New York: John Wiley & Sons, 1966, pp. 59–66.

17. Cox, D. F., ed., *Risk-Taking and Information Handling in Consumer Behavior,* Boston: Graduate School of Business, Harvard University, 1967.

18. Crow, J. H., "Financial Management in Relation to Family Values and Concepts of Financial Security," unpublished Ph.D. thesis, Cornell University, 1961.

19. Davis, H. L., "Determinants of Marital Roles in Consumer Purchase Decisions," unpublished working paper, Graduate School of Business, University of Chicago, October 1970.

20. ———, "Dimensions of Marital Roles in Consumer Decision-Making," *Journal of Marketing Research* 7, May 1970, pp. 168–177.

21. ———, and Alvin Silk, "Small Group Theory," in Robert Ferber, ed., *Handbook of Marketing Research,* New York: McGraw-Hill, forthcoming.

22. Davis, M. J., "Decision-Making in Relation to the Performance of Household Activities in New York State Homes," unpublished Ph.D. dissertation, Cornell University, 1957.

23. Dix, L. C., "Decision-Making in the Farm Family," unpublished master's thesis, Cornell University, 1957.

24. Duesenberry, James, *Income Savings and the Theory of Consumer Demand,* Cambridge: Harvard University Press, 1949. A very similar exposition, though from a broader point of view, appeared about the same time by Franco Modigliani, "Fluctuations in the Saving-Income Ratio: A Problem in Economic Forecasting," National Bureau of Economic Research Studies in Income and Wealth 11, 1949, pp. 371–443.

25. E. I. Dupont de Nemours & Company, *Consumer Buying Habits Studies,* 1945, 1949, 1954, 1959.

26. Edwards, K. P., "A Theoretical Approach to Goal-Oriented Family Behavior," *Journal of Home Economics* 62, November 1970, pp. 652–655.

27. Farber, Bernard, *Family Organization and Interaction,* San Francisco: Chandler Publishing Co., 1964, pp. 299–300.

28. Farley, J. U., " 'Brand Loyalty' and the Economics of Information," *Journal of Business* 27, October 1964, pp. 370–381.

29. Fawcett Publications, *Male versus Female Influence on the Purchase of Selected Products,* New York, 1958.

30. Feldman, S. P., and M. C. Spencer, "The Effect of Personal Influence in

the Selection of Consumer Services," in Holloway, Mittelstaedt, Vankatesan, eds., *op. cit.,* pp. 247–257.

31. Ferber, Robert, "Research on Household Behavior," *American Economic Review* 52, March 1962, pp. 19–63.

32. ———, *Factors Influencing Durable Goods Purchases,* Urbana: University of Illinois Bureau of Economic and Business Research, 1955.

33. ———, and F. N. Nicosia, "Newly Married Couples and Their Asset Accumulation Decisions," in *Human Behavior in Economic Affairs,* forthcoming.

34. Freeman, R. C., and J. M. Due, "Influences of Goals on Family Financial Management," *Journal of Home Economics* 53, June 1961, pp. 448–452.

35. Fults, A. C., and M. Zunich, "Money Management Practices of Teenagers from Low-Income Families," *Journal of Home Economics* 59, January 1967, pp. 45–47.

36. Gibbs, M., "Decision-Making Procedures by Young Consumers," *Journal of Home Economics* 55, May 1963, pp. 359–360.

37. Granbois, D. H., "Decision Processes for Major Durable Goods," in George Fisk, ed., *New Essays on Marketing Theory,* Boston: Allyn & Bacon, 1971, pp. 172–205.

38. Henell, Olaf, *Marketing Aspects of Housewives' Knowledge of Goods,* Göteborg, Sweden: Institute for Marketing and Management Research, 1953.

39. Hill, Reuben et al., *Family Development in Three Generations,* Cambridge, Mass., Schenkman Publishing Company, 1970, pp. 127–133, 135–137.

40. Honey, R. R., *Family Financial Management Experiences,* Pennsylvania State University, College of Home Economics, Research Publication 141, 1957.

41. ———, V. Britton, and A. S. Hotchkiss, *Decision-Making in the Use of Family Financial Resources,* Pennsylvania State University, College of Home Economics, Research Publication 163, 1959.

42. ———, and W. M. Smith, Jr., *Family Financial Management Experiences, as Reported by 179 College Students,* Pennsylvania State College, School of Home Economics, Research Publications 113, 1952.

43. Howard J. A., and J. N. Sheth, *The Theory of Buyer Behavior,* New York: John Wiley and Sons, 1969.

44. ———, ———, *The Theory of Buyer Behavior,* New York: McGraw-Hill, 1970.

45. Jaffe, L. J., and H. Senft, "The Roles of Husbands and Wives in Purchasing Decisions," in Lee Adler and Irvin Crespit, eds., *Attitude Research at Sea,* Chicago: American Marketing Association, 1966, pp. 95–110.

46. Juster, F. T., *Anticipations and Purchases,* Princeton: Princeton University Press, 1964. See especially pp. 24–26.

47. Katona, George, *The Mass Consumption Society,* New York: McGraw-Hill, 1964, pp. 176–177.

48. ———, *The Powerful Consumer,* New York: McGraw-Hill, 1960, pp. 14, 92–93; also George Katona, *The Mass Consumption Society,* New York: McGraw-Hill, 1964, chapters 18–19.

49. ———, *Private Pensions and Individual Saving,* Ann Arbor: Institute for Social Research, 1965.

50. ——— and Eva Mueller, "A Study of Purchase Decisions," in L. H. Clark, ed., *Consumer Behavior: The Dynamics of Consumer Reaction,* pp. 30–87.

51. Katz, Elihu, and P. F. Lazarsfeld, *Personal Influence,* Glencoe, Illinois: The Free Press, 1955.

52. Kenkel, W. F., "Influence Differentiation in Family Decision-Making," *Sociology and Social Research* 42, September–October 1957, pp. 18–25.

53. King, C. W., and J. L. Summers, "Overlap of Opinion Leadership Across Consumer Product Categories," *Journal of Marketing Research* 7, February 1970, pp. 43–50.

54. Komarovsky, Mirra, "Class Differences in Family Decision-Making in Expenditures," in N. N. Foote, ed., *Household Decision-Making*, New York: New York University Press, 1961, p. 260.

55. Kuehn, A. A., "Consumer Brand Choice—A Learning Process," in R. E. Frank, A. A. Kuehn, and W. F. Massy, eds., *Quantitative Techniques in Marketing Analysis*, Homewood, Illinois: Richard D. Irwin, Inc., 1962.

56. Kyrk, Hazel, *The Family in the American Economy*, Chicago: University of Chicago Press, 1953, chapter 16; also, J. N. Morgan, *Consumer Economics*, Englewood Cliffs, N.J.: Prentice-Hall, 1955, chapters 4 and 16. See also pp. 323–324.

57. Lazarsfeld, P. F., B. Berelson, and H. Gaudet, *The People's Choice*, New York: Columbia University Press, 1948.

58. Lewin, Kurt, "Group Decision and Social Change," in Newcomb, Hartley, et al., eds., *Readings in Social Psychology*, New York: Henry Holt & Company, 1947, pp. 330–344.

59. Life Insurance Agency Management Association, *The Family Financial Officer*, Hartford, Connecticut, Research Report No. 5, 1966.

60. Massy, W. F., D. B. Montgomery, and D. G. Morrison, *Stochastic Models of Buying Behavior*, Cambridge, Mass.: MIT Press, 1970.

61. Miller, D. L., "The Life Cycle and the Impact of Advertising," in L. H. Clark, ed., *The Life Cycle and Consumer Behavior*, New York: New York University Press, 1955.

62. Morse, R. L. D., "Family Financial Security: Survey of Kansas Rural Families," *Journal of Home Economics* 54, October 1962, pp. 711–713.

63. Mueller, Eva, "Desire for Innovations in Household Goods," in L. H. Clark, ed., *Consumer Behavior: Research on Consumer Reactions*, New York: Harper & Brothers, 1958, pp. 13–38.

64. Munn, Mark, "The Effect on Parental Buying Habits of Children Exposed to Children's Television Programs," *Journal of Broadcasting* 2, Summer 1968, pp. 253–258; reprinted in R. J. Holloway, R. A. Mittelstaedt, M. Vankatesan, eds., *Consumer Behavior, Contemporary Research in Action*, Boston: Houghton Mifflin Company, 1971, pp. 267–271.

65. Newman, J. W., and R. Staelin, "Multivariate Analysis of Differences in Buyer Decision Time," *Journal of Marketing Research* 8, May 1971, pp. 192–198.

66. Newton, A. E., and D. L. Gilmore, "Consumer Behavior in Carpet Purchasing," *Journal of Home Economics* 61, February 1969, pp. 110–113.

67. Oberly, J. A., "Major Financial Decisions and Changes in the Family Life Span," unpublished Ph.D. thesis, Purdue University, 1967.

68. Phelan, G. K., and J. D. Sehvaneveldt, "Spending and Saving Patterns of Adolescent Siblings," *Journal of Home Economics* 61, February 1969, pp. 104–109.

69. Phelan, J. M., and R. R. Ruef, *Values Expressed and Realized in Family Financial Plans*, University Park, Pennsylvania: College of Home Economics Research Publication 176, Pennsylvania Agricultural Experiment Station Bulletin 685, 1961.

70. Pratt, R. W., Jr., "Consumer Buying Intentions as an Aid in Formulat-

ing Marketing Strategy," in R. L. King, ed., *Marketing and the New Science of Planning*, Chicago: American Marketing Association, 1968 Fall Conference, pp. 296–302.

71. Rayburn, M. B., "A Study of Money Management Practices of Selected Rural Families in Pontotoc County, Mississippi," unpublished master's thesis, University of Mississippi, 1956.

72. Roberts, J. B., *Sources of Information in Food Buying Decisions*. Southern Cooperative Series, Kentucky Agricultural Experiment Station Bulletin 85, 1963.

73. Schomaker, P. K., "Financial Decision-Making as Reported by One Hundred Farm Families in Michigan," unpublished Ph.D. thesis, Michigan State University, 1961.

74. ——— and A. C. Thorpe, "Financial Decision-Making as Reported by Farm Families in Michigan," *Quarterly Bulletin*, Michigan State University 46, November 1963.

74a. Sharp, H., and P. Mott, "Consumer Decisions in the Metropolitan Family," *Journal of Marketing*, 21, October 1956, pp. 149–156.

75. Stern, H., "The Significance of Impulse Buying Today," *Journal of Marketing* 26, April 1962, pp. 59–62.

76. Thorp, R. C., "Dimensions of Marriage Roles," *Marriage and Family Living* 25, November 1963, pp. 389–404.

77. Townsend, Peter, *The Family Life of Old People*, London: Routledge & Kegan, Paul, 1961, p. 68.

78. Udell, J. G., "Prepurchase Behavior of Buyers of Small Electrical Appliances," *Journal of Marketing* 30, October 1966, pp. 50–52; reprinted in S. H. Britt, ed., *Consumer Behavior in Theory and in Action*, New York: John Wiley & Sons, 1970, pp. 461–464.

79. Van Syckle, Carla, *Practices Followed by Consumers in Buying "Large Expenditure" Items of Clothing, Furniture and Equipment*, East Lansing: Michigan State Agricultural Experiment Station Bulletin 222, 1951.

80. Wells, H. L., "Financial Management Practices of Young Families," *Journal of Home Economics* 51, June 1959, pp. 439–443.

81. West, C. J., "Results of a Two-Year Study of Impulse Buying," *Journal of Marketing* 15, January 1951, pp. 362–363.

82. Wilkening, E. A., "Joint Decision-Making in Farm Families," *American Sociological Review* 23, April 1958, pp. 187–192.

83. ———, and L. Bharadwaj, "Dimensions of Aspirations, Work Roles and Decision-Making of Farm Husbands and Wives in Wisconsin," *Journal of Marriage and the Family* 29, November 1967, p. 711.

84. Willis, Elizabeth, *Family Financial Security*, Iowa State Agricultural and Home Economics Experiment Station Special Report 36, North Central Regional Research Publication No. 131, Ames, Iowa, 1964.

85. Whyte, W. H., Jr., "The Web of Word of Mouth," *Fortune*, November 1954, reprinted in L. H. Clark, ed., *The Life Cycle and Consumer Behavior*, New York: New York University Press, 1955, pp. 113–122.

85a. Wolgast, E. G., "Do Husbands or Wives Make the Purchasing Decisions?" *Journal of Marketing*, 23, October 1958, pp. 151–158.

86. Young, M., "Distribution of Income Within the Family," *British Journal of Sociology* 3, December 1952, pp. 305–321.

87. Zunich, M., and A. C. Fults, "Teenage Economic Behavior: Earning and Saving," *Journal of Home Economics* 59, November 1967, p. 739.

3

Economic Life-Styles, Values, and Subjective Welfare—

AN EMPIRICAL APPROACH

Author's note: This research was financed by grant GS-3244 from the National Science Foundation. Valuable advice from Lutz Erbring, Gerald Gurin, and George Katona is gratefully acknowledged. Richard T. Curtin and M. Susan Schwartz, who also worked on this paper, are assistant study directors in the Institute for Social Research at Michigan.

BURKHARD STRUMPEL

Introduction

The theoretical purposes of the ensuing paper, "Economic Life-Styles, Values, and Subjective Welfare—An Empirical Approach," by Burkhard Strumpel, are largely descriptive in character:

1. To describe how households adapt to, and interact with, the changing economic system in America.
2. To explain productive behavior and satisfaction with economic life-style.
3. To describe the differential value-orientations and economic life-styles of socioeconomic groups.

Strumpel not only described the phenomena in which he is interested and the patterns they take, but also attempted to construct a causal explanation for them. Although he was working with data in a historically-bound context (contemporary America), the explanation he sought is abstract enough to be considered deductive in the way we are using that term.

Strumpel's objectives were ambitious and Martin Pfaff, of Wayne State University, his formal discussant, noted that more attention was directed toward explaining the dependent variable, economic satisfaction or subjective welfare, than toward explaining productive behavior. The behaving units Strumpel studied are heads of households and not all the household, let alone family, members.

Several empirical generalizations can be adduced from Strumpel's paper:

EG10. Subjective welfare is in part a function of reality-bound goals, aspirations, expectations, and values, as well as self-efficacy/fate-control.

EG11. Subjective welfare and relative accomplishment are an inverse function of the discrepancy between aspirations and accomplishments.

EG12. An exciting life, important work, a nonmaterial orientation, and achievement characterize the values of upper occupational status groups; a high level of subjective welfare and fate-control also characterize upper occupational status groups. Security, prosperity, a material orientation, and affiliation with others in the same group characterize the values of lower occupational status groups; a moderate level of subjective welfare and a low level of fate-control also characterize lower occupational status groups.

EG13. If aspirations exceed perceived accomplishments (*i.e.,* low relative accomplishment) and fate-control and expectations are low, goal reduction will result.

EG14. An increase in economic satisfaction reflects an increase in accomplishment when fate-control and expectations are high, and reflects a decrease in aspirations (*i.e.,* goal reduction) when fate-control and expectations are low.

EG10 begins to outline the boundaries of Strumpel's theoretical explanation, but does not move very far. EG11 is essentially a statement that introduces the relativity concept, relative accomplishment or relative achievement. It is also interrelated with EG10 in that both generalizations share the concept of subjective welfare. It is interesting to note that Strumpel did not consider the logical possibility of accomplishment exceeding aspirations or the consequences of such a condition. A. Marshall Puckett explicitly considered this possibility, as we shall see later. EG12 compresses the rich discussion of group differences in value systems to the point that it probably does injustice to Strumpel's analysis. Nevertheless, it serves as a parsimonious statement of the essential features of that analysis.

EG13 and 14 are speculative interpretations that Strumpel inferred when economic satisfaction is higher than one might otherwise expect. Strumpel was quick to point out that a longitudinal study would be required to check out these interpretations. Although EG13 and 14 are not empirically derived, they are so crucial to Strumpel's causal scheme that we have included them on the list with this reservation noted. As an adjunct to EG14, Strumpel declared that an increase in accomplishment may be achieved through increased productive effort or a redistribution of economic rewards. If expectations are high despite low economic satisfaction, pressures to redistribute these rewards may be exerted. It is because of this situation, which Strumpel hypothesized is in fact occurring, that he concluded as follows:

> Weak goals for advancement of those who have high expectations for income increases certainly are a potentially explosive combination in a period of declining growth rates . . . (and) claims for the rewards of the system are rising faster than the willingness to provide inputs.

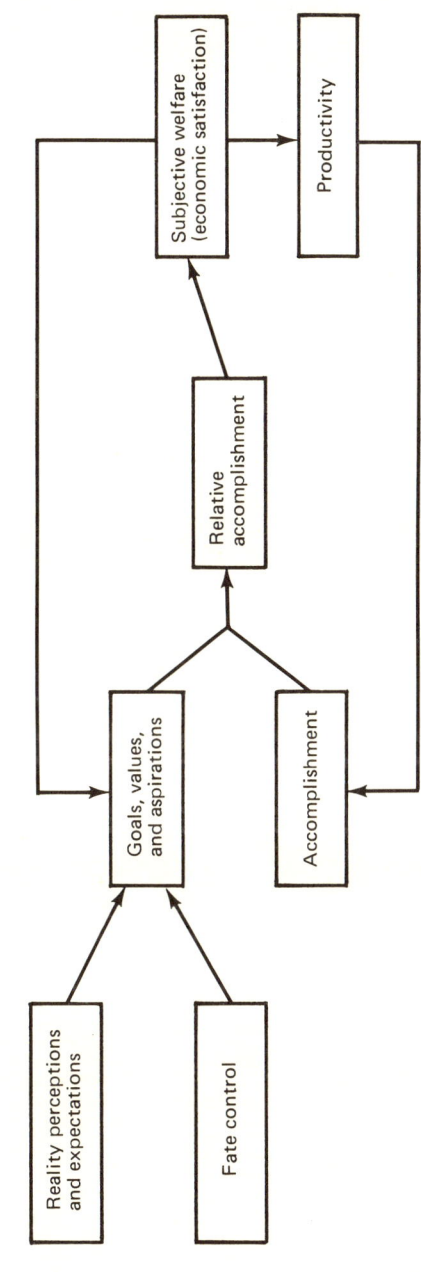

CHART 1.
STRUMPEL'S MODEL OF SUBJECTIVE WELFARE

Strumpel relied on conventional language to express his ideas. In his rapporteur notes, Murray Straus, University of New Hampshire, suggested that Strumpel's general strategy was to demonstrate that economic and sociological variables interact to produce subjective welfare (a psychological variable), which in turn affects productive behavior. Pfaff presented two conceptual models that help organize Strumpel's theoretical formulation. In Chart 1 we present an alternative model that emphasizes different aspects of the adaptive nature of economic life-styles.

The central feature of the model is the *comparison* between goals-values-aspirations and accomplishment, symbolized by the split-tailed arrow. This "cognitive event" reflects the discrepancy notion in EG11 and 13. The curved arrows leading back to the goal and accomplishment blocks reflect the feed-back processes that may be utilized to correct the discrepancy when it exists. Expectations and fate-control are crucial variables whose values aid in the prediction of the consequences of a particular level of economic satisfaction, as EG14 suggests.

All of the concepts represented in Chart 1, with the exception of accomplishment and productivity, are of the dispositional variety. For the purpose of simplification we have left out the objective environmental antecedents of the four blocks on the left side of Chart 1. Among the concepts Strumpel included in this category are socioeconomic status, skills and opportunities, economic climate, age, ideology, public opinion, and reference groups. Knowing an individual's occupational status and his expectation, fate-control, and goal structures, Strumpel hoped to be able to predict subjective welfare, productivity, and their consequences for the individual and the social system.

There is no reason to believe that Chart 1 is the optimum formalized expression of Strumpel's theory of subjective welfare. It undoubtedly raises many more questions than it answers. For example, is fate-control a constant personality trait or does it vary according to routinized levels of relative accomplishment? Our attempt to formalize Strumpel's very complex deductive explanation has convinced us, at least, that additional trials at systematizing the theory will be necessary before all of its implications are easily understood.

Reuben Hill and David M. Klein

Economic Life-Styles, Values, and Subjective Welfare — An Empirical Approach

By Burkhard Strumpel
With the assistance of Richard T. Curtin and M. Susan Schwartz

I. Social Change

The economic scene of the late sixties and early seventies has been dominated by a dual concern: the functioning of the national economy plagued by persistent inflation and unemployment, and the impact of economic growth on the quality of people's lives.

There are forebodings of more and potentially painful changes. Young workers are said to be bored with their highly routinized work roles and to lack identification with the organization; low morale and high absenteeism, known as "blue-collar blues," have been noted particularly in the automobile industry. One of the rallying points of the youth protest is the rebellion against what is alleged to be the materialism of the older generation. An increasing number of college-educated young people have been questioning traditional economic and material values and rejecting occupational careers (mainly business) that express these values [5]. Among the middle-aged and older generation, the proportion of people wanting to retire early and actually doing so is rapidly on the increase [1].

According to both scholarly and impressionistic interpretations of social change there is a widespread notion that things have become or are becoming worse: the citizens are more restive, dissatisfied, and more vociferous in making demands on the system. The markets are less able to direct scarce societal resources in accordance with the expectations and aspirations of the public. These widely perceived problems notwithstanding, there is a deplorable dearth of microdata about the effect of social change on people's behavioral dispositions: their economic goals, motivations, satisfactions. We lack systematic knowledge about people's satisfactions with their economic situation, with their future prospects, with their opportunities, and much less about the changes in these perceptions. We know very little about their incentive structures; is there a weakening of productive or acquisitive motivation under way accompanied by unchanged or enhanced aspirations for goods and services?

The understanding, not just statistical description, of national trends of this kind requires an analysis of differences between subgroups of society. Social change is a process of diffusion. Sometimes it starts with the young; with accelerated rates of societal change, age differences widen into generational gaps [14]. Alternatively, it may start with people best adapted to or favored by change. Economic historians point to the pioneer role of the entrepreneurial class in early industrialization. The transmission of knowledge to the general society may make professionals or college graduates most likely to be innovators in economic life-styles and behavior. In particular, economic incentives and satisfactions of subgroups whose status is low and/or is changing relatively or absolutely merit continuous attention. At present, this applies particularly to the lower-skilled workers and non-white populations. The research reported here tries to lay the groundwork for continuous measurements by analyzing cross-sectional data on people's interaction with and adaptation to the economic system.

Economic and demographic variables have had limited success in explaining the rapid changes in the ways in which people respond to prosperity. This is hardly surprising. Rising mass incomes and short work hours make it possible for many to choose between saving or spending, between work or leisure. For some, a steady and continuous improvement in real income, common in modern society, is a reason to relax and to enjoy the fruits of prosperity. For others, it is a challenge to extend their range of goals even further and to strive toward them. Thus, the majority of private households in Western societies make their decisions in a setting characterized by discretion relating to income allocation—choice of various consumer goods, saving/spending—as well as to income acquisition—job, work/leisure, educational choice.

The individual choices, on which behavioral differences and trends are based, are not made frequently and suddenly. They emerge as the result of experiences and information. They are reflected in values, goals, and aspirations which are formed in advance of action. The most crucial behavior patterns—educational and career decisions, and to a lesser degree consumption and saving habits—are formed early and stabilized between the ages of 20 and 35 years. It is thus of particular importance to explore the minds of younger adults for whom the conflicting pressures and aspirations of the worlds of work, consumption, and leisure are fully present and not yet tempered by accommodation to reality and goal reduction characteristic of older people. Accordingly, our sample has been drawn from a universe of young households (see Appendix page 115).

Our approach to identifying and analyzing economic life-styles builds upon various lines of inquiry in psychological economics, each relating particular psychological concepts to specific areas of economic behavior. The approach, identified with the name of George Katona, relies on attitudes and expectations about one's personal economic situation and the economy as a whole in order to analyze short-term changes in aggregate spending [9]. James N. Morgan used the theory of achievement motivation developed by McClelland and Atkinson to predict labor-force participation, job status, and the amount of education parents plan for their children [20]. Gerald Gurin, Patricia Gurin, and others applied recently developed measures of expectancy and fate-control to the explanation of occupational aspirations and performance of unemployed and minority students [7].

The research reported here draws together various psychological approaches. People's productive behavior and their satisfactions are assumed to be shaped by goals or values (what do people want?), reality perceptions and expectations (how do they evaluate their situation in relation to their goals?), and self-efficacy/fate-control (to what extent are they confident of their ability to move closer to their goals?). The application of values and satisfaction to microeconomic analysis is new and will therefore receive special emphasis.

Surprisingly, value concepts have not yet been used empirically to explain differences or changes in economic behavior. Economists tend to think of "tastes" or "preferences" as stable, or as satellites of income and its changes. The objective of Katona's cyclical model is not to explain and predict interindividual differences but rather short-term aggregate fluctuation in spending behavior. Therefore, he could legitimately disregard tastes, preferences, and aspirations, as well as all attributes of a person other than those which could be assumed to change in the short run in response to economic or noneconomic news, events of public concern, or changes in the economic and political situation. However, there are important analytical objectives in behavioral economics which do not permit us to disregard differences and changes in people's tastes or preferences. This is true for long-term behavioral change, intercultural comparisons of behavior—so crucial for dealing with economic growth—and for cross-section analysis within a population [24].

Satisfaction scores have been devised as subjective measures of quality of life or economic welfare in our survey. Economists have traditionally understood welfare primarily as command over material resources. Consequently, the measurement of welfare and its distribution was undertaken in terms of income or the ratio of income to assumed needs (welfare ratios). In a society where subsistence levels are far exceeded for the majority, income differences are only one of the important criteria for assessing the distribution of welfare. With rising affluence other situational advantages such as social status, job and income security, fringe benefits (especially pension rights), moderate and convenient working time, availability of opportunities for advancement, choices of alternatives to unsatisfactory conditions, and a favorable human and physical environment in the workplace, gain in importance.

Consequently, we will be concerned with the distribution of these advantages and how this distribution is perceived and evaluated. We shall see how income advantages spill over to situational, motivational, and behavioral advantages and are thus reinforced. Higher status subgroups are more confident of their ability to master their own fate; consequently, they have a clearer sense of purpose and direction and are more active in pursuing their goals. Moreover, they are behaviorally better adapted in that they provide for the future as well as profit from their own and their parents' provisions in the past by saving more, providing higher education for their children, and purchasing housing and durables to a larger extent [25].

A realistic and comprehensive concept of economic welfare requires more than just the inclusion of "metaeconomic" situational rewards or their absence. There are good reasons to pay attention to subjective measures of affect, adaptation, and satisfaction. Welfare is in the eye of the beholder. Subjective measures give us a chance to view the perceived importance of various life domains and to assess potential problem areas. Extreme dissatisfaction, withdrawal, lack of motivation, or fate-control reflect the inability of individuals to cope with their economic environment. We will deal below with the implications of such maladaptation for both the individuals and the system.

In the next section, we will present data on economic satisfactions in relation to people's objective situation. Section III will introduce empirical data on values and analyze their distribution. In Section IV satisfactions, values, and goals are analyzed for several subgroups of the population: white professionals, managers, and clerical/sales workers; white blue-collar workers; and black blue- and white-collar workers. Section V points to some implications of our findings for society and the economic system.

II. Economic Satisfactions

We will report an extensive range of survey items relating to various aspects of economic satisfaction administered to almost 600 young, employed heads of households in the Baltimore and Detroit Metropolitan areas (see Appendix page 116). The questions relate to evaluations of their own standard of living, recent and future financial changes, job, and education.

We look at satisfaction ratings as representing the distance between reality and goal. People are assumed to evaluate their situation with the yardstick of their goals; thus these ratings can be seen to summarize their assessment. There are several reasons why satisfaction ratings alone should not be used as approximations to well-being in the particular area to which they refer; much of the paper will develop these reasons.

One reason emerges on the basis of theoretical considerations. There is far less consensus about the desirability of satisfaction than about the concept of well-being. Economic satisfaction will be considered undesirable by many if it represents accommodation or acquiescence to a constraining reality. Dissatisfaction, for some, may be an attitude developed in response to opportunities—it may then be the concomitant of optimism.

Even consciously many people know they will not be satisfied tomorrow with what would satisfy them today. If they have made progress, they most probably are not satisfied today with what they had or wanted to have yesterday. If they lost ground, or discovered their earlier goals to be unrealistic, they may well reduce them. Goals are bound by reality. If this is so, and if our conceptual definition of satisfactions is appropriate, dissatisfaction may be a symptom as often of impending success as of failure or maladaptation.

Another caveat should be added. The degree of dissatisfaction does not yield any information about the goal in a quantitative manner. If somebody expresses dissatisfaction with an income of $10,000, we don't know the amount of additional income that would satisfy him. We also know little about the importance he attaches to his income deficit. Possibly, the extent of expressed dissatisfaction may be considered a function of both distance and importance.

A tested theory of goal formation and adjustment does not yet exist; there are only fragments of theories, each capturing certain aspects of what really occurs. Closest to the economist's heart is the concept of tastes or preferences which are assumed to be independent of income changes. If "preference functions" stay constant, rising accomplishment must increase the individual's satisfaction.

Evidence about people's self-assessment of happiness, recently summarized by Richard A. Easterlin [4], indeed points to a noticeable positive association between income and happiness within societies, emerging from cross-section analyses of individuals. However, hardly any such positive association is found among countries at a given time [2]; for example, mean self-rating scores of happiness are higher in Egypt and Israel than in West Germany, and only insignificantly lower in Yugoslavia, Nigeria, Brazil, and Poland.[1] Americans rank somewhat higher in happiness and much higher in income, but are joined on the first score by Cubans. However, if United States data are studied in time series, rising real incomes do not appear to be accompanied by greater happiness. Self-assessed happiness is related to other expressions of socioeconomic status beyond the economic situation such as education, occupational status, etc. Yet material ingredients play a prominent role in people's conception of happiness;

when asked about the reasons for being happy or unhappy, personal economic concerns have been most frequently mentioned by Americans [8].

To explain the aforementioned findings, relative status considerations of the Duesenberry type have been put forward. According to this line of reasoning, the level of aspirations—and we imply economic satisfaction—depends on relative accomplishment; interpersonally relative to others within the same society and intertemporally relative to one's own standing in the past. Immediately the question arises: how are reference groups and past reference points chosen? Is this choice not simply tantamount to or a function of the level of aspirations? [2]

Goals are bounded not only in the sense of being related to accomplishment; they are also related to expectations [11]. Those expecting financial progress are likely to raise their aspirations further than those who expect income stagnation. On a more general level, perceived chances for remedying an unsatisfactory situation may accentuate its importance and saliency, and reduce the patience to endure it. De Tocqueville remarked nearly 150 years ago:

> The evil which is patiently endured as long as it is considered inevitable, becomes intolerable as soon as a remedy is in sight. And after substantial improvement has set in, there is more clamor than ever before.

Changes in expectations may be prompted by shifts in ideology or by trends in public opinion. To realize how aspirations, goals, and satisfactions as well as conceptions of their importance may be formed, shaped, and changed with no manifest relationship to changes in the economic environment, one may think of the dominant issues of the sixties: aid to poor nations, racial inequality, domestic poverty, urban problems, pollution, war and peace.

As a result, there is little hope that a parsimonious hypothesis relating present or past economic/environmental variables to goals or satisfactions alone can do the job of explaining various people's satisfaction with their well-being and its changes. These approaches will have to be supplemented by psychological and sociological explanations relating to values, aspirations, and expectancy which in turn are culturally or subculturally determined. Therefore, we will relate our satisfaction scores to variables of this kind as well as to economic situational measures.

Our respondents were men in their most productive years and accustomed to income increases. Almost three-quarters of them reported being better off financially than they had been the previous year, although the interviews were conducted in a period of recession. Given the special nature of the group, the prevalently favorable economic self-assessment is less notable than the differences between areas of satisfaction and subgroups of respondents. Our respondents seemed to be better adjusted to the exigencies of their work than to their standard of living (Tables 1 and 2). A consid-

TABLE 1. SATISFACTION WITH INCOME AND STANDARD OF LIVING BY RACE AND OCCUPATION OF HEAD[a]

	All Respondents	White, White-Collar[b]	White, Blue-Collar[b]	Black
Satisfaction with financial changes				
Satisfied	35%	38%	32%	27%
Moderately satisfied	37	36	36	43
Not satisfied	15	16	15	19
Income decreased during past twelve months	13	10	16	11
Not ascertained; do not know	*	*	1	*
Total	100%	100%	100%	100%
Family income sufficient to meet bills				
Yes	86%	91%	88%	68%
No	14	9	12	31
Not ascertained; do not know	*	*	*	1
Total	100%	100%	100%	100%
Family income sufficient to live comfortably				
Yes	42%	48%	42%	25%
No	57	52	57	74
Not ascertained; do not know	1	*	1	1
Total	100%	100%	100%	100%
Satisfaction with standard of living				
Satisfied	34%	39%	36%	21%
Moderately satisfied	50	50	50	48
Not satisfied	16	11	14	31
Total	100%	100%	100%	100%
Satisfaction in case standard of living five years hence is not better				
Satisfied	15%	14%	19%	11%
Moderately satisfied	27	25	30	17
Not satisfied	58	61	51	72
Total	100%	100%	100%	100%

TABLE 1. SATISFACTION WITH INCOME AND STANDARD OF LIVING BY RACE AND OCCUPATION OF HEAD (Cont.)

		Race and Occupation		
	All Respondents	White, White-Collar[b]	White, Blue-Collar[b]	Black
Concern for future standard of living				
Very concerned	41%	31%	43%	60%
Somewhat concerned	36	42	35	26
Not too concerned	18	24	16	8
Not at all concerned	4	3	5	5
Not ascertained; do not know	1	*	1	1
Total	100%	100%	100%	100%
Number of cases[c]	574	238	235	88

* Less than .05 per cent.
[a] For wording of question and definition of satisfaction categories see Appendix C, questions C9-C13.
[b] White-collar workers include professionals, managers and officials, and clerical and sales workers.
 Blue-collar workers include craftsmen and foremen, operatives, and laborers.
[c] Totals of race and occupation subgroups do not add to 574 because race and occupation were not ascertained for all respondents.

erable and rising extent of job satisfaction has been reported elsewhere.

A recent American study based on interviews with a representative cross section of members of the labor force revealed a significant positive relationship between change in technology and job satisfaction [21]. Working conditions in industrial economies have steadily improved in the last fifty years or more; there is a trend toward reduced physical effort, improvement in the work environment, increased security against personal injury, and more rewarding social relations with supervisors and fellow workers. This has resulted partly from the specific efforts of government, unions, and employers, and partly from the intersectoral shifts in employment and technological changes. After looking at more data, we will ask if the high extent of job satisfaction must be seen also as a symptom of goal reduction or withdrawal, rather than only as a recognition of a favorable working environment.

In contrast to high job satisfaction, 57 per cent of our sample of employed men did not feel their income was large enough for them to live as comfortably as they would have liked at the time. Although the large majority reported being better off than they had been a year ago, less than half of those were satisfied with the changes in their financial situa-

TABLE 2. SATISFACTION WITH JOB AND EDUCATION BY RACE AND OCCUPATION OF HEAD[a]

	All Respondents	Race and Occupation		
		White, White-Collar[b]	White, Blue-Collar[b]	Blacks
Satisfaction with main job				
Satisfied	62%	66%	59%	61%
Moderately satisfied	30	29	32	25
Not satisfied	8	5	9	13
Not ascertained; do not know	*	*	*	1
Total	100%	100%	100%	100%
Recommend job to a friend				
Strongly recommend	69%	75%	67%	60%
Have doubts	19	19	18	21
Strongly advise against	8	5	12	10
Not ascertained; do not know	4	1	3	9
Total	100%	100%	100%	100%
Work is just a way of making money				
Agree	37%	20%	45%	61%
Disagree	62	79	53	38
Not ascertained; do not know	1	1	2	1
Total	100%	100%	100%	100%
Worry about unemployment				
Yes	23%	17%	30%	24%
No	75	82	69	73
Not ascertained; do not know	2	1	1	3
Total	100%	100%	100%	100%
Satisfaction with education				
Satisfied	31%	47%	19%	16%
Moderately satisfied	35	36	34	30
Not satisfied	34	17	47	54
Total	100%	100%	100%	100%
Number of cases[c]	574	238	235	88

* Less than .05 per cent.

[a] For wording of question see Appendix C, questions B5, C6, D34, D35, D39.

[b] White-collar workers include professionals, managers and officials, and clerical and sales workers.

Blue-collar workers include craftsmen and foremen, operatives, and laborers.

[c] Totals of race and occupation subgroups do not add to 574 because race and occupation were not ascertained for all respondents.

tion. Felt needs are rapidly expanding in this stage of the life cycle. Rising wants are projected into the future and readily translated into a sliding level of aspirations, expanding over time. What is enough today is not satisfactory tomorrow, and what is already unsatisfactory today will be much more so tomorrow. There are drastic differences between over-all satisfaction with the present level of living and the widespread disenchantment about the hypothetical prospect of no change in this level over the next five years (Table 1). We encounter here a symptom of the peculiar American economic culture. Americans, much more frequently than Europeans, demand and expect progress and change. Impatience goes along with optimism and thus is conducive to the reinforcement of wants. This pattern was not found to prevail in other affluent societies [13].

A well-known observer of the American scene concluded:

> In the American Dream there is no final stopping point. . . . At each income level . . . Americans want just about 25 per cent more (but of course this "just a bit more" continues to operate once it is obtained). . . . The family, the school, and the workplace—the major agencies shaping the personality structure and goal formation of Americans—join to provide the intensive disciplining required if an individual is to retain intact a goal that remains elusively beyond reach [16].

What determines economic satisfaction? First of all, expressed satisfaction goes along with higher socioeconomic status. Satisfaction with one's job and living standard responds to reality; actual income correlates positively with measured satisfaction in standard of living (Table 3); and job satisfaction, as Tables 2 and 4 suggest, correlates with the factual "quality" of a job, working conditions, job status and autonomy, and monetary rewards. These findings are in line both with a naive saturation model and with the above mentioned "relativity" thesis—in a Western society ideologically committed to equality and opportunity, the whole nation serves as a reference group in some, albeit limited, sense.

There is a strong correlation between satisfaction with standard of living and satisfaction with recent income increases.[3] This relationship is theoretically revealing. Recent income increases have moved the individual closer to his goals. Although he tends to respond to improvement by extending his levels of aspirations, this expansion is a slow and gradual process. Thus, recent improvements are particularly likely to be greeted with satisfaction, if only temporarily.

While blue-collar workers receive their peak income early in life and may suffer income losses as early as in their forties or fifties, white-collar workers, especially professional workers and managers, begin their working life at relatively low salaries and reach their peak income only late in life, often just before retirement. They are permanently on the rise financially, and their ranks are expanding. In 1950 the number of blue-collar workers in the United States was slightly higher than that of white-collar

TABLE 3. SATISFACTION WITH INCOME AND STANDARD OF LIVING WITHIN DEMOGRAPHIC GROUPS[a]

	All Respondents	Income of Head					Age of Head		
		Under $7500	$7500 –9999	$10,000 –12,499	$12,500 –14,999	$15,000 or more	19–25	26–30	Age 31 or older
Satisfaction with financial changes									
Satisfied	35%	23%	28%	36%	37%	47%	29%	34%	36%
Moderately satisfied	37	49	36	33	34	40	44	32	38
Not satisfied	15	14	16	18	19	10	12	19	15
Income decreased during past twelve months	13	13	20	12	9	3	14	14	11
Not ascertained; do not know	*	1	*	1	1	*	1	1	*
Total	100%	100%	100%	100%	100%	100%	100%	100%	100%
Family income sufficient to meet bills									
Yes	86%	73%	79%	92%	97%	92%	88%	82%	88%
No	14	26	21	8	3	8	12	17	11
Not ascertained; do not know	*	1	*	*	*	*	*	1	1
Total	100%	100%	100%	100%	100%	100%	100%	100%	100%
Family income sufficient to live comfortably									
Yes	42%	25%	28%	46%	52%	68%	27%	42%	51%
No	57	75	72	54	47	31	72	57	48
Not ascertained; do not know	1	*	*	*	1	1	1	1	1
Total	100%	100%	100%	100%	100%	100%	100%	100%	100%
Satisfaction with standard of living									
Satisfied	34%	21%	29%	30%	38%	57%	25%	28%	46%
Moderately satisfied	50	52	49	58	50	39	52	58	42
Not satisfied	16	27	22	12	12	4	23	14	12
Total	100%	100%	100%	100%	100%	100%	100%	100%	100%

TABLE 3. SATISFACTION WITH INCOME AND STANDARD OF LIVING WITHIN DEMOGRAPHIC GROUPS *(Continued)*

		White					Black		
	All Respondents	Professionals, Technical	Managers, Officials	Clerical, Sales	Craftsmen, Foremen	Operatives, Laborers	Professionals, Managers, Clerical, Sales, Craftsmen, Foremen		Operatives, Laborers
Satisfaction in case standard of living five years hence is not better									
Satisfied	15%	13%	13%	12%	15%	23%	6%	11%	25%
Moderately satisfied	27	21	25	28	29	30	23	23	32
Not satisfied	58	66	62	60	56	47	71	66	43
Total	100%	100%	100%	100%	100%	100%	100%	100%	100%
Concern for future standard of living									
Very concerned	41%	60%	48%	39%	24%	27%	44%	40%	39%
Somewhat concerned	36	28	33	37	47	43	40	37	34
Not too concerned	18	7	14	19	24	26	10	17	23
Not at all concerned	4	4	5	5	1	4	4	5	4
Not ascertained; do not know	1	1	*	*	4	*	2	1	*
Total	100%	100%	100%	100%	100%	100%	100%	100%	100%
Number of cases	574[a]	85	167	147	68	90	140	214	220
Satisfaction with financial changes									
Satisfied	35%	42%	38%	29%	34%	28%	36%		22%
Moderately satisfied	37	36	36	34	31	41	28		52

Not satisfied	15	11	20	20	15	16	22	16
Income decreased during past twelve months	13	11	6	17	18	14	14	10
Not ascertained; do not know	*	*	*	*	2	1	*	*
Total	100%	100%	100%	100%	100%	100%	100%	100%
Family income sufficient to meet bills								
Yes	86%	92%	91%	88%	90%	84%	64%	70%
No	14	7	9	12	10	16	36	28
Not ascertained; do not know	*	1	*	*	*	*	*	2
Total	100%	100%	100%	100%	100%	100%	100%	100%
Family income sufficient to live comfortably								
Yes	42%	52%	40%	46%	50%	30%	28%	20%
No	57	47	60	54	49	68	69	80
Not ascertained; do not know	1	1	*	*	1	2	3	*
Total	100%	100%	100%	100%	100%	100%	100%	100%
Satisfaction with standard of living								
Satisfied	34%	45%	29%	34%	39%	30%	17%	22%
Moderately satisfied	50	44	62	51	51	50	53	46
Not satisfied	16	11	9	15	10	20	30	32
Total	100%	100%	100%	100%	100%	100%	100%	100%

TABLE 3. SATISFACTION WITH INCOME AND STANDARD OF LIVING WITHIN DEMOGRAPHIC GROUPS (Continued)

	Total							
Satisfaction in case standard of living five years hence is not better								
Satisfied	15%	18%	13%	7%	24%	17%	5%	14%
Moderately satisfied	27	22	14	39	27	31	17	16
Not satisfied	58	60	73	54	49	52	78	70
Total	100%	100%	100%	100%	100%	100%	100%	100%
Concern for future standard of living								
Very concerned	41%	26%	33%	41%	37%	50%	64%	58%
Somewhat concerned	36	44	45	32	39	31	25	26
Not too concerned	18	28	20	19	15	15	11	6
Not at all concerned	4	1	2	8	8	3	*	8
Not ascertained; do not know	1	1	*	*	1	1	*	2
Total	100%	100%	100%	100%	100%	100%	100%	100%
Number of cases	574	122	55	59	113	107	36	50

[a] Totals of income subgroups and age subgroups do not add to 574 because income and age were not ascertained for all respondents.

* Less than .05 per cent.

TABLE 4. SATISFACTION WITH JOB AND EDUCATION WITHIN DEMOGRAPHIC GROUPS[a]

	All Respondents	Income of Head					Age of Head		
		Under $7500	$7500–9999	$10,000–12,499	$12,500–14,999	$15,000 or more	19–25	26–30	Age 31 or older
Satisfaction with main job									
Satisfied	62%	55%	58%	59%	69%	72%	49%	65%	66%
Moderately satisfied	30	27	31	36	26	26	37	29	27
Not satisfied	8	18	11	5	3	1	14	6	6
Not ascertained; do not know	*	*	*	*	2	1	*	*	1
Total	100%	100%	100%	100%	100%	100%	100%	100%	100%
Recommend job to a friend									
Strongly recommend	69%	54%	65%	72%	78%	76%	67%	69%	70%
Have doubts	19	24	20	21	18	14	21	19	19
Strongly advise against	8	15	13	4	3	6	9	8	7
Not ascertained; do not know	4	7	2	3	1	4	3	4	4
Total	100%	100%	100%	100%	100%	100%	100%	100%	100%
Work is just a way of making money									
Agree	37%	55%	49%	33%	26%	15%	45%	37%	31%
Disagree	62	44	50	66	74	83	53	63	67
Not ascertained; do not know	1	1	1	1	*	2	2	*	2
Total	100%	100%	100%	100%	100%	100%	100%	100%	100%
Worry about unemployment									
Yes	23%	26%	27%	25%	24%	12%	29%	24%	20%
No	75	71	72	74	75	86	71	75	78
Not ascertained; do not know	2	3	1	1	1	2	*	1	2
Total	100%	100%	100%	100%	100%	100%	100%	100%	100%

[a]For wording of question see Appendix C, questions C2, C9–C13.

[83]

TABLE 4. SATISFACTION WITH JOB AND EDUCATION
WITHIN DEMOGRAPHIC GROUPS (Continued)

				Race and Occupation of Head					
	All Respondents	White					Black		
		Professionals, Technical	Managers, Officials	Clerical, Sales	Craftsmen, Foremen	Operatives, Laborers	Professionals, Managers, Clerical, Sales, Craftsmen, Foremen		Operatives, Laborers
Satisfaction with education									
Satisfied	31%	19%	19%	28%	43%	58%	21%	28%	40%
Moderately satisfied	35	25	43	35	28	31	42	35	29
Not satisfied	34	56	38	37	29	11	37	37	31
Total	100%	100%	100%	100%	100%	100%	100%	100%	100%
Number of cases	574	85	167	147	68	90	140	214	220
Satisfaction with main job									
Satisfied	62%	68%	73%	52%	66%	47%	61%		64%
Moderately satisfied	30	29	24	36	28	39	33		16
Not satisfied	8	3	3	12	5	14	3		20
Not ascertained; do not know	*	*	*	*	1	*	3		*
Total	100%	100%	100%	100%	100%	100%	100%		100%

Recommend job to a friend									
Strongly recommend	69%	78%	80%	65%	72%	63%	72%	54%	
Have doubts	19	18	14	22	17	19	14	22	
Strongly advise against	8	3	2	10	10	14	8	12	
Not ascertained; do not know	4	1	4	3	1	4	6	12	
Total	100%	100%	100%	100%	100%	100%	100%	100%	
Work is just a way of making money									
Agree	37%	13%	20%	34%	42%	52%	47%	70%	
Disagree	62	87	78	63	57	45	53	28	
Not ascertained; do not know	1	*	2	3	1	3	*	2	
Total	100%	100%	100%	100%	100%	100%	100%	100%	
Worry about unemployment									
Yes	23%	22%	9%	14%	27%	34%	28%	22%	
No	75	77	87	85	73	65	69	74	
Not ascertained; do not know	2	1	4	1	*	1	3	4	
Total	100%	100%	100%	100%	100%	100%	100%	100%	
Satisfaction with education									
Satisfied	31%	61%	29%	34%	26%	14%	25%	10%	
Moderately satisfied	35	27	51	37	36	34	33	26	
Not satisfied	34	12	20	29	38	52	42	64	
Total	100%	100%	100%	100%	100%	100%	100%	100%	
Number of cases	574	122	55	59	113	107	36	50	

* Less than .05 per cent.
^a For wording of question see Appendix C, questions B5, C6, D34, D35, D39.

workers. In 1965, however, the latter outnumbered the former by 20 per cent.

Satisfaction with standard of living in the United States is largely a response to a dynamic phenomenon: to the change rather than to the level of income and standard of living. It is in this context that the strongly held goal for a higher standard of living in the future has to be seen. It is the more affluent segment of society (professionals and managers) which harbors the most dynamic orientation. Although these people are most satisfied with the present, the idea not to improve their standard of living during the next five years is particularly disturbing (Table 3). Both the secular rise in prosperity and the increasing proportion of white-collar workers in the labor force make real income increases a normal and expected phenomenon for most people. This of course is particularly true for our sample of young heads of households. The psychological dependence on improvements in living standards may raise serious problems for subjective well-being in the instant of protracted economic stagnation or even of declining growth rates.

The older our respondents, the more satisfied they were, both with their living standards and with their job. This relationship holds if controlled for income. One may look at age as a proxy for realism. The options of the young become the constraints of the old and are so perceived. Unattainable goals are abandoned or reduced as time passes.[4]

The variables mentioned up to this point (with the partial exception of age) represented various features of the past, present, and future economic situation and its changes. There is considerable virtue in linking measures of economic well-being to manifest (and possibly manipulable) aspects of the environment or situation rather than to psychological predispositions. Yet after the situational variables have been introduced, there remains much unexplained variance in people's expressed satisfactions. With the loosening of social control and the saturation of physiological needs, people's goals and behavior are increasingly freed from economic and role constraints. Environmental data consequently do not suffice to predict people's reactions [10].

Another indication of systematic variance in goals are the remarkable differences in satisfactions between occupational subgroups similar in social status (Tables 3 and 4). We find, for instance, that white managers are more dissatisfied with their standard of living than white professionals, and also take a much more negative attitude toward the prospect of real income stagnation over the next five years. Black blue-collar workers are considerably more dissatisfied with living standards than white blue-collar workers in the same income situation. Different professions cherish different goals and values due to common experience, belongingness, and the camaraderie that shapes their members, or to recruitment that is in effect value-selective.

Various occupational subgroups also structure their environment and perceive the choices open to them differently. This is not to deny that differences in occupation within the white-collar and the blue-collar stratum partly represent different environments. However, these environments are only partly determined by income and its trends, and partly by occupational opportunities, availability of housing, transportation, etc. There are other reasons rooted in people's background, past experiences, present affiliations, or communication networks by which people are differently satisfied with the same reality. Even if we cannot hope to capture many of these rather diffuse and interpersonally heterogeneous sources of influences dispersed over time, we can identify their effects as reflected in people's values and orientations.

III. Values

This section is devoted to the analysis of values for two reasons: first, to gain a better understanding so as to interpret the differences in satisfactions between occupational and race categories; second, because values are an important ingredient of life-styles and of substantial significance for society and the direction it is taking. Much of the theory of social change has been cast in terms of values (See Max Weber, Talcott Parsons, David Riesman [15]). Thus it seemed worthwhile to introduce this concept empirically and utilize it in the context of research dealing with people's reaction to the economic system and its changes.

Values are relatively stable personality attributes, affective states, and generalized concepts. As Milton Rokeach says [23]:

> While attitude and value are both widely assumed to be determinants of social behavior, value is a determinant of attitude as well as of behavior. . . . If we further assume that a person possesses considerably fewer values than attitudes, then the value concept provides us with a more economical analytic tool for describing and explaining similarities and differences between persons, groups, nations, cultures.

We distinguish values from aspirations, the latter representing the images people have about a good life, as in the economic sphere, quality of housing, the range of durables, job status, money, and savings accounts. Aspirations are assumed to change more readily with accomplishment, with reference groups, with the environment. Values, being more enduring, offer greater promise for analyzing persistent inter- and intragroup differences and trends in economic life-styles. Applying some of Rokeach's basic value categories to people's economic orientations, several survey questions were developed. The first of them assesses life goals; the second, "guiding principles"; the third, criteria for evaluating a job or occupation generally; and the fourth, criteria for job change. The wording is as follows:

> I would like you to tell me what you have found important in life. Would you please look at this card and tell me which of these is most important to you as a goal in your life, which comes next in importance, which is third, and so forth? A prosperous life (having a good income and being able to afford the "good" things in life); an important life (a life of achievement that brings me respect and recognition); a secure life (making certain that all basic needs and expenses are provided for); an exciting life (a stimulating, active life); a family life.

Would you please look at this card and tell me which of these is most important to you as a guiding principle in your life, which comes next in importance, which is third, and so forth? To be ambitious (a hard-working, aspiring person); to be well-liked (a friendly, pleasant person); to be independent (a self-reliant, self-sufficient person); to be helpful (working for the welfare of others); to be responsible (a dependable, reliable person).

Would you please look at this card and tell me which things on this list about a job (occupation) you would most prefer, which comes next, which is third, etc.? Income is steady; income is high; there's no danger of being fired or unemployed; working hours are short; chances for advancement are good; the work is important, gives feeling of accomplishment.

Suppose you were offered a different job. Which thing on this list would most tempt you to take the new job, which would be second in importance, which third and so forth? Income is steadier; income is higher; there's less danger of being fired or unemployed; working hours are shorter; chances for advancement are better; the work is more important.

The conservative value "security" as a goal in life was widely acclaimed as most important (46 per cent) (Table 5). "Prosperity" ranked second in people's minds, and "self-actualizing" (Maslow) values like "important" or "exciting life" were ranked third (22 per cent). "Prosperous life" was rarely selected by respondents with a college degree, or by professionals (largely identical groups, of course). It appeared most frequently among such diverse groups as blacks and managerial workers. Conversely, images like "important" or "exciting life" were most attractive to persons with a college degree (52 per cent compared with only 17 per cent in the rest of the population).

The distribution of the rankings of important job attributes was similar to that of the more general life-goal rankings (Table 6). "Income is steady" and "There is no danger of being fired or unemployed" accounted for 39 per cent of the preferences mentioned first. References to job advancement were given by 17 per cent and to high income by 14 per cent of the respondents. "Important work" was mentioned by 29 per cent. Few respondents ranked "short working hours" either first or second.

The question, "Suppose you were offered a different job—which thing on this list would most tempt you to take the new job?" aims at the differ-

TABLE 5. GOALS IN LIFE WITHIN DEMOGRAPHIC GROUPS

Goal Ranked First by Family Head [a]

	Prosperous Life	Secure Life	Important Life	Exciting Life	D.K. N.A.[b]	Total	Number of Cases
All family heads	30%	47%	13%	10%	*	100%	574
Age of family head							
19–25 years	30	52	6	11	1	100	140
26–30 years	35	45	10	9	1	100	214
31 years or older	25	45	20	10	*	100	220
Education of family head							
0–11 grades	40	46	8	6	*	100	134
High school	30	55	10	5	*	100	177
College, no degree	30	51	8	11	*	100	140
College	16	31	30	22	1	100	121
Race and occupation of family head							
White professionals	20	34	24	20	2	100	122
White managers	38	35	14	13	*	100	55
White clerical, sales	29	46	12	13	*	100	59
White craftsmen, foremen	27	59	10	4	*	100	113
White laborers, operatives	30	58	3	9	*	100	107
Black professionals, managers, clerical, sales, craftsmen, foremen	42	47	8	3	*	100	36
Black operatives, laborers	48	38	12	2	*	100	50

* Less than .05 per cent.

[a] For wording of question see Appendix C. Forty per cent of all respondents ranked Family Life first. We feel that this large number of responses was due to perceived normative expectations on the part of the respondents and did not represent a true choice. Accordingly, that goal was deleted; for those respondents who ranked Family Life first, the response above is the goal ranked second.

[b] Category includes: do not know, not ascertained, and respondents who ranked two or more values first.

TABLE 6. JOB CHARACTERISTIC WITHIN DEMOGRAPHIC GROUPS

Job Characteristic Ranked First by Family Head[a]

	Income Steady	Income High	No Danger of Being Fired	Hours Short	Advancement Good	Work Important	DK NA[b]	Total	No. Cases
All family heads	29%	14%	10%	1%	17%	29%	*	100%	574
Age of family head									
19–25 years	27	17	16	1	17	22	*	100	140
26–30 years	30	11	9	1	21	27	1	100	214
31 years or older	30	16	7	1	11	35	*	100	220
Education of family head									
0–11 grades	39	24	19	1	7	10	*	100	134
High school	39	10	9	1	17	23	1	100	177
College, no degree	24	16	11	1	23	25	*	100	140
College	8	8	1	1	18	63	1	100	121
Race and occupation of family head									
White professionals	11	7	4	1	20	56	1	100	122
White managers	9	13	4	2	27	45	*	100	55
White clerical, sales	36	20	5	3	14	22	*	100	59
White craftsmen, foremen	37	9	12	1	15	26	*	100	113
White laborers, operatives	39	23	19	2	9	8	*	100	107
Black professionals, managers, clerical, sales, craftsmen, foremen	28	25	14	*	16	17	*	100	36
Black operatives, laborers	42	14	16	*	16	10	2	100	50

* Less than .05 per cent.
[a] For wording of question see page 88.
[b] Category includes do not know, not ascertained, and respondents who ranked two or more values first.

ence between a present job and one desired in the future; it tells us something about which values the respondent considers least implemented or realized in his present job. The answer to this question thus may be closer to behavioral dispositions; it says where the person would like to go from where he is. The results were significantly different (Table 7). "Higher income" was the most important attraction by far, while security of income and job decreased precipitously in frequency. There was also less interest in "work is important." An analysis of the different meaning of these two questions has not yet been undertaken.

There are strong and characteristic differences between three subgroups: white white-collar workers, white blue-collar workers, and blacks. Although all of these differences need further specification and disaggregation, we present this trichotomy here as a first approximation to keep in mind. White blue-collar workers are strongly attracted to values related to material security; white professionals, to nonmaterial values like important or exciting life. The blacks in our sample, most of them operatives and laborers, were clearly oriented toward "prosperous life" and "high income." They also tended to emphasize affiliative values like "being helpful" and "being well-liked," although these differences are far less pronounced. I have not presented these data; however, see distribution of composite factor achievement versus affiliation in Table 8. With respect to important features in a job, professionals and managers differed significantly from the rest of the sample by referring much more frequently to self-actualizing values and job advancement, somewhat less frequently to high income, and much less frequently to income or job security.

In order to reduce the rich set of variables available in our study, we made use of the psychometric technique for content validation and index construction, called factor analysis. Factor analysis is a generalized procedure, based on correlation matrices, for determining the minimum number of dimensions (factors) necessary to reproduce adequately the observed variance between respondents within a set of variables. This technique enables us to see whether some underlying pattern of relationship between variables exists; if so, a multitude of variables may be rearranged or reduced to a smaller set of factors or components.[5] Thus, the distinguishing feature of factor analytic techniques is their capability of reducing data. In the following, we use this technique both as a measuring device for constructing indices to be used as new variables in later analysis, and in an exploratory fashion for the detection and patterning of variables for the discovery of the meaning of concepts.[6]

The questions concerning goals, guiding principles in life, and preferred job characteristics yielded a range of 16 items ranked by respondents. To reduce this extensive and unmanageable number of variables, an initial correlation matrix was developed into a factor matrix. The following discrete factors emerged:[7]

TABLE 7. IMPORTANT CHARACTERISTIC IN CHOOSING NEW JOB WITHIN DEMOGRAPHIC GROUPS

Most Tempting Characteristic of Different Job as Ranked by Family Head[a]

	Income Steadier	Income Higher	Less Danger of Being Fired	Hours Shorter	Advancement Better	Work More Important	DK NA[b]	Total	No. Cases
All family heads	10%	40%	7%	2%	18%	22%	1%	100%	574
Age of family head									
19–25 years	8	50	10	2	14	14	2	100	140
26–30 years	9	39	7	1	22	21	1	100	214
31 years or older	12	34	6	2	17	27	2	100	220
Education of family head									
0–11 grades	18	48	13	1	12	8	*	100	134
High school	12	40	11	3	19	15	*	100	177
College, no degree	6	46	4	1	21	18	4	100	140
College	2	24	1	1	21	50	1	100	121
Race and occupation of family head									
White professionals	3	26	3	2	21	43	2	100	122
White managers	5	40	*	*	24	31	*	100	55
White clerical, sales	7	44	3	3	24	17	2	100	59
White craftsmen, foremen	13	46	9	2	16	12	2	100	113
White laborers, operatives	13	46	13	1	14	13	*	100	107
Black professionals, managers, clerical, sales, craftsmen, foremen	11	58	*	*	17	14	*	100	36
Black operatives, laborers	22	36	20	2	14	4	2	100	50

* Less than .05 per cent.
[a] For wording of question see page 88.
[b] Category includes do not know, not ascertained, and respondents who ranked two or more values first.

TABLE 8. MEAN SCORES ON VALUE FACTORS
WITHIN VARIOUS SUBGROUPS

Value Factors

Race-occupation of family head	Income Security Orientation	Prosperity Orientation	Achievement versus Affiliation [a]	Cases
White white-collar	−0.480	−0.133	0.147	234
White blue-collar	0.379	0.003	−0.062	235
Black	0.340	0.405	−0.212	85
Significance tests	$F=57.8$[b] $p=.001$	$F=9.2$[c] $p=.001$	$F=4.7$[d] $p=.01$	
Race-occupation of family head				
White professional	−0.674	−0.411	0.174	119
White managers	−0.560	0.164	0.243	55
White clerical	−0.001	0.124	0.014	58
White craftsmen, foremen	0.209	0.018	0.070	113
White operatives, laborers	0.549	0.063	−0.207	107
Black professional, manager, clerical, craftsmen, foremen	0.249	−0.411	−.063	36
Black operatives, laborers	0.423	−0.396	−0.416	48
Significance tests	$F=20.9$ $p=.001$	$F=5.7$ $p=.001$	$F=2.9$ $p=.01$	
Age of family head				
19–25 years	0.117	−0.109	−0.053	138
26–30 years	0.071	−0.017	0.083	213
31–35 years	−0.195	−0.101	−0.111	129
36–40 years	−0.192	0.422	0.059	53
41 years or older	0.118	0.217	0.153	34
Significance tests	$F=2.6$ $p=.05$	$F=3.5$ $p=.01$	$F=1.0$ $p=NS$*	
Education of family head				
9–11 grades	0.416	−0.341	−0.438	133
High school	0.136	−0.049	0.137	314
College degree	−0.833	0.501	0.182	118
Significance tests	$F=67.0$ $p=.001$	$F=24.1$ $p=.001$	$F=17.8$ $p=.001$	

[a] Positive values indicate achievement orientation.
[b] The difference between the first and the second categories is significant at the .001 level, and between the first and third categories at the .001 level.
[c] The difference between the first and third categories is significant at the .001 level, and between the second and third categories at the .001 level.
[d] The difference between the first and second categories is significant at the .025 level, and between the first and third categories at the .005 level.
* Not significant.

Value Factor 1: Income security-orientation. The factor is heavily loaded on the positive side for "steady income" and "no danger of being fired or unemployed," and on the negative side for "work important" and "exciting life."

Value Factor 2: Prosperity-orientation. The factor is, on the positive side, loaded most highly for "prosperous life" and "high income." On the negative side, for the guiding principles "helpful" and "responsible," for the goal "family life," and for the job characteristic "important work," as in Factor 1.

Value Factor 3: Achievement versus affiliation. The factor on the positive side is loaded toward job advancement, and toward the guiding principles "responsible" and "ambitious." On the negative side, we find the guiding principles "helpful" and "well-liked" and the job value "hours short."

It is remarkable and reflective of the pervasiveness of human values across life spheres that each of the three factors combines heavily loaded items from at least two of the three questions.

The plotting of race/occupation subgroups summarizes much of the information on value differences between socioeconomic segments.

Chart 1 plots various subgroups of our sample on Factors 1 and 2. The white professionals were the most extreme group. They tended to emphasize strongly the job value "important work" and the life value "exciting life." The other extreme was represented by white operatives and laborers and by lower-status blacks. The former were highest in security, the latter in prosperity orientation. White clerical workers and white foremen or craftsmen were close to each other and not far from average along both dimensions. Managerial occupations were much higher than professionals in prosperity orientation, but equally low in material security orientation.

To summarize: blacks were high, and white professionals were low, in prosperity orientation. Blue-collar workers, regardless of race, were high in security orientation, and white high-status occupations were low. White lower-status white-collar workers and upper-status blue-collar workers (craftsmen, foremen, etc.) were about average on both factors.

Using the high correlation between subgroup scores in prosperity and income security orientation shown in Chart 1, Chart 2 summarizes these scores to form a new composite dimension "material orientation" which is plotted on Chart 2 against Factor 3: achievement versus affiliation. Blue-collar blacks were, as we already know, relatively very high in material orientation. They were also highest in value-related affiliation, as measured by Factor 3. White operatives and laborers, although with less extreme scores, were to be found in the same quadrant. White professionals, managers, and black white-collar workers differed little in

CHART 1. MEAN SCORES ON VALUE FACTORS FOR OCCUPATIONAL SUBGROUPS

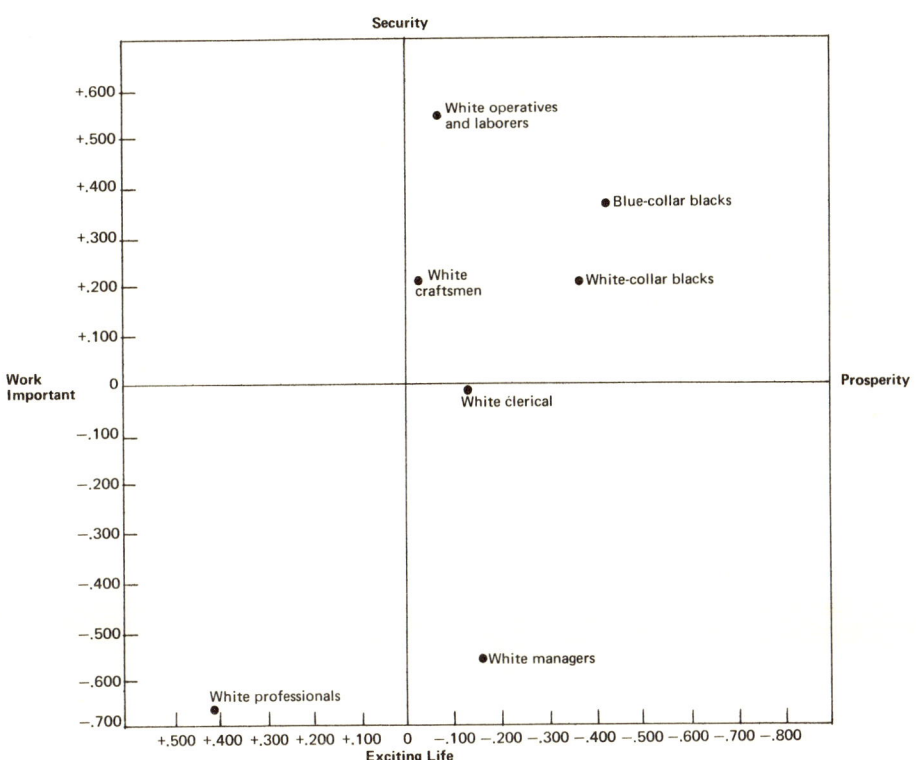

Note. Negative scores on the prosperity orientation dimension indicate a **greater** prosperity orientation.

CHART 2. MEAN SCORES ON VALUE FACTORS FOR OCCUPATIONAL SUBGROUPS

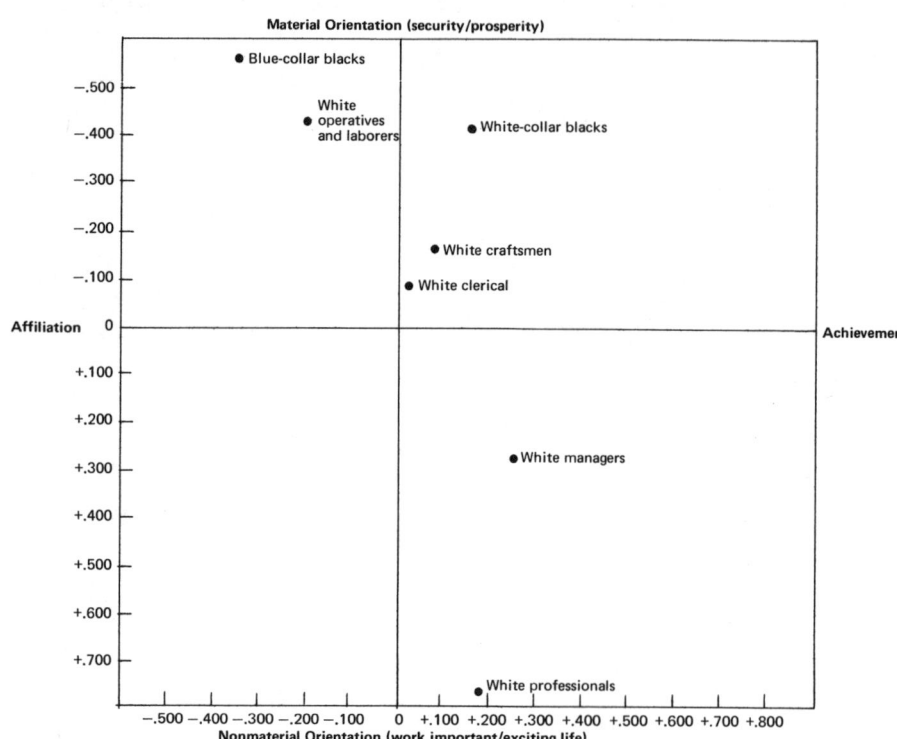

Note: Negative scores on the material orientation dimension indicate a greater material orientation.

their achievement orientation, which was positive throughout. However, as we know, they differed radically in their material-mindedness: professionals most strongly voiced values like important and exciting; managers much less frequently, but still more than the average worker; white-collar blacks were clearly prosperity—and, to a somewhat less degree, security-minded. With the exception of the black white-collar workers, achievement orientation accompanied a stress on nonmaterial goals in work and life, while the groups most attracted to material payoffs scored below average in achievement orientation. We will look at these and other findings in the last section of this paper.

IV. Satisfactions, Values, Goals

The preceding section was intended to make the reader aware of the substantial and subgroup-specific diversity of economic values within the American society. The distribution of these values seems, at least partly, to be related to socioeconomic status. It correlates much more highly with proxy variables for status—education, income,[8] occupation—than with variables distinguishing various individuals within one stratum, age for example.[9] It also differs considerably between blacks and whites.

In this section, we look at people's orientation to their economic environment and situation for several separate characteristic segments of our sample: blacks; white professionals; white managers, clerical and sales workers; white blue-collar workers. Each group appears to exhibit a particular style of coping with its economic problems. These "economic lifestyles" will be documented by our data on values, satisfaction, and fate-control. The question could be raised, what additional information do we gain by looking at people's values and other psychological predispositions? Is not the way people think just an outgrowth of what they are, what roles they play on the job, how much income they have to spend, etc.?

There are two answers. First, even if these psychological variables follow from people's function in society, which can be measured by easily identifiable categories, we want to know the considerations and mechanisms through which roles are translated into behavior as well as quality of life. Second, people's way of thinking—or, to speak in Marxian terms, consciousness—is not just the product of their present situation and environment; it embodies their past experiences and thus the culture of their ethnic group or social stratum.

The black worker

We will first consider the blacks in the sample. Mainly because of limited sample range and size (88 blacks, 122 white professionals, 114 managerial and clerical workers), interpretations are meant as suggestive rather than definitive. In particular, the stress on subgroup differences serves a methodological purpose; namely, to add a note of caution to the application of identical quality of life measures to the whole society.

Fifty-seven per cent of the blacks and 23 per cent of our white sample were operatives, laborers, or service workers. It was not possible or expedient to draw separate conclusions for the craftsmen/foremen category or for the smaller segment of blacks (26 per cent of the blacks in our sample) which did not belong to the blue-collar stratum. Therefore, much of what will be said on the basis of the data will not apply to blacks as a subgroup, but primarily to the blue-collar blacks, outside of the foreman/craftsman categories.

Dealing with blacks as one of our subgroups implies the recognition that this segment is characteristically different. Our data suggest that there exists a distinct black subculture which is expressed in distinctive economic life-styles. The low average income and job status of blacks does not alone account for their economic life-style, although it certainly contributes to and reinforces it. It should also be noted that the special character of our sample (only employed heads of households, only "complete" families with children) excludes a much larger part of blacks, particularly lower-class blacks, than whites from our sample.

It is well known that a large part of black workers in the unskilled categories have irregular employment. "Last hired and first fired" still is a common part of black experience. In this segment of the population, "Life is crisis-life constantly trying to make do with string where rope is needed" [17]; "Got a job but I got sick and lost it"; and "We managed until the baby got sick." As long as the present is in jeopardy, there is little attention and energy left to consider or provide for the future [18].

Blacks tend to be disadvantaged by virtue of both social class and race. They encounter serious and unique obstacles not only in the area of work (the so-called "job ceiling") but also in areas of income allocation, housing discrimination, and, regionally, overt or hidden discrimination in public facilities. On the other hand, blacks' full participation in the educational revolution of the last decades [6], reflecting the American ideology of equal opportunity, and the more recent stress (and publicity) on black identity and advancement have contributed to high aspirations for and expectations of improvements. How is this reflected in the economic orientations and satisfaction of the young black heads of households in the sample?

Our survey makes use of the concepts of self-efficacy/fate-control or internal/external control which have now gained prominence in many diverse areas of research [3], and have been shown to be particularly crucial orientations for groups confronted with severe handicaps.

Gerald Gurin and Patricia Gurin in a set of studies concerning groups disadvantaged by economic and/or minority status—black college students, manpower trainees, "hard-core" unemployed youth—have attempted to analyze the motivational determinants of occupational aspirations and performance. These studies have focused on an "expectancy" orientation, stressing that behavior depends not only on the motives and incentives that define what a person values and desires, but also on the expectancy, or the person's estimate of the probability, that the behavior will help him obtain what he is striving for. These studies have separated and measured different components of motivation and suggest that for economically disadvantaged and minority groups, the expectancy component of motivation may be more crucial than achievement motives or values. The bases as well as the level of an individual's expectancies seem important. That is, there is not just the question of the degree of confidence or optimism about one's opportunities and possibilities, but also relevant are such issues as the extent to which a person feels his chances are dependent on his own skill and resources, the extent to which he feels they are affected by the social system, and the extent to which he feels these system-imposed constraints can be influenced by his own or group efforts.[10]

A substantial number of fate-control items were factor analyzed. The factors which emerged corresponded to the underlying theoretical concepts:

Fate-Control Factor 1: Self-efficacy. Main loadings: the individual's ability to do things that are difficult and challenging, "can make plans work."

Fate-Control Factor 2: "Generalized" fate-control. Belief that lack of skills, abilities, and motivation (rather than lack of job or bad luck) keep people back or unemployed. The items used here refer to the perception of what all or most people (rather than the individual himself) can do to master their fate.

Fate-Control Factor 3: Future orientation. Person plans ahead, thinks much about the future, would rather save for the future than spend the money to enjoy life today.

Fate-Control Factor 4: Trust in people. Belief that people are generally trustworthy.

Considering the existing research, which is mainly centered on students and unemployed people, it comes as no surprise that the blacks in our sample come out significantly lower than whites on virtually all of our fate-control measures. They are extremely low on self-efficacy. They are low on future orientation, and significantly lower on generalized fate-control and trust in people (Table 9).

Gerald Gurin and Patricia Gurin suggested that a high sense of general-

TABLE 9. MEAN SCORES ON FATE-CONTROL FACTORS WITHIN RACE-OCCUPATION

Race-occupation of family head	Self-Efficacy Scale	Generalized Fate-Control	Future Orientation	Trust in People	Number of Cases
White professional	0.657	−0.345	−0.216	0.424	119
White managers	0.720	0.573	0.247	0.326	54
White clerical	0.197	0.162	−0.112	0.053	58
White craftsmen, foremen	0.103	0.267	0.165	0.037	113
White operatives, laborers	−0.630	0.040	0.179	−0.227	106
Black professional, manager, clerical, craftsmen, foremen	−0.317	−0.455	−0.416	−0.349	36
Black operatives, laborers	−1.105	−0.345	0.082	−0.847	50
Significance tests	F=13.689 p=.001	F=4.379 p=.001	F=1.719 p=NS *	F=5.476 p=.001	

* Not significant

ized fate-control may aggravate the task of coping with adverse economic experience. "When associated with success, an internal orientation (such as high generalized fate-control) can lead to feelings of competence and efficacy. When associated with failure, however, it can lead to self-derogation and self-blame" [7]. Conversely, the recognition of adverse circumstance —be it poverty, discrimination, or an unfavorable labor market, etc.—can open the way for collective action to change or alleviate the unsatisfactory conditions. The blacks in our sample were partly but not entirely successful with this kind of realism, adaptation, or mental self-defense. To be sure, they were high in system-blame, but they were also very high in self-blame (Table 10).

All of this is strongly suggestive of the difficulties of blacks in coping with the adverse circumstances they encounter both as members of the lower class and by virtue of their race. The evidence from our measures of satisfaction is more complex. There is, as was previously noted, particularly strong expressed dissatisfaction with standard of living and education, but no deviation from the generally favorable perception of job satisfaction in the population as a whole. Each of these themes is evidenced by a variety of data (Tables 1 and 2): 31 per cent of the blacks felt their total family income was not enough to meet usual monthly expenses and bills, as opposed to only 12 per cent of white blue-collar workers; barely 25 per cent of blacks felt their income was enough for them to live as comfortably as they would like at the time, as opposed to 42 per cent of white blue-collar workers. And if in five years their standard of living were the same as

TABLE 10. REASONS FOR "NOT DOING WELL" WITHIN RACE AND OCCUPATION GROUPS[a]

	All Respondents	White					Black	
		Professionals, Technical	Managers, Officials	Clerical, Sales	Craftsmen, Foremen	Operatives, Laborers	Professionals, Managers, Clerical, Sales, Craftsmen, Foremen	Operatives, Laborers
Not using good breaks I have had								
True	26%	22%	7%	17%	25%	33%	33%	46%
Not true	74	78	93	83	75	67	67	52
Not ascertained; do not know	*	*	*	*	*	*	*	2
Total	100%	100%	100%	100%	100%	100%	100%	100%
Not having enough ability								
True	26%	19%	16%	22%	22%	32%	33%	50%
Not true	74	80	84	78	78	68	67	50
Not ascertained; do not know	*	1	*	*	*	*	*	*
Total	100%	100%	100%	100%	100%	100%	100%	100%

* Less than .05 per cent.
[a] For wording of question see Appendix C, question D40.

now, only 28 per cent of the blacks would be satisfied or moderately satisfied as opposed to 49 per cent of white blue-collar workers. As a warning against any straightforward interpretation of the uncharacteristic outcome of the work satisfaction question, the comparatively low work involvement expressed by the blacks should be mentioned: 61 per cent of them agreed with the statement, "Work is just a way of making money" as opposed to 45 per cent of the white blue-collar workers and 20 per cent of the white white-collar workers. We also may recall the high scores of blacks on the value factor, prosperity versus important work; 40 per cent of our blacks considered "income is high" the thing about a job they would most prefer, compared to 26 per cent of blue-collar whites.

At this point, we introduce factor analysis again, this time not as a data reduction and measuring device for constructing indices, but for detecting the peculiar patterning of variables and meaning of concepts for different subgroups. In contrast to the value data, the satisfaction data proved not to be amenable to composite factoring for the whole sample. The patterns of covariance between variables, and thus the factor formation, were divergent between blacks, white professionals, white managers, and blue-collar workers. Graphic presentation of the factor loadings permits a visual representation of these structures. Chart 3 plots the variables representing the satisfaction syndrome. These variables are:

1. Satisfaction with financial changes in the recent past
2. Satisfaction with present standard of living
3. The question of whether present income is enough to meet family expenses
4. The question of whether present income is enough for the family to live comfortably
5. Concern about threats to future standard of living
6. Satisfaction with main job
7. The question of whether the person would continue to work at the same job if he did not need the income
8. The question of whether main interests in life are work
9. The question of whether work is just a way of making money
10. Concern about unemployment
11. Chances of finding a comparable job if present job is lost
12. The question of whether actual work is in equilibrium with desire to work [11]
13. Satisfaction with own education

The emerging factor dimensions are "satisfaction with the standard of living," "job satisfaction," and "optimism/concern."

Naturally, the meaning of these factors follows from the dominant vari-

CHART 3. SATISFACTION FACTORS FOR BLACKS (BLUE COLLAR AND WHITE COLLAR)

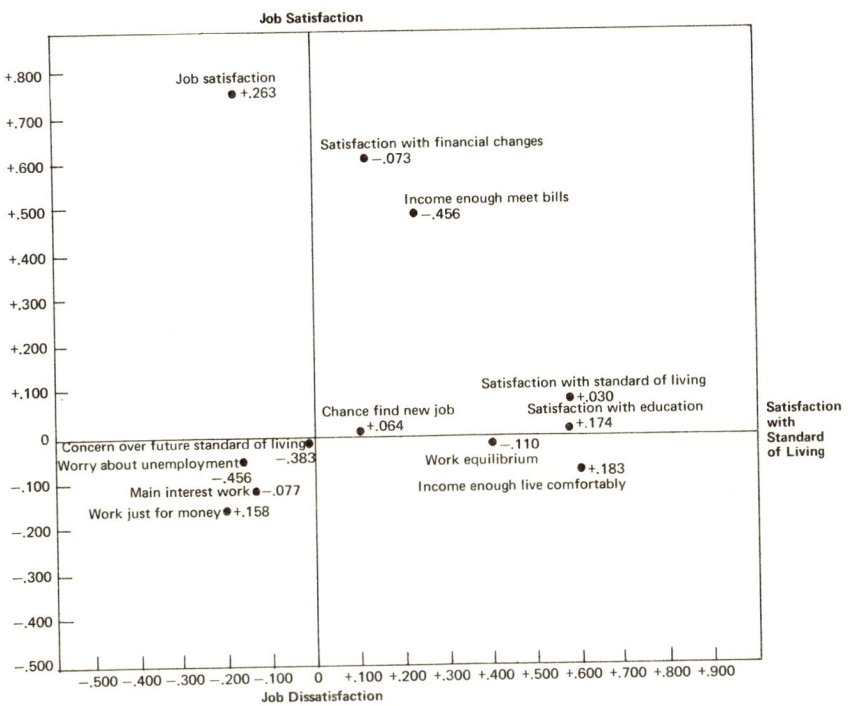

Note: Scores adjacent to points on this chart and charts 4 and 6 refer to the third factor: optimism vs. concern. Positive scores indicate optimism, negative scores indicate concern. The coefficients plotted in this and the following three charts represent both the factor pattern and structure (orthogonal factors).

ables of which they are composed. We are operating here, for the sake of clarity, with only three dimensions, the third factor being expressed by plus or minus scores attached to each variable. This third factor is positively loaded on job satisfaction, "income enough to live comfortably," "satisfaction with education, and work involvement" (work is not just a way of making money), and is negatively loaded on worry about unemployment and concern with future standard of living. One might call this factor optimism/concern.

The main theme which catches the eye is the fragmentation of the black image of economic life-style between job and standard of living (Chart 3). A job tends to be looked at as a short-term affair, as a way of procuring the means for making ends meet, possibly of providing steady income (viz. the negative correlation between job satisfaction and worry about unemployment). A good job is a job which pays well, offers some continuity, and fills the most pressing needs for meeting expenses and paying bills, as demonstrated by the vicinity of the three variables. However, a decent standard of living means a radically different way of life which, as evidenced by the lack of correlation between the respective configuration of variable points, is not linked to and cannot be expected from a job, even if it is considered good by the more realistic standards set by the daily and often dismal struggle for livelihood. Satisfaction with standard of living among black workers is contingent upon a satisfactory education [12] and upon "living as comfortably as one would like to," both states largely unattainable for the majority of blacks.

These differences add up to a consistent picture. The younger blacks were particularly attracted to a "prosperous life." Yet most of them realized a "comfortable" life was out of their immediate reach; it could not be achieved on their present terms of trade, within the constraints of low skills and social status, ghetto existence, and limited opportunities. It could only come through a basic change in their terms of trade, to be brought about primarily by education, and through changes in their opportunities.

These considerations should warn us against accepting the relatively high job satisfaction of blacks at face value. Such satisfaction is not an expression of a desirable or desired state of affairs. Given the high incidence of unemployment experience among blacks, to have a job (and all our respondents are at present employed) means to be ahead of others operating within similar constraints and possibly serving as reference persons. However, the world of work is not where the involvement is expected—and this in itself may give rise to social concern. The vision of betterment is linked to the desire for education from which, however, only the next generation can benefit. Given the quoted internal and external constraints, high consumption aspirations find little outlet in increased labor-force participation or job advancement, certainly in the short and medium run; housing discrimination adds to discontent in the highly emphasized sphere of consumption and leisure. Constructive responses through behavioral coping are largely blocked by the system. The data suggest how the environmental handicaps are mirrored and reinforced through psychological adjustments which can serve as impediments in the world of work (self-blame, low sense of efficacy, low job involvement). On a methodological level, our results cast more doubt on the suitability of aggregated satisfaction scores for measuring the quality of economic life across subcultures.

Professionals

In choosing the subgroups, we refrained from applying statistical methods for maximizing the between-group variance in economic life-styles. We instead selected subgroups which, in addition to being very different with respect to our subject matter, are easily identifiable and distinct with respect to socioeconomic status and their function in the production process. Occupational categories fit these requirements the best. Therefore, we will analyze professionals, managerial occupations, and blue-collar workers separately with respect to whites.

In Section III, we found professionals (comprising medical and paramedical occupations, accountants and auditors, teachers, natural scientists, technicians like airplane pilots, foresters, public advisors like clergymen, welfare workers, lawyers, and judges, etc.) to be most attached to nonmaterial "self-actualizing" values like "important work" and "exciting life," and at the same time to be higher on our measure of achievement versus affiliation. The deviations within the former measure were substantially higher than within the latter.

Professionals, comparatively speaking, appeared most adapted to our economic system. They were most satisfied with their job, their education, their living standard. Their job involvement was the highest, they were the most attached to its intrinsic rewards (Table 4). Together with the managerial workers, they were most advancement minded (Table 6). They were outstanding in satisfaction with their present standard of living, and although they were more likely to expect income increases, they would not be significantly more unhappy than others if their standard of living remained the same over the next five years (Table 3). They also harbored the strongest sense of fate-control in its various facets. This was not contradicted by their relatively low score on generalized fate-control (Is it fate or the system which keeps somebody unemployed?). These questions were phrased to fit the lower-class situation. Professionals recognized more frequently than white blue-collar workers that, at the bottom of society, the environment is less controllable.

All in all, the present society and economy appeared to be a congenial medium for professionals to live in. Although most of them were working as employees in organizations, their special skills and expert status provided them with a degree of autonomy. Their social status relieved them from some of the pressures felt by other segments to strive for status through increasing income and standard of living.

How was their particular economic life-style reflected in the configuration of components of satisfaction? Chart 4 shows that the variable job satisfaction was somewhat loaded on the factor "satisfaction with standard of living," and the variable satisfaction with standard of living was somewhat loaded on the factor "job satisfaction." Thus in the evaluation of professionals, both spheres of economic well-being were distinct, but not segregated from each other as in the perceptions of the blacks. Likewise, financial considerations marginally affected both satisfaction with job and living

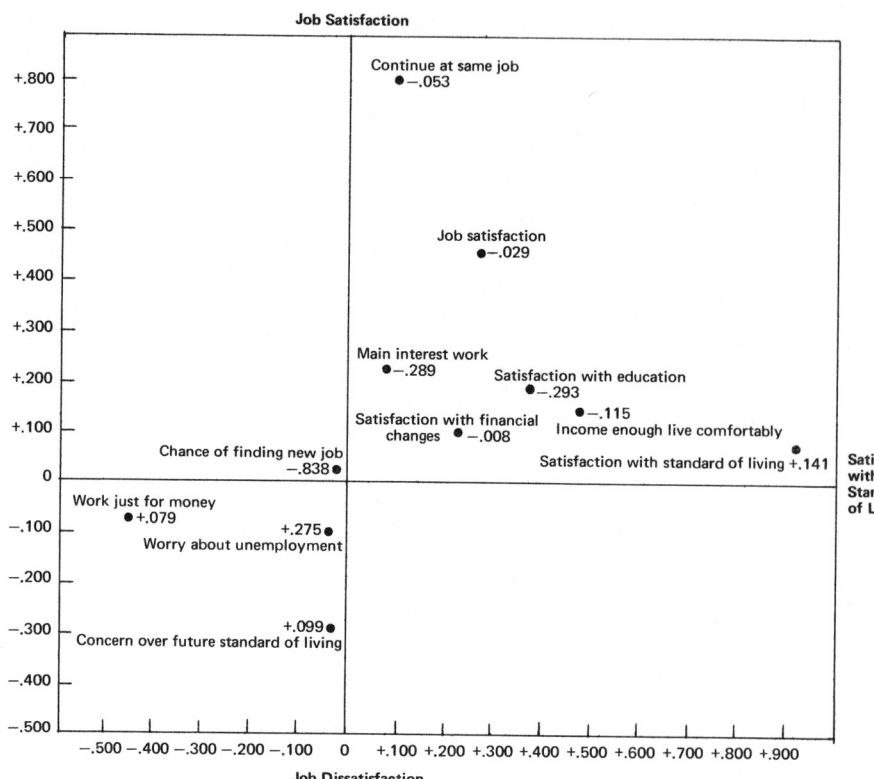

CHART 4. SATISFACTION FACTORS FOR WHITE PROFESSIONALS, TECHNICAL AND KINDRED WORKERS

standard but, unlike the black case, did not dominate it. The role of education in the subjective economic well-being of professionals came out most clearly in the third dimension (optimism/concern) which was not plotted but indicated by the signed scores. Education quite plausibly played a most crucial role in counterbalancing concern for future well-being. The main concern of professionals, as evidenced by the relative loadings of the variables on the third dimension, was not the worry of unemployment (as for blacks), but the concern for finding a comparable job. Furthermore, the neutrality of the job concern variables on the dimension of satisfaction with the standard of living made it clear that security or concern for the professional future was not considered an ingredient of job satisfaction. Professionals, in evaluating their future well-being, did not rely primarily on their present employers but on the marketability of their skills.

The organization men

Among the subgroups, blacks (including all occupations) and white professionals provided the most clearly contrasting images of economic lifestyles. The profiles of white managers, clerical or sales workers, and blue-collar workers of various status categories emerged as somewhat less distinct. In much of the following discussion, we emphasize some common traits within two larger segments of the white labor force: combining managerial with clerical (including sales) workers on the one hand, and skilled with unskilled blue-collar workers on the other. Needless to say, important variations within these two categories will remain unrecognized and undescribed, partly due to the small size of the sample.

Managerial and clerical workers appeared to be less well adjusted to their present economic setting than did professionals. Managers have a strong preoccupation with financial success and a large and a highly dynamic margin of aspirations over accomplishments. For clerical and sales workers, the high standards set by more successful organization men appeared to reduce this group's satisfaction with the respectable status they have achieved within society as a whole.

In sharp contrast to professionals, managers were highly oriented toward the values of prosperity and income maximization (Table 6). Profit is the most visible success criterion for a business organization; this emphasis, imparted by the occupational role, filters through to the private sphere. Another symptom of the American business creed came out in the attitude of managerial workers toward the unemployed. Financial success is more than just instrumental; it vindicates the whole person. Economic failure, in turn, tends to be viewed as a failure to react properly to the opportunities offered by society. Managers were highest of all subgroups in generalized fate-control: one who really tries, will get ahead (Table 9). Furthermore, managers were most likely to expect and demand future improvements in their standard of living. The idea of a stagnant income made them more unhappy than any other group except blacks (Table 3).

The clerical and sales workers, who incidentally were relatively low in job satisfaction (second only to the operatives and laborers), appeared less ready to internalize the values of the world of organizations but still felt subject to its standards. They approached blue-collar workers in emphasizing security and, to a lesser degree, affiliation-oriented values. They were lower than managers in all facets of fate-control. However, almost as eagerly as managers they embraced the American dream of constant progress. They would be most unhappy if five years from now they would not be more prosperous. With regard to satisfaction with present living standard, both groups were considerably less satisfied than professionals and somewhat less satisfied than the foremen/craftsmen segment (Table 3).

The structure of satisfactions among managerial and clerical/sales occupations (Chart 5) both documented these thoughts and allowed us to add to them. In conspicuous contrast to the configurations for blacks and professionals, the technique was in a position to accommodate job satisfaction and satisfaction with standard of living on one dimension: over-all *economic* satisfaction. The third dimension of the other charts (optimism/concern) could therefore be represented on the vertical axis. Occupational success, for an organization man, was reflected in financial success; a good job was a job that paid well, enabled him to live comfortably, and recognized successful effort through income increases. Security appeared to play a minor role in the generation of job satisfaction.

Interestingly, both satisfaction with job and with standard of living were *negatively* loaded on the optimism factor; they accompanied concern about the future, the negation of chances to find a new comparable job, and underemployment. Satisfaction appeared to be part of a coping mechanism, a symptom of accommodation, the second-best response of people who were finding themselves in the role of "getting ahead" and who tried to move away from that role. Managerial and clerical/sales occupations, according to our interpretation, were readily provided by their peer groups and work organizations with relatively high and rapidly expanding material goals. The high level of goals, in spite of respectable achievements in social and material status, seemed to tax their sense of economic well-being. However, mechanisms were available to them for coping with failure or the threat of it to a certain extent, and if the need arose, they managed to withdraw from the dominant values of their group by reducing their goals.

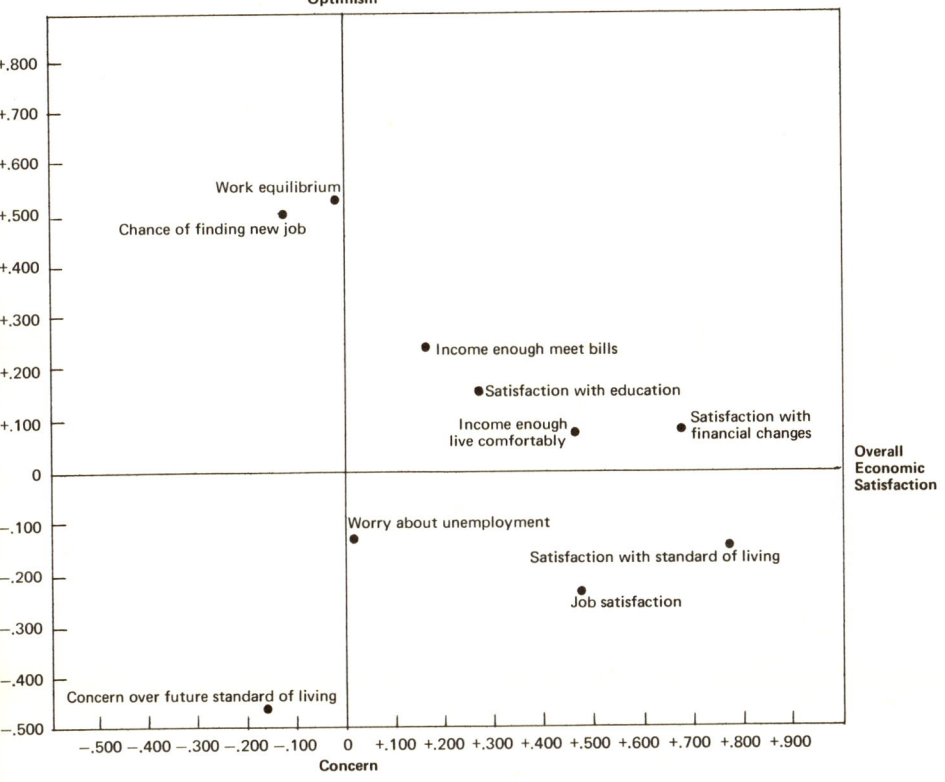

CHART 5. SATISFACTION FACTORS FOR WHITE MANAGERS, OFFICIALS, CLERICAL AND SALES WORKERS

Blue-collar workers

The main concern of white blue-collar workers, except for the lowest strata, was not their low and comparatively stagnant income; our data suggest that they were no less satisfied with their standard of living than the more affluent white-collar groups [19]. However, they were more worried. Many of them expressed concern about unemployment, and they were more likely than white-collar workers to be "very concerned" about societal developments threatening their standard of living (Table 3). Their dominant concern was security, which was also indicated by the value-scores charted in Section III.

The insecurity expressed by the white blue-collar segment has been observed often and has recently been dealt with mainly under the heading of alienation from a complex and rapidly changing society which increasingly relies on higher educated manpower.

> Strongly desiring education for his children, he [the blue-collar worker] feels alienated from the teachers, the schools, as well as many institutions in society. The working-class world is a simple world.... The working-class family's perspective is, in general, severely truncated. Situations and alternatives typically are seen in black and white and people are classified as either "in" or "out," in "we" and "they" terms [22].

Insecurity and worry are closely related to their lack of fate-control. Blue-collar whites were significantly lower in self-efficacy and trust in people than professionals and managers. Yet, they were more hesitant than either professionals or blacks to blame the system or "bad luck" in the case of an individual who was unemployed or otherwise unsuccessful (Table 9). The latter was particularly true for skilled workers. The refusal to hold fate or the system responsible for their perceived difficulties may cause the same type of problems for an individual in his coping behavior and self-esteem which we pointed to in dealing with the black subgroup. Failure would then lead to self-blame. With respect to self-blame, the white blue-collar group was indeed located between blacks and white-collar whites (Table 10).

Whether or not these difficulties for the economic adaptation of white blue-collar workers are becoming more serious cannot be determined on the basis of one small survey. Yet the contours of the characteristic coping mechanisms of this segment emerge from our data.

Indications are that blaming the system is on the increase. Trust in government and in its ability to solve economic and social problems, as numerous surveys have shown, has declined dramatically during the past decade [26] and a sizable blue-collar protest vote has emerged in recent years. Second, there may be a withdrawal from identification with work and employer. The recent problem of "blue-collar blues," mentioned pre-

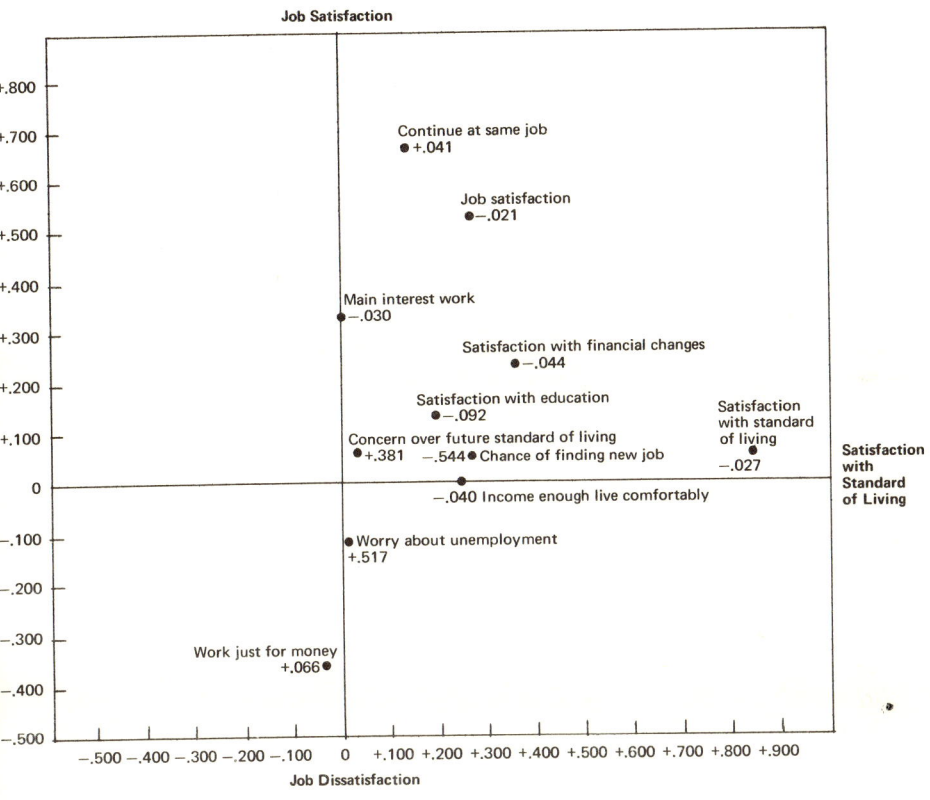

CHART 6. SATISFACTION FACTORS FOR WHITE BLUE COLLAR

viously along with our data on the frequency of a purely instrumental attitude toward work ("work is just a way of making money") expressed by almost half of white blue-collar workers (Table 2), supports this point. Third, there appears to be a limitation of goals. The emphasis on defensive goals like "secure life" and "job and income security" leads to this interpretation, as well as the remarkably high satisfaction with standard of living in the face of concerns about past progress, future income trends, and worries to that effect.

Chart 6 maps the configuration of satisfaction variables for white blue-collar workers. There was, as with professionals, a moderate correlation between the variables of job satisfaction and satisfaction with living standards. Unlike the mapping for professionals, satisfaction with education contributed little to either the dimension representing satisfaction with standard of living or that representing job satisfaction. Satisfaction with financial change contributed to both. Interestingly, concern about the future (mainly fear of unemployment) had little relationship to job satisfaction or job involvement. One who was highly satisfied with his job was as likely as the next fellow to be worried about unemployment and his future standard of living. This is consistent with our line of argument. The problems bothering blue-collar whites are societal problems, and not so much the problems of the individual's work setting. We cannot resist pointing to the apparent mirror image between our interpretations for the blacks and the white blue-collar workers. The blacks tended to be very dissatisfied with what they had and entertained a vision of the good, prosperous, and comfortable life, quite unrelated to their position. In contrast, the blue-collar whites were reasonably satisfied with their situation, but tended to be preoccupied with the vision of a threat to their livelihood and status, in most cases no less distant from their present reality. It should be noted, however, that the blacks were not significantly less pessimistic than white blue-collar workers in our measures for future concern and expectations.

V. Implications for Society

The economic orientations we are dealing with are, at the same time, measures of societal resources and of individual adaptation. We will now briefly and in a summary fashion look at our results both from the system and the individual perspective.

How does change in economic life-styles, values, and subjective welfare affect the society? The variables we dealt with in detail have manifest behavioral consequences for consuming, saving, working, and choosing an occupation. Some of those relationships have been documented elsewhere [13] and thus have implications for aggregate consumer demand and for the supply of labor and financial capital. Furthermore, the more dissatisfied people are with the range of available economic choices, with their given terms of trade on the labor, credit, and commodity markets, the more they or their representatives will try to alter their terms of trade through collective bargaining, strikes, voting, and other inputs into the institutional sphere. The present economic difficulties—most prominently inflation coupled with high rates of unemployment—testify to the inability of markets to accommodate demands for rewards of the system within the existing rules of the game.

The 574 young American men in our sample were greatly satisfied with their jobs, and less satisfied with their standard of living and education. People's aspirations clearly revolved around the sphere of consumption and domestic living. Is this a fairly new phenomenon, a characteristic of the "affluent" or "mass consumption" society, or does it reflect a more basic condition? The documented increase in job satisfaction over the last 10 to 15 years would suggest the presence of a trend. We may interpret the high job satisfaction as resulting from a relative stagnation of vocational goals in a setting of improving working conditions, of relative increase in the proportion of comfortable white-collar and related jobs, and rising real incomes even for the nonadvancing employee. This type of satisfaction appears to be of a fairly passive kind. Only 17 per cent of the sample considered chances for advancement the most important attribute of a job. In contrast, 39 per cent listed job and income security. Asked what would tempt them most to change their jobs, most chose higher income while fewer people chose career advancement.

Higher incomes were impatiently desired. The classic mechanism for coping with high and unfulfilled consumption aspirations is the stepping-up of effort—working more or striving for advancement. Yet in the blue-collar stratum, progress seemed to be expected from a general increase in wage and salary levels rather than from changes of the individual roles within the sphere of production. Work was seen primarily in an instrumental way, and those subgroups most dissatisfied with their standard of living and most desirous (and in need) of higher incomes, were least actively oriented toward goal attainment. Higher status groups were more achievement oriented and appeared to be motivated by nonmaterial rewards.

In other words, the link between the need for, or expectation of, financial increases and motivation to work for this increase has at least become tenuous. Weak goals for advancement among those who had high expectations for income increases were certainly a potentially explosive combination in a period of declining growth rates. Time series data are needed to test our hypothesis that claims made upon the system are rising faster than the willingness to provide the necessary inputs.

How did the people in our sample adapt to their environment? Clearly, the data warn us against establishing summary indices of well-being to be used for cross-segment comparisons. The main argument against doing so is provided by the factor analysis of satisfactions within occupational and racial groups. This analysis suggested that various satisfaction concepts have entirely different meanings across groups. The same must be said about variables like job involvement, concern with the future, and satisfaction with education.

Yet the rich data base collected permits us to evaluate the characteristic problems experienced by a subgroup along several dimensions of well-being. After doing so, one general conclusion emerges: Higher socioeconomic status spills over to a fuller sense of well-being, no matter how you measure it. The syndrome of the humble but happy life could not be identified in any segment. High-status people, mainly professionals, were generally more satisfied with what they had and more confident about their future. And even the managers, who were more likely to be dissatisfied, tended to be optimistic about their ability to improve their situation. Lower-strata respondents in our sample of men in their most productive years not only were more dissatisfied with virtually all aspects of their economic situation, but also were more worried about their well-being, were less involved in their work, and were less confident in their ability to master their fate.

The literature suggests that relative rather than absolute status shapes satisfactions. Only in a very limited sense can professionals and managers be considered reference groups for blue-collar workers. Therefore we propose to use the notion of relativity in a temporal sense. Higher-status people were subjectively better off partly because they were more likely to experience substantial real income increases. These increases, as we know from other research, [12] were only slowly incorporated into the individual's routine level of living and current expenditures and thus tended to provide a sense of financial latitude. It was these income increases that tended to be allocated to the purchases of durables and to saving. The former use plays a large role in symbolizing a high standard of living, the latter in providing a sense of security. Americans, in contrast to Western Europeans, place an unusually heavy emphasis on progress.

No less than 84 per cent of our sample of young heads of households expected they would be better off a year from now. If five years from now their standards of living were the same, 58 per cent would be outright dissatisfied. But a large part of the sample, particularly in the lower-status groups, at the same time expected improvements from the future and worried about it. The expectation of progress, or what we call the "sliding scale of aspirations," made them quite vulnerable to even small setbacks. Apart from low levels of income, the absence of progress as experienced by many more blue-collar than white-collar workers must already have had a detrimental effect on economic satisfaction. Where stagnation is considered bad news, good news may become a scarce commodity.

The nonattainment of goals can be handled in a more or less constructive and painful way. It can be handled by stepping up efforts to bring reality in line with goals. It can be handled by goal reduction. Even if neither is the case, recognition of failure may still coexist with a sense of self-efficacy and optimism; things will be better tomorrow. Dissatisfaction has many more serious psychological, behavioral, and system consequences where none of these avenues is open. Our data on self-efficacy, self-blame, and trust in people describe the psychological choices by which people mainly of low status are confined. Their means and opportunities for getting out of an unsatisfactory job, neighborhood, or financial situation are severely limited. They usually are subject to closer social control. If they are dissatisfied, they are, rightly or wrongly, less confident in their ability to do something about it. They also, as we have seen, have less reason to view the future with optimism. They remain more worried about changes even if they reduce their goals so as to be satisfied with what they have—a trend observable among white blue-collar workers.

The line of inquiry presented here can only be fully utilized through applications on larger samples and through time series data. This will allow us to test the propositions developed in the present exploratory study in a more definitive manner. While the concern with subgroup differences in economic motivation and subjective welfare is justified, it is by no means clear to what extent these variables are amenable to change through public policy and situational trends generally. Time series data would allow us to relate such external changes to their subjective and motivational consequences. This would be a first step towards identifying sources of motivation and satisfaction. The monitoring of people's economic wants, aspirations, and satisfaction can play an important role as a sensitive feed-back and warning mechanism for public policy.

Appendix
Part A

Sampling and interviewing

Birth records and other official sources were used for a random selection of households who had their first child during the 1960s (oldest child under 10 years of age) from the Detroit and Baltimore SMSA's. Additionally, only those family units which were complete with employed heads were actually interviewed. The resulting sample consisted of 574 heads and their wives. Only 6 per cent of the heads were more than 40 years old. The survey was conducted in the spring of 1971.

Since our sample was selected from a restricted sampling frame, a determination of the effects of our sampling bias was deemed essential for an adequate interpretation of our data. To this end, a comparison was made on selected demographic characteristics of our sample to a comparable subgroup of the 1971 Survey of Consumer Finances conducted by the Survey Research Center during the first quarter of 1971. The sampling design for the 1971 Survey of Consumer Finances used the method of multistage area probability-sampling to select a sample of dwelling units representative of the population living in private households in the United States. Comparisons between the two samples generally yielded similar distributions among the various demographic characteristics. However, a small but systematic income bias (underrepresentation of low-income families) in our sample was detected, which is summarized in the following table:

Total Family Income	Our Data	1971 SCF
Less than $ 7,500	10%	16%
$ 7,500– 9,999	23	20
$10,000–12,499	26	24
$12,500–14,999	17	13
$15,000 or over	24	27
Total	100%	100%

Appendix
Part B

TABLE B1. PRINCIPAL FACTOR SOLUTION FOR 16 VALUE-GOAL ITEMS[a]

	Common Factors		
Variables	Security Orientation	Prosperity Orientation	Achievement vs. Affiliation
Prosperous life	−.142	.738	.033
Family life	−.311	−.335	−.079
Important life	.434	−.116	.038
Secure life	−.522	−.197	−.302
Exciting life	.545	−.106	.308
Ambitious person	−.107	.417	−.354
Well-liked person	−.253	.160	.424
Independent person	.358	.172	−.095
Helpful person	.042	−.400	.535
Responsible person	−.120	−.393	−.437
Income steady	−.642	−.146	.041

Appendix · 117

	Common Factors		
Variables	Security Orientation	Prosperity Orientation	Achievement vs. Affiliation
Income high	.292	.539	.063
No danger of being fired	−.570	.009	.205
Hours short	.037	.080	.445
Advancement good	.298	.095	−.559
Work important	.563	−.495	−.106

[a]This factor solution was obtained by using the squared multiple correlation coefficient of each variable as initial estimates of the communalities for all principal components whose eigenvalues were greater than one. The coefficients in this table represent both the factor pattern and structure (orthogonal factors). In the following chart (Chart B1) this solution is represented graphically.

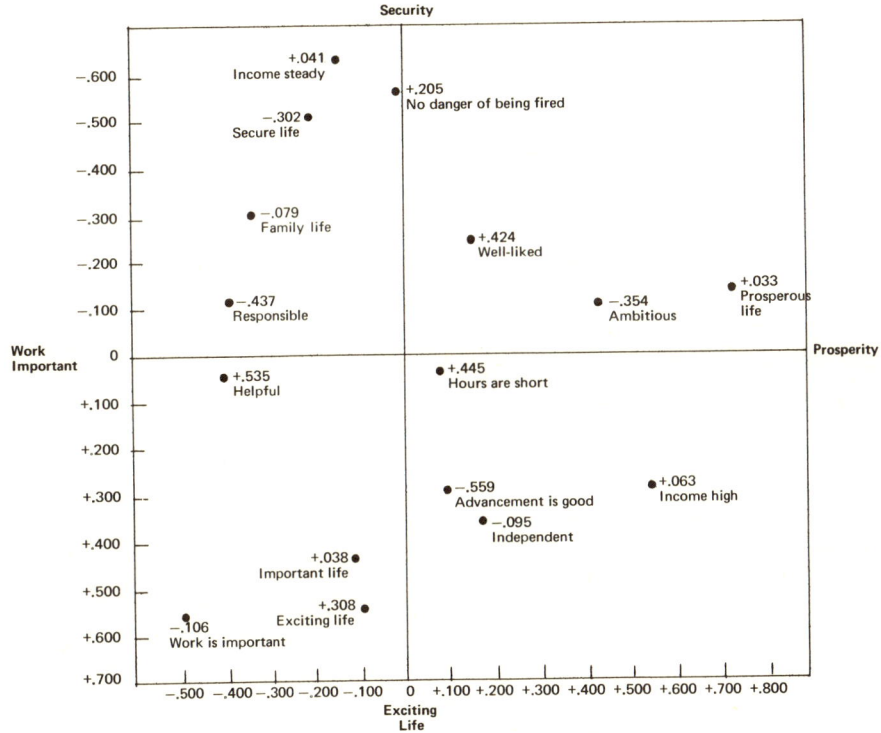

CHART B1. VALUE FACTORS FOR ALL RESPONDENTS

Note. Scores adjacent to points on this chart refer to the third factor: achievement vs. affiliation. Negative scores indicate achievement, positive scores indicate affiliation.

TABLE B2. OBLIQUE FACTOR SOLUTION FOR 17 FATE-CONTROL ITEMS[a]

	Common Factors			
Variables	Self Efficacy	Generalized Fate-Control	Future Orientation	Trust in People
I plan life ahead	.102	.032	.587	.109
I do difficult things	.432	.068	−.029	−.015
I trust people	.157	−.021	−.127	.571
I am hard working	.071	−.052	.041	.027
Most people help others	−.080	.038	.061	.500
I think a lot about future	−.010	.032	.491	−.038
I spend money today	−.003	.015	−.311	.140
I have little influence	.017	.010	−.013	.033
Success requires hard work	.122	−.040	−.061	.044
I can make plans work	.421	−.123	.127	.015
What happens to me is my own doing	.172	−.163	.079	.053
One must know the right people to get ahead	.081	.014	.025	−.113
People who do not do well lack breaks	−.140	.352	.056	.074
I felt sure life would work out well	.277	−.078	.125	.112
Poor people have less chance to get ahead	.269	.341	.043	.042
If people had skills, they could get jobs	.033	−.374	−.012	.054
Most unemployed have not had good breaks	.145	.640	−.007	.061

[a] This factor solution was obtained by using the squared multiple correlation coefficient of each variable as initial estimates of the communalities for all principal components whose eigenvalues were greater than one. The initial factor solution was then rotated obliquely (oblimin criterion). The coefficients in this table represent the pattern matrix (*i.e.* factor "loadings").

Appendix
Part C Questionnaire

The three questions used to construct value factors are listed in Section III (text). Please note that the second question on occupational goals ("What would tempt you most?") was not used for factor construction.

The following group of questions was used to construct fate-control factors:

A3. Now I have some questions about how you feel about things. In these next questions I will read you two statements and I would like you to tell me which statement comes closest to the way you feel.

Are you the kind of person that
> plans his life ahead all the time—or—
> lives more from day to day?

A4. Would you rather
> do things that are difficult and challenging—or—
> do things that you're sure you know how to do?

A5. Would you say that
> most people can be trusted—or—
> you can't be too careful in your dealings with people?

A6. Would you say that you were
> always hard-working—or—
> somebody who sometimes takes things easy?

A7. Would you say that
> most people are more inclined to help others—or—
> most people are more inclined to look out for themselves?

A8. Do you
> think a lot about things that might happen in the future—or—
> usually just take things as they come?

A9. Would you rather
> spend your money and enjoy life today—or—
> save more for the future?

A10. In each of the next questions, I am going to read you two sentences. These statements are listed on this sheet so that you can follow along as I read them. Tell me the one that comes closest to the way you feel things actually are in life. Be sure it is the way things *actually are* in life, *not* the way you would like them to be.

Which of these first two statements is closest to the way you feel things actually are?
> Many times I feel that I have little influence over the things that happen to me.
> It is impossible for me to believe that chance or luck play an important role in my life.

A11. Which of these two?
> Becoming a success is a matter of hard work; luck has little or nothing to do with it.
> Getting a good job depends mainly on being in the right place at the right time.

A12. And these?
> When I make plans, I am almost certain that I can make them work.
> It is not always wise to plan too far ahead because many things turn out to be a matter of good or bad luck anyhow.

A13. Which of these?
> What happens to me is my own doing.

Sometimes I feel that I do not have enough control over the direction my life is taking.

A14. And these?

Knowing the right people is important in deciding whether a person will get ahead.

People will get ahead in life if they have the skills and do a good job; knowing the right people has nothing to do with it.

A15. How about these?

People who do not do well in life often work hard, but the breaks just do not come their way.

Some people just do not use the breaks that come their way; if they do not do well, it is their own fault.

A16. And these?

I have usually felt pretty sure my life would work out the way I want it to.

There are times when I have not been very sure that my life would work out the way I wanted it to.

A17. Now I have a few questions concerning poverty and unemployment. People have different ideas about poverty and unemployment. I would like to ask you about your ideas.

Which of these two statements is closer to the way you feel?

People who are born poor have less chance to get ahead than other people.

People who have the ability and work hard have the same chance as anyone else, even if their parents were poor.

A18. Which of these two statements is closer to how you feel?

It is the lack of skills and abilities that keep most unemployed people from getting a job; if they had the skills most of them could get a job.

Many people with skills can not get a job; there just are not any jobs for them.

A19. Which of these?

Most people who are unemployed just have not had the right breaks in life.

Most people who are unemployed have had the opportunities; they have not made use of the opportunities that came their way.

The following questions were used in determining the satisfaction configurations in Charts 3–6 and the distributions presented in Tables 1–4.

B5. How satisfied are you with the amount of formal education you have? (IF NECESSARY) Which letter comes closest to how satisfied you feel?

C2. How satisfied are you with the changes in your financial situation over the past year? (IF NECESSARY) Which letter comes closest to how satisfied you feel?

C6. Do you worry at all about the possibility of being laid-off or unemployed?

C6a. Why is that? Why do you worry about that?

C6b. Is this something you worry about more now than you did a year ago?

C6c. Why is that? Why do you feel you do not have to worry about that?

C9. Do you feel that your total family income is enough to meet your family's usual monthly expenses and bills?

C10. Do you feel that your total family income is enough for you and your family to live as comfortably as you would like at this time?

C11. The things people have—housing, car, furniture, recreation, and the like—make up their standard of living. Some people are satisfied with their standard of living, others feel it is not as good as they would like. How satisfied are you with your standard of living?

C11a. What are you dissatisfied with?

C11b. Is there anything you can do to improve your standard of living? (PROBE: What can you do? OR Why not?)

C12. Suppose five years from now your standard of living was the same as now—you were managing to live on your income pretty much the same—how satisfied would you be then?

C13. Thinking of the future, how concerned are you that some sort of political, economic, or social situation may come up which would threaten *your* future standard of living? Would you say that you are *very concerned, somewhat concerned, not too concerned,* or *not at all concerned?*

D20. Is there more work available on your job/any of your jobs so that you could work more if you wanted to?

D21. Would you like to work more if you could find more work?

D22. Could you work less if you wanted to?

D23. Would you prefer to work less even if you earned less money?

D29. If you should lose your present job, what would you say are your chances of finding another job that is just as good as your present job in all respects? Would you say very good, good, not so good, or not good at all?

D34. All in all, how satisfied would you say you are with your main job?

D35. If a good friend of yours told you he was interested in working in a job like yours for your employer, what would you tell him? Would you *strongly recommend* this job, would you have doubts about recommending it, or would you *strongly advise him against* this sort of job?

D36. If you were to get enough money to live as comfortably as you'd like for the rest of your life, would you continue to work?

D36a. Would you continue to work at the same job you have now?
D38. Do you agree or disagree with the statement:
"My main interests in life are connected with my work"?
D39. And this one: "Work is just a way of making money?"

For the satisfaction questions, respondents were handed a card with a seven-point (A, B, C, D, E, F, G) satisfaction scale. The end points were labeled "Very Satisfied" and "Not at All Satisfied." Respondents were asked to choose the letter on the scale which most closely represented how satisfied they were. In Tables 1–4, we summarized A and B under "Satisfied," C and D under "Moderately Satisfied" and E, F, and G under "Not Satisfied."

The following question was used in Table 10:

D40. Even people who are pretty satisfied with how they are doing sometimes feel they could have done even better. These are some reasons people give for not doing as well as they might have done. Are any of these reasons true for you? (Which reasons are true for you?)
Not using the good breaks I have had.
Not having enough ability.

Notes

1. Cantril's happiness scores, which were collected around 1960, are used here.
2. Duesenberry uses the highest earlier reached status as reference point.
3. The product-moment correlation between the measures is .371. A large part of this correlation persists even after the socioeconomic level is controlled. See Charts 3–6.
4. Age, of course, may also stand for social trends, which often gain a foothold among the young and extend to society as a whole only through intergenerational changes. Our data are not extensive enough to test Richard A. Easterlin's hypothesis expounded in his paper for this conference which links people's level of aspirations to their parents' level of living.
5. By rotating the factor structure around the origin we may shift our analytic goal from factors which maximize the total observed variance to factors which separate groups of highly intercorrelated variables. In general, two types of rotations may be employed: orthogonal rotation, which will require the factors to delineate statistically independent variation, and oblique rotation, in which the factors are allowed to become correlated. In our analysis we made use of both types of rotations. For details see R. R. Rummel, *Applied Factor Analysis,* Evanston: Northwestern University Press, 1970; Norman H. Nie and others, *Statistical Package for the Social Sciences,* New York: McGraw-Hill, 1970; and H. H. Harmon, *Modern Factor Analysis,* ed. Chicago: University of Chicago Press, 1967.
6. The constructed indices provide a description of the factors in terms of the observed variables. This procedure differs as follows from the "naive" scoring or indexing by building composite variables with arbitrary weights:
1) The variables contributing to a factor (*i.e.* the composite variable) emerge as the result of the factor analytic routine, not by virtue of arbitrary selection. Naturally, the usefulness of the resulting factor depends on the construct validity in the theoretical context.

2) The weights to be assigned are determined on the basis of the factor structure of the variables.

3) The procedure is not applicable if covariance matrices, on the basis of which the factors and their loadings emerge, differ strongly between subgroups. When the subgroup configurations differ significantly within the given set of variables, it is inappropriate to apply common indices to the entire population since the factors do not possess enough common content validity across the subgroups which are of interest to the investigator. The latter was the case with the whole satisfaction complex in our data (but not with the value and fate-control complexes). For the former, we were left with the possibility of utilizing differences in the configurations of factors for analytic purposes (see Charts 3–6). However, serious methodological problems were raised for the comparison across subgroups, with which this paper deals in Sections II, IV, and V.

7. See Appendix Part B for the factor loadings as well as a graphic representation of the factor structure.

8. Data available but not presented.

9. We experimented with measures of individual social mobility, and income relative to that of occupational subgroup; these data are not presented here.

10. One striking example of the relevance of the value-expectancy distinction to social policy has been the approach to the training of the hard-core unemployed, particularly those programs directed to ghetto youth. Most early approaches were based on the assumption that the problem lay in the goals and values of these youth —that they lacked the traditional achievement values and motives. Consequently most early programs had a heavy "resocialization" emphasis, teaching trainees the "proper" attitudes and behaviors that would supposedly enable them to go out into the job world. Today there is more inclination to view the problem in "expectancy" terms, seeing the trainees' problems of motivation as tied to their assessment of the job market and the payoff from the training program. This has led to a much greater investment in on-the-job training programs, with an emphasis on clear job payoffs rather than individual value changes.

11. This variable describes respondents as working the number of hours they would like to work, or preferring more or fewer hours of work. It was constructed from questions D20–D23 as listed in Appendix Part C.

12. Questions about educational aspirations suggest blacks rank relatively high on expectations for the education of their children.

References

1. Barfield, Richard, and James N. Morgan, *Early Retirement: The Decision and the Experience,* Ann Arbor, Michigan: Survey Research Center, Institute for Social Research, University of Michigan, 1969.

2. Cantril, H. Easterlin relies partly on the work of Cantril in *The Pattern of Human Concerns,* New Brunswick, New Jersey: Rutgers University Press, 1965, and N.M. Bradburn, *The Structure of Psychological Well-Being,* Chicago: Aldine Publishing Company, 1969.

3. Coleman, J.S., and staff, *Equality of Educational Opportunity,* Washington, D.C.: U.S. Government Printing Office, 1966; more recently, and for a detailed discussion of the relevant theoretical issues, see Patricia Gurin, Gerald Gurin, and others, "Internal-External Control in the Motivational Dynamics of Negro Youth" in *Journal of Social Issues* 25, No. 3, 1969, pp. 29–53.

4. Easterlin, Richard A., "Does Economic Growth Improve the Human Lot?" mimeographed draft.

5. Feldman, Kenneth A., and Theodore M. Newcomb, *The Impact of Col-*

lege on Students, San Francisco: Jossey-Bass, Series in Higher Education, 1969.

6. Flax, Michael J., *Blacks and Whites—An Experiment in Racial Indicators*, Washington, D.C.: The Urban Institute, 1971.

7. Gurin, Gerald, and Patricia Gurin, "Expectancy Theory in the Study of Poverty," in *Journal of Social Issues*, 26, No. 2, 1970.

8. ———, Joseph Veroff, and Sheila Field, *Americans View Their Mental Health*, New York: Basic Books, 1960, p. 24.

9. Katona, George, "On the Theory of Expectations," in James N. Morgan, Burkhard Strumpel, and Ernest Zahn, eds., *Human Behavior in Economic Affairs: Essays in Honor of George Katona*, Amsterdam, Holland: Elsevier Publishing Company, 1972.

10. ———, *Psychological Analysis of Economic Behavior*, New York: McGraw-Hill, 1951; and more recently Daniel Bell, "American Culture and the Concept of Change" in Edward D. Sullivan, ed., *Change or Revolution?* New York: Institute of Life Insurance, 1971.

11. ———, *The Mass Consumption Society*, New York: McGraw-Hill, 1964.

12. ———, and Eva Mueller, *Consumer Response to Income Increases*, Washington, D.C.: Brookings Institution, 1968.

13. ———, Burkhard Strumpel, and Ernest Zahn, *Aspirations and Affluence: Comparative Studies in the United States and Western Europe*, New York: McGraw-Hill, 1971, pp. 171 f. These conclusions are based mainly on expectations and aspirations measured in the United States and several European countries, as well as on consumption and saving data. This book is also helpful in explaining the relationship between economic optimism and purchasing and saving behavior or aspirations in various industrial countries.

14. Katz, Daniel, "Psychology and Economic Behavior," in James N. Morgan, Burkhard Strumpel, and Ernest Zahn, eds., *Human Behavior in Economic Affairs: Essays in Honor of George Katona, op. cit.* Amsterdam, Holland: Elsevier Publishing Company, 1972.

15. McClelland, David C., in *The Achieving Society*, Princeton, New Jersey: Van Nostrand, 1961. He comments on the sociological thinking about the role of psychological variables in economic development with reference to Talcott Parsons, "It has never been really seriously attempted to bridge the gap between idealized pattern variables as tools of analysis, and social norms as present in the minds of men. Stated another way, it is not always clear just how a characteristic of social structure like stress on 'achieved' versus 'ascribed' status should be reflected in the attitudes of members of that social structure so that one can check empirically whether those attitudes are in fact present in a society. . . . The theoretical relationship between questionnaire and interview data and the social structure variable they are supposed to be getting at has not as yet been perfectly worked out" (p. 17).

16. Merton, Robert G., *Social Theory and Social Structure*, 9th printing, New York: McGraw-Hill, 1962, pp. 136–137.

17. Miller, S. M., "The American Lower Classes: A Typological Approach," in Arthur B. Shostak and William Gomberg, eds., *Blue Collar World: Studies of the American Worker*, Englewood Cliffs, New Jersey: Prentice-Hall, 1964, p. 9.

18. ———, and Frank Riesman, "The Working Class Subculture: A New View," *ibid.*, p. 24.

19. ———, and ———, ibid., p. 29: "[The blue collar worker] while desiring a good standard of living is not attracted to the middle-class style of life with its accompanying concern for status and prestige. . . . He looks horizontally for his norms."

20. Morgan, James N., "The Achievement Motive and Economic Behavior," in John W. Atkinson, ed., *A Theory of Achievement Motivation*, New York: John Wiley and Sons, 1966.

21. Mueller, Eva L., et al., *Technological Advance in an Expanding Economy: Its Impact on a Cross-Section of the Labor Force*, Ann Arbor, Michigan: Survey Research Center, Institute for Social Research, the University of Michigan, 1969.

22. Patterson, James N., "Marketing and the Working Class Family," in Arthur B. Shostak and William Gomberg, eds., *Blue Collar World: Studies of the American Worker, op. cit.*, p. 76.

23. Rokeach, Milton, "A Theory of Organization and Change Within Value and Attitude Systems," unpublished manuscript of a talk, 1970, pp. 2–4.

24. Strumpel, Burkhard, "Economic Behavior and Economic Welfare—Models and Interdisciplinary Approaches," in Morgan, Strumpel, and Zahn, eds., *Human Behavior in Economic Affairs: Essays in Honor of George Katona, op. cit.*

25. ———, "Higher Education and Economic Behavior," in Stephen Withey, ed., *A Degree and What Else? Correlates and Consequences of a College Education*, New York: McGraw-Hill, 1971, p. 62.

26. ———, Jay Schmiedeskamp, and M. Susan Schwartz, "The Function of Consumer Attitude Data Beyond Econometric Forecasts," paper presented to the tenth conference of CIRET (International Conference of Business Tendency Surveys), Brussels, September 1971; to appear in Lewis Mandell, George Katona, James N. Morgan, and Jay Schmiedeskamp, eds., *Surveys of Consumers 1971*, Ann Arbor: Institute for Social Research, 1972.

Economic Life-Styles, Values, and Subjective Welfare — An Empirical Approach
A Response

By Martin Pfaff

I. An Overview

In recent years, increasing attention has been focused onto the phenomenon of poverty amidst plenty, and of social unrest and revolt by some groups of society at a time when others "never had it so good." As a corollary, some have questioned the meaningfulness of physical measures of growth. They place a high premium on the understanding of how values and subjective welfare relate to the over-all economic attainment of different groups in society.

Strumpel's paper is a pioneering effort in exploring the correlates of subjective welfare and the attending values and life styles. He noted that the distribution of welfare is not simply a function of income but of other social and economic factors, including social status, job and income security, opportunities for advancement, and a favorable environment. Ultimately, he noted, "welfare is in the eye of the beholder." He analyzed the results of a survey of different socioeconomic groups' pattern of values and subjective welfare, as expressed by their avowed satisfaction with various facets of life. His foray into an area of social measurement may have ramifications for economic and social policy.

Not surprisingly, Strumpel found large differences in the aspirations and the degree of dissatisfaction felt by different occupational and racial subgroups. This, indeed, is the major contribution of his paper. He provided some interesting sociological insights by relating measures of work satisfaction to the individual's satisfaction with his general standard of living; and by pointing out the degree of relationship between the different clusters of satisfaction which by themselves are an expression of the degree of integration of these groups within society at large.

As part of an implicit model, he postulated a wide range of hypotheses on individual behavior and adaptation to economic, social, and other rewards. Many of these hypotheses are only loosely related. By the very limited nature of the exploratory survey, many hypotheses could not be tested. They are thus at best suggestive of a more general theory of subjective adaptation to the economic and social landscape. Strumpel's introductory question, which concerns the way people's demands for the output of the system relate to their willingness to provide inputs in the form of labor and other efforts, was posed occasionally but not answered by any empirical evidence. He did describe patterns of attitudes including satisfaction and expectations regarding economic and other attainments. But there was no conclusive evidence presented as to how these demands for a given share of the output of the economic and social system relate to the willingness of different groups to participate in the production system.

Indeed, any attempted criticism of the paper could be based largely on some of the handicaps that methodological constraints impose on the author. While he did indeed formulate a range of indicators of economic motivation, economic values, and subjective well-being or satisfaction, he did not live up fully to his claim that these measures are validated by the analysis. His conclusions were based mainly on frequency distributions and cross-tabulations of responses, and on factor analysis. While the latter represents a powerful descriptive technique to organize a wealth of data, it did in no way validate the measures which are summarized thereby. Such validation can only be forthcoming in the context of a broader theory within which individual hypotheses are tested.

A further methodological critique may be levied against the formulation of the typologies themselves. No doubt, the subgrouping of individual responses is based on the traditional sociological categories of professionals, white-collar and blue-collar workers, and the racial distinction of blacks and whites. The results are very striking and intuitively quite convincing in terms of *a priori* images. Strumpel missed, however, the opportunity to infer alternative clusters inductively from the structure of responses. Such alternative subgroups could only be inferred from communality of responses; these could have gone across the dividing lines between white- and blue-collar individuals, on the one hand, and black and white individuals, on the other.

On the basis of the pattern of responses of these different groups, one is tempted to place these groups into a "hierarchy-of-needs" typology which is reminiscent of Maslow and McGregor. These different groups can be viewed as being "frozen" at different levels of a motivational hierarchy of values.

There is little surprise in the finding that socioeconomic groups are most immediately concerned with the particular step of this motivational ladder which they have not yet climbed successfully, or which they would like to take in the future. Measures of satisfaction and dissatisfaction, accordingly, relate to the needs that particular subgroups have been able to satisfy and those that are yet to be satisfied within the over-all hierarchy of needs.

II. Theoretical Framework

Strumpel placed his work in the context of other approaches to the study of economic behavior made by his colleagues at the Survey Research Center at the University of Michigan. He postulated that changes in behavior are a function of values, reality perception, expectations, and self-efficacy/fate-control. He then proceeded to hypothesize how some of these factors might influence each other without, however, completing the interrelationship in the context of a model of individual behavior. I have proceeded, however, to explicate and extend some of these relationships in order to provide a visual representation of this implicit model of economic behavior.

In Chart 1 values, productive behavior, the environment, attainment of aspirations, and reality perception and satisfactions are depicted on a two-stage feed-back control diagram. The individual's values are shown as inputs into a transformation process that leads to productive behavior; the latter, in turn, has an impact on the environment—his own behavior becomes an input into the economic process which leads to a set of outputs which, in turn, relate to his individual values. The perception of one's own behavior in relationship to one's values represents feed-back relationship No. 1. The impact of one's economic attainment (the share of the output of the system accruing as a reward for productive effort) feeds back on values. (This is shown through feed-back process No. 2.) Similarly, subjective welfare has an immediate and direct impact on productive behavior as shown through reality perception and through feed-back process No. 3.

Alternatively, one could view these feed-back processes as manifestations of the different kinds of satisfaction or dissatisfaction an individual experiences from interacting with or adapting to his environment. Feed-back process No. 1 could denote satisfaction with the job; or, more generally, evaluation of one's own state, patterns of internal consistency, etc. Feed-back process No. 2 relates to satisfaction with the rewards that the system has to offer. More generally, it refers to self-efficacy and fate-control which one can exercise through one's productive behavior and, indirectly, to the rewards that the system will pass out in exchange for productive effort. Finally, feed-back process No. 3 may pertain to the satisfaction with economic and social incentives to productive effort which are provided in order to solicit participation in the system's operations.

We may now contemplate Strumpel's first major hypothesis: He postulated that the distribution of welfare is a function of (1) income, (2) social status, (3) job and income security, (4) fringe benefits, (5) working time, (6) opportunities for advancement, (7) choices of alternatives to unsatisfactory conditions, and (8) favorable human and physical environment. He went on to point out that income advantages may spill over into situa-

CHART 1. DIAGRAMMATIC MODEL OF INDIVIDUAL ADAPTATION TO ENVIRONMENT

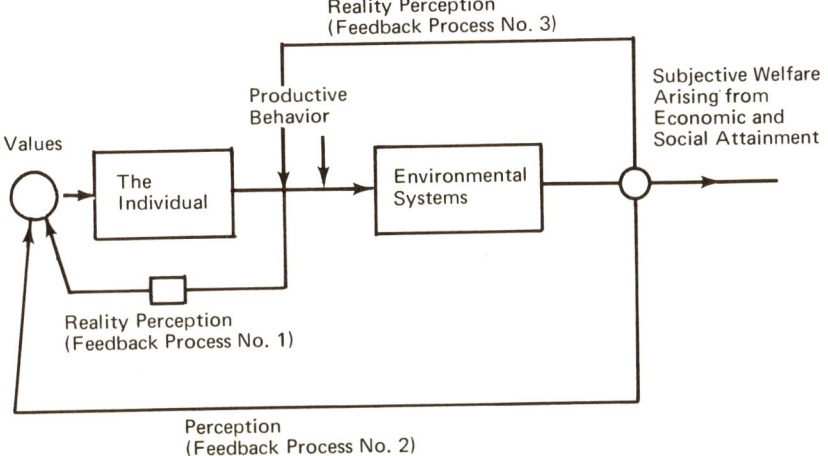

Sources of Satisfaction/Dissatisfaction

Feedback Process No. 1: a. Satisfaction with job
b. Evaluation of one's own state

Feedback Process No. 2: a. Satisfaction with rewards of the system
b. Sense of self-efficacy/fate-control

Feedback Process No. 3: Satisfaction with economic and social incentives to productive effort (system participation)

---

tional, motivational, and behavioral advantages. They, in turn, tend to reinforce income advantages.

A diagrammatic representation of Strumpel's implicit model of the welfare of an individual or a group, relative to other individuals or other groups, is found in Chart 2. It should be evident that *relative welfare* is influenced both by differential income as well as by differences in situational, motivational, and behavioral advantages of an individual or group. Differential income tends to reinforce differences in other aspects which, in turn, feed back on differential income. We have thus a phenomenon of positive feed-back—a process whereby changes tend to lead to cumulative changes in the future. This kind of a model might be in fact called a "benevolent circles" model. It represents the converse image of the notion of "vicious circles" of income disadvantage and poverty, which are similarly

CHART 2. STRUMPEL'S IMPLICIT MODEL OF RELATIVE WELFARE

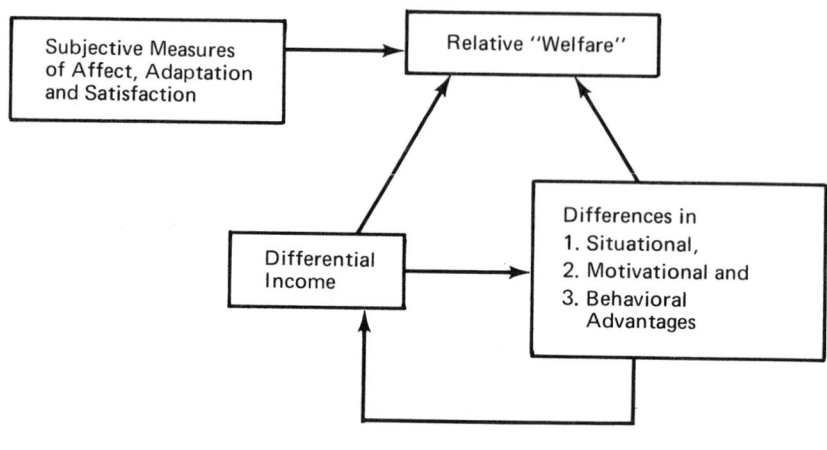

related to disadvantages in the situational, motivational, and behavioral aspects. However, to the differences in income and the differences in these "metaeconomic" situational rewards, Strumpel added the impact of subjective measures of affect, adaptation, and satisfaction as explanators of welfare. Here we notice his implicit value judgment: "Economic satisfaction by many will be considered *undesirable, if it represents accommodation or acquiescence to a constraining reality*. And dissatisfaction for some may be an attitude developed *in response to opportunities—it may then be the concomitant of optimism*. . . . [And] if this is so, and if our conceptual definition of satisfactions is appropriate, *dissatisfaction may often be a symptom of impending success as of failure or maladaptation*."

My first response to this contention is somewhat irreverent: "So what?" How are we to judge whether one kind of satisfaction is "good" or "bad"? In order really to know whether such a discrepancy between aspiration level and actual perception of one's attainment has been due to the lowering of the aspiration level or due to the subjective evaluation of progress in one's own attainment, one would have to have time-series data. A cross-section study cannot make any judgment about the uses of satisfaction scores as welfare measures even if some indirect questions probe the time process of adaptation which preceded this measure. Furthermore, even if time-series measures were available, one could still postulate that the lowering of aspiration levels in response to relative failure may itself be a sign of wisdom and a general expression of satisfaction with one's present life, rather than a response to failure. In any case, whenever one associates some meaning with satisfaction scores, one no doubt imposes one's own value judgment on the respondent's subjective evaluation of his own welfare.

Strumpel recognized some of this when he maintained that the level of satisfaction is not only influenced by the distance between reality and goals but also by the importance of, say, an income deficit. This highlights the necessity of inferring the weighting—or importance—that an individual associates with a particular area in the over-all context of his satisfaction pattern. One can only agree with Strumpel when he noted that in economics the concept of tastes and preferences is generally assumed to be independent of the system and therefore not influenced by changes in the income of the individual studied. However, if social scientists could attain a better understanding of economic behavior, they would surely have to recognize that preference functions are influenced by individual attainment, as well as by a communications process between the individual and his environment.

It is thus relative status within a group or a country which influences satisfaction and well-being. However, the interdependence of utilities implied in a Duesenberry-type model is only one form of interdependence. It is based on the assumption that an individual's well-being is influenced negatively by another individual's well-being. Or, in other words, the higher one's income in relation to another individual's income, the better one is off and vice versa. One must note, however, positive utility interdependence; the better others are off, the better we feel, too. This type of interdependence results from identification with others in primary and secondary groups. Subjective welfare can result therefore also from similarity rather than dissimilarity of attainment. (This is indeed the approach that underlies the body of economics which has been termed Grants Economics [see, 1, 2, 3, 4, 8].)

I concur partly with the author: "There is little hope that a parsimonious hypothesis relating present or past economic/environmental variables to goals or satisfactions alone can do the job of explaining various people's satisfaction with their well-being and exchanges." There is, however, no reason why we should not formulate a more rigorous model in which several hypotheses are interrelated.

III. Empirical Results

I shall comment here on some of the empirical patterns that Strumpel inferred from the respondents. He noted, above all, a prevalently favorable self-assessment and rising satisfaction with the job. However, these individuals would not be satisfied if their situation were not to change over time. Strumpel thus attempted to measure expectations and satisfactions with time-related attainment, by asking hypothetical questions about future satisfaction. I question, however, an individual's ability to specify how satisfied he will be at any point in the future, based on his general expectation about his satisfaction if there were to be no change in his position. This is not to deny that the contemplation of the prospect of not experiencing progress is unpleasant to people, and that they are likely to be dissatisfied with such a prospect. However, there is no substitute for taking repeated measures of satisfaction in order to make a judgment about changes in welfare. The same is true for the more affluent, who tend to be more satisfied with their present state and who have the highest expectations of future changes.

Older respondents are generally more satisfied. Over time they may have learned to scale down their aspirations. It may also be true that they are generally more satisfied with life in general, so that any specific area is not likely to be so important to their over-all satisfaction pattern. One could argue that this kind of adaptive response is just as good as any other kind of adaptive response which results from changes in one's economic attainment for maintaining one's level of satisfaction.

Of great interest are the systematic differences in goals and satisfactions between occupational subgroups. When the patterns for responses are evaluated, a hierarchy of values emerges. "Security" is placed first, followed by "prosperity" and "self-actualization," expressed by adjectives such as "important" or "exciting life." "Prosperous life" is mentioned largely by such groups as blacks and managerial workers and not by professionals or individuals with a college degree. An "exciting life" or images like "important" appear most attractive to college-educated individuals. It appears to me that these groups occupy particular levels in the hierarchical ladder of needs. The lower social status individuals are also those with less income; they are likely to strive first for income changes. Conversely, professionals and individuals with higher education are also those more likely to have satisfied these basic aspirations; they are, therefore, more concerned with self-actualization and with other needs as described, for example, in Maslow's or McGregor's hierarchy of needs. This is confirmed by the observed pattern which indicates that white blue-collar factory workers are more attracted to material security, while black operatives and laborers aim at prosperous lives and at high incomes.

These patterns appear to be confirmed in general by the results of the factor analysis reported by Strumpel. Three discrete value factors are cited; namely, (1) income-security-orientation, (2) prosperity-orientation, and (3) achievement versus affiliation. When prosperity and income-security-orientation are combined on the basis of a composite dimension termed "material orientation," blue-collar blacks emerge as being high on material orientation and high in terms of their expressed needs for affiliation. Socioeconomic status therefore emerges as the major determinant of value emphasis among the various groups studied.

In his Section 4, Strumpel turned to look at these subgroups separately. He examined their orientation to their economic environment and situation. The whole conglomerate of values and satisfactions associated with blacks, white professionals, managers, clerical and sales workers, and blue-collar workers, were identified in terms of their "life-styles." Thereby an attempt was made to infer something about the mechanisms whereby social roles are translated into behavior, as well as about the "consciousness" of different socioeconomic groups. In studying the behavior of groups disadvantaged by economic or minority status, the author followed Gurin's lead in emphasizing the "expectancy orientation" according to which "behavior depends not only on the motives and incentives that define what a person values or desires, but also on the expectancy of the person's estimate of the probability that the behavior will help him obtain what he is striving for." Implicit in this view is a set of hypotheses, represented in Chart 3, according to which both motives and incentives are "translated" through the intervening forces of expectancy into economic and social behavior.

In the context of this over-all model the author cited a plethora of hypotheses on the behavior of minority groups. By his own admission, Strumpel refrained from applying statistical methods in order to maximize the between-group variance in economic life-styles and thus from arriving at a typology which would deviate from the conventional racial and occupational categories. Accordingly, he proceeded to analyze professionals. They were most satisfied with their job, their education, and their living

CHART 3. "EXPECTANCY" AND ECONOMIC BEHAVIOR

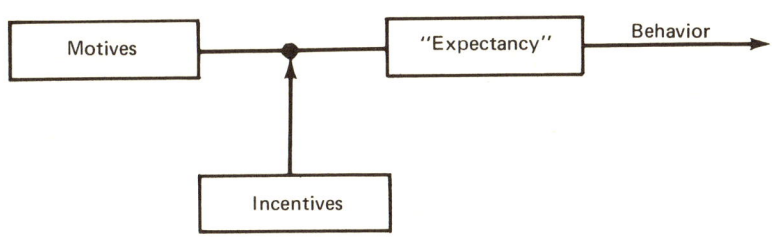

standard. Their job involvement was the highest. The same was also true for their sense of fate-control. Interestingly enough, while job satisfaction was viewed distinctly from satisfaction with standard of living, these two areas are not separate, as in the perception of blacks. Having thus identified the two polar extreme types, namely the black workers and the white professionals, Strumpel then proceeded to place white managers, clerical sales workers, and blue-collar workers within this over-all typology.

One of Strumpel's major conclusions about managers and clerical workers follows: "Optimism about future well-being and the reassuring belief that good opportunities are available elsewhere, makes for dissatisfaction with job and standard of living. Conversely, satisfaction appears to be part of a coping mechanism, a symptom of accommodation, the second-best response of people who are finding themselves in the role of getting ahead and have tried to move away from the role by reducing their goals." Here again crops up this attempt to evaluate dissatisfaction on the basis of a set of information which is too limited. Perhaps the strongest argument in favor of the author's theoretical model results from the behavior of these two subgroups. However, a variety of hypotheses on the nature of society, general awareness of social crises, and social problems, as well as appreciation of the current state of the economy may have given rise to many of these measures as well.

Strumpel concluded the description of the empirical patterns by comparing the problems that concern blue-collar whites and those that concern blacks: "We cannot resist pointing to the apparent mirror-image symmetry between our interpretations for the blacks and the white blue-collar workers; the blacks tend to be very dissatisfied with what they have and entertain an unreal vision of the good-prosperous-comfortable life, quite unrelated to their position. In contrast, blue-collar whites are generally satisfied with their position, but tend to be not a little preoccupied with the vision, in most cases no less distant from the present reality, of their livelihood and status." It is this contrast which is most vivid and adds the greatest amount of conviction to the analysis and the findings. Furthermore, it tends to confirm what I had postulated about the hierarchy of needs at the outset. After the individual has satisfied a certain type of need, he tends to be concerned with the need-level next on his hierarchy. Insofar as different racial and occupational subgroups have attained different levels on this social status and need hierarchy, they are concerned with different aspects of life. Since society itself can be viewed as a continuum, at least as defined by Strumpel's subgroups, we can in fact perceive an explicit hierarchy in the patterns that describe the values and satisfactions, or briefly the economic life-styles, of these various groups.

IV. Conclusions

In the final section, Strumpel attempted to draw the implications of these findings for the subjective welfare of the total society. He maintained that "the present economic difficulties—most prominantly inflation—testify to the inability of markets to accommodate the demands for the material rewards of the system within existing rules of the game." This contention does not directly follow from the analysis; hence it must the author's own *Weltanschauung*. No doubt, markets do not satisfy the expectations of low-income blacks for a more prosperous and high-income life, and only partly satisfy the expectations of other groups. But blacks are generally more satisfied with specific market goods than whites [7]. Moreover, as soon as one gets into self-fulfillment goals, say of professionals, one would be hard pressed to expect markets to provide the kind of "social good" that is implied in their implied needs. Indeed, the very fact that most individuals are satisfied with their jobs—the area of most immediate involvement with markets on the input side of the economic system—would contradict this over-all conclusion. This satisfaction, then, is more with distributive consequences of the socioeconomic system, with their standard of living, and with their educational attainment, than with the operation of the factor markets. If high job satisfaction, as Strumpel concluded, is largely due to the "relative stagnation of vocational roles in a setting of improving working conditions, of relative increase in the proportion of comfortable white-collar and related jobs, and rising real incomes," then I see little quarrel with this measure of satisfaction. I do not concur with the author, who claimed that "this type of satisfaction appears to be of a fairly passive kind." His conclusion, no doubt, followed from his willingness to impose his own value judgment on the type of dissatisfaction observed for different groups.

Similarly, Strumpel analyzed the motivation of the blue-collar stratum of society; apparently, it expects progress from an increase in wage and salary levels rather than from changes of its particular role in the productive process. It may very well be true that this expectation is based on a great measure of realism; apparently the increase in the economic attainment of the lower socioeconomic group was largely due to the general rise in salary and wages experienced in the last twenty-five years, and only secondarily due to any distributive aspects of the government or any other agency [3]. These groups accordingly would be doing nothing else than projecting their own experience into the future.

In another major conclusion, Strumpel warned against the use of summary indices of well-being for cross-segment comparisons, on the basis of differences of the analytic results of satisfactions among occupational and racial groups. There is little doubt that various satisfaction concepts have different semantic meanings from group to group. Against this contention, however, stands empirical evidence provided, for example, by Inkeles [5], which indicates that happiness "may be translated fairly well from one language to another."

The second major implication of Strumpel's contention, if it were accepted, is that it expresses certain caveats about possibilities of aggregating responses. His paper provided insufficient information to help me answer some questions of interest in this regard. He gave no indication of the "goodness" of various factor solutions; the general procedure of arriving at three factors may or may not have been good and representative of the whole structure.

Strumpel stated, "In contrast to the value data, the satisfaction data proved not to be amenable to composite factoring for the whole sample." Exactly what does this assertion mean? Does factoring over all individuals increase complexity? What kinds of data does he have to justify rejecting the hypothesis that the data are factorable over all subgroups? Of the thirteen variables listed, a number are concerned with satisfaction; nevertheless, the author decided to do the factoring within specified groups; e.g., blue-collar and white-collar blacks, white professionals, technical and kindred workers. If the author has some basis for rejecting factoring over all individuals, then he should have consistently applied the same criteria within those groups that he did select. For a sufficiently large sample, he may very well have found a covariance matrix different from white-collar blacks. And if we push this argument to its ultimate conclusion, we would *never* be able to make comparisons by virtue of each individual's absolute differences from his fellows. Actually, Strumpel disregarded his own explicit caveats by selecting such well-defined groups for the analysis. He assumed, in fact, *homogeneity of individuals within groups,* an assumption made without benefit of some kind of test akin to the one that he applied to the total group.[1]

Another criticism of Strumpel's paper is more basic and philosophic. Be it stated explicitly or implicitly, all scores are composite. Though it has not been built-up mathematically, "Satisfaction with jobs" is not a simple, but a composite, score. The score is a function of one's satisfaction with all the attributes and relevant factors bearing upon job satisfaction. And the existence of different covariance structures, of different patterns and correlations, does not suffice in and of itself to determine whether composites should be derived on the basis of any one particular sample.

Logically considered, and given that it were possible, a particular score matrix should be inspected (take the rows as individuals and the columns as variables); it should be partitioned both by individuals and by variables in such a way as to maximize homogeneity within a subset of individuals and a subset of variables. Whenever similarity or covariation is measured over a group of variables, the problem of how to weight them in computing the index of relationship arises. Had some other variables been used, individuals found dissimilar in one study might be found similar in another. The problem is always present. Although particular subgroups of people may be of interest, on *a priori* grounds, it would seem that pushing the argument to its logical conclusion requires finding that subset of people or of variables that is homogeneous. Only in this fashion do we obtain a substantial foundation for compiling composite scores [6].

But, pushing the argument to the logical conclusions again, it may be that these variables, though they be homogeneous for all individuals, might have patterns which differ among their subgroups. If we lack knowledge of how to break up the individuals and the variables simultaneously, then analysis must proceed in a step-wise fashion. Having found the set of variables that is homogeneous, the analysis is free to measure all individuals with respect to this, and to determine whether indeed some *a priori* groups (blacks, or whites, or blue-collar, etc.) differ with respect to this unified concept or measure.

The criticism of measures of aggregation brought forth in Strumpel's paper doubtless does not appear to be specific to this particular context. In very much the same way it could be applied to any economic aggregation problem involving objective measures as well. In any aggregation, by necessity, a loss of information occurs with respect to the distributional aspects and to particular subgroupings that appear more homogeneous, and within which more similarity can be found than between groups.

Strumpel finally arrived at the conclusion that higher socioeconomic status is generally associated with a fuller sense of well-being and with generally higher satisfaction and a greater level of confidence about the future, than is lower socioeconomic status. In this sense then the over-all hypothesis that relative rather than absolute status will determine satisfaction appears not to be rejected. However, Strumpel chose to interpret the higher subjective well-being of higher status groups differently—they tend to "experience substantial real income increases," rather than absolute differences. This conclusion appears more plausible than the general relativity hypothesis, insofar as American culture emphasizes the idea of progress and the concept of achievement as related to progress. Lower levels of satisfaction of the lower-income groups may thus be explained by their absence of felt progress. I have no quarrel with this explanation.

The final conclusions of the paper relate to the coping mechanisms available to different socioeconomic groups. Strumpel associated more serious psychological, behavioral, and system consequences with the dissatisfaction of those individuals who, because of their socioeconomic status, cannot expect to change their situation by the mechanisms available to the upper socioeconomic groups.

When all is said and done, the author provided us with an incisive insight into the psychological make-up of socioeconomic groups based on their values, aspirations, and satisfaction with different aspects of economic and social experience. The empirical picture which emerged from the factor analysis technique and his incisive interpretations was striking indeed. Often, however, the conclusions which he drew were based perhaps on his deep insight into the nature of these phenomena rather than on the empirical evidence presented. This is particularly true for his conclusion on the nature of satisfaction.

One can but wholeheartedly agree with the author that time-series data are required to get at some of these dynamic processes and adaptive mechanisms. They are likely to offer additional explanations of the empirical patterns which emerged in the cross-section analysis of Strumpel's valuable paper.

Note

1. Homogeneity is essentially an index of the average correlation—the squared correlation ratio—existing among the variables scaled. If we wish to aggregate across variables or individuals, then we should attempt to maximize homogeneity [6].

References

1. Boulding, Kenneth E., *The Economy of Love and Fear: A Preface to Grants Economics*, Belmont, California; Wadsworth Publishing Company, 1973.
2. ———, Janos Horvath, and Martin Pfaff, eds., *The Grants Economy in International Perspective*, Belmont, California; Wadsworth Publishing Company, (forthcoming).
3. ———, and Martin Pfaff, eds., *Redistribution to the Rich and the Poor*, Belmont, California; Wadsworth Publishing Company, 1973.
4. ———, ———, and Anita B. Pfaff, eds., *Transfers in an Urbanized Economy*, Belmont, California; Wadsworth Publishing Company, 1973.
5. Inkeles, A., "Industrial Man: The Relations of Status to Experience, Perception, and Value," *American Journal of Sociology* 66, 1, July 1960, pp. 1–31.
6. Lingoes, James C., and Martin Pfaff, "The Measurement of Subjective Welfare and Satisfaction," paper presented at the 84th Annual Meeting of the American Economic Association held jointly with the Association for the Study of the Grants Economy, at New Orleans, December 27, 1971.
7. Pfaff, Anita, "An Index of Consumer Satisfaction," paper presented at the 84th Annual Meeting of the American Economic Association held jointly with the Association for the Study of the Grants Economy, New Orleans, December 27, 1971.
8. Pfaff, Martin and Anita B. Pfaff, with an introduction by Kenneth Boulding, *The Grants Economy*, Belmont, California: Wadsworth Publishing Company, (forthcoming).

4
Social Stratification and Family Economic Behavior

Authors' note: The study on which this paper is based was supported by a grant from the Consumer Research Institute, Inc. We are grateful to Robert W. Hodge, Paul M. Siegel, David Knoke, and E. Daniel Ayres for their advice and assistance in this study. Our data were provided by the Economic Behavior Program at the University of Michigan and the Inter-University Consortium for Political Research. This study was completed during the senior author's tenure as visiting social scientist at the James K. Pollock Research Program, Bonn-Bad Godesberg, Germany. Elizabeth Douvan, Albert Hermalin, George Katona, and Eleanor Sheldon contributed useful suggestions for the revision of this paper.

DAVID R. SEGAL and MARCUS FELSON

Introduction

The theoretical purposes of the Segal-Felson paper, "Social Stratification and Family Economic Behavior," may be viewed as follows:

1. To test the historical proposition that social class differences are decreasing in the United States.
2. To identify the determinants of social class identification.
3. To identify the social structural antecedents of material consumption and activity in the credit market.

Segal and Felson descriptively and historically explored the antecedents of various aspects of material life-style. Their mode of expression is conventional, and their findings can be summarized in a single but complex empirical generalization.

EG15. As income and class consciousness distinctions among social classes are narrowing, material life-styles are converging while status differences are maintained by different proportional saving-spending patterns, with white-collar workers emphasizing credit mobilization and blue-collar workers emphasizing consumption.

In more elaborate terms, Segal and Felson found an increasing convergence toward a middle-majority in material life-style and class identification by occupational categories. They ascribed this effect to the fact that spreading affluence (discretionary income), occupational rank, and educational level have become less useful differentiators of social stratification. Upward social mobility through education, and geographical mobility to the suburbs, as well as the acquisition of status durables, are all becoming increasingly open possibilities for blue-collar families. On the other hand, status cultures persist via reference groups, shared values, and increased relative deprivation due in part to differential manipulation of the credit market. Upper-class families are investing more in the future and lower-class families more in the present, making for potential life-style gaps in the future.

Segal and Felson interpreted their findings as being more in line with a Weberian multi-dimensional conceptualization of social stratification than a Marxian single-factor orientation. It remains an open question, however, as to which is the most appropriate overarching deductive theoretical framework for explaining such findings. The Segal-Felson study appears to be compatible with at least a functionalistic interpretation of social stratification. Such an orientation starts from the premises that social stratification is a functional prerequisite of a society's social structure and, while the indicators of stratification may vary, some meaningful form of status differentiation is always present.

Reuben Hill and David M. Klein

Social Stratification and Family Economic Behavior

By David R. Segal and Marcus Felson

The foundations of stratification theory

The analysis of social stratification in modern industrial nations is largely built upon a history of ideas imbedded in the theories of Karl Marx and Max Weber. Marx saw social stratification being simplified through the processes of industrialization. The manifold gradation of social ranks that had existed in preindustrial feudal society was converted into two antagonistic economic classes with opposing interests: a numerically large, unskilled, and economically disadvantaged proletariat alienated from the means of production; and a smaller, economically advantaged capitalist bourgeoisie owning the means of production.

Assuming that relationship to the means of production was the base upon which all social relations were built, the Marxian model of social stratification in industrial society had a pyramidal configuration. The bulk of the labor force—the blue-collar proletariat—occupied the base, and the structure tapered toward the capitalist bourgeoisie at the top. Great differences were presumed to exist between the two classes [27].

Weber, like Marx, drew his data primarily from the European experience. He therefore shared with Marx the assumption that large gaps existed between the working class and the middle class. At the same time, he had a more complex view of class relations than did Marx. For Weber [49, pp. 926–940] class derived both from the possession of material goods and from the opportunity to get them. Thus, where Marx emphasized the labor market as the basis of economic relations, Weber attended to the operation of three economic markets: labor, commodity, and credit. Weber also departed from Marx in his view of social status. The deterministic Marxian view saw status as a reflection of economic class relations. Weber, on the other hand, suggested that while there was an empirical relationship between economic class and social status, status groups could and did cut across economic class lines. Unlike economic classes based on similar market positions, he saw status groups as characterized both by a sense of membership and by a common life-style.

In dealing with the relationship between social stratification and family economic behavior in modern America, we shall be concerned with two basic issues raised by these early theorists. First, we shall consider the degree to which the pyramidal model of stratification fits mature, in contrast to early, industrial society. Second, we shall study the degree to which lifestyle, as manifested by certain kinds of economic behavior, is influenced by social status, in contrast to economic class.

The Convergence of Occupational Classes

A variety of processes associated with industrialization mitigate against the perpetuation of the pyramidal structure assumed by classical social stratification theory. In the working class, new technologies of production have, on the one hand, replaced much manpower with machine power; and have, on the other hand, required higher levels of skill of those workers remaining in the manual-labor strata. In the middle class, the growth of large-scale bureaucracies and of service industries (as opposed to extraction and manufacturing) has produced a large corps of white-collar functionaries in clerical and sales occupations who, despite their white-collar status, earn relatively low incomes. Additionally, the increased scale of production units, and the increasingly specialized skills required to run them, have replaced the independent bourgeois entrepreneur with a class of professionals and technicians who, in terms of ownership of productive enterprise, are as alienated from the means of production as are the workers [32, pp. 71–72]. Table 1 presents these changes in the occupational structure of the American nonfarm labor force between 1900 and 1970.

TABLE 1. OCCUPATIONAL DISTRIBUTION OF THE AMERICAN NONFARM LABOR FORCE, 1900, 1950, 1970

Occupation	1900	1950	1970
Managers, proprietors, owners	9.3	9.9	11.7
Professional, technical, and kindred	6.9	9.7	15.0
Clerical, sales	12.0	21.8	23.9
Service	14.4	11.8	14.5
Craftsmen, foremen	16.8	16.1	13.1
Operatives	20.5	23.1	17.0
Laborers	20.0	7.5	4.7
Total	99.9%	99.9%	99.9%
(N)	(18,288,900)	(52,509,110)	(74,081,810)

Sources: 1900 and 1950, United States Bureau of the Census, *Historical Statistics of the United States,* Series 1772-88; 1970, United States Bureau of the Census, *Current Population Reports,* Series P. 60, No. 80, October 4, 1971.

In 1900, the American labor force did approximate a pyramid. Fifty-seven per cent of the urban labor force were in manual labor occupations, including 20 per cent of the total who were laborers. By 1950, the percentage in manual occupations had declined to 47 per cent, of which 7.5 per cent were laborers. During this 50-year period, there was an increase of almost 10 per cent in the clerical and sales categories. By 1970, less than 5 per cent of the urban work force was composed of laborers, and only 35 per cent of the total labor force were in manual occupations. The clerical and sales categories increased only an additional 2 per cent in these two decades, but the percentage in professional, technical, and kindred occupations increased markedly over the 1950 figure and more than doubled the percentage of the labor force in these occupations at the turn of the century.

The pyramidal structure of the American labor force was thus lost. Instead, it came to resemble a diamond-shaped distribution, tapered less at the top than at the bottom of the occupational distribution, and broadest in the middle categories—service workers and unpropertied white-collar workers—whose income was based on salaries rather than profits. In contrast to the conflicting economic interests of groups located at the extremes of a pyramidal distribution, this new distribution is characterized by a consensual "middle-mass," within which the distinction between working-class and middle-class interests has become blurred [48].

The Convergence of Income

If, as the data in Table 1 indicate, the occupational distribution of the American labor force has become more dense in the middle of the structure and less dense at the extremes, we would anticipate that the great differences between the economic well-being of the working class and that of the middle class that was assumed by classical stratification theorists would not be characteristic of modern American society. Contemporary market research operates largely on the postulate that "you are what you earn" [9]. According to this postulate, we would expect the economic behavior of the working class and middle class to diverge insofar as income differentials were maintained or increased. To the extent that working-class and middle-class income converged with the growth of the middle-mass, however, the market research perspective would anticipate a convergence in economic behavior as well.

Two major trends have been noted in the distribution of income in the United States. First, many scholars have pointed to increases in the income gap between the richest and the poorest segments of American society [30, 24, 4]. At the same time that the range of income has been increasing, a convergence of the income of the upper working class and that of the lower middle class—the segments of the labor force that comprise the middle-mass—has also been suggested. Hamilton [17] attempted to refute this assumed convergence. He demonstrated that in 1960, the median income of skilled workers was about $1,900 greater than the median income of clerical and sales personnel. By controlling for a number of variables he reversed the direction of this relationship, giving the clerical and sales workers an $88 advantage.

In an attempt both to bring these data more up to date and to identify existing trends, we calculated the ratio of the income of clerical workers relative to that of craftsmen, foremen, and kindred workers from 1939 to 1968. Table 2 compares median wage and salary income of males, 14 years or older, in the full-time year-round labor force, in these occupations, for selected years. We found that clerical workers declined in relative income between 1939 and 1950, but that no appreciable changes took place from 1950 to 1968.

TABLE 2. COMPARISON OF MEDIAN WAGE AND SALARY INCOME OF MALE CLERICAL WORKERS WITH MALE CRAFTSMEN, FOREMEN, AND KINDRED WORKERS, FOR SELECTED YEARS

Year	Index for Clerical Workers *
1939	109
1950	88
1960	88
1968	89

* Median income of craftsmen, foremen, and kindred workers for each year = 100.

While clerical workers have trailed craftsmen, foremen, and kindred workers in wage and salary income for at least the past two decades, their relative position is not quite so bad when total family income is taken into account. In this case, the income of families headed by clerical personnel lags only about five points behind that of families headed by craftsmen or foremen. The over-all picture, then, suggests considerable overlap in income between these two occupational categories, with the skilled manual workers experiencing a slight financial advantage. It should be emphasized that the income superiority of the upper working class over the lower middle class is not a phenomenon of the 1950s and 1960s. Douglas [10] has previously demonstrated that during the period 1890–1926 clerical workers declined in income position relative to manual workers. What these several bodies of data suggest is that there has at the very least been a convergence of income of those strata of the labor force that comprise the middle-mass. This being the case, we would anticipate finding no difference in economic behavior between these strata if income were itself the determinant of such behavior. It is an empirical question whether class-based differences exist despite the convergence of income in the middle-mass.

The Convergence of Subjective Class Identification

To this point, we have been concerned with more or less objective elements of the stratification system—economic class and income. Let us now turn to a subjective aspect of social stratification—where people see themselves in that system.

Centers' [6] early study of subjective class identification in the United States suggested that occupation was the single most important determinant of Americans' perceptions of their position in the stratification system. Recent research by Hodge and Treiman [20] and by Segal, Segal, and Knoke [44] indicated that this is still the case.

The middle-mass perspective challenges the continued primacy of occupation. Wilensky [50], for example, suggested that class consciousness is a transitional phenomenon among manual workers in the industrialized nations, and that "much behavior and many attitudes said to be rooted in class are instead a matter of race, religion, ethnic origin, education, age, and stage in family life cycle" [cf. 43]. Wilensky pointed out that, with the convergence of income and life-styles between manual and nonmanual occupations, about 20 per cent of manual workers regard themselves as middle class; while more than 20 per cent of professional, business, and white-collar people see themselves as working class. Hamilton [18] showed that a little over half of the clerical and sales workers consider themselves working class rather than middle class, and attributed this to the effects of income.

The decline in working-class identification asserted by Wilensky and by Tucker [47] was challenged by Lane [25] and by Hamilton [18 and 19]. Schreiber and Nygreen [42] attempted to resolve this difference through the analysis of the electoral series data collected by the Survey Research Center, University of Michigan. They concluded that there has been no decline in working-class identification in the United States, and that Tucker's results are an artifact of the form of the class–identification question that he used.

The important point to note is that within the middle-mass, there are people in working-class occupations who consider themselves to be middle class, and people in middle-class occupations who consider themselves to be working class. This provides additional evidence for a blurring of the distinction between working-class and middle-class occupational groups. It also portends a convergence of life-styles between middle-class and working-class occupations to the extent that subjective placement rather than objective position determines life-style.

Consumption as a Status Attribute

If economic class differences *per se* become less important, status distinctions may assume added import. Since economic class is subject to change through individual achievement, Weber suggested that those in privileged positions seek to dissociate class from status in order to deny social honor to the *nouveaux riches*. Occupations come to be differentiated on the basis of their prestige, above and beyond their economic returns [15]. Similarly, claims to status based upon education, religion, and ethnic background become important in social stratification. These claims to status become manifested in life-styles.

The material expression of life-style is consumption pattern. Sewell [45] and Chapin [7], among others, studied the association between household furnishings and socioeconomic status. More recently, Laumann and House [26] have found a striking relationship between living-room furnishings and socioeconomic status. The *nouveaux riches* in this study did not wholly emulate the material consumption patterns of the established upper class. Where the latter had very traditional furnishings, the former sought to establish their claims to status on material living-styles that were modern and chic. In our own analysis, we shall attend to this finding, and focus on quality of material consumption, defined in terms of housing, automobile, and durable goods spending, rather than on stylistic preferences.[1]

We have little data on status-linked economic behavior in the United States. Economists have studied the process of family budgeting, but by and large they have focused on how much money is spent, rather than what it is spent on. This reflects their primary concern with the condition of the national economy rather than with individual behavior [40]. Where ownership of specific consumption items was considered, the variables that were used to predict such ownership were almost wholly restricted to those that could be measured in standard monetary units [2] [8, p. 29; 37].

One of the major reasons for undertaking the present study is that in using economic variables to explain consumer behavior, market researchers and economists have left most of the variance in consumer behavior unexplained. We are interested here in ascertaining whether consideration of nonmonetary characteristics of the social stratification system would increase the power of contemporary models of economic behavior by accounting for some of the previously unexplained variance.

Social Stratification and Economic Behavior

It is clear from the discussion above that several forms of relationship can be posited between social stratification and economic behavior. Four of these are presented in Chart 1. The models presented in Chart 1 will not be tested in a formal sense. Indeed, they are for the most part in forms that are not directly testable. Neither do they exhaust the possible relationships between social stratification and economic behavior. Rather, they are presented to illustrate graphically the range of relationships that may be inferred from the theoretical and empirical literature.

Chart 1, line a is what might be called the market research model. It asserts simply that how people behave economically is determined by how much they earn. The determinants of income are not themselves important.

Line b represents the Marxian orientation. Here economic behavior, income, social status, and subjective class identification are all determined by a single underlying factor. Economic class is the base upon which all other social phenomena are built.

Line c reflects the Weberian conceptualization. Here economic behavior,

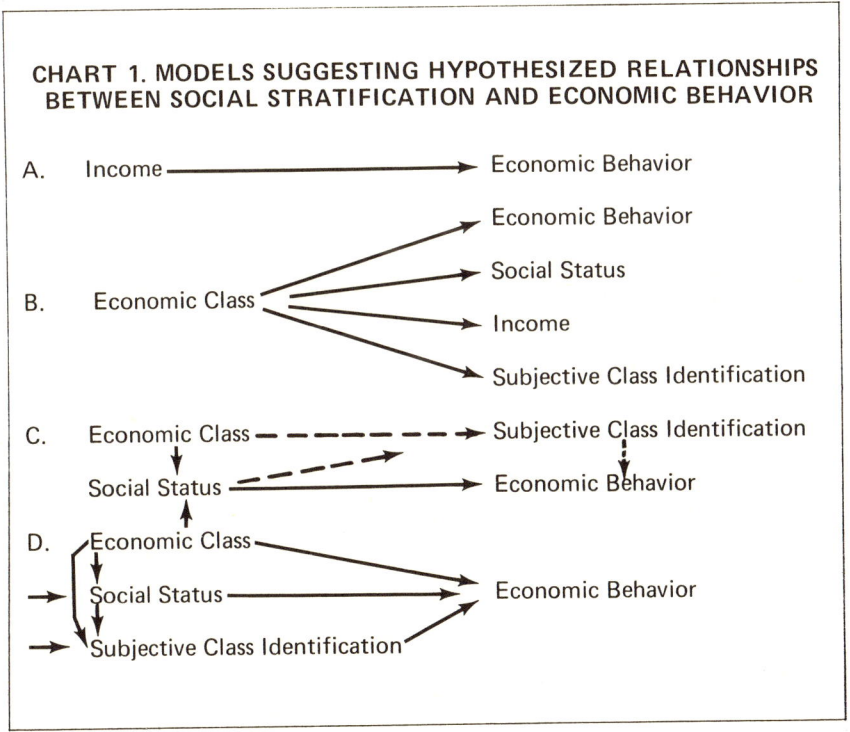

CHART 1. MODELS SUGGESTING HYPOTHESIZED RELATIONSHIPS BETWEEN SOCIAL STRATIFICATION AND ECONOMIC BEHAVIOR

as a reflection of life-style, is seen rooted in social status rather than in economic class. A linkage is noted between economic class and social status, but other determinants of status are recognized as well. The issue of whether subjective class identification really reflects economic class or social status is left unresolved. To the extent that it reflects the latter, it has a bearing on economic behavior as life-style.

In line d, subjective class identification assumes a more important role. Although the influences of social status and economic class upon it are noted, it is not wholly determined by them. Thus aspirations for occupational mobility and processes of past socialization or anticipatory socialization may lead to forms of economic behavior inconsistent with objective measures of economic class and social status, but consistent with an individual's perception of his system in the stratification system.

Note that our concern is primarily with social structural antecedents of economic behavior; *i.e.,* class and status. While we admit the operation of psychological processes to the extent that they are reflected in subjective judgments about one's position in the stratification system, we do not dwell on social psychological factors. We recognize the legitimacy of such an approach, but leave it to other scholars [see for example Strumpel paper].

Data

The sample.—Between November 9, 1966, and December 15, 1966, the field staff of the Survey Research Center, University of Michigan, interviewed a random probability sample of 1,291 citizens of voting age in the continental United States, excluding residents of Alaska, institutionalized persons, and persons residing in hotels, rooming houses, etc. This survey was the fourth-quarter survey on consumer attitudes conducted by the Economic Behavior Program of the Survey Research Center for 1966.

In January 1967, 1,127 of these respondents were re-interviewed in the course of the ninth survey in the Survey Research Center's electoral series. We were able to merge these data files, producing a single set of data containing extensive documentation on economic behavior and social class identification.

Index construction.—We constructed indices to measure the three economic markets (credit market, commodity market, and labor market) that Weber argued were important. The Weberian dichotomy between debtors and creditors is not the relevant issue in our modern credit market. Rather, the important distinction is that between people who can mobilize resources in our credit market and those who cannot. Since not all resources that are convertible to credit are highly liquid, the same people tend to be both debtors and creditors. Thus the relevant dimension in the modern economy is participation in financial transactions, or the finance market. We considered the following variables for inclusion in the financial transaction index: (1) ownership of stock; (2) borrowing of money; (3) purchasing of bonds; (4) withdrawal of money from banks; (5) ownership of house and/or a farm; (6) ownership of a certificate of deposit; (7) amount (in dollars) saved or invested. The interrelationships among these items are presented in Table 3.

TABLE 3. INTERRELATIONSHIPS (TAU-B) AMONG ITEMS IN FINANCIAL TRANSACTION INDEX

	2.	3.	4.	5.	6.	7.
1. Stock ownership	−.038	.187	.197	.138	.192	.414
2. Borrowing		−.003	.073	.064	−.084	*
3. Bond purchase			.071	.132	.076	.295
4. Bank withdrawal				.003	.125	.190
5. Home and/or farm ownership					.023	.217
6. Certificate of deposit						.180
7. Amount saved/invested						

* Variable was dropped before this statistic was computed.

Items 1–6 represent resources available either for liquidation or for use as collateral. Item 7, which was coded in seven categories, reflects the amount that could easily be mobilized.

Among the first six items, stock ownership (Item 1) was the most highly correlated with the others, and thus was double-weighted in the index. Borrowing money (Item 2) was the least correlated, and was dropped from the index. Points were added for the number of types of bonds purchased (up to two); withdrawal of money from banks; ownership of a certificate of deposit, a farm, or a home; and for the total amount of money saved or invested. The resulting index ranged from 0–14 with a mean of 3.63 and a standard deviation of 2.90. Where necessary for statistical analysis, a square root transformation was used to approximate the normal distribution.[3]

We also adapted Weber's notion of the structure of the commodity market to fit modern economic conditions. Weber initially distinguished between those people who produce goods and those who do not. Following in Weber's tradition, but reflecting a view of industrial organization that could benefit from hindsight, Lipset and Rokkan [28, p. 14] suggested that the real cleavage was between the primary economy based on extraction (landed interests) and the secondary economy, based on manufacturing (industrial entrepreneurs). Data presented by Murphy and Morris [36] suggested that the distinction between secondary and tertiary economic organization (service) may be equally important, with location in the secondary sector being related to working-class identification and Democratic

Party preference, while placement in the tertiary sector is related to middle-class identification and Republican Party preference [35]. Given these considerations, we specified whether our respondents were employed in the primary, secondary, or tertiary sectors of the economy. The distribution of our sample across these industrial sectors is presented in Table 4.

TABLE 4. INDUSTRIAL AFFILIATION OF HOUSEHOLD HEADS

	Primary (Extractive)	Secondary (Manufacturing)	Tertiary (Service)
Per cent	13.2	32.0	54.7
(n) *	116	281	480

* Excluding the unemployed.

Position in the labor market was indexed by the dichotomy mentioned by both Marx and Weber—employers (including self-employed) and employees. Almost 13 per cent of our respondents were members of households whose heads were self-employed. An additional 1.7 per cent of the household heads were both self-employed and employed by someone else. They were coded as self-employed.

In addition to these measures of economic class position we included measures of two achieved status attributes in our analysis—occupational prestige and education. Occupational prestige was measured both by a crude blue-collar/white-collar distinction and by the Duncan Index of Socioeconomic Status [11]. For statistical analysis involving assumptions of normality, a logarithmic transformation of Duncan's index was used. Education was originally coded in terms of years completed and degree earned. We recoded these data in terms of the following eleven categories: 0–2 years, 3–4 years, 5–6 years, 7 years, 8 years, 9–11 years, 12 years, 12 years + noncollege training, some college, bachelor's degree, advanced degree.

Income was entered into our analysis as an additional dimension of the stratification system. Specification of income as an indicator of social status or of economic class is difficult. On the one hand, income is clearly an indicator of economic position. On the other hand, social honor does accrue to persons of high income; and the effects of income on a wide range of dependent variables tends to be monotonic, suggesting status gradations rather than discrete economic classes.

Respondents had been asked to report their expected 1966 incomes in terms of a ten-category scheme (less than $1,000; $1,000–$1,999; $2,000–$2,999; $3,000–$3,999; $4,000–$4,9999; $5,000–$7,499; $7,500–$9,999; $10,000–$14,999; $15,000–$24,999; more than $25,-

000).[4] Although income data in single dollar intervals could not be recaptured, we treated this variable as continuous. Where necessary for analysis, a logarithmic transformation was used as a better approximation of normality.

Two status attributes were considered as consequences of objective class, status, and income position—subjective social-class identification and consumer behavior. Our respondents were asked whether they thought they belonged to the working class or the middle class, and then whether they belonged to the average or upper strata in their chosen classes. For purposes of analysis, we combined those respondents who refused to answer the second part of the question (less than 4 per cent of the sample) with those who said they were average, producing the distribution in Table 5. Obviously this distribution was far from normal, and no conventional transformation could normalize it.

TABLE 5. DISTRIBUTION OF SUBJECTIVE CLASS IDENTIFICATION

Subjective Class Identification	%	N
Average working class	48.0	525
Upper working class	10.2	112
Average middle class	33.0	361
Upper middle class	8.8	96
Total	100.0%	1,094*

* 33 respondents were coded D.K. or N.A.

In measuring consumption, we were attempting to measure the quality of anticipated material well-being, rather than simply the amount of money spent on consumer goods or the stylistic preference of our respondents. The items that we initially considered for inclusion in this index were plans to buy a home, plans for home improvement, plans to buy a car and whether it will be new or used, automobiles bought in the past year and whether they were new or used, plans to buy various durable goods (furniture, refrigerator, stove, washing machine, air conditioner, television set, other). That is, we were concerned with recent and anticipated major expenditures.

On the basis of analysis of relationships among these items, they were combined and weighted in the following manner: planned purchases of durable goods (up to two coded) were given three points each, regardless of the nature of the goods; automobile purchases either in the last year or planned for the current year were given two points (used car), four points (new car) or six points (two cars in two-year period); two points were assigned for the planned purchase of a home; one point was assigned for planned improvements of the home.

The points were cumulated for each respondent, with index values ranging from 0–15. The mean score was 2.75 with a standard deviation of 3.18. A square root logarithmic transformation was used to reduce skewness.

Results

Since our measures of labor market and industrial affiliation were nominal scales, we performed our initial analysis using Multiple Classification Analysis (MCA). MCA is a linear analysis model capable of handling missing data, nonlinear data, and nominal independent variables with the accuracy of least squares methods. It can be conceived of as a form of dummy variable multiple regression [46]. The coefficients obtained through MCA are analogous to those obtained through dummy variable regression, and the coefficients derived by either of these techniques may easily be converted to the other by the addition or subtraction of a constant for each predictor. MCA has the advantage of requiring no conversion of basic data. All variables are automatically dealt with as dummy variables [Andrews, et al., 1967].

TABLE 6. MULTIPLE CLASSIFICATION ANALYSIS OF SUBJECTIVE SOCIAL CLASS IDENTIFICATION

Independent Variable	Eta_1	$Beta_2$
Labor market	.036	.025
Industrial affiliation	.166	.061
Financial transactions	.322*	.104
Education	.516*	.328*
Income	.387*	.210*
Duncan SES	.484*	.216*

Multiple r^2 (adjusted for degrees of freedom) = .331 *
* $p < .05$
1. Eta measures gross relationships
2. Beta measures partial relationships

Neither position in the labor market nor industrial affiliation has an affect on subjective class identification (Table 6). Participation in financial transactions has a significant relationship to subjective class identification at the zero-order. When all other factors are taken into account, however, the relationship disappears. The zero-order and the partial relationships of our two status indicators and of income to social-class identification are all

TABLE 7. MULTIPLE CLASSIFICATION
ANALYSIS OF MATERIAL
CONSUMPTION

Independent Variable	Eta	Beta
Labor market	.006	.030
Industrial affiliation	.111	.098
Financial transactions	.170	.076
Education	.283*	.214
Income	.325*	.285*
Duncan SES	.212	.089

Multiple r^2 (adjusted for degrees of freedom) = .104 *
* p<.05

significant, suggesting that class identification is a reflection of status and income gradations rather than of discrete economic classes.

The importance of status and affluence, as opposed to economic class position, in defining material life-style, is shown in Table 7. Education and income are the only attributes related to material consumption at the zero-order; and when all other factors are controlled, income stands alone as a determinant of material consumption.

Because our first multiple classification analysis had suggested that subjective social-class identification is an indicator of social *status,* we added this variable to our analyses of consumer behavior. Class identification was significantly related to the dependent variable (p < .05) at the zero-order. The betas for class identification were not significant, however, and the mutliple r^2 was not increased significantly.

On the basis of these results, we decided to reject the labor market and industrial affiliation as explanatory variables, and to reclaim the data lost by imposing an assumption of nominal scaling on interval variables by turning to regression analysis.

Hodge and Treiman's [20] regression of subjective class identification on education, occupation of household head, and family income had produced a multiple r^2 of .196. With our financial transaction index added to these, our multiple r^2 was .268. The betas suggest that education is the most important determinant of subjective class identification, but they must be interpreted in the light of a multicollinearity problem, the extent of which is suggested by the magnitude of the zero-order correlations presented in Table 8. These data do suggest, however, that status, as measured by education and Duncan SES, is a more important determinant of subjective class identification than are such economic variables as income and participation in financial transactions. These findings are similar to the results of our earlier Multiple Classification Analysis.

TABLE 8. REGRESSION COEFFICIENTS AND ZERO-ORDER CORRELATIONS FOR ANALYSIS OF SOCIAL-CLASS IDENTIFICATION

	Beta	Zero-order correlation				
		1.	2.	3.	4.	5.
1. Education	.272		.524	.421	.135	.446
2. Duncan SES	.175			.432	.400	.411
3. Income	.096				.412	.339
4. Finance	.130					.328
5. Subjective class identification						

Our earlier analysis had suggested that, unlike subjective class identification, material consumption was primarily determined by income. Our regression analysis confirmed this finding, as shown in Table 9. The regression of our consumer index on education, income, Duncan SES, and position in the credit market yielded a multiple r^2 of .193. The betas for income and education, respectively, were .408 and .111. Adding class identification to the equation increased r^2 to .195, an insignificant increment. The addition of subjective class identification also increased the betas for education and income.

TABLE 9. REGRESSION COEFFICIENTS FOR ANALYSIS OF CONSUMPTION INDEX AND ITS COMPONENTS

	Dependent Variables			
Independent Variables	Consumer Index	Automobile Purchase	Durable Purchase	Home Ownership
Education	.125***	.048	.006	−.131***
Duncan SES	−.004	−.008	.081**	.079**
Income	.412***	.326***	.123***	.307***
Financial transactions	−.038	*	*	*
Subjective class identification	−.055	.028	.039	−.008
Multiple r^2	.195***	.128***	.039***	.091***

* Variable omitted from analysis
** $p < .01$
*** $p < .001$

Our findings with regard to consumption, then, agreed with those of economists concerned with the effects of affluence. Income explains the lion's share of the relatively small proportion of variance in economic behavior that social scientists have been able to account for. As a corollary, we suggest that increases in income will be matched by increases in consumption spending (cf. Katona and Mueller, [23], who argued that while some consumption spending lags behind income increases, this is not true for discretionary expenditures). Given the income overlap between upper working-class and lower middle-class occupations, we argue that material life-styles overlap as well.

Table 9 presents regression coefficients for the component parts of our consumption index. These were taken as indicators of potential value differentials within our sample. Within some segments of the American population, for example, great importance is placed on owning one's own home [51]. Similarly, other segments of the population might place value priorities on the mobility afforded by automobile ownership, or the convenience furnished by major labor-saving electrical appliances.

As Table 9 shows, with regard to all three components, income stands out as the primary determinant, and the only one that is statistically significant in every case. The pattern is somewhat different with regard to home ownership than with regard to the other components in that in the former case, the coefficient for eduction is negative, while in the others it is positive but not significant. The primacy of income is unqestionable.

Financial transactions, which we have to this point been using as an indicator of economic class serving as an antecedent to material consumption, represent an alternative arena of economic behavior as well. That is, one can choose to purchase stocks or bonds, or to save available money, rather than spend it on durable goods (see Ferber page 30). Our previous analyses have suggested that our financial transactions index is not related to consumer behavior as a structural antecedent. We shall now take the financial transactions index as a supplementary dependent variable.

As Table 10 indicates, education, Duncan SES, income, and social-class identification have different relationships to financial behavior than to material consumption. Income is still the most powerful determinant of this form of economic behavior. However, the regression coefficients for Duncan SES and class identification are also highly significant, suggesting that financial behavior is a far more status-rooted phenomenon than is material consumption. Again, these data may be interpreted in terms of the perma-

TABLE 10. REGRESSION COEFFICIENTS FOR ANALYSIS OF FINANCIAL BEHAVIOR INDEX

Independent Variable	Beta
Education	.053
Duncan SES	.199*
Income	.248*
Subjective class identification	.153*
Multiple r^2	.192

* $p < .001$

158 · Social Stratification and Family Economic Behavior

nent income concept;[4] and again, we remain unconvinced that an argument in terms of permanent income effects is superior to an argument in favor of social status effects.

Bourgeoisie or Proletariat?

Given the convergence of the labor force on middle-status occupations (upper working class and lower middle class) and the income overlap between these occupations, the primacy of income in determining consumption suggests a convergence of material life-styles as well. However, we have not yet defined the nature of the material life-style that they share. Does the affluent working class manifest a bourgeois life-style, or does the lower middle class live like the working class? The data on financial behavior suggest that there are still economic differences between the working and middle classes, economic convergence notwithstanding. This differentiation suggests that the middle class may possess some unique economic attributes to which the affluent worker might aspire. The question remains whether these are reflected in material consumption as well as financial behavior.

We inspected the graphs of our consumer index by income for white-collar and blue-collar occupations. There was a tendency for white-collar workers to have higher index scores in the range $1,000–$3,999, and for blue-collar workers to have higher scores in the range $4,000–$14,999, as shown in Table 11. Above this range there were only 16 blue-collar respondents, and no comparisons were possible.

Clearly the greatest effect on material consumption is that of income. These data do reflect, however, a marginal effect of status (occupation and its correlates) at the lower end of the income distribution. This is rapidly overtaken and surpassed by working-class affluence. The status effect is reflected in the regression analysis of these data, with white-collar workers

TABLE 11. MEAN CONSUMER INDEX SCORES ($\bar{C}$), BY OCCUPATIONAL CLASS AND INCOME

Income	Blue Collar		White Collar	
	$\bar{C}$	N	$\bar{C}$	N
$ 1,000	.52	25	.74	4
$ 1,000–$ 1,999	.93	60	1.29	14
$ 2,000–$ 2,999	.79	48	1.64	14
$ 3,000–$ 3,999	1.81	69	2.17	24
$ 4,000–$ 4,999	2.20	66	2.00	31
$ 5,000–$ 7,499	3.02	128	2.84	85
$ 7,500–$ 9,999	3.94	107	3.20	101
$10,000–$14,999	4.88	51	4.51	83

having a higher intercept and blue-collar workers a steeper slope. The regression of consumer index (Y) on income (X) for blue-collar workers was
$$Y = -1.066 + 1.269X.$$
For white-collar workers, the equation was
$$Y = -0.855 + 1.075X.$$
The standardized betas for blue-collar and white-collar workers respectively were .441 and .362.

We conclude from these data that material consumption is almost solely a function of income, with minor occupational differences that in fact change in direction. Behavior in the financial market, by contrast, while necessarily (and tautologically) related to economic well-being, reflects the status gradation of occupations, and people's perceptions of their positions in the stratification system as well.

Conclusion

The major question with which this study has been concerned is whether social stratification has an effect on economic behavior over and above the effect of income that has previously been demonstrated. Since material consumption is a component of life-style, and since life-style has been regarded by sociologists largely as a function of placement in the social stratification system, we as sociologists anticipated that social stratification would indeed make a contribution to the explanation of economic behavior.

Our major finding is that stratification does not in fact make such a contribution. Here there is a lesson for sociology to learn from economics. The theories regarding man in industrial society upon which sociologists draw, starting from Marx and Freud, assume that one's occupation is central to one's self-concept, and hence to one's style of life. Our analysis does not allow us to rule on the truth of this assumption for years past. Neither can we speak of the nature of this relationship at the extremes of the occupational distribution in the contemporary world. In the middle of the occupational distribution, however, where the bulk of the labor force is concentrated, the distinction between blue-collar and white-collar lifestyles as manifested through money spent on durable goods, housing, and automobiles, seems not to exist except within net of income differentials. While we have dealt with only a limited set of expenditures, other research dealing with a wider range of consumer behavior is consistent with our findings on the primacy of income [41].

Sociology does seem to have something to offer to economics in the understanding of differentials in financial, as opposed to consumer, behavior. Here, we found that both occupational status and subjective class identification contributed to the explanation of participation in financial transactions over and above the effect of income. The higher an individual's occupational prestige, and the higher his subjective placement on the stratification system, the more likely he is to engage in financial transactions. To the extent that involvement in financial transactions has an effect on dollar income, we would of course expect this relationship to contribute to differentials in consumer behavior among social strata. Our analysis would mask this stratification effect by assigning the variance indirectly due to status differentials in financial transactions to the direct relationship between dollar income and consumer behavior. In an effort to deal with such potential biases built into our methodology, we tested a variety of stratification models that essentially stacked the deck in favor of social stratification variables. That is, we used indirect least squares methods to test models that explicitly assigned shared variance to the social class and social status variables rather than to income [12]. That stratification variables could not win even with a stacked deck gives us increased confidence in our original findings.

None of this is to say that sociological variables have no contributions to make to the understanding of consumer behavior. Our purpose was to determine whether conceptualizations that see economic behavior as a function of social stratification hold true. We were not on a fishing expedition to find sociological variables that help explain economic behavior. Indeed, we know from previous research that marital status, family size, age of children, position in the life cycle, and other sociological variables do have effects on the quality and quantity of consumption [33]. Our study, however, was concerned with gleaning a set of independent variables from the field of social stratification, not the sociology of the family.

In closing, let us note that recent research in the fields of political science and consumer psychology add support to our conclusion that changes in the social stratification system do not currently have great implications for changes in consumer behavior. Inglehart [22] has confronted the issue of the emergence of a "counter culture" [38] in the context of European industrial society. Inglehart characterized the value priorities of the contemporary middle-mass as "acquisitive" (in a material sense), and suggested that the children of the middle-mass, who, unlike their parents, were born into affluence, might manifest "post-bourgeois" values. His data, reflecting the value priorities of adolescents in six European nations, suggest that the majority of the children of the acquisitive middle class are themselves acquisitive. Moreover, while he suggested a trend toward increased incidence of post-bourgeois humanistic values in the future in the industrial nations, he did not see this trend reflecting a rejection of the bourgeois materialism of the parental generation. Rather, he saw it rooted in the fact that bourgeois materialism *qua* economic security can be taken for granted by the ascending generation. While Inglehart's own concern was with the political implications of such value change, some scholars have noted the potential import of his findings for understanding economic behavior, and are attempting to measure the effects of acquisitive and post-bourgeois value priorities in a current survey.

A second set of findings suggest a set of psychological processes that intervene between placement in the stratification system and economic behavior. Demby [9], for example, argued that people in the same occupational groups, or in the same income categories, have very different attitudes about their occupations and incomes. The crucial determinant of purchasing behavior, he argued, is the degree to which an individual can visualize experiences beyond his immediate environment. Such breadth of vision might, of course, be associated with education or occupational status. However, the correlation is far enough from unity to make exploration of this variable in its own right fruitful. The point to be emphasized is that while theories of social stratification derived from Marx and Weber have little to offer economics in the explanation of consumer behavior, the variation in such behavior that is currently unexplained need not remain so.

Notes

1. There are in fact two important senses in which the quality of material consumption can be seen as an attribute of status. On the one hand, consumption may be merely a reflection of a man's position—achieved or ascribed—in the stratification system. On the other hand, it may be a claim to increased status through conspicuous consumption. We did not initially differentiate between these positions, and our data do not allow us to choose between them.

2. Few economists studying consumption have considered social status variables in their research. Among the exceptions, Millican [31] found that budgetary variations are related to education and occupation, Katona and Mueller [23] have studied the zero-order relationship between economic attitudes and occupation, and Burk [5] has utilized indicators of social status in her analysis of food expenditures by upper income families. Market researchers are more interested in sociological variables than economists, but seldom make careful use of sophisticated measures to partial out different stratification dimensions [16, 29, 39, 13, 3].

3. In all cases of mathematical transformation of data, analysis was performed using both the transformed and untransformed variables. Differences appeared only in the third decimal place, and were not significant. Thus, our findings are not an artifact of the transformations used. The transformations, while helping us meet the assumptions of the statistical techniques used, really made little difference in our findings.

4. As an alternative approach, we might have attempted to estimate permanent income, rather than annual income, as a predictor [14]. Indeed, to anticipate some of our results, an economist might argue that a predictive model for economic behavior that includes annual income, occupational prestige, and education merely indicates that annual income is an imperfect indicator of permanent income. In this view, permanent income is the crucial independent variable, and the inclusion of occupation and education in the model merely improves the estimation of permanent income. We find recent research which indicates that the consumption function is at least as sensitive to current as to permanent income more convincing than Friedman's formulation [21, 2, see also Arak and Spiro, 1971]. We would therefore view

status characteristics in such a model as reflections of real status effects rather than as corrections of income estimation.

References

1. Andrews, Frank, James Morgan, and John Sonquist, *Multiple Classification Analysis,* Ann Arbor: Survey Research Center, University of Michigan, 1967.
2. Arak, M. V., and Alan Spiro, "The Relationship Between Permanent Income and Measured Variables," *Journal of Political Economy* 79, May–June 1971, pp. 652–660.
3. Bass, Frank M., Douglas Tigert, and Ronald Lonsdale, "Market Segmentation: Group versus Individual Behavior," *Journal of Marketing Research* 5, August 1968, pp. 264–270.
4. Budd, Edward C., ed., *Inequity and Poverty,* New York: W. W. Norton, 1967.
5. Burk, Marguerite C., *Food Expenditures by Upper Income Families,* Technical Bulletin 269, University of Minnesota Agricultural Experiment Station, 1969.
6. Centers, Richard, *The Psychology of Social Classes,* Princeton: Princeton University Press, 1949.
7. Chapin, F. Stewart, *Contemporary American Institutions,* New York: Harper, 1935.
8. Cramer, J. S., *The Ownership of Major Consumer Durables,* Cambridge: Cambridge University Press, 1962.
9. Demby, Emanuel H., "Over-the-Counter Life-Style." *Psychology Today* 5, April 1972, pp. 75 ff.
10. Douglas, Paul H., *Real Wages in the United States: 1890–1926,* Boston: Houghton Mifflin, 1930.
11. Duncan, Otis Dudley, "A Socioeconomic Index for All Occupations" and "Properties and Characteristics of the Socioeconomic Index," pp. 109–131, 1961 and 263–275 in Albert J. Reiss, Jr., ed., *Occupations and Social Status,* New York: Free Press of Glencoe, 1961.
12. Felson, Marcus, "Conspicuous Consumption and the Embourgeoisement Question," unpublished Ph.D. dissertation. Department of Sociology, University of Michigan, 1973.
13. Frank, Ronald E., William F. Massey, and Harper W. Boyd, "Correlates of Grocery Product Consumption Rates," *Journal of Marketing Research* 4, May 1967, pp. 184–190.
14. Friedman, Milton, *A Theory of the Consumption Function,* Princeton: Princeton University Press, 1957.
15. Galbraith, John Kenneth, *The Affluent Society,* New York: New American Library, 1958.
16. Gottleib, Morris J., "Segmentation by Personality Types," chapter 10 in James U. McNeal, *Dimensions of Consumer Behavior,* New York: Appleton-Century-Crofts, 1965.
17. Hamilton, Richard F., "Income, Class and Reference Groups," *American Sociological Review* 29, August 1964, pp. 576–579.
18. ———, "The Marginal Middle-Class," *American Sociological Review* 31, April 1966, pp. 92–199.

19. ———, "Reply to Tucker," *American Sociological Review* 31, December 1966, p. 865.

20. Hodge, Robert W., and Donald J. Treiman, "Class Identification in the United States," *American Journal of Sociology* 73, March 1968, pp. 535–547.

21. Holmes, James M., "A Direct Test of Friedman's Permanent Income Theory," *Journal of the American Statistical Association* 65, September 1970, pp. 1159–1962.

22. Inglehart, Ronald, "The Silent Revolution in Europe," *American Political Science Review* 65, December 1971, pp. 991–1017.

23. Katona, George, and Eva Mueller, *Consumer Expectations: 1953–1956*, publication of Survey Research Center, University of Michigan, 1957.

24. Lampman, Robert, *The Share of Top Wealth Holders in the National Wealth*, Princeton: Princeton University Press, 1962.

25. Lane, Robert E., "The Politics of Consensus in an Age of Affluence," *American Political Science Review* 59, December 1965, pp. 875–894.

26. Laumann, Edward O., and James S. House, "Living Room Styles and Social Attributes: the Patterning of Material Artifacts in a Modern Urban community," *Sociology and Social Research* 54, April 1970, pp. 321–342.

27. Lefebvre, Henri, *The Sociology of Marx*, New York: Random House, 1968.

28. Lipset, Seymour M., and Stein Rokkan, *Party Systems and Voter Alignments*, New York: Free Press, 1967.

29. Martineau, Pierre, "Social Classes and Spending Behavior," *Journal of Marketing* 23, October 1968, pp. 121–130.

30. Miller, Herman P., *Income Distribution in the United States*, Washington: U.S. Bureau of the Census, 1960.

31. Millican, Richard D., *A Consumption Expenditure Study of Eight United States Cities*, University of Illinois mimeograph, 1957.

32. Mills, C. Wright, *White Collar*, New York: Oxford University Press, 1951.

33. Modigliani, Franco, and Albert Ando, "The 'Permanent Income' and 'Life Cycle' Hypotheses of Saving Behavior," pp. 29–174 in Vol. 2 of Irwin Friend and Robert Jones, eds., *Study of Consumer Expectations, Incomes and Savings*, Philadelphia: Wharton School, 1960.

34. Morgan, James N., Ismael A. Sirageldin, and Nancy Baerwaldt, *Productive Americans*, Survey Research Center Monograph 48, Ann Arbor: University of Michigan, 1966.

35. Morris, Richard T., and Raymond J. Murphy, "The Situs Dimension in Occupation Structure," *American Sociological Review* 24, April 1959, pp. 321–239.

36. Murphy, Raymond J., and Richard T. Morris, "Occupational Situs, Subjective Class Identification and Political Affiliation," *American Sociological Review* 26, June 1961, pp. 303–392.

37. Perrot, Marguerite, *Le Mode de Vie des Familles Bourgeoises, 1873–1953*, Paris: Libraire Armand Colin, 1960.

38. Roszak, Theodore, *The Making of a Counter Culture*, Garden City: Doubleday, 1969.

39. Samli, A. Coskun, "Segmentation and Carving a Niche in the Market Place," *Journal of Retailing* 44, Summer 1968, pp. 35–49.

40. Schipper, Lewis, *Consumer Discretionary Behavior*, Amsterdam: North Holland Publishing Company, 1964.

41. Schlinger, M. J., and W. D. Wells, "Social Stratification and Life Style," University of Chicago, mimeograph.

42. Schreiber, E. M., and G. T. Nygreen, "Subjective Social Class in America: 1945–1968," *Social Forces* 48, March 1970, pp. 348–356.

43. Segal, David R., and David Knoke, "Political Partisanship: Its Social and Economic Bases in the United States," *American Journal of Economics and Sociology* 29, July 1970, pp. 253–262.

44. Segal, David R., Mady W. Segal, and David Knoke, "Status Inconsistency and Self-Evaluation," *Sociometry* 33, September 1970, pp. 347–356.

45. Sewell, William H., "The Construction and Standardization of a Scale for the Measurement of the Socioeconomic Status of Oklahoma Farm Families," Technical Bulletin No. 9, Agricultural Experimental Station, Oklahoma Agricultural and Mechanical College, Stillwater, Oklahoma, 1940.

46. Suits, Daniel B., "Use of Dummy Variables in Regression Equations," *Journal of American Statistical Association* 52, 1957, pp. 548–551.

47. Tucker, Charles W., "A Comparative Analysis of Subjective Social Class: 1945–1963," *Social Forces* 46, June 1968, pp. 508–514.

48. Veblen, Thorstein, *The Theory of the Leisure Class*. New York: Viking Press, 1931.

49. Weber, Max, *Economy and Society*, Guenther Roth and Claus Wittich, eds. New York: Bedminster Press, 1968.

50. Wilensky, Harold L., "Class, Class Consciousness and American Workers," pp. 12–28 in William Haber, ed., *Labor in a Changing America*, New York: Basic Books, 1966.

51. Wood, Robert C., *Suburbia*, Boston: Houghton Mifflin, 1958.

5

Relative Economic Status and the American Fertility Swing

Author's note: The research on which this paper is based was supported by National Institute of Child Health and Human Development grant 1 RO1 HD-05427-01 and by National Science Foundation grant GS-1563. I am especially grateful for assistance and comments from Duane E. Ball, Gretchen A. Condran, and Betty A. Rippel. Some Bureau of Census data which are as yet unpublished were kindly made available to me by Conrad Taeuber, Paul C. Glick, Wilson H. Grabill, Herman P. Miller, and Campbell Gibson. I have benefited from conversations or correspondence with T. R. Balakrishnan, Yoram Ben-Porath, J. D. Durand, Paul C. Glick, Wilson H. Grabill, Peter Hicks, J. F. Kantner, Allen C. Kelley, L. R. Klein, S. Kuznets, R. M. McInnis, G. S. Masnick, Ann R. Miller, G. Oja, N. B. Ryder, Eleanor B. Sheldon, and M. L. Wachter. I should like also to record here the debt which this paper owes generally to prior work on the topic by demographers (see references at the end of the paper).

RICHARD A. EASTERLIN

Introduction

The theory-related purposes of Richard A. Easterlin's paper, "Relative Economic Status and the American Fertility Swing," are explanatory, both historically and deductively. As outlined below, he sought

1. To provide a historical explanation for two events, the decade-long decline and recent upturn of fertility rates in the United States.
2. To provide a general causal explanation for fertility patterns.

Easterlin hoped to be able to place his historical interpretation in the context of a deductive explanation. The aggregate fertility rate was his dependent variable, and his mode of expression was conventional.

The most important empirical generalization derived from Easterlin's study is the following:

EG16. A family's relative economic status, or the discrepancy between the labor-market experiences of a son and his father, produces the marriage and fertility patterns of the family members.

Because the causal paths to fertility experience are much more complex than EG16 alone can handle, we have constructed a conceptual model that interrelates several of the author's key concepts.

The first thing to recognize in Chart 1 on Easterlin is the *comparison* phenomenon that is hypothesized to produce relative economic status. It has features noticeably similar to those expressed in Chart 1 summarizing Strumpel's study (page 67). The comparison here is between tastes and economic status and not directly between the labor-market experiences of sons and fathers. Easterlin emphasized that material aspirations reflect earlier economic socialization experiences, and presumably a father's work experience is an input to the socialization process. Easterlin also allowed for other factors in formation of taste, although he did not explore them in any detail.

The intervening links between fathers' labor-force experience and tastes should serve as a warning that "contaminating" factors may operate to deflect relative economic status away from its expected value, given only information about fathers' labor-force experiences. In this light, it is espe-

CHART 1. EASTERLIN'S EXPLANATION OF FERTILITY PATTERNS

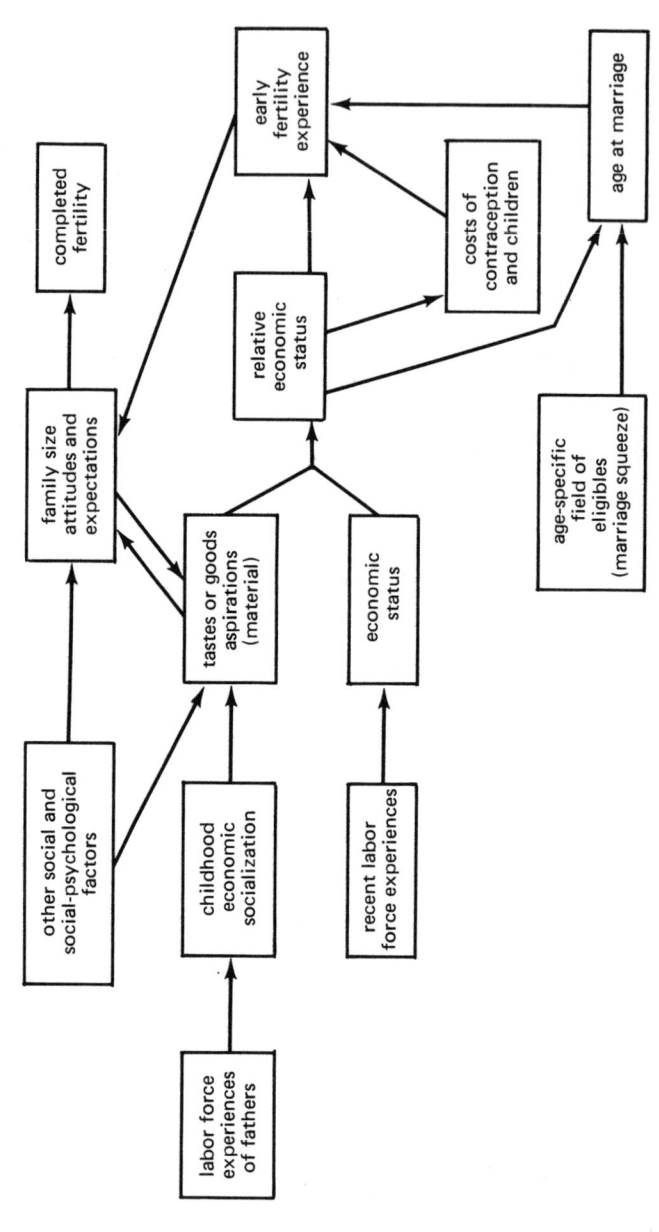

cially surprising that Easterlin's measures of relative economic status appeared to work so well as fertility predictors.

Easterlin acknowledged that the objective and subjective costs of contraception and children may operate independently and in opposite directions to influence fertility rates. He suggested, however, that relative economic status itself plays a major role in determining these costs.

It is interesting to note that EG16 does not account well, or at least directly, for the inducements for women to marry and bear children. Chart 1 suggests that one determinant of the female's impact on fertility decisions is the "marriage squeeze" phenomenon, which Easterlin observed is historically quite variable in its significance.

A relationship deserving special attention is the causal relationship from early fertility experience to attitudes and expectations regarding size of the family. It reflects an hypothesized feed-back mechanism. Easterlin proposed that before the first child is born attitudes concerning size of the family are weak or flexible, and that only after children are born do these attitudes firm up in a direction congruent with that experience. Easterlin called on the "cognitive dissonance theory" of social psychology to explain this sequence of events. It is apparently easier to adjust one's attitudes about family size than to "make up" for deferred childbearing or psychologically to disown unwanted children. Easterlin also employed this reasoning to explain in part the social movement of population control.

We feel that this particular feature of the fertility model is the most tenuous. In spite of the evidence he presented to demonstrate that "changes in behavior precede those in attitudes," more empirical research into this phenomenon is clearly called for. We suspect that to the extent the population stabilization movement is a youth movement, its adherents maintain less flexible family-size ideals ("maximum of two natural children") than the supposed "two-to-four norm," and plan their fertility experiences accordingly. If their social concern is with environmental quality, then temporary profertility economic conditions may indeed provide very shallow incentives for increasing family size. Increased resources may instead be invested or expended on other economic alternatives.

Reuben Hill and David M. Klein

Relative Economic Status and the American Fertility Swing

By Richard A. Easterlin

In two earlier papers, I presented arguments and evidence to show that economic factors played an important role in the postwar baby boom and subsequent downturn in American fertility [15]. A half dozen years have now elapsed and the accumulation of additional experience and new data offers an opportunity to test and develop this line of analysis further. This is the purpose of the present paper. Interest in such an inquiry is heightened by the recent appearance of articles both generally critical of economic explanations of fertility and specifically questioning my earlier interpretation of fertility swings [8, 55].[1]

As in the previous papers, the analysis focuses on women in early childbearing ages. The fertility behavior of the white population is, strictly speaking, the subject of interest, but the more readily available data for all classes of the population have often been used since these data are, in any event, dominated by the behavior of the white population. The basic time span of the analysis is the period from the Great Depression, since it seems reasonable to suppose that the explanation of the recent decline in fertility must be generally consistent with that of the earlier baby boom, though new factors may, of course, appear from one time to another.

While the additional data now available make it possible to go further than was previously possible, limitations will quickly become apparent. Demographers, in particular, may be disturbed by the use here of relatively unsophisticated measures of fertility. However, as will also become apparent, there is a serious problem of appropriately matching economic measures with the fertility observations. While I feel that the present study has made an advance in matching better these two sets of data, there is much room for improvement. Also, the assumptions used in the analytical model, particularly with regard to how aspirations are formed and earnings prospects estimated, obviously require much fuller exploration. The present analysis, therefore, should be viewed chiefly as suggesting a general approach to the explanation of the recent swing in fertility, and providing a crude empirical test of the promise of this approach. The fertility patterns are described first, after which the analysis proceeds to the question of causation. Finally, the relation of period fertility rate changes to family-size attitudes and completed fertility rates is discussed.

Fertility Patterns and Characteristics of Young Adults

The fertility pattern

A summary picture of American fertility over the past half century is provided by the total fertility rate. As an indicator of movements in the rate of childbearing from one year to another, this measure is superior to others such as the crude birth rate and general fertility rate, because it is unaffected by variations in the relative number of women at high and low childbearing ages. Conceptually, the rate is the sum for a given year of the age-specific birth rates for women in each single year of age between 14 and 49. As such, it indicates the total number of births per thousand women that would be produced by a hypothetical cohort of women which experienced these age-specific rates in successive years during the course of its reproductive career.

By this measure, American fertility, after declining in the 1920s, reached an all time low during 1933-39 (Chart 1). In the next eighteen years, it moved upward, reaching a peak in 1957. In that year the rate was about 75 per cent higher than at its mid-thirties trough. Subsequently, it turned down, and within thirteen years returned almost four-fifths of the way toward the previous low. Although there is evidence of long swings in fertility in the century prior to World War I [15], such a precipitous rise and fall within a mere three decades is unparalleled.

For the most part, this entire movement was a remarkably smooth one. Annual series relating to economic magnitudes, such as output or unemployment, show much more marked variations. For fertility, however, the most noticeable fluctuations were concentrated in war and early postwar years.

A look at the birth rates by age of woman shows that the general movement in fertility since the mid-thirties is common to all five-year age groups of women between 15 and 39, but that there are differences in timing and amplitude [75, p. 5]. The age groups of special interest here, females 15-19 and 20-24 years old, accounted in 1968 for over half of total births (Table 1). For both of these groups the amplitude of the fertility rise and fall is fairly similar to that in the total fertility rate (Chart 1). There is, however, a difference in the timing of the downturn. For those 15-19 years old, it starts after 1957; for those 20-24, there is no clear indication of a decline until after 1960.

For both age groups, the fertility swing arises from underlying changes in both marital status and marital fertility. In general, the number of births

CHART 1. TOTAL FERTILITY RATE OF FEMALES AGED 14-49, AND AGE-SPECIFIC BIRTH RATE AND MARITAL FERTILITY OF FEMALES AGED 15-19 AND 20-24, VARYING PERIODS, 1917-1970 (RATE PER 1,000 WOMEN)

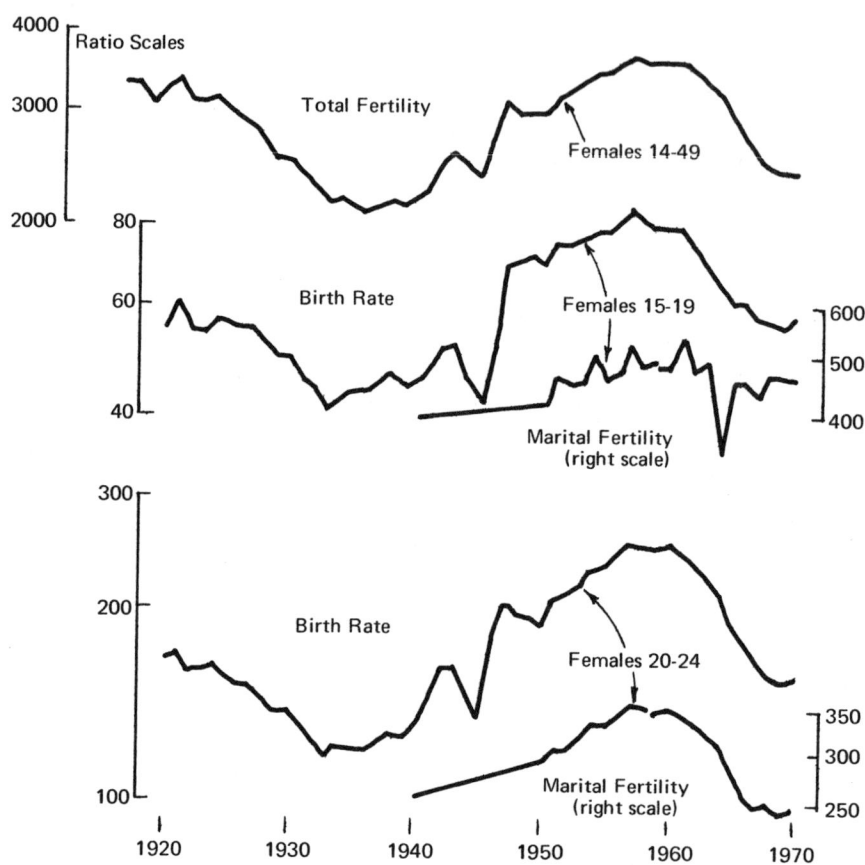

Sources: Total fertility (all classes) from [75, p. 6]; age-specific birth rates, 1920-1939 (native white), from [26, p. 31], 1940-1967 (total white), from [80, Table 1-6]. These series were extrapolated to 1970 on the basis of estimates of total fertility rates and age-specific birth rates of all classes for 1968 in [71, Vol. 18, No. 11 Supplement (January 30, 1970, p. 41)] and 1969-1970 by Campbell Gibson. I am grateful to Dr. Gibson for making his preliminary estimates available. Marital fertility (all classes) for 1940 is from [77, p. 83] and 1950-1967 from [80, Table 1-7]. An extrapolation to 1970 was made on the basis of movements in marital fertility 1967-1970 as estimated from the age-specific birth rates obtained above divided by the proportions ever-married in each age class as reported in the annual marital status reports through March 1970 of [58].

TABLE 1. PER CENT DISTRIBUTION
OF BIRTHS BY AGE, WHITE
FEMALES, 1968

Age	Per Cent
10–49	100.0
10–14	—
15–19	14.6
20–24	38.3
25–29	27.1
30–34	12.2
35–39	5.9
40–44	1.7
45–49	0.2

Source: [71, Vol. 18, No. 11, Supplement (January 30, 1970) p. 4].

to a given age group of women depends on the fertility rate of married women, the rate for unmarried women (the illegitimacy rate), and the relative proportions of women who are married and unmarried. Although illegitimacy is a subject of interest in itself, it is of minor importance in the fertility swing. Even for the two youngest age groups, the rise in illegitimacy rates since 1940 can account for only a very small part of the rise in total fertility. Moreover, the subsequent downturn in total fertility occurred while illegitimacy rates were stable or rising slowly [75, 76].

Of the principal factors in the swing in total fertility—that is, marital fertility and the proportion of women married—the former has played the more important role. However, there is an important difference between the 20–24-year-olds and 15–19-year-olds in the relative weight of these two components. For the 20–24-year-olds, marital fertility at the end of the sixties was at about the same level as thirty years earlier (Chart 1). While there was a decline during the sixties in the proportion of females in this age group who were married, it was only a mild reversal of the earlier uptrend, and the total birth rate for the group remained higher than its 1940 level. For the 20–24-year-olds, therefore, the recent fertility decline was overwhelmingly due to a decline in marital fertility.

For the 15–19-year-olds, even though the decline in total fertility is similar to that for those 20–24 years old, the decline in marital fertility is considerably less. By the end of the sixties, marital fertility for this group was about halfway between its previous trough and peak values (Chart 1). It follows that a decline in the proportion married played a correspondingly greater role in the total birth-rate decline for this group.

A noteworthy feature apparent in the data for both age groups that has heretofore received little notice is the leveling off of fertility in the latter part of the 1960s, though for the 15–19-year-olds, the timing of this is somewhat ambiguous because of the marked fluctuations in the marital fertility series.[2] Hence for these two groups, at least, the sizable recent decline in fertility was largely accomplished in a relatively short time span, roughly between 1961 and 1966.

TABLE 2. ESTIMATED TYPICAL MARITAL DURATION AND HUSBAND'S AGE OF EVER-MARRIED WHITE FEMALES 14–19 AND 20–24 YEARS OLD, AND TYPICAL AGE OF HUSBAND'S FATHER AND WIFE'S FATHER FOR EVER-MARRIED WHITE FEMALES 20–24, 1960 AND 1970

	(1) 1960	(2) 1970
A. Ever-Married White Females 14–19 Years Old		
1. Median age at survey date, ever-married white females	18.8	18.8
2. Median age at first marriage, ever-married white females	16.9	17.6
3. Estimated duration of marriage, (1) − (2)	1.9	1.2
4. Husband's age minus wife's age, estimated median difference	+3.4	+3.0
5. Estimated median age of husband at survey date, (1) + (4)	22.2	21.8
B. Ever-Married White Females 20–24 Years Old		
1. Median age at survey date, ever-married white females	22.8	22.8
2. Median age at first marriage, ever-married white females	19.1	19.4
3. Estimated duration of marriage, (1) − (2)	3.7	3.4
4. Husband's age minus wife's age, median difference	+3.2	+2.7
5. Estimated median age of husband at survey date, (1) + (4)	26.0	25.5
6. Estimated median age of father at birth of children in 1940	29.8	29.8
7. Estimated age at survey date of husband's father	55.8	55.3
8. Estimated age at survey date of wife's father	52.6	52.6

Sources and methods: 1960, line 1, from [63, p. 13]; line 2, from [62, p. 6]. 1970, lines 1 and 2 from [58, No. 212 (February 1, 1971) pp. 9, 36]. Both dates, line 3 from [*ibid.*, p. 38, data for all classes]. For line 3, the 1960 difference between husband's age and wife's age was estimated from the 1970 data for wives who had been married five years or more. The figure for those 14–19 years old was estimated as the median of the data for wives who were 19 or under at first marriage; for those 20–24, as the median of the data for wives who were 21 or under at first marriage. The same estimating procedure was used for 1970, except that the basic data were for wives married less than five years. Line 6 was estimated by adding to the 1950 figure for median age of mother at birth [78, p. 1–2] the estimated difference in age of husband and age of wife in 1930 [58, *op. cit.*, p. 1]. Line 7 is the sum of lines 1, 4, and 6; line 8 of lines 1 and 6.

Characteristics of young adults

An explanatory analysis requires as an essential first step an understanding of the circumstances of the young adults who were responsible for these developments. In what follows an attempt has been made to construct a rough sketch of the typical situation of young married adults in the 1960s, but a more complete picture, and for the period as a whole, is needed.

Since 14-year-olds account for only about 3 per cent of married women 14–19 years old, data for married females 14–19 years old may be used to approximate the situation of those 15–19. The average age of married women 14–19 was 18.8 years in both 1960 and 1970 (Table 2, line 1). In 1960, the typical age at marriage of women in this group was slightly under 17 years and the average duration of marriage consequently almost two years (lines 2 and 3). In 1970 the average age at marriage was more than 6 months greater than in 1960, and the duration of marriage correspondingly less.

As shown in column 1 of Table 3, relatively few of these women were married to husbands in the same age group—almost two-thirds of the husbands were in the 20–24 bracket. On the average, husbands were about three years older than wives, the representative age being about 22 years (Table 2, line 5).

Corresponding figures for 20–24-year-old married women are given in panel B of Table 2. Most of these women were nearly 23 years old; their husbands, about 26; and they had been married three and a half to four years.

TABLE 3. PER CENT DISTRIBUTION OF HUSBANDS BY AGE FOR WHITE WIVES OF SPECIFIED AGE, 1960

	(1)	(2)	(3)
		Age of Wife	
	14–19	20–24	25–29
Number of Wives (000)	888	3,509	4,516
Age of Husband			
14+	100.0	100.0	100.0
14–19	18.0	0.8	0.1
20–24	63.9	41.3	3.3
25–29	13.0	44.5	42.9
30–34	2.5	10.1	40.1
35+	2.6	3.3	13.7

Source: [63, p. 139].

TABLE 4. PER CENT DISTRIBUTION BY YEARS OF SCHOOL COMPLETED, EVER-MARRIED WHITE FEMALES 15–24 YEARS OLD, 1960 AND AVERAGE FOR 1969–71

	(1) 1960	(2) 1969–71
Number of Women (000)	4,418	5,691
Years of School Completed		
Elementary school:		
less than 8 years	5.5	2.7
8 years	7.0	4.2
High school:		
less than 4 years	30.6	21.3
4 years	44.3	51.6
College:		
less than 4 years	9.6	14.3
4 years	3.1	6.0
Total	100.0	100.0

Source: [61, p. 65], [58, No. 205 (July 22, 1970), p. 13], and unpublished 1970 and 1971 tabulations.

Several new tabulations from the *Current Population Survey,* which have recently become available, provide further information on the characteristics of these wives and their husbands. In this case, however, the age classification relates to the 15–24-year-old group as a whole. As shown in columns 1 and 2 of Table 4, most of the wives in this age group had had

TABLE 5. PER CENT DISTRIBUTION BY LABOR FORCE STATUS, EVER-MARRIED WHITE FEMALES 15–24 YEARS OLD, 1960 AND AVERAGE FOR 1969–71

Labor Force Status	(1) 1960	(2) 1969–71
Number of Women (000)	4,418	5,691
In labor force	32.0	46.8
Not in labor force	67.9	53.2
Total	100.0	100.0

Source: [61, p. 90], [58, No. 205 (July 22, 1970), p. 13], and unpublished 1970 and 1971 tabulations.

no college education—even by 1970 only one in five had received some education beyond high school. The typical amount of schooling was a high school education, but a substantial proportion of these young women had had even less schooling than this—for 1960 and 1970 together the average proportion who had not completed high school was one in three.

The majority of the wives were not in the labor force (Table 5, columns 1 and 2). There was, however, a noticeable change in this respect between 1960 and 1970. In 1960, only one wife in three was in the labor market; by 1970 the proportion had risen to almost one in two.

TABLE 6. EMPLOYMENT STATUS AND OCCUPATION OF HUSBANDS OF MARRIED WHITE FEMALES 15–24 YEARS OLD, WITH HUSBAND PRESENT, 1960 AND AVERAGE FOR 1969–71

	(1) 1960	(2) 1969–71
A. Employment Status		
Number of Husbands (000)	3,791	5,049
Total	100.0	100.0
In labor force	96.8	95.9
Employed	87.2	85.4
Unemployed	4.0	4.0
In armed forces	5.6	6.6
Not in labor force	3.2	4.2
B. Major Occupation Group of Employed Husbands		
Number of Husbands (000)	3,304	4,308
Total	100.0	100.0
Professional, technical and kindred workers	11.8	14.4
Managers, officials, and proprietors, except farm	6.2	8.8
Clerical and kindred workers	8.4	8.3
Sales workers	6.8	5.8
Craftsmen, foremen and kindred workers	21.2	21.4
Operators and kindred workers (not elsewhere classified)	29.1	26.8
Service workers	3.6	4.8
Laborers, except farm and mine	7.3	6.8
Farmers and farm managers	3.1	1.4
Farm laborers and foremen	2.4	1.5

Source: [61, p. 104] and [58, No. 205 (July 22, 1970), p. 19], and unpublished 1970 and 1971 tabulations.

Almost all of the husbands were in the labor market, and at the beginning and end of the decade the proportions of those unemployed or in the armed forces were quite similar (Table 6). Of those employed, only about one-third were in white-collar jobs; that is, professional, managerial, clerical, or sales work. The rest were in blue-collar, service, or farm occupations, with about one-half in craftsmen's and operatives' jobs.

TABLE 7. MEDIAN INCOME OF HUSBAND AND FAMILY FOR MARRIED WHITE FEMALES 15–24 YEARS OLD, WITH HUSBAND PRESENT, 1959 AND AVERAGE FOR 1968–70
(income in 1964 dollars)

	(1) 1959	(2) 1968–70
1. Husband's income	$4,221	$5,279
2. Family income	$5,172	$6,619
3. Line (1) as per cent of (2)	81.6	79.8

Source: [61, pp. 112, 114], [58, No. 205, (July 22, 1970), p. 19] and unpublished 1969 and 1970 tabulations.

These husbands earned about four-fifths of the family income (Table 7). Between 1960 and 1970 both husband's income and that of the whole family rose in real terms by about one-fourth. In 1969, the median total income of these young families was somewhat below the national average —about four-fifths of that for white families of all ages.

It appears that the group whose behavior we are seeking to understand consists principally of persons of the high-school-education/blue-collar work/lower middle-income category.[3]

Fertility differentials

Although this paper is not primarily concerned with differences in fertility among subgroups of the population, it is pertinent to ask whether the fertility decline has been concentrated among certain socioeconomic classes. Table 8, which shows the 1960–70 fertility change for young married women classified by occupation of husband, demonstrates strikingly the pervasiveness of the fertility decline. In every one of the 10 occupational classes, there is a sizable drop in fertility and for 8 of the 10, the declines are within 6 percentage points of the average. The remaining two

TABLE 8. OWN CHILDREN UNDER 5 YEARS OLD
PER 1,000 MARRIED WHITE FEMALES
15-24 YEARS OLD WITH HUSBAND
PRESENT, BY OCCUPATION OF
EMPLOYED HUSBAND, 1960
AND AVERAGE FOR 1969-71

Occupation	(1) 1960	(2) 1969-71	(3) (2)÷(1) Per Cent
Total	1,085	820	75.6
Professional, technical, and kindred workers	904	592	65.5
Managers, officials, and proprietors, except farm	1,072	767	71.5
Clerical and kindred workers	951	757	79.6
Sales workers	981	680	69.3
Craftsmen, foremen, and kindred workers	1,155	905	78.4
Operators and kindred workers (not elsewhere classified)	1,155	935	81.0
Service workers	1,088	792	72.8
Laborers, except farm and mine	1,132	870	76.8
Farmers and farm managers	1,253	908[a]	72.5
Farm laborers and foremen	1,211	714[a]	59.0

[a] Average for 1970-71
Source: Same as Table 6.

—the professional and farm laborer categories—show somewhat larger declines. This suggests that rather similar factors were operating on all segments of the young adult population to alter fertility. Other evidence points to the same conclusion for the previous baby boom [26].

By level of education of females, some interesting differences appear (Table 9). For marital fertility there is a noticeable association between the level of education and the fertility decline—the higher the level of education, the greater the decline (column 6). For total fertility, however, this association virtually disappears (column 3). The implication is that reductions in marriage proportions played a more important part in the fertility decline among less-educated women. This is shown in column 3 of Table 10, where the three highest educational classes are seen to have the smallest declines in proportions married. Thus it appears that although women at all levels of education participated significantly in the fertility reduction, among the less well-educated a reduction in proportions marrying was a major factor, while among those with a high-school education or better, lower marital fertility was the component chiefly responsible.

TABLE 9. OWN CHILDREN UNDER 5 YEARS OLD PER 1,000 TOTAL AND EVER-MARRIED WHITE FEMALES 15–24 YEARS OLD, BY YEARS OF SCHOOL COMPLETED, 1960 AND AVERAGE FOR 1969–71

	(1)	(2)	(3)	(4)	(5)	(6)
	Per 1,000 Total Females			Per 1,000 Ever-Married Females		
Years of School Completed	1960	1969–71	(2)÷(1) %	1960	1969–71	(5)÷(4) %
Total	427	287	67.2	1,023	772	75.5
Elementary school:						
less than 8 years	488	393	80.5	1,186	1,167	98.4
8 years	438	233	53.2	1,195	993	83.1
High school:						
less than 4 years	345	218	63.2	1,152	1,024	88.9
4 years	577	433	75.0	979	766	78.2
College:						
less than 4 years	308	180	58.4	775	505	65.2
4 years	265	114	43.0	475	231	48.6

Source: Same as Table 4.

TABLE 10. EVER-MARRIED FEMALES AS PER CENT OF TOTAL WHITE FEMALES 15–24 YEARS OLD, BY YEARS OF SCHOOL COMPLETED, 1960 AND AVERAGE FOR 1969–71

	(1)	(2)	(3)
	Per Cent of Ever-Married to Total Females		
Years of School Completed	1960	1969–71	(2)÷(1) %
Total	41.7	37.2	89.2
Elementary school:			
less than 8 years	41.2	33.7	81.8
8 years	36.6	23.6	64.5
High school:			
less than 4 years	29.9	21.3	71.2
4 years	59.0	56.5	95.8
College:			
less than 4 years	39.5	35.7	90.4
4 years	54.9	49.6	90.3

Source: Same as Table 4.

Causes of the Changing Fertility of Young Adults

Analytical viewpoint

The interpretation developed here focuses on the changing balance between the income earning possibilities of young adults and their desired living levels. The approach is similar to that of some sociologists who seek to explain fertility in terms of the changing relation between aspirations and living levels. Related notions, such as "relative deprivation" in sociology and social psychology, and "relative income" in economics, have gained increasing attention in recent decades [4, 39, 82, 83].

The basic idea is that if young men—the potential breadwinners of households—find it easy to make enough money to establish homes in the style desired by them and their actual or prospective brides, then marriage and childbearing will be encouraged. On the other hand, if it is hard to earn enough to support the desired style of life, then the resulting economic stress will lead to deferment of marriage and, for those already married, to the use of contraceptive techniques to avoid childbearing, and perhaps also to the entry of wives into the labor market.

A young man's view of his earning potential is likely to be shaped by his labor-market experience. If times have been good and jobs easy to come by, then his assessment of his income prospects is likely to be correspondingly favorable. On the other hand, while recent experience may play some part, the material aspirations of a young adult are probably largely formed by his earlier economic socialization experience. Thus young persons who have been raised in households where goods were abundant are likely to have developed relatively high standards of consumption. The state of affluence of one's parents' household depends, in turn, on the parents' income, and this is typically a function of the labor-market experience of the father. Thus, the balance between income-earning possibilities of young adults and their desired living levels may be seen as depending largely on the comparative earnings experience (or labor-market experience) of young adults and their parents. In the subsequent discussion, this comparative situation will be termed the "relative economic status" of young adults.

The foregoing obviously does not exhaust the factors relevant to changes in fertility over time.[4] For example, it is possible that the cost of children may increase, perhaps because of better earnings possibilities for wives, and this may discourage childbearing and rearing. Or there may be new developments in contraceptive techniques which lower the effective cost of employing such practices, and their consequent wider adoption reduces the number of children born. In both cases, however, it is important to establish that new influences really are operating independently of the relative status factor.

For example, a deterioration in relative status and associated economic stress would in itself tend to induce increased adoption of fertility control and increased participation in the labor force by wives. In this case it would be a mistake to take an observed rise in contraceptive practice and wives' labor-force participation as reflecting influences making for reduced fertility independently of the change in relative economic status. On the other hand, if there were no change in relative economic status, and new female employment opportunities opened up or a less costly contraceptive became available, then these factors would independently tend to lower fertility.

The possibility of testing the foregoing approach is seriously hampered by the limited data available. However, a reasonable attempt can be made for two subjects—the marital fertility of females 20–24 years old and the marriage patterns of young adults. While the resulting analysis is not as thorough as one might like, it provides a fuller idea of the general approach and of its potential value as an explanation of the fertility swing.

Marital fertility of females 20–24 years old

Relative economic status since the late fifties—Although a fair amount of economic data by age is available for the postwar period, it is not in the most useful form for analyzing fertility behavior. One of the major problems is that of determining whether the economic data relate to essentially the same persons or families as those whose marriage or fertility behavior is being studied. The matching of economic and demographic data in the present study is at best only partially successful, and there is undoubtedly scope for much improvement, especially if one were to go back to the original unpublished data.

With regard to marital fertility the problem is this. The fertility data are classified by age of wife. We wish to analyze these in relation to the labor-market experience of the husband, who is typically at least three years older, and also in relation to the economic status of the parents of both the husband and wife. The data for the parents should relate to the period prior to the marriage of the husband and wife, when each was living at home.

On the basis of the characteristics of husbands and wives sketched earlier, an attempt has been made to develop a rough picture of what one might call the "representative household." In the illustration in Table 11, the behavior to be explained is taken to be the marital fertility of wives 20–24 years old in 1960. As shown in line 3 of the table, the husbands of these women had typically been in the labor market since around 1952. Their experience over the period through 1959 would be pertinent to fertility decisions in 1959 and to observed fertility in 1960.

TABLE 11. ILLUSTRATIVE SKETCH OF LIFE-CYCLE RELATIONSHIPS RELEVANT TO EXPLANATION OF 1960 MARITAL FERTILITY OF FEMALES 20–24 YEARS OLD

Item	(1)	(2)	(3)	(4)	(5)	(6) Year	(7)	(8)	(9)	(10)	(11)
	1950	1951	1952	1953	1954	1955	1956	1957	1958	1959	1960
Husband											
1. Age[a]	16.0	17.0	18.0	19.0	20.0	21.0	22.0	23.0	24.0	25.0	26.0
2. Household and marital status	......Living at parents' home......								....Married, own home....		
3. School and labor force status	....In school..../			......In labor force......							
4. Estimated income experience[b]						*Family Income, Head 14–24 Years Old*					
				$3,670	$3,630	$3,848	$4,331	$4,301			
5. Father's age[a]	45.8	46.8	47.8	48.8	49.8	50.8	51.8	52.8	53.8	54.8	55.8
6. Father's income[b]					*Family Income, Head 45–54 Years Old*						
	$4,769	$4,863	$5,102	$5,670	$5,583	$5,899	$6,186				
Wife											
7. Age[a]	12.8	13.8	14.8	15.8	16.8	17.8	18.8	19.8	20.8	21.8	22.8
8. Household and marital status	......Living at parents' home......								....Married, own home....		
9. School and labor force status	........In school........					/ In LF ./			....In or not in labor force....		
10. Father's age[a]	42.6	43.6	44.6	45.6	46.6	47.6	48.6	49.6	50.6	51.6	52.6
11. Father's income	See line 6.										

[a] Age assumed to be midyear estimate.
[b] Income in 1964 dollars.

Sources and methods: Lines 1, 5, 7, and 10 from Table 2, column 1, panel B, lines 5, 7, 1, and 8 respectively. Lines 2 and 8 from *ibid.*, line 3. Lines 3 and 9, school enrollment status and labor force status were assumed as shown. Lines 4 and 6 from [66, pp. 57–62].

Prior to their marriage in 1956, both spouses were living at home with their parents and were either in school or at work (lines 2, 3, 8, and 9). During the period from 1950 to 1956, the husband's father was in the 45–54-year-old age bracket; and midway in the period, the wife's father moved into this bracket (lines 5 and 10). Thus representative data on the economic status of the parents before the son and daughter left home would be those for households headed by persons 45–54 years old in the 1950–56 period.

Line 4 is an attempt to approximate the husband's earnings experience. It gives the annual figures during 1953–57 of the constant-dollar value of total money income of household heads 14–24 years old (most of whom were actually around 23 years old). Clearly these figures have a number of shortcomings for our purpose. The data are for the same 14–24-year-old age group in each year, 1953–57, even though the males for whom we would like information were from 19 to 23 years old during this time and were household heads only toward the end of the period. Moreover, nothing is included on the income experience of these cohorts in 1958 and 1959—income data for the next available age class, 25–34, seem of dubious relevance. At best, therefore, we are obtaining a rough idea of how these men might have been succeeding over a five-year period that ended two years before the year in which the pertinent fertility decision was made and three years before the fertility observation which is to be explained. Even then the income concept is an imperfect measure of the husband's earning potential. It counts income from all sources, including, for example, the wife's contribution to family income as well as unemployment compensation, and since it is a before-tax measure, it fails to allow for the changing incidence of taxation on take-home pay from one time to another.[5]

As shown in line 6, for the economic status of the parents, we used the total money income of families whose head was 45–54 years old in the period 1950–56, during which time the young persons in whom we are interested were living at home. Clearly there are various shortcomings with this measure also, among them, that the period chosen as relevant to the formation of young persons' aspirations is rather arbitrary.

Dividing the 1953–57 average income estimate for the husbands by the 1950–56 average for the parents, one obtains an estimate of the economic status of the second generation relative to the first for the cohort of wives whose fertility behavior was observed in 1960. In this case, the quotient is 72.7 per cent. Similarly derived estimates for other years for which the necessary data are available are presented in Table 12, and plotted in Chart 2 (broken line).

The economic status and fertility observations are matched as in the illustration above; that is, the relative economic status measure for a given year is linked to observed fertility three years later. It should be emphasized that since our interest is in explaining the temporal movement in fertility, it is the change through time in the relative status measure that is of interest here. One can clearly find fault with the estimate for a given year regarding the assumptions used in estimating both earnings potential and aspirations. The real question, however, is whether these assumptions cor-

TABLE 12. ANNUAL AVERAGE TOTAL MONEY INCOME OF FAMILIES WITH HEAD 14–24 YEARS OLD AS RELATIVE OF THAT OF FAMILIES WITH HEAD 45–54, SPECIFIED PERIODS, 1947–1970; AND MARITAL FERTILITY OF FEMALES 20–24 YEARS OLD, 1940 AND 1950–1970
(income in 1964 dollars)

(1)	(2)	(3)	(4)	(5)	(6)	(7)
Head 14–24 Years Old		Head 45–54 Years Old		(2) ÷ (4)	Marital Fertility	
Period	Income	Period	Income	Per Cent	Year	Per Thousand
					1940	254
					1950	288
					1951	304
					1952	306
					1953	313
					1954	335
					1955	333
					1956	345
1950–54	3,596	1947–53	4,917	73.1	1957	356
1951–55	3,687	1948–54	5,028	73.3	1958	353
1952–56	3,814	1949–55	5,203	73.3	1959	350
1953–57	3,956	1950–56	5,439	72.7	1960	354[a]
1954–58	4,033	1951–57	5,641	71.5	1961	349
1955–59	4,132	1952–58	5,830	70.9	1962	335
1956–60	4,210	1953–59	6,011	69.7	1963	326
1957–61	4,222	1954–60	6,204	68.0	1964	310
1958–62	4,241	1955–61	6,404	66.2	1965	280
1959–63	4,282	1956–62	6,602	64.8	1966	256
1960–64	4,414	1957–63	6,795	65.0	1967	247
1961–65	4,625	1958–64	7,019	65.9	1968	250
1962–66	4,824	1959–65	7,288	66.2	1969	243
1963–67	5,032	1960–66	7,564	66.5	1970	247

[a] Values for 1960 on are not adjusted for underregistration. Unadjusted 1959 value was 347 compared with adjusted value of 350.

Source: Annual income data for 1947–64 from [66, pp. 57–62]; for subsequent years from appropriate annual issues of [57], adjusted to 1964 dollars by consumer price index in [17, p. 249]. For marital fertility see source note for Chart 1.

CHART 2. MARITAL FERTILITY OF FEMALES AGED 20-24, ESTIMATED ABSOLUTE AND RELATIVE INCOME EXPERIENCE OF YOUNG ADULTS, AND PER CENT OF WOMEN MARRIED LESS THAN FIVE YEARS NOT USING ORAL CONTRACEPTION, VARYING PERIODS, 1940-1970

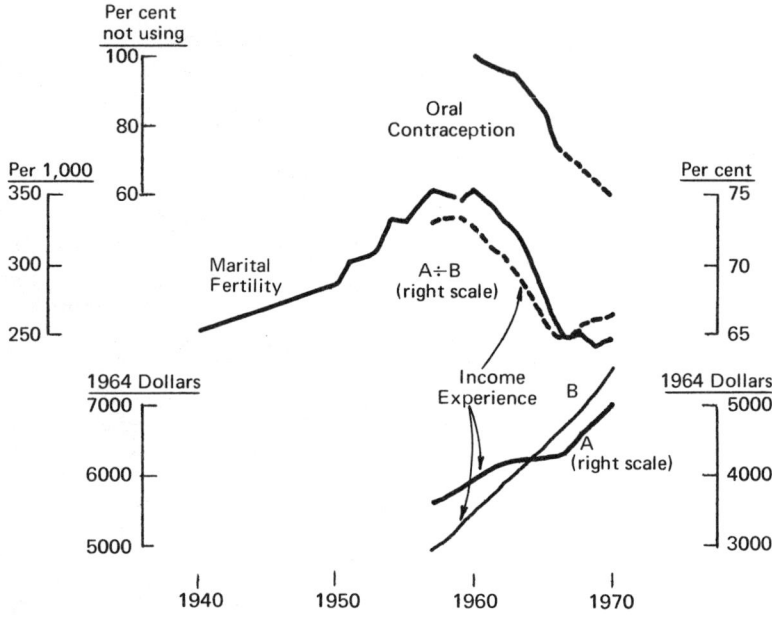

A. Annual average total money income of families with head aged 14-24 for five-year period ending three years before date at which average is plotted (see Table 11).

B. Annual average total money income of families with head aged 45-54 for seven-year period ending four years before date at which average is plotted (see Table 11).

Source: Tables 12 and 15.

---

rectly identify the forces dominating the change during our period in the relative economic status of young adults.

To judge from a comparison of the fertility and relative status curves in Chart 2, the answer is encouraging. The similarity in the movement of the two curves is striking. Both show a pronounced downward movement concentrated in a period of about seven years, though the economic status series appears to lead the fertility series by one year. However, the amplitude of the decline is somewhat greater for the fertility series, and in the later sixties it levels off rather than turns upward as does the status curve. It is interesting to note that the relative status curve is rather smooth in appearance, like the fertility curve. This lends support to the view underlying the present analysis that the decisions determining fertility reflect a cumulation of economic experience over a span of years, not just experience in the single year preceding that to which the fertility observation relates.

What is responsible for the movement shown by the relative economic status curve? In my earlier study three considerations were advanced—aggregate demand, and the relative quantity and quality of young persons [15, pp. 130 ff.]. The association between fertility and relative number of young persons has been noticed by others—for example, Norman B. Ryder observed that "the five years with the lowest total fertility rates were the years 1933–37; the five cohorts with the highest total fertility rates are the cohorts born in 1933–37" [45, p. 591].

However, a cursory look at recent economic data suggests that while aggregate demand is clearly important in determining relative economic status, there is some question as to the channels through which the influence of relative numbers is exerted. Thus, taking the national unemployment rate as indicative of the state of aggregate demand, one finds that the unemployment rate of young persons moves in close correspondence with aggregate demand. In contrast, if one compares years in the 1960s when the relative number of young persons was comparatively large with years in the 1950s when their relative number was comparatively small, holding the national unemployment rate constant, the difference in the relative number of unemployed young persons seems quite small [67, p. 221]. There may be other ways that the relative number variable exerts its influence on the relative well-being of the young, but this result suggests that more work is needed before the importance of this factor can be taken as established.

The oral pill—In public discussion of the recent decline in fertility there is frequent speculation that the introduction and diffusion of oral contraception has been a major causal factor. Professional analysts, while giving some credit to this argument, have been rather cautious in their judgments. It is pointed out, for example, that the decline in fertility started in 1958, but that the oral pill was not authorized for contraceptive use until June 1960, and could not have had a noticeable influence on fertility until 1962 at the earliest [75, p. 9; 34, p. 53].

In their comprehensive 1965 *National Fertility Study,* Ryder and Charles F. Westoff compared year-by-year declines in total fertility from 1960 through 1965 with annual changes in the per cent of married women using oral contraception and found that "the decline in total fertility is well in advance of the increase in pill use" [46, p. 152; cf. also 48]. Their general conclusion was that "it is likely that the direction, if not the degree, of change in marital fertility in the 1960s would have been the same even if the oral contraceptive had not appeared on the scene. However, the tempo of decline at mid-decade can probably be attributed in part to the availability of this highly efficient and highly acceptable method of fertility regulation." [*ibid.*, p. 153] However, immediately following this rather reserved judgment on the effect of the pill in the fertility decline for all women of reproductive age, they went on to state that "its contribution to fertility decline among recently married couples is already substantial. The young American wife has clearly shown an extraordinary enthusiasm for oral contraception." [*ibid.*] Since this last generalization relates precisely to the group in which we are interested, it calls for careful consideration.

In principle, there are two ways in which the pill may have contributed to fertility decline. First, it may have led to greater growth in the use of contraception than would otherwise have occurred. Second, among those who would have been using some form of contraception anyway, the pill might replace less effective methods of fertility control, with a consequent decrease in unintended or unwanted pregnancies.

The data brought together by Ryder and Westoff from the 1955, 1960, and 1965 national surveys of American reproductive behavior throw some light on these issues. Let us consider first the possibility that the pill may have accelerated the trend toward greater use of contraceptives. Table 13 documents the wide extent of contraceptive practice in the United States at all three dates. The lower panel shows that throughout this decade at least 7 out of 10 white wives 20–24 years old had used contraception. In the period when the oral pill was coming into use—between 1960 and 1965—there was an increase in use of contraceptives among these women amounting to about 6 percentage points. But the increase is actually somewhat smaller than the 8 percentage point increase which occurred between 1955 and 1960. This raises some doubt that the pill accelerated the growth of contraceptive practice.

However, as the detail by religion shows, Catholic women are an exception. For them, the percentage point change in the second quinquennium is double that in the first, a development consistent with a positive stimulus from the pill. It is possible, of course, that even among young Protestant wives, the growth in contraceptive use from 1960 to 1965 would have been less if the pill had not been available. One might further argue that contraceptive practice was already so widespread among Protestant women —in 1960 four out of five had used contraception—that much further growth was unlikely, especially if one allows for the possible existence of sterility and subfecundity among nonusers. But this amounts to recognizing that for these women contraceptive use was already so high that the introduction of the oral pill could not have done much to accelerate the growth of contraception.

TABLE 13. PER CENT OF WHITE COUPLES WHO HAVE USED CONTRACEPTION, BY AGE OF WIFE, MARITAL DURATION, PARITY, AND RELIGION, 1955-65

	(1) 1955	(2) 1960	(3) 1965
	Females 18–39 years old		
Total	70	81	84
Married less than 5 years	65	75	82
Parity			
0	42	55	56
1	71	74	81
2	78	89	89
	Females 20–24 years old		
Total	71	79	85
Religion			
Protestant	76	83	88
Catholic	58	·65	79

Source: [46, pp. 107, 109].

It is known that the use of contraception tends to grow in the course of marriage [34, p. 42]. The greater ease of using the pill as a contraceptive might encourage the adoption of contraception earlier in marriage and in this way accelerate the trend toward contraception. Is there evidence that this has been the case? The figures by parity in the upper panel of Table 13 raise doubt that this effect occurred to any substantial extent. There was a noticeable increase between 1955 and 1960 in contraceptive use among couples with no children. Between 1960 and 1965, however, there was little change for this group. All in all, therefore, the possibility of any substantial acceleration in the trend toward contraception due to the pill appears to be confined to Catholic women.

The second way in which the pill might lower fertility is by replacing less effective methods of contraception. Again, Ryder and Westoff provide data relevant to this issue. As shown in Table 14, among Protestants the rise in the use of the pill has been accompanied by declines primarily in the use of the diaphragm and condom. These last two methods are generally considered quite effective, and therefore their replacement by oral contraception would not ordinarily be expected to have much effect on fertility. For Catholics, Table 14 shows that the rise in use of the pill has been accompanied by a decline in the fairly inefficient rhythm method. (For Protestants there was also a small shift of this sort.) For this group,

TABLE 14. PER CENT DISTRIBUTION OF WHITE WIVES 18–39 YEARS OLD BY METHOD OF CONTRACEPTION USED MOST FREQUENTLY AND BY RELIGION, 1955 AND 1965

Method	(1) Total White[a] 1955	(2) Total White[a] 1965	(3) Protestant 1955	(4) Protestant 1965	(5) Catholic 1955	(6) Catholic 1965
Total	100	100	100	100	100	100
Pill[b]	0	27	0	30	0	20
Diaphragm	25	10	29	12	12	4
Condom	27	18	30	19	15	15
Jelly alone	4	2	5	3	—	1
Withdrawal	7	5	7	5	8	7
Rhythm	22	13	12	4	54	36
Douche	8	6	9	7	4	4
All other[c]	7	19	8	20	7	13

[a] Includes all religions.
[b] Includes 3 per cent reporting use of pill in combination with some other method.
[c] Includes other methods used singly and all multiple usage involving both alternate and combined use.
Source: [46, p. 124].

therefore, there is a stronger presumption that the pill did have an effect on fertility through raising the effectiveness of contraceptive practice.[6]

All in all, the evidence available through 1965 suggests that the introduction of the pill may have had a noticeable impact on the fertility of young Catholic women; for non-Catholics, however, the effect would seem to be small at best. Since Catholics comprise less than three-tenths of females 20–24 years old the implication is that the effect of the pill on the birth rate of the group as a whole was probably quite limited.

In Chart 2, data on the adoption of oral contraception have been plotted with a one-year lead over fertility. The per cent not using the pill is shown; hence, a downward movement in the pill series would lead one to expect a corresponding movement in fertility. The series relates to use among women who have been married less than five years. Of the annual series available this seems most relevant to the 20–24-year-old women whose fertility is being analyzed here. I have made a rough extrapolation of the series from 1965 to 1969 on the basis of preliminary information from the 1970 fertility survey reported to me by Norman B. Ryder (Table 15).

As shown in the chart, throughout the 1960s there was a marked trend

TABLE 15. PER CENT OF MARRIED WOMEN (HUSBAND PRESENT) BORN SINCE MID-1920 CURRENTLY USING ORAL CONTRACEPTION, BY MARITAL DURATION, SPECIFIED YEARS 1959–1969

	(1)	(2)
	Marital Duration	
Year	0–19 years	0–4 years
1959	0	0
1960	0.5	n
1961	1.1	3.9
1962	2.7	5.5
1963	6.3	10.9
1964	10.9	15.1
1965	17.9	25.6
1969	25.5?	40.0?

Source: [48, p. 2], except 1969 which is my tentative estimate based on preliminary information from the 1970 National Fertility Survey reported to me by Norman B. Ryder.

toward adoption of the pill. Presumably this would have exerted a depressing influence on fertility, but as the foregoing discussion suggests, a much smaller influence on fertility than one would expect from data on adoption of the pill alone. Of particular interest is the fact that (by our estimate) the rise in the use of oral contraception between 1965 and 1969 was as great as between 1963 and 1965 (about a 15 percentage point change in each period). Between 1966 and 1970, however, marital fertility hardly changed, whereas from 1964 to 1966 marital fertility dropped by one-sixth. This raises further doubt about the pill being a dominant influence in the fertility movement of the 1960s.

Considering the fertility decline in the light of the changes in both economic status and oral contraception, one is led to the conclusion that relative economic status has been the dominant factor in the fertility movement since the late fifties. However, its influence has been modified by the appearance and spread of the pill. Thus, due to the negative impact of the pill, the fertility decline to 1966 was somewhat greater than might have been expected on the basis of the change in relative economic status alone. Similarly, after 1966, fertility tended to level off, rather than to rise, as one would have expected from the movement in the status series alone. However, when more and better data are available for both oral contraception and economic status, a multivariate analysis would obviously be desirable.

Relative economic status since the thirties—With regard to the complete movement in fertility since the 1930s, oral contraception is obviously an inadequate explanation, since it has no bearing at all on the period of the baby boom. The economic status argument is, in principle, potentially relevant; but testing of the hypothesis for the longer period, including the baby boom, is handicapped by the lack of income data.

Some limited information which is available, cited in my previous study, does suggest a gain in the relative economic status of young adults from around 1940 to 1950. Thus, between 1941 and the late forties income of younger age groups grew substantially more rapidly than for others [15, pp. 116–117, cf. also pp. 105–107].

If one is willing to accept a rather simple assumption, it is possible to construct a time series of the relative economic status of young adults that may at least indicate major shifts over the period since 1930. The assumption is that the relative well-being of young adults depends on how the general unemployment rate during the period in which the sons were in the labor market compares with that during the period their fathers were in the market. For example, if a given cohort of sons experiences much poorer labor-market conditions than did their fathers and a second cohort experiences better conditions than did their fathers, then one would expect that the relative economic status of the first cohort of sons would be lower than that of the second.

The life-cycle relationships shown in Table 11 were again used as a guide in implementing this approach. Thus, to obtain a measure of relative economic status pertinent to the fertility of females 20–24 years old in 1960, I computed average unemployment rates, as follows:

A. For the son (the fathers of the 1960 babies): an average from 1952–59 when the sons, 18 to 25 years old, were in the labor market.

B. For the son's father: an average from 1937–56, when the father was from 33 to 52 years old, and the son from 3 to 22 and was living in his parents' home.

I have used longer period averages for both items A and B than in the income analysis. In the case of item A, the unemployment data, unlike the income data previously used, were available for the entire period of the son's labor-market experience. With regard to item B, it was felt that the longer period average of the unemployment data would give a better index of the economic status of the father. For example, a son who was 26 in 1940 would have come from a household in which the father by 1930 was already 45. The high employment situation of the 1920s would have benefited the parents' household—perhaps, for example, by fostering home ownership—and this experience should be reflected in an index of the father's economic status. However, the specific periods chosen here and else-

CHART 3. BIRTH RATE OF FEMALES AGED 20-24 AND ESTIMATED ABSOLUTE AND RELATIVE UNEMPLOYMENT EXPERIENCE OF YOUNG ADULTS, 1930-1970

A. Average unemployment rate (inverted) during eight-year period ending one year before date at which average is plotted. Data for 1942-45 excluded from average.

B. Average unemployment rate (inverted) during twenty year period ending four years before date at which average is plotted.

Source: Table 16.

where in the analysis are obviously arbitrary to some extent, and there is need for further exploration in this area.

The unemployment averages, calculated as above, are plotted (inverted) in Chart 3. The use of general unemployment rates, rather than rates more relevant to the specific age groups, is a shortcoming of the approach. However, the general rate may move in roughly the same way as the true cohort rates. A crude check of this for the mid-fifties onward suggests this is so.

The fertility series in Chart 3 is that for total rather than marital fertility of those 20–24 years old, since the latter is not available for the longer period analysis. The series starts in 1930. As shown in my earlier study, an adequate explanation of fertility movements in the 1920s and before requires separate study of the foreign-born white, rural native white, and urban native white populations, each of which was subject to rather different influences. The decade of the 1930s represents a transition to the more homogeneous population situation of the post-World War II era, so that even for the 1930s the present analytical framework is only of limited relevance.

Series A in Chart 3 shows the eight-year average of the unemployment rate, indicating the general labor-market conditions in the period during which the sons had been in the market; series B shows the twenty-year average, relating to the father's experience. In series A, for the younger men, the average is computed excluding the 1942–45 values, on the grounds that at this time most of the young men were in the armed forces at low pay, and that the very low civilian unemployment rates prevailing during the period were not germane to their income experience. These wartime years are included, however, in the father's average since they are relevant to his experience, though it might be argued that because of wartime rationing these rates exaggerate the prosperity of fathers.

In the middle panel of Chart 3, series A has been subtracted from series B to obtain a measure of the labor-market experience of sons relative to their fathers, and hence implicitly of the relative economic status of sons. For example, the 1935 value of −8.6 per cent (Table 16) implies that men reaching age 26 in that year had encountered a labor market in the preceding eight years in which the unemployment rate was on the average 8.6 percentage points worse than that experienced by their fathers when the sons were growing up. Correspondingly the 1955 value of +5.6 signifies that the men reaching 26 at that date had experienced considerably better average labor market conditions than their fathers had. Implicitly, therefore, the economic status of sons compared with fathers was much better in 1955 than in 1935.

The movement of the relative status series indicates a decline in the relative position of sons in the 1930s, a marked improvement to the 1950s and then a noticeable decline to the mid-sixties. In the latter period, how-

Causes of the Changing Fertility of Young Adults · 195

TABLE 16. AVERAGE UNEMPLOYMENT RATE, SPECIFIED PERIODS THROUGH 1969, AND AGE-SPECIFIC BIRTH RATE, WHITE[a] FEMALES 20–24 YEARS OLD, 1930–1970

(1)	(2)	(3)	(4)	(5)	(6)	(7)
\multicolumn{4}{l}{Unemployment Rate, Per Cent of Civilian Labor Force}			
Eight-Year Average Ending in Specified Year		Twenty-Year Average Ending in Specified Year			Age-Specific Birth Rate	
Year	Rate[b]	Year	Rate	(4)−(2)	Year	Rate Per Thousand
1929	4.2	1926	5.3	1.1	1930	139
1930	4.3	1927	5.5	1.2	1931	131
1931	6.0	1928	5.2	− 0.8	1932	126
1932	8.2	1929	5.1	− 3.1	1933	118
1933	10.8	1930	5.2	− 5.6	1934	122
1934	13.3	1931	5.7	− 7.6	1935	121
1935	15.3	1932	6.7	− 8.6	1936	121
1936	16.9	1933	7.7	− 9.2	1937	124
1937	18.3	1934	8.4	− 9.9	1938	128
1938	19.6	1935	8.9	−10.7	1939	125
1939	19.7	1936	9.5	−10.2	1940	131
1940	18.6	1937	10.0	− 8.6	1941	142
1941	16.7	1938	10.9	− 5.8	1942	163
1942	16.0	1939	11.6	− 4.4	1943	161
1943	15.3	1940	12.1	− 3.2	1944	148
1944	15.0	1941	12.1	− 2.9	1945	135
1945	15.2	1942	11.9	− 3.3	1946	180
1946	11.4	1943	11.8	0.4	1947	208
1947	8.1	1944	11.6	3.5	1948	196
1948	5.4	1945	11.5	6.1	1949	195
1949	4.4	1946	11.6	7.2	1950	190
1950	4.6	1947	11.6	7.0	1951	206
1951	4.4	1948	11.6	7.2	1952	213
1952	4.2	1949	11.7	7.5	1953	220
1953	4.0	1950	11.6	7.6	1954	231
1954	4.2	1951	10.9	6.7	1955	236
1955	4.3	1952	9.9	5.6	1956	247
1956	4.3	1953	8.8	4.6	1957	254
1957	4.1	1954	8.0	3.9	1958	251
1958	4.3	1955	7.2	2.9	1959	253
1959	4.6	1956	6.5	1.9	1960	253[c]
1960	4.9	1957	6.1	1.2	1961	248
1961	5.3	1958	5.4	0.1	1962	238
1962	5.3	1959	4.9	− 0.4	1963	225
1963	5.5	1960	4.4	− 1.1	1964	213

TABLE 16. (Continued)

(1)	(2)	(3)	(4)	(5)	(6)	(7)
Unemployment Rate, Per Cent of Civilian Labor Force						
Eight-Year Average Ending in Specified Year		Twenty-Year Average Ending in Specified Year			Age-Specific Birth Rate	
Year	Rate[b]	Year	Rate	(4)−(2)	Year	Rate Per Thousand
1964	5.7	1961	4.2	− 1.5	1965	190
1965	5.7	1962	4.3	− 1.4	1966	180
1966	5.3	1963	4.5	− 0.8	1967	169
1967	5.1	1964	4.7	− 0.4	1968	159
1968	4.9	1965	4.8	− 0.1	1969	156
1969	4.4	1966	4.8	0.4	1970	158

[a] Native white, 1930–39. (1940 value for native white equals that for total white.)

[b] Averages ending in 1942 through 1952 exclude yearly values for 1942 through 1945.

[c] Values for 1960 on are not adjusted for underregistration. Unadjusted 1959 value was 252 compared with adjusted value of 253.

Sources: Annual unemployment rates for 1890–99 from [36, p. 522], for 1900–1928, from [35, p. 215], and for 1929–1969 from [17, p. 222]. For birth rate, see source note for Chart 1.

ever, the relative status of sons was still considerably higher than it had been in the 1930s. As a comparison with the birth series shows, these movements accord reasonably well with the ups and downs shown by the fertility rate. There is some suggestion that the economic series leads the fertility series in timing in the post-World War II period, but in view of the much greater crudity of this relative status index than that used in Chart 2, it is probably best not to make much of this timing difference. What is noteworthy is that the amplitude of the recent fertility decline leaves the series at present in much the same position relative to its preceding trough and peak as the relative status series.

It is also worth pointing out that the relative unemployment rates of young males (the differences between series A and B) correspond better to the fertility movement than do the absolute unemployment rates (series A alone). The relative series is the one which, like the fertility series, shows a pronounced hump in the postwar period, with a peak much above the beginning and ending levels. In contrast, the absolute series has a postwar peak not much different from its 1930 and late sixties values, and the decline from the peak to the sixties is very mild. It seems, therefore, that the evidence, crude as it is, is consistent with the hypothesis that shifts in the relative economic status of young adults have played a major role in the swing in their fertility performance since the 1930s.

In closing this section, it is perhaps worth emphasizing that this "economic" analysis of fertility sees economic conditions as influencing fertility through both the income and taste variables of the economic theory of consumer choice. In presenting a general theoretical framework for fertility analysis several years ago, I explicitly argued for the inclusion of taste variables in economic analyses of fertility on the grounds that this would make it possible to merge the contributions of both sociology and economics [16, cf. also 51]. Despite this, the view persists that economic explanations preclude the possibility of taste changes.[7] In his recent critique of my work, Alan Sweezy concluded:

> I am not suggesting that people take no account of income, employment opportunities, etc., in deciding how many children to have. That would be to fly too blatantly in the face of common sense. What I am suggesting is that such considerations have been relatively minor in their influence and that changes in fertility have for the most part been the result of changes in attitudes—changes in 'tastes' rather than in the constraints of income and price, to use the economist's language [55, p. 266].

As the present section should make clear, my argument is in fact that the taste variable is an important fertility determinant, which interacts with current and recent income experience, to influence the fertility behavior of young adults.[8] But the change in tastes—that is, in the goods aspirations of young adults—is itself seen as determined chiefly by economic circumstances; namely, those experienced by young adults in their parents' households as they are growing up.

At the same time, recent and current economic conditions operate too on the fertility of young adults via the "income" variable, by shaping the "permanent income" estimates of young adults. Thus, both income and taste variables are influenced by economic conditions, though not by identical ones. The relative status variable is thus a composite of both the taste and income variables of economic theory. If my earlier papers failed to make this entirely clear, I hope the current one will set the matter straight. Although Sweezy asserted that the taste variable is important he did not make clear what mechanism of taste formation or evidence of change in tastes he had in mind—the only empirical reference is to the attitudes expressed in conversations with him by "a number of women who were in college just before or during World War II" [*ibid.*, p. 263]. To say the least, this seems like a somewhat dubious basis for generalization.

Marriage behavior of young adults

Marriage patterns—The analysis of marriage patterns focuses on males 20–24 and 25–29 years old and females 18–19 and 20–24 years old, the age-sex groups in which most marriages begin and among whom the principal changes in marriage behavior since 1940 have occurred. (In 1960, the number of those who had ever been married was 77 per cent for males 25–29 years old, and 71 per cent for females 20–24 years old.) These groups are, in addition, those whose behavior is most relevant to the fertility changes in which we are interested.

The basic data used here are annual sample survey observations on the per cent that has ever been married. A problem with these data is that the dates of occurrence of the actual marriages are uncertain—the reported proportion of males 25–29 years old who had ever been married in 1960 relates to marriages of these men which may have taken place at any time during the preceding decade or more. We have dealt with this problem as follows. Since relatively few males marry before the age of 20, it is assumed that the time reference of the series for males 20–24 years old is to marriages over the preceding five-year period. (In effect, the per cent ever-married for this cohort is assumed to be zero five years earlier.)

Similarly, since relatively few females marry before the age of 18, the time reference of the series for females 18–19 years old is assumed to be the preceding two years.[9] For males 25–29 years old and females 20–24 years old the change in the per cent ever-married during the preceding five years is obtained by subtracting the observed or estimated values for the cohort at the start of the quinquennium. For example, for males 25–29 years old in 1960 the 1955–60 change in per cent ever-married is obtained as the difference between the per cent ever-married for males 20–24 years old in 1955 and 25–29 years old in 1960. Hence, three of the four basic series relate to marriage behavior in the preceding quinquennium, and the fourth—that for females 18–19 years old—in the preceding two years.

The series are shown in Table 17 and plotted in Chart 4. The original data relate to March or April of a particular year—for example, 1960—and in the form used here, they refer to behavior during the preceding five-year period—strictly speaking, from March 1955 to March 1960. The observations have been plotted at the terminal date of the quinquennium to which they most nearly relate. For example, that for March 1955–March 1960 is plotted at 1959 since it relates chiefly to 1955–59, rather than 1956–60.

There are noticeable three- to four-year fluctuations in the series. (As noted earlier, for women under 20, these movements are probably responsible for the fluctuations shown by the series on marital fertility.) In the original marital-status data these fluctuations appear principally in the series for males 20–24 years old and females 18–19 years old, and, as can be seen from the chart, are similar in timing. Their appearance here in the series for the two older age groups is largely a consequence of the differencing procedure employed in deriving the figures for the older groups. Whether the fluctuations reflect real world developments or are a statistical artifact is unclear. Since our concern is with the longer term movements, we have used where possible a four-item moving average (shown by the broken line) to bring out the underlying tendencies more clearly.

The series for males 20-24 years old and females 18-19 years old show that there was a noticeable upward movement in the proportions marrying between 1939 and the 1950s. The four series available for the

TABLE 17. PER CENT EVER-MARRIED, MALES 20-24 YEARS OLD AND FEMALES 18-19 YEARS OLD, 1939 AND 1948-1969, AND CHANGE IN PER CENT EVER-MARRIED DURING PRECEDING QUINQUENNIUM MALES 25-29 YEARS OLD AND FEMALES 20-24 YEARS OLD, 1953-1969

	(1)	(2)	(3)	(4)	(5)	(6)	(7)	(8)
			Change During Preceding Quinquennium in					
	Per Cent Ever-Married		Per Cent Ever-Married		Four Item Moving Average of			
Year	Males 20-24	Females 18-19	Males 25-29	Females 20-24	(1)	(2)	(3)	(4)
1939	27.8	22.2						
1948	44.3	32.1						
1949	43.9	32.1						
1950	48.3	32.1						
1951	51.7	32.2			47.1	32.1		
1952	51.3	33.8			48.8	32.6		
1953	45.8	29.8	32.5	52.7	49.3	32.0		
1954	51.2	33.0	28.0	53.1	50.0	32.2		
1955	50.8	34.0	28.4	54.8	49.8	32.7		
1956	48.2	30.3	25.1	54.5	49.0	31.8	28.5	53.8
1957	47.9	33.6	25.9	53.5	49.5	32.7	26.9	54.0
1958	48.6	34.1	29.5	55.4	48.9	33.0	27.2	54.6
1959	45.3	29.1	25.8	52.9	47.5	31.8	26.6	54.1
1960	44.9	28.3	26.9	53.2	46.7	31.3	27.0	53.8
1961	47.6	30.4	30.4	54.8	46.6	30.5	28.2	54.1
1962	46.4	29.0	30.8	52.3	46.1	29.2	28.5	53.3
1963	44.1	27.9	32.2	51.6	45.8	28.9	30.1	53.0
1964	47.1	26.6	37.5	52.7	46.3	28.5	32.7	52.9
1965	48.2	26.0	38.4	55.5	46.5	27.4	34.7	53.0
1966	46.2	23.8	37.2	52.4	46.4	26.1	36.3	53.1
1967	44.9	23.2	32.8	50.1	46.6	24.9	36.5	52.7
1968	45.4	22.7	37.9	50.6	46.2	23.9	36.6	52.2
1969	44.8	24.5	33.2	51.3	45.3	23.6	35.3	51.1

Source: Annual marital status reports in [58].

CHART 4. PER CENT EVER-MARRIED, MALES AGED 20-24 AND FEMALES AGED 18-19, AND CHANGE IN PER CENT EVER-MARRIED DURING PRECEDING FIVE YEARS, MALES AGED 25-29 AND FEMALES AGED 20-24, AND PERCENTAGE RATIO OF MALES AGED 20-29 TO FEMALES AGED 18-24, VARIOUS DATES, 1939-1969

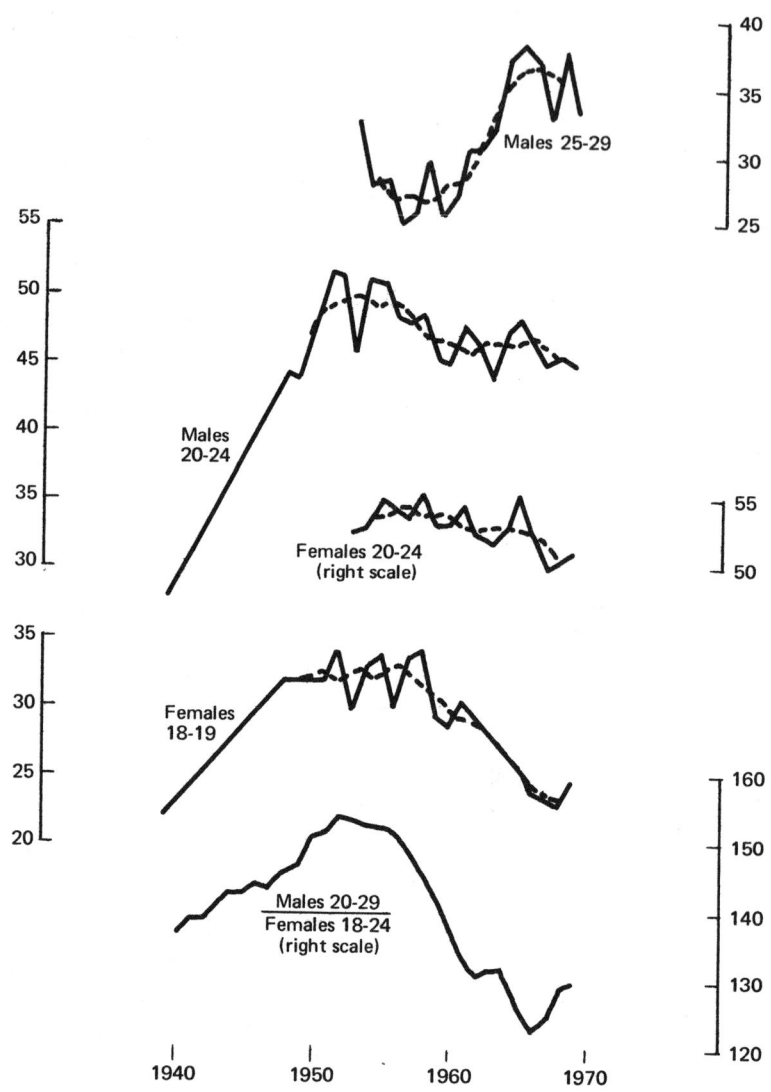

Note: Broken line is four item moving average of series.
Source: Tables 17 and 18.

subsequent period show some divergence in the patterns for the two sexes. The proportions marrying have turned downward for females, especially among those 18-19 years old. For males 20-24 years old, there is a downturn to the early sixties, and then a leveling off or slight rise. Among males 25-29 years old the proportion marrying has continued to rise. The extent of the rise since the fifties shown for this group is perhaps somewhat exaggerated, since the relatively low proportions marrying in the fifties partly reflect the exceptionally high proportions of this cohort which had married five years earlier at age 20-24.

Determinants of marriage patterns—The factor which has attracted most attention in connection with developments since the 1950s, and particularly the declining marriage proportions among young females, is the so-called "marriage squeeze." The basic idea is that at a given time the proportion of a given sex-age group marrying—for example, females 18-24 years old—depends in part on the proportion of males to females in the appropriate age groupings [1, 12, 24, 30].[10] Since women typically marry men somewhat older than they are, the postwar baby boom has produced a situation in which an upsurge in the number of young females eligible for marriage has not been matched by a contemporaneous rise in the number of males available for marriage. The resulting "marriage squeeze," it is argued, has consequently led to a decline in the proportions of young women marrying.

Various indicators of the marriage squeeze have been developed [*ibid.*]. None of these fit the observed marriage patterns very closely, in part because of shifts in marriage behavior within the component age-sex groups which are themselves partly induced by changes in the relative sizes of the groups. For our purposes, a ratio of males 20-29 years old to females 18-24 years old provides a reasonably satisfactory indicator of the squeeze (Table 18). As shown in Chart 4 this shows a noticeable drop since the late fifties consistent with the hypothesis that the growing shortage of young males has been at least partly responsible for the declining proportion of young females marrying. The figure also shows that the incidence of this has been especially concentrated among females 18-19 years old. Reference to our earlier discussion of Tables 9 and 10 further suggests that this decline has been particularly large among women with less than high school education, the group which is probably in the weakest competititve position in the marriage market.

It is clear, however, that the marriage squeeze is far from a complete explanation of the marriage movements since 1939. The squeeze ratio does move upward from 1939 to the 1950s, and this is consistent with the marriage trends for young females in that period. However, the ratio cannot explain the movement in the proportion of young males marrying, es-

TABLE 18. RATIO OF WHITE MALES 20–29 YEARS OLD TO WHITE FEMALES 18–24 YEARS OLD, 1940–1969
(per cent)

(1) Year	(2) Ratio	(3) Year	(4) Ratio
1940	137	1955	153
1941	139	1956	152
1942	139	1957	149
1943	141	1958	146
1944	143	1959	142
1945	143	1960	138
1946	144	1961	133
1947	144	1962	131
1948	146	1963	132
1949	147	1964	132
1950	151	1965	126
1951	152	1966	123
1952	154	1967	125
1953	154	1968	129
1954	153	1969	130

Source: [59, Nos. 311 (July 2, 1965), 314 (August 19, 1965), 385 (February 14, 1968), and 441 (March 19, 1970)]. Data are for population including armed forces overseas.

pecially the noticeable rise in marriages among young males between 1939 and the 1950s. It seems clear that an adequate explanation of marriage patterns must take account not only of the numerical proportions between the relevant age-sex groups, but also of the economic circumstances of young adults. In particular, the economic status of young males, who are typically the initiators of marriage bids, may be taken as critical.

A test of this view is again handicapped by the scarcity of data. However, following the line of reasoning in the preceding fertility analysis, I have constructed from national unemployment rates a crude index of the relative economic status of young males 20–24 years old, the age group of males most relevant to the marriage behavior of females under the age of 20 (Table 19). This status measure differs from that used in the preceding section in two respects. As an indicator of the labor-market conditions of young males, a five-year average rather than an eight-year average has been used because the former more nearly reflects the duration of the labor-market experience of these young men prior to marriage (Table 11). For older men, I have again used a 20-year average but the terminal date is the same as for the younger men, rather than three years earlier, on the grounds that the sons were at home until their marriage. As in the earlier section, values for 1942–45 have been omitted from the average for younger men.

As shown in Chart 5, the series on relative economic status of sons versus fathers traces a path broadly similar to that in the proportion of males 20–24 years old who were ever married. Associated with the marked improvement in economic status between 1939 and the early 1950s there was a marked rise in the percentage of males 20–24 years old who were ever married. Subsequently, there was a downturn in both series. The decline in the status series leads that in the fertility series; but as in the earlier analysis, it is hard to know whether this is real or simply a reflection of the crudity of the status indicator. In the sixties the relative status series moved upward. A corresponding movement appeared to be taking place

TABLE 19. AVERAGE UNEMPLOYMENT RATES, SPECIFIED PERIODS THROUGH 1969

(1) Year	(2) Five-Year Average Ending in Specified Year	(3) Twenty-Year Average Ending in Specified Year	(4) Difference (3)−(2)
1939	17.5	11.6	−5.9
1948	3.9[a]	11.6	7.7
1949	4.4[a]	11.7	7.3
1950	4.6	11.6	7.0
1951	4.4	10.9	6.5
1952	4.3	9.9	5.6
1953	4.1	8.8	4.7
1954	4.0	8.0	4.0
1955	3.8	7.2	3.4
1956	4.0	6.5	2.5
1957	4.2	6.1	1.9
1958	5.0	5.4	0.4
1959	5.0	4.9	−0.1
1960	5.2	4.4	−0.8
1961	5.8	4.2	−1.6
1962	6.0	4.3	−1.7
1963	5.8	4.5	−1.3
1964	5.7	4.7	−1.0
1965	5.5	4.8	−0.7
1966	4.9	4.8	−0.1
1967	4.6	4.8	0.2
1968	4.2	4.8	0.6
1969	3.8	4.7	0.9

[a] Excludes values for 1944 and 1945.
Sources: Same as for Table 16.

CHART 5. PER CENT EVER-MARRIED, MALES AGED 20-24, AND ESTIMATED ABSOLUTE AND RELATIVE UNEMPLOYMENT EXPERIENCE OF YOUNG ADULTS, 1939-1969

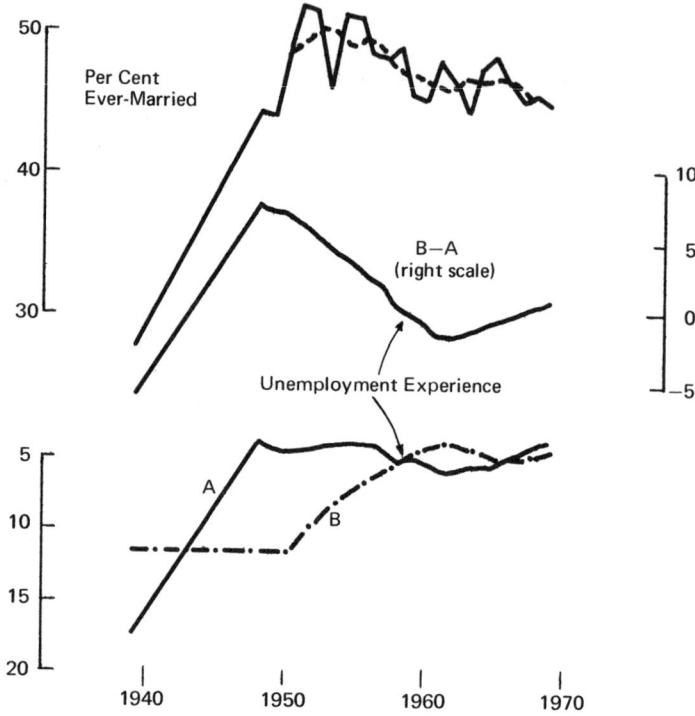

A. Average unemployment rate (inverted) during five-year period ending with year at which average is plotted.

B. Average unemployment rate (inverted) during twenty-year period ending with year at which average is plotted.

Sources: Table 17, columns 1 and 5, and Table 19.

for the marriage series, but then it turned downward toward the end of the period, reflecting a drop in the proportions marrying in the years after 1965. This disparate movement in the two series at the end of the period may reflect a rise in the percentage of young men in military service as a result of the Vietnam War. Between 1965 and 1968 the proportion of the male noninstitutional population 20–24 years old in the armed forces rose sharply from around 15 to 22 per cent.[11] The evidence appears broadly consistent with the hypothesis that economic circumstances play a part in determining the marriage behavior of young males.

In conclusion, the implications of this discussion for the fertility behavior of females 15–19 years old should be noted. The earlier analysis showed that the fertility of this group was noticeably influenced by changes in the proportions of women marrying. The present analysis suggests that these changes in marriage behavior have been partly due in turn to a marriage-squeeze phenomenon, and, until 1965, partly to changes in the relative economic status of males in their early twenties. Moreover, the rough conformity of the marital fertility series for those 15–19 years old and our crude status index (Charts 1 and 5) suggests that the status factor may also have operated on fertility within marriage. However, the available data do not permit an adequate testing of this hypothesis.

Relations Between Period Fertility Rates,
Attitudes Regarding Family Size,
and Completed Fertility Rates

The last two decades have seen the development of cohort analysis as a tool of fertility research. Cohort fertility measures are designed to follow the historical experience of groups of women as they proceed through the childbearing years, whereas period measures, the type used in the preceding analysis, relate to fertility in specific calendar years.

With the development of cohort analysis there has come a tendency to discount the importance of analyzing period rates. Cohort analysis sees period rates as the result of two types of household decisions, one relating to the total number of children wanted and one to the timing of births. A typical statement is the following:

> The number of children borne by a cohort in a particular year may be regarded as the product of two variables: the number of children the women of the cohort will have by the end of the childbearing period, and the proportion of children they have in the specified year. If it were known, for example, that the women of the 1930 cohort would have 3,100 births per 1,000 women by the end of the childbearing period and that they would have 2 per cent of these births during age 35, attained in 1965, then one would know that the central birth rate for the 1930 cohort during 1965 would be 62 births per 1,000. In brief, cohort analysis views annual fertility rates as the resultant of two factors: completed fertility and the distribution of births over the ages of the reproductive period.
>
> In the process of analyzing trends in fertility, attempts are made to state the extent to which changes in each of these factors are responsible for changes in annual measures of fertility [34, p. 256].

This view has been carried over into work on fertility projections—indeed, interest in this application was an important stimulus to the development of cohort analysis. The essential idea is to couple survey results on the expectations of women of childbearing age as to their completed family size with assumptions about the timing of childbearing, so as to derive projections of annual fertility rates [59, No. 381; 47, 50]. Note that in this approach the period rate is again taken partly as a function of the completed rate.

Still another illustration of this viewpoint was presented in Judith Blake's analysis of the survey results on ideal family size from 1936 through 1961 [7]. She found an uptrend in family-size ideals over this period, and concluded that the postwar upsurge in fertility was partly an effect of this trend: "Apparently, the baby-boom experience in the United States has been at least in part a result of a long-term shift in preferences among women from families of two and three children to families of three and four" [*ibid.*, p. 166]. Blake did not inquire into possible causes of the trend in ideal family size, though this is obviously an important issue.

Historical experience

Despite the prevalence of the view that period fertility is in part determined by completed fertility, various considerations suggest that the opposite is more nearly correct; that is, that the period rate, especially among young adults, partly determines attitudes toward family size and eventual completed fertility. In my earlier study, I pointed out that there is a high positive correlation between cumulative fertility through age 29 and completed fertility [15, p. 136]. I noted also a suggestion by Freedman, Goldberg, and Bumpass that what may be initially viewed by young persons simply as postponement of births may, as such postponement continues, lead to a downward revision of views about completed family size and eventually lower actual completed fertility [22; cf. also 20, p. 189]. Additional evidence and analysis now make possible a fuller development of this view.

The basic proposition is that the ongoing fertility experience of young adults tends to shape their statements of expectations and ideals as to completed family size as well as their eventual completed fertility. For example, as current marriage and childbearing tapers off among young adults, this leads with some lag to a downward shift in their attitudes toward completed family size and eventually in actual completed size. The reasoning is as follows:

1. Evidence from surveys over the past few decades of the family size ideals, desires, and expectations of Americans have repeatedly shown what Judith Blake termed a "remarkable consensus" among

the great majority of Americans for a two- to four-child family [6, p. 67].
2. This repeated finding has led Freedman, Coombs, and Bumpass to suggest that below and above this range "social sanctions must operate . . . to discourage 'too few' or 'too many' children but that the *differences between two, three, or four are socially less important."* [21, p. 253, my emphasis]. A study of the intensity of family-size preferences by Goldberg and Coombs supports this conclusion that Americans do not differentiate strongly between the desirability of two, three, and four children [25].
3. If the social norm regarding family size does in fact comprise a range of almost equally acceptable numbers from two to four children, then it seems likely that early adult experience plays a critical role in determining where within that range a cohort will ultimately end up. If relative status circumstances induce early marriage and childbearing, a cohort will tend to fall higher within the socially sanctioned range than if relative status circumstances encourage deferment of marriage and childbearing. Important differences between cohorts in their economic circumstances during the later childbearing ages might modify this tendency, but such differences would ordinarily be rare.
4. Similarly, variations from one cohort to another in relative status circumstances will tend through their effect on early childbearing experience to produce shifts, chiefly within the two- to four-child range, in ideals and expectations about completed family size. Changes in attitudes toward completed family size would tend to lag behavior changes because the latter would at first be viewed as changes in the timing of childbearing, rather than in completed size of family, as suggested by Freedman, Goldberg, and Bumpass [op. cit.].

Evidence supporting this reasoning is provided by the recent downturn in fertility. (The series on attitudes does not extend far enough back in time to permit a corresponding analysis for the earlier upturn.) The upper two curves of Chart 6 show two of the historical series compiled by Judith Blake on ideal family size (extended by me to 1970) [6, 7]. The top curve shows that since at least 1936 the proportion of young white women considering two to four children ideal has been, almost without exception, between 85 and 95 per cent, with little indication of any trend. However, as is shown by the second curve, that on mean ideal family size, within this range there was an uptrend and then a decline in ideal family size. Because of sampling variability and the intermittent timing of the observations, precise dating of the peak is difficult—in the present data, the indicated date is 1961 (Table 20).

CHART 6. IDEAL AND EXPECTED NUMBER OF CHILDREN, AND AGE-SPECIFIC AND CUMULATIVE BIRTH RATE, WHITE FEMALES, SPECIFIED AGE GROUPS UNDER 30, 1936-1970

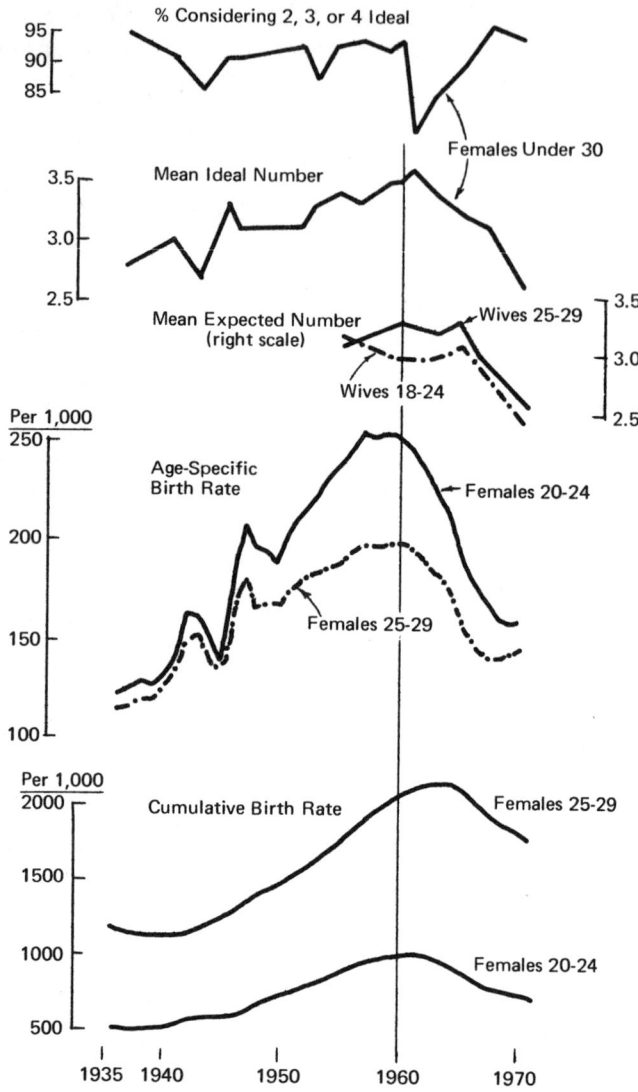

Source: Ideal size, from Table 20; expected size, from Table 21. Age-specific birth rates (white women), see source note for Chart 1. Cumulative birth rates as of January 1 of specified year (all women), for 1936-1958, from [81, pp. 46-47]; 1959-1963, from [72, p. 61]; 1964-68, from [80, Table 1-15]; 1969, January [58, No. 178], November [58, No. 196]; 1971, [58, No. 232].

TABLE 20. NUMBER OF CHILDREN CONSIDERED IDEAL BY WHITE FEMALES UNDER 30 YEARS OLD, 1936–1970

Survey Date	(1) Per Cent Considering 2, 3, or 4 Children Ideal	(2) Mean Ideal Number of Children
November 1936	95	2.8
March 1941	91	3.0
May 1943	85	2.7
November 1945	91	3.3
January 1947	91	3.1
October 1948	92	3.1
March 1952	93	3.1
May 1953	87	3.3
April 1955	93	3.4
February 1957	94	3.3
December 1959	92	3.5
May–July 1960	94	3.5
May 1961	78	3.6
April 1963	85	3.4
January 1966	91	3.2
December 1967	96	3.1
December 1970	94	2.6

Source: 1936–1961 from [7, p. 167], 1963 and 1966 from [6, p. 69], and 1967 and 1970 from unpublished tables from American Institute of Public Opinion polls Nos. 755 and 821. The age group covered in most surveys is 21–29, but there are a few deviations from this (see sources).

The other attitude series in Chart 6 is on family-size expectations as reported in surveys conducted at various dates since 1955 (Table 21). These data, which relate only to married women, indicate little change in expectations through 1965, after which a downturn occurs.

Consider now the series on the actual fertility experience of the women responding to these attitude surveys (the four lowest curves in the figure). The annual age-specific birth rates, those relating to current fertility performance, level off and turn down before the downturns in both family-size ideals and expectations.[12] The downturn in cumulative fertility rates tends to lag behind that in family-size ideals, but leads the downturn in expectations. On balance, then, the evidence is more consistent with the view that changes in behavior precede those in attitudes, rather than vice versa.

TABLE 21. MEAN NUMBER OF CHILDREN EXPECTED BY WHITE WIVES 18–24 AND 25–29 YEARS OLD, 1955–1971

	(1) Age of Wife	(2)
Year	18–24	25–29
1955	3.2	3.1
1960	3.0	3.3
1962–1964	3.0	3.2
1965	3.1	3.3
1967	2.9	3.0
1971	2.4	2.6

Source: 1955, 1960, 1965, 1967, from [60, p. 48], 1962–1964 from [20, p. 185], 1971 from [58, No. 232, p. 1].

It is interesting to speculate whether we are not witnessing in this relationship an illustration of "cognitive dissonance," the concept developed and tested by Festinger, Aronson, and other social psychologists [86]. In this case, psychological dissonance would be experienced by individuals who find themselves in a situation of growing disparity between expressed attitudes on completed family size and actual childbearing behavior. This disparity might be rationalized simply as postponement of childbearing, but as the condition persists and the disparity grows, attitudes would be revised downward to conform with behavior, as would be predicted by the theory of cognitive dissonance. In principle, dissonance could also be removed by changing behavior (catching up on childbearing) rather than by revising attitudes. However, since Americans tend to view two, three, or four children as almost equally preferable, a change in attitudes would seem to be a much less costly way of removing dissonance.

According to dissonance theory, persons who are under pressure to revise attitudes will try to marshal support for this action from the environment. One wonders if a phenomenon of this sort may not partly account for the recent evidence of a marked upsurge in public concern about population growth. According to a 1971 survey of American attitudes on population growth:

> More than half [of those surveyed] think government should try to slow population growth . . .
> An equally large number believe people should voluntarily limit the size of their families even if they can afford more children [42, p. 22].

These results may be due in part to a genuine concern about population arising from the widespread publicity given to the "population problem" in the past decade or so. But it is possible that they also partly reflect a greater willingness of at least a part of the population to seize an opportunity for justifying its lower rate of childbearing, thereby reducing the dissonance caused by the disparity between this behavior and previously expressed attitudes on family size. To the extent this is so, such expressions of concern about the "population problem" might prove evanescent if economic circumstances changed in a pro-fertility direction.

To this point we have been concerned with the relation between fertility behavior and *attitudes* about completed family size. There remains the question whether changes in period rates of fertility foreshadow corresponding movements in *actual* completed family size, as anticipated in the reasoning sketched earlier. For the period rate decline of the 1960s, it is not possible to answer with certainty, since the women involved have not yet completed their reproductive careers. Nevertheless, a reasonable judgment is possible, based on recent studies.

When period fertility rates of young females turned down sharply in the early sixties, demographers at first hesitated to infer from this that the completed fertility of these women would be lower, in part because at that time the data for these women on expected family size indicated little change, as we have just seen. With the persistence of the decline and further analysis of the relation between period and completed fertility rates, however, the view grew that the period rate decline did portend a reduction in completed fertility. For example, Ryder, by linking period and completed rates via the mean age of fertility of a cohort, compared movements of period and completed rates in three periods—World War I to 1933-40; 1933-40 to 1954-61; and 1954-61 to 1967. He found for these successive periods that "a decline of 50 per cent in period terms represented a decline of 30 per cent in cohort terms; a subsequent rise of 60 per cent for periods represented a rise of 40 per cent for cohorts; and the recent decline of 30 per cent in the period total fertility rate would appear to have represented a decline of 10 per cent in the corresponding cohort measure" [45, p. 588].[13]

A simulation analysis of the fertility decline by Siegel and Akers, done in 1968, concluded that the period rate decline from 1960 to 1965 implied a "moderate to substantial decrease" in completed rates [50, p. 107]. The sharp downturn now shown by the more recent data on expected family size reinforces this inference. Thus, so far as it is possible to judge at the present time, the recent decline in period rates will eventuate in lower completed rates. This correspondence between major changes in period and completed rates is in keeping with the earlier experience described by Ryder, and is in line with the theoretical expectations sketched at the start of this section. Not only family-size attitudes, but actual completed fertility as well, is partly shaped by the ongoing fertility experience of young adults.

This conclusion, combined with the preceding explanation of period rates of young adults, suggests that both fertility attitudes and fertility behavior, current as well as completed, are all influenced in part by relative economic status. The impact of the latter on attitudes and completed family size occurs with a lag, however, and is constrained by the persistent tendency for preferences to center on the two- to four-child range. This range might itself change, of course, due to other economic or noneconomic developments, and independently influence fertility behavior. There is little indication, however, of such changes in the record for the last three and a half decades.

Outlook for period rates of young adults

With regard to projections of fertility, this view implies that it may be worthwhile to explore methods that take account of the dependence of completed rates on period rates, rather than vice versa. If this is so, the outlook for period rates in the coming decade takes on added interest. Current reports on fertility during 1971 indicate a noticeable drop [43]. Does this imply a resumption of the decline of the sixties? Or is this a temporary phenomenon, largely attributable to the sharp economic downturn which started in 1970, the first since the recession of 1960–61?

The present analysis suggests caution in treating the 1971 drop as the inception of a new decline. As we have seen, the economic expansion of the 1960s was starting to generate an improvement in the relative economic status of young persons, and there was an accompanying leveling off of fertility. Estimates of relative status for more recent dates than those presented in Chart 2 show an interruption in this recovery. But if the economy were to move vigorously forward in the 1970s, one might expect a resumption of the improvement, in relative status, and a corresponding upward pressure on fertility. As for the marriage squeeze, its negative influence seems exhausted, and this factor should move in a pro-fertility direction in the future—the exact timing of this varies with the marriage-squeeze measure used. Furthermore, diffusion of the pill, another negative factor, may have largely run its course [3], though new methods for fertility control are continuing to emerge, such as the legalization of abortion. Finally, regarding the crude birth rate—as opposed to age-specific and age-adjusted period rates of fertility, our concern to this point—there will be a strong upward stimulus due to a growing concentration of women in the prime ages of childbearing. On balance, these considerations raise doubts about the likelihood of a continued decline in the age-adjusted fertility rates in the seventies, and suggest the probability of a rise in the crude birth rate.

Indeed, if a major and sustained economic boom were to develop in this decade, the possibility of an upturn in age-specific birth rates of young persons cannot be ruled out. As I suggested a decade ago, the most confident assertion that seems possible with regard to future fertility is that it is likely to show longer term fluctuations [13, p. 900; cf. also 45]. Experience so far has been consistent with this. It is likely, however, that such movements will be dampened in magnitude, unless another Great Depression occurs. This is because the biggest changes in relative economic status of young adults, as indicated by series such as those in Charts 3 and 5, have been bound up with the Great Depression, either through its immediate effects on the earning power of young adults, or through its echo effects via the formation of desired living levels.

It is perhaps worth emphasizing again that American fertility is likely to be characterized by long-term fluctuations. During the baby boom, there was a tendency to view high fertility as a persisting phenomenon. Similarly, some have seized on the recent decline as portending a movement toward stabilization of population size. If an upturn of fertility takes place in the seventies, one can readily imagine the prophecies of impending doom that would ensue. The present analysis indicates, however, that it is difficult to infer long-term fertility trends from changes over periods as lengthy even as three decades. To those who are fearful of the consequences of further population growth and anxious for a guide to future trends, this may seem dismaying counsel. For reasons I have stated elsewhere, I think such concerns are exaggerated [14; cf. also 33]. But if one's interest is in the long-term outlook for fertility, the most obvious course of action is to advocate intensive research into the factors responsible for the historical trend. This position is much more consonant with the state of knowledge than the current tendency to project ongoing experience into the future.

Other explanations of the fertility swing

In view of the unparalleled magnitude of the fertility swing, the scarcity of attempts to explain it is surprising. While cohort analysis has helped to clarify the relations among different fertility measures, it leaves unanswered the basic question of the causes of the movements described by these measures. Two causal factors that have figured prominently in professional discussions of the fertility decline, the marriage squeeze and oral contraception, have already been discussed at length above. Mention was also made of Judith Blake's view that the baby boom was partly due to an upward trend in desired family size (though she has not advanced this argument regarding the period of the fertility decline), and the point made that the evidence is more consistent with the opposite cause-effect relation;

that is, that the change in period fertility rates was the cause rather than the effect of the change in attitudes.

Ryder's review of American fertility experience since World War I mentions economic conditions as a determinant along with the marriage squeeze and contraceptive developments, but since no data were presented on the independent variables other than for oral contraception (in a separate analysis [46, 48]), it is difficult to be sure of the precise meaning he attaches to these concepts and how he assesses their relative causal importance [45]. To judge from his discussion of the fertility outlook, he attached special importance to developments in fertility regulation. His prediction of a further decline in fertility in the seventies is predicated almost entirely on a discussion of prospective contraceptive developments, and no attention at all is given to the outlook for economic conditions.

In connection with the recent fertility decline, various explanations appear from time to time in popular discussion. Factors other than those previously mentioned are the increasing cost of children; growing proportions of young men and women remaining in school; and greater employment opportunities for women.

The principal problem with such arguments, aside from the absence of any systematic presentation of empirical support, is that they cannot be applied consistently to the explanation of both the baby boom and fertility decline. School enrollments and female employment opportunities have been rising throughout the period since 1940, but despite this, the fertility of young women rose markedly, and then fell. As for the relative cost of children, its movement in the past few decades is uncertain. It seems doubtful, however, that it declined to the mid-fifties and subsequently rose, as would be necessary if it were to play a major role in causing the observed fertility movement. Below are index numbers, on 1960 as a base, for the price of food and housing, and the wage rate per hour for year-round full-time female workers (an approximation to the opportunity cost of prospective mothers), items that dominate the usual estimates of cost of children: [14]

	Consumer Price Index	Food	Housing	Female Wage Rate
1939	47	39	58	24
1960	100	100	100	100
1970	131	131	132	164

The greater rise from 1939 to 1960 in the food and female wage rate indices than in the Consumer Price Index suggests that a time-series estimate of the relative cost of children would quite likely show an increase during the period when fertility rose dramatically. This increase continues in the period of fertility decline, 1960 to 1970, with regard to the female wage-rate index only and at a lower annual rate, suggesting a slower growth in the relative cost of children in the period of fertility decline than in the period of fertility increase.

Another popular explanation of the fertility decline current today is the growth of the Women's Liberation Movement. It seems doubtful that this quite recent development has much relevance to the behavior of the socio-economic group which dominates the fertility performance of young adults —namely, women with no college education who are married to husbands engaged in other than white-collar jobs. In any event, the fertility decline was largely concentrated in the period through 1966. Since then, in the period when Women's Liberation has gained prominence, fertility has been largely stable.

Summary and Research Implications

The principal conclusions suggested by the present analysis are these:

1. The dramatic swing since the 1930s in the fertility of young adults was due primarily to a corresponding movement in the relation between the income earning possibilities of young men and the desired living levels of them and their actual or prospective brides. This relationship is termed here the "relative economic status" of young persons, on the grounds that the material aspirations of young persons were formed largely in their parents' households. Therefore the balance between earning possibilities and desired living levels is largely a function of the income or labor-market experience of sons relative to that of their fathers. A rise in the relative economic status of young persons, such as occurred between the 1930s and 1950s, induces earlier marriage and childbearing, and a corresponding rise in fertility. Conversely, a decline in relative economic status, like that which occurred from the 1950s through the latter part of the 1960s, encourages deferment of marriage and childbearing, and correspondingly lower fertility.

2. A marriage squeeze—that is, a shifting balance between the number of young males and young females of appropriate ages eligible for marriage—also played a part in the swing in marriage behavior of young females. Since marital fertility rather than marriage is the principal factor in the fertility swing, it follows that this demographic factor cannot be accorded prime importance as an explanation of the total fertility swing. It is possible, however, that the marriage squeeze was an important initiating factor in the fertility decline after 1957 among females 15–19 years old. But a change in relative economic status may have been operating concurrently as well, discouraging the marriage of young men in their early twenties. With regard to our measures of both the marriage squeeze and

relative status, it is difficult to make confident statements about the precise timing of movements.

3. In the recent decline in the marital fertility of females 20–24 years old, the diffusion of oral contraception played a part. One must be wary, however, of exaggerating the importance of this factor, because in many cases there appears to have been merely substitution of the pill for other quite effective contraceptive methods. Clearly the pill had nothing to do with the prior upsurge in fertility. On the whole, the role of oral contraception appears to have been to modify in a negative direction the basic pattern of fertility change since 1960 attributable to the movement of relative economic status.

4. The ongoing fertility experience of young adults, as determined chiefly by movements in relative economic status, in turn influences their statements of expectations and ideals as to completed family size, as well as their eventual completed fertility. The drop in the annual fertility performance of young persons in the 1960s preceded a downward shift in their statements about ideal and expected family size, and it now seems clear that their completed fertility will also show a noticeable decline.

5. It seems unlikely that over the next decade age-specific birth rates of young persons will decline much below the level at the beginning of the decade. If a sustained and vigorous economic boom were to take place and produce an upward movement in young adults' relative economic status, a rise in these rates is possible. The changing composition of the population in regard to age will be an additional upward pressure on the crude birth rate.

Research needs

As stated in the introduction, this paper basically presents an approach to the analysis of the fertility swing. Clearly there are many opportunities for improvement of this approach and further exploration of the argument. What then is most needed (and at least partly feasible if one goes back to the primary data) is an attempt to reconstruct the life-cycle experience—both economic and demographic—of various cohorts. Particular attention should be paid to the young adult ages. How plentiful were jobs? What rates of pay were available? How rapidly did one move up the occupational ladder? Do the early years of labor-market experience play a disproportionate part in forming one's career and income expectations, or is such experience rapidly discounted? Does persistent unemployment have a greater or lesser effect on long-term income expectations than does fluctuating employment around the same average level?

The longitudinal studies of current labor-market experience directed by Herbert S. Parnes are providing valuable detailed data relevant to such questions [68]. But it should be possible to do rough reconstructions of cohort experience for earlier periods from Census and *Current Population Survey* data and such materials as those of the University of Michigan Survey Research Center, and to combine them with available cohort studies of demographic behavior [34, 85].

There is need to develop alternative and more refined measures of the economic status of parents, and to explore the effect of varying the periods for which the status measures for both generations are computed. Occasionally I encounter the view that if one tries manipulating the economic data in enough different ways, eventually a measure will be obtained that corresponds reasonably well to the fertility pattern. Having initially tried a fair amount of mechanical manipulation, I can testify that this has not been my experience. Only after working out the intergenerational and intragenerational relationships shown in Table 11, did I obtain a measure that fit the data as well as in Chart 2. Nevertheless, the matching of data for husbands with those for wives, and of both of these sets with those for parents, could doubtless be improved.

More generally, there are important research opportunities on how the aspirations of young people are formed. A variety of influences are at work. Along with family economic background there are factors such as peer group, religious, and ethnic influences. Education may play a role, for example, by fostering ambitions to do better than one's parents. The emphasis on family economic background in the present empirical analysis reflects the judgment that this has been the factor principally responsible for long-term fluctuations in the aspirations of young adults during the period studied. But clearly this calls for further investigation. Research along these lines might draw on pertinent studies in sociology and social psychology, as well as economic studies such as those of the University of Michigan Survey Research Center, and demographic inquiries into desired size of the family [7, 32, 46].

Much more work is needed too on the relation of completed family size to early childbearing experience, and on the role of the latter in modifying desires and expectations regarding completed fertility. This line of investigation forms an obvious complement to the call at the start of this section for a reconstruction of both economic and demographic aspects of life-cycle experience.

There is also the need to test the present interpretation against the experience of other countries. A recent fertility analysis notes a number of parallels between Finnish and American patterns [54]. Canada has shown a fertility swing much like that of the United States. My impression is that the explanation developed for American experience would be applicable to Canadian as well. In Australia, an amazing decline has occurred during the postwar period in the age at marriage. Could this be due, in effect, to the establishment as a permanent situation of the type of high employment conditions for young men which the United States enjoyed as a transient phenomenon in the post-World War II economic boom? For both Canada and Australia, however, an analysis of fertility would need to take account of the much greater importance of foreign immigration.[15]

The foregoing does not exhaust the list of possibilities. But it should suffice to demonstrate that the present problem offers an exciting opportunity for combining the research skills of demography, economics, and sociology to study the experience of a number of countries.

Notes

1. Alan Sweezy's effort, for instance, to go into the historical record and my analysis of that record, is a welcome addition to a much neglected subject. But there is little point in attempting an item-by-item rejoinder. Much of his argument dealt with fertility differentials, which were not my concern, while the issue of the causes of the recent fertility decline seems most usefully advanced by further research like that attempted here. A basic conceptual confusion in his article is discussed in this paper.

2. As is noted in the discussion of Chart 4 below, these fluctuations in the marital fertility estimates appear to be due chiefly to fluctuations, not in the birth data, but in the current population survey returns on the marital status of females in this age group. The exceptionally low marital fertility estimate published for 1964 is almost surely wrong.

3. For wives 25–29 years old, the proportion with some college education rises to about one-fourth; and the proportion of husbands in white-collar work, almost to one-half. This suggests that the fertility patterns for the 25–29 age group might usefully be viewed as a composite of those for two subgroups—one essentially blue collar in nature and fairly well advanced in its childbearing career, and the other primarily white collar in nature and only fairly recently started in the family life cycle.

4. A general statement of the theoretical viewpoint underlying the present paper is given in [16]. Other recent contributions by economists include [11, 41, 49, 51, 53, 56].

5. According to the Current Population Survey source cited in Table 7, while family income in 1970 was about 5 per cent higher (in constant dollars) than in 1966, husband's income had hardly changed. For a fuller discussion of the theoretically appropriate income concept, see [16, pp. 128–130, 142, 147–148, and 155, n. 44].

6. The Toronto Fertility Study shows a number of similarities between the United States and Canada in adoption of the pill [2, 3, 31]. I am grateful to T. R. Balakrishnan for allowing me to see some preliminary chapters from a monograph reporting on the study.

7. As I have previously noted, Judith Blake's criticism of the economic theory of fertility confuses the effect on fertility of income with that of tastes, the factor to which her evidence actually relates [8; 16, p. 156]. A recent sociological study which correctly distinguishes between income and tastes is that by Geoffrey Hawthorn [27].

8. This is not to claim that the present treatment of tastes cannot be improved upon. Some of the shortcomings are noted in my earlier theoretical article [16, especially pp. 147–148].

9. For males 15–19 years old, the proportion ever-married was around 3 to 4 per cent in the postwar period; for females 14–17, around 3 to 6 per cent.

10. An illustration of this type of influence in earlier United States experience is provided by the changing marriage proportions of foreign born women from 1890 to

1930 [see 15, pp. 92–95]. The term "marriage squeeze" first appeared in print in [23, p. 38].

11. It is possible that deferment procedures under the draft laws had some effect on marriage behavior. Throughout the period since 1948, fatherhood was an effective basis for deferment, but marriage alone was a valid basis for deferment only through June 19, 1951, and then again from September 1963 through August 1965. The outbreak of the Korean War in June 1950 may have spurred marriages in the period to June 1951. Whether the availability of deferment on the basis of marriage in 1963–65 was much of an incentive in the absence of sizable involvement in war is hard to say. The possibility of such deferment in this period does mean, however, that the upturn of marriages for young males in the 1960s might be partly due to deferment procedures rather than economic factors.

12. The survey population for the two expectation series is narrower than that for the others, but this conclusion would hold for the more restricted population as well. (See the marital fertility series for females 20–24 years old in Chart 1.)

13. Another valuable comparison of period and completed rates appears in [34, pp. 261–264].

14. The price index numbers are from [17]; the wage rate estimate was obtained by dividing the figure on median wage and salary income for year-round full-time workers, as reported in [57], by 2000, the assumed number of hours worked per year.

15. For recent studies of Canadian fertility, see [2, 3, 10, 28, 29, 31, 37]; of Australian, see [5, 9, 52].

References

1. Akers, Donald S., "On Measuring the Marriage Squeeze," *Demography* 4, No. 2, 1967, pp. 907–924.

2. Allingham, J. D., T. R. Balakrishnan, and J. F. Kantner, "Time Series of Growth in Use of Oral Contraception and the Differential Diffusion of Oral Anovulants," *Population Studies* 23, 1, March 1969, pp. 43–51.

3. ———, ———, and ———, "The End of Rapid Increase in the Use of Oral Anovulants? Some Problems in the Interpretation of Time Series of Oral Use Among Married Women," *Demography* 7, No. 1, February 1970, pp. 31–41.

4. Banks, J. A., *Prosperity and Parenthood*, London: Routledge, 1954.

5. Basavarajappa, K. G., "The Influence of Fluctuations in Economic Conditions on Fertility and Marriage Rates, Australia 1920–21 to 1937–38 and 1946–47 to 1966–67," *Population Studies* 25, No. 1, March 1971, pp. 39–53.

6. Blake, Judith, "Family Size in the 1960's—A Baffling Fad?" *Eugenics Quarterly* 14, No. 1, March 1967, pp. 60–74.

7. ———, "Ideal Family Size Among White Americans: A Quarter of a Century's Evidence," *Demography* 3, No. 1, 1966, pp. 154–173.

8. ———, "Income and Reproductive Motivation," *Population Studies* 21, 3 (November 1967), pp. 185–206.

9. Borrie, W. D., "Fertility in Australia: A Review of Recent Trends," *International Population Conference 1*, International Union for the Scientific Study of Population, London: 1969.

10. Burch, Thomas K., "The Fertility of North American Catholics: A Comparative Overview," *Demography* 3, No. 1, 1966, pp. 174–187.

11. Cain, Glen G., and Adriana Weininger, "Economic Determinants of Fertility: Results from Cross-Sectional, Aggregative Data," mimeographed paper, no date.

12. Carter, Hugh, and Paul C. Glick, *Marriage and Divorce: A Social and Economic Study*, Cambridge, Massachusetts: Harvard University Press, 1970.

13. Easterlin, Richard A., "The American Baby Boom in Historical Perspective," *American Economic Review* 51, 5, December 1961, pp. 896–911.

14. ———, "Does Human Fertility Adjust to the Environment?" *American Economic Review Papers and Proceedings* 61, 2, May 1971, pp. 399–407.

15. ———, *Population, Labor Force, and Long Swings in Economic Growth: The American Experience*. New York: Columbia University Press, 1968.

16. ———, "Towards a Socio-Economic Theory of Fertility: A Survey of Recent Research on Economic Factors in American Fertility," in S. J. Behrman, L. Corsa, Jr., and R. Freedman, eds., *Fertility and Family Planning: A World View*, Ann Arbor: University of Michigan Press, 1969.

17. *Economic Report of the President*, Washington, D.C.: 1971.

18. Elliott-Jones, M. F., "Population Growth and Fertility Behavior," *The Conference Board Record* 5, No. 9, September 1968, pp. 34–43.

19. Freedman, Deborah, "The Relation of Economic Status to Fertility," *American Economic Review* 53, 3, June 1963, pp. 414–426.

20. Freedman, Ronald, and Larry Bumpass, "Fertility Expectations in the United States, 1962–64," *Population Index* 32, No. 2, April 1966, pp. 181–197.

21. ———, ———, Lolagene C. Coombs, "Stability and Change in Expectations About Family Size: A Longitudinal Study," *Demography* 2, 1965, pp. 250–275.

22. ———, David Goldberg, and Larry Bumpass, "Current Fertility Expectations of Married Couples in the United States: 1963," *Population Index*, January 1965, pp. 3–20.

23. Glick, Paul C., David M. Heer, and John C. Beresford, "Family Formation and Family Composition: Trends and Prospects," in Marvin B. Sussman, ed., *Sourcebook on Marriage and the Family*, Boston: Houghton Mifflin Co., 1963.

24. Goldberg, David, "Some Observations on Recent Changes in American Fertility Based on Sample Survey Data," *Eugenics Quarterly* 14, No. 4, December 1967, pp. 255–264.

25. ———, and Clyde H. Coombs, "Some Applications of Unfolding Theory to Fertility Analysis," in *Emerging Techniques in Demographic Analysis*, Milbank Memorial Fund Round Table, 1962.

26. Grabill, Wilson H., Clyde V. Kiser, and Pascal K. Whelpton, *The Fertility of American Women*, New York: John Wiley & Sons, Inc., 1958.

27. Hawthorn, Geoffrey, *The Sociology of Fertility*, London: Collier-Macmillan, 1970.

28. Henripin, J., "Evolution de la Fecondité au Canada Depuis la Dernière Guerre Mondiale," International Union for the Scientific Study of Population, *International Population Conference 1*, London: 1969.

29. ———, Jacques Legare, "Recent Trends in Canadian Fertility," *Canadian Review of Sociology and Anthropology* 8, No. 2, 1971, pp. 106–118.

30. Hirschman, Charles, and Judah Matras, "A New Look at the Marriage Market and Nuptiality Rates, 1915–1958," *Demography* 8, No. 4, November 1971, pp. 549–569.

31. Kantner, J. F., J. D. Allingham, and T. R. Balakrishnan, "Oral Contraception and the Fertility Decline in Canada, 1958–1968: A First Look at a

Crucial Component in the Argument," mimeographed paper presented at Annual Meeting of Population Association of America: Boston, April 1968.

32. Katona, George, Burkhard Strumpel, and Ernest Zahn, *Aspirations and Affluence*, New York: McGraw-Hill, 1971.

33. Kelley, Allen C., "Demographic Changes and American Economic Development: Past, Present, and Future," mimeographed paper prepared for the Commission on Population Growth and the American Future, October 12, 1971.

34. Kiser, Clyde V., Wilson H. Grabill, and Arthur A. Campbell, *Trends and Variations in Fertility in the United States*, Cambridge, Massachusetts: Harvard Press, 1968.

35. Lebergott, Stanley, "Annual Estimates of Unemployment in the United States, 1900–1954," in *The Measurement and Behavior of Unemployment*, Universities-National Bureau Conference Series 8, Princeton: Princeton University Press, 1957.

36. ———, *Manpower in Economic Growth: The United States Record Since 1800*, New York: McGraw-Hill, 1964.

37. Long, Larry H., "Fertility Patterns Among Religious Groups in Canada," *Demography* 7, 2, May 1970, pp. 135–149.

38. Mayer, Lawrence A., "Why the U.S. Population Isn't Exploding," *Fortune*, April 1967, pp. 162–166, 186–192.

39. Morgan, James N., "The Supply of Effort, the Measurement of Well-Being, and the Dynamics of Improvement," *American Economic Review* 58, 2, May 1968, pp. 31–39.

40. Parke, Robert, Jr., and Paul C. Glick, "Prospective Changes in Marriage and the Family," *Journal of Marriage and the Family* 29, 2, May 1967, pp. 249–256.

41. Robinson, Warren C., and David E. Horlacher, "Population and Welfare," *Reports on Population/Family Planning*, No. 6, 1971.

42. Rosenthal, Jack, "Survey Finds 50% Back Liberalization of Abortion Policy," *New York Times*, October 28, 1971, pp. 1, 22.

43. ———, "U. S. Population Growth Rate Found Sharply Off," *New York Times*, November 5, 1971, pp. 1, 25.

44. Ryder, Norman B., "The Character of Modern Fertility," *Annals of the American Academy of Political and Social Science* 369, January 1967, pp. 26–36.

45. ———, "The Time Series of Fertility in the United States," International Union for the Scientific Study of Population, *International Population Conference Vol. 1*, London: 1969, pp. 587–597.

46. ———, and Charles F. Westoff, *Reproduction in the United States 1965*, Princeton: Princeton University Press, 1971.

47. ———, and ———, "The Trend of Expected Parity in the United States: 1955, 1960, 1965," *Population Index* 33, 2, April–June, 1967, pp. 153–168.

48. ———, and ———, "The United States: The Pill and the Birth Rate, 1960–1965," *Studies in Family Planning*, No. 20, June 1967.

49. Schultz, T. Paul, "An Economic Model of Family Planning and Fertility," *Journal of Political Economy* 77, 2 March/April 1969, 153–180.

50. Siegel, J. S., and D. S. Akers, "Some Aspects of the Use of Birth Expectations Data from Sample Surveys for Population Projections," *Demography* 6, 2, May 1969, pp. 101–115.

51. Simon, Julian L., "The Effect of Income on Fertility," *Population Studies* 23, 3, November 1969, pp. 327–341.
52. Spencer, Geraldine M., "Fertility Trends in Australia," *Demography* 8, 2, May 1971, pp. 247–259.
53. Spengler, Joseph J., "Values and Fertility Analysis," *Demography* 3, 1, 1966, pp. 109–130.
54. Sweetser, Frank L., and Paavo Peipponen, "Postwar Fertility Trends and Their Consequences in Finland and the U.S.," *Journal of Social History*, 1, 2, Winter 1967, pp. 101–118.
55. Sweezy, Alan, "The Economic Explanation of Fertility Changes in the United States," *Population Studies*, 25, 2, July 1971, pp. 255–267.
56. Tabarrah, Riad B., "Toward a Theory of Demographic Development," *Economic Development and Cultural Change* 19, 2, January 1971, pp. 257–277.
57. U. S. Bureau of the Census, *Current Population Reports: Consumer Income*, Series P-60.
58. U. S. Bureau of the Census, *Current Population Reports: Population Characteristics*, Series P-20.
59. U. S. Bureau of the Census, *Current Population Reports: Population Estimates and Projections*, Series P-25.
60. U. S. Bureau of the Census, *Current Population Reports: Special Studies: Fertility Indicators: 1970*, Series P-23, No. 36, Washington, D.C.: 1971.
61. U. S. Bureau of the Census, *Census of Population: 1960, Subject Reports PC(2)-3C: Women by Children under Five Years Old*, Washington, D.C.: 1968.
62. U. S. Bureau of the Census, *Census of Population: 1960, Subject Reports PC(2)-4D: Age at First Marriage*, Washington, D.C.: 1966.
63. U. S. Bureau of the Census, *Census of Population: 1960, Subject Reports PC(2)-4E: Marital Status*, Washington, D.C.: 1966.
64. U. S. Bureau of the Census, *Census of Population: 1960, Subject Reports PC(2)-6A: Employment Status and Work Experience*, Washington, D.C.: 1963.
65. U. S. Bureau of the Census, *Census of Population: 1960, United States Summary*, Washington, D.C.: 1963.
66. U. S. Bureau of the Census, *Trends in the Income of Families and Persons in the United States: 1947–1964*, Technical Paper No. 17, Washington, D.C.: 1967.
67. U. S. Department of Labor, *Manpower Report of the President*, Washington, D.C.: 1971.
68. U. S. Department of Labor/Manpower Administration, *Career Thresholds Vol. 3*, Manpower Research Monograph No. 16, Washington, D.C.: 1971.
69. U. S. Public Health Service, National Center for Health Statistics, *Marriage Statistics Analysis: United States—1963*, Series 21, No. 16, Washington, D.C.: 1968.
70. U. S. Public Health Service, National Center for Health Statistics, *Marriages: Trends and Characteristics: United States*, Series 21, No. 21, Washington, D.C.: 1971.
71. U. S. Public Health Service, National Center for Health Statistics, *Monthly Vital Statistics Report*.
72. U. S. Public Health Service, National Center for Health Statistics, *Natality Statistics Analysis: United States—1962*, Series 21, No. 1, Washington, D.C.: 1964.

73. U. S. Public Health Service, National Center for Health Statistics, *Natality Statistics Analysis: United States—1963*, Series 21, No. 8, Washington, D.C.: 1966.
74. U. S. Public Health Service, National Center for Health Statistics, *Natality Statistics Analysis: United States—1964*, Series 21, No. 11, Washington, D.C.: 1967.
75. U. S. Public Health Service, National Center for Health Statistics, *Natality Statistics Analysis: United States—1965–1967*, Series 21, No. 19, Washington, D.C.: 1970.
76. U. S. Public Health Service, National Center for Health Statistics, *Trends in Illegitimacy: United States—1940–1965*, Series 21, No. 15, Washington, D.C.: 1968.
77. U. S. Public Health Service, *Vital Statistics of the United States, 1950* 1, Washington, D.C.: 1960.
78. U. S. Public Health Service, *Vital Statistics of the United States, 1960* 1, Washington, D.C.: 1962.
79. U. S. Public Health Service, *Vital Statistics of the United States, 1965* 1, Washington, D.C.: 1967.
80. U. S. Public Health Service, *Vital Statistics of the United States, 1967* 1, Washington, D.C.: 1969.
81. U. S. Public Health Service, *Vital Statistics—Special Reports: Fertility Tables for Birth Cohorts of American Women* 51, 1, Washington, D.C.: 1960.
82. Wachter, M. L., "A Labor Supply Model for Secondary Workers," University of Pennsylvania, Wharton School of Finance and Commerce, Discussion Paper No. 194, Revised July 1971.
83. ———, "A New Approach to the Equilibrium Labor Force," University of Pennsylvania, Wharton School of Finance and Commerce, Discussion Paper No. 226, November 1971.
84. Westoff, Charles F., and Norman B. Ryder, "United States: Methods of Fertility Control, 1955, 1960 & 1965," *Studies in Family Planning*, No. 17, February 1967.
85. Whelpton, Pascal K., *Cohort Fertility: Native White Women in the United States*. Princeton: Princeton University Press, 1954.
86. Zajonc, Robert, "Thinking: Cognitive Organization and Processes," *International Encyclopedia of the Social Sciences* 15, New York: Macmillan, 1968, pp. 618–621.

Relative Economic Status and the American Fertility Swing A Response

By Allen C. Kelley

In spite of the extensive research on the determinants of family size, there is still no widely accepted and consistent theory of family size and population growth which commands strong empirical support. Economists have long held that the decision regarding family size can be analyzed in an economic framework, where parents compare the costs and benefits of children with alternative uses of family resources. While the results of cross-section studies have been mixed in revealing the nature of such an association, problems of model specification and data have been cited to discount the inability to obtain unbiased estimates of the relevant parameters in an economic model of family formation.

For economists, however, possibly the greatest difficulty in analyzing American family-size patterns has been the problem of explaining the secular trend in the fertility rate. In particular, how does one reconcile the long-run decline in the American fertility rate with the secular expansion of economic well-being? Explanations have rested on the rising costs of children—in particular, the costs of education—and the foregone market earnings of mothers as opportunities for female employment have risen. In addition, the improvement in health of children from the time of birth is cited as a reason for minimal effects of income on the fertility rate. Finally, the shift of population into urban areas, where both the benefits of children diminish and their relative costs increase, has been cited as accounting for a major portion of the secular decline in the birth rate.

Possibly the most significant single contributor to the literature on American economic-demographic interactions has been Richard Easterlin, whose studies have focused largely, but not exclusively, on long-run variations, or long swings, in economic and demographic activity. He has combined standard economic analysis, some imaginative hypotheses of his own, and an increasing stock of empirical evidence to demonstrate that the family-size decision is, and has been, sensitive to economic and environmental conditions. But sociologists and demographers (as well as some economists) have remained less than fully convinced.

They cite, for example, the dramatic postwar surge and subsequent decline in birth rates as a phenomenon yet unexplained by the slowly changing secular trends in economic benefits and costs of children which economists have emphasized in their theories of family formation. Easterlin's present paper represents not only another significant addition to his list of carefully compiled research reports, but also a major input into the continuing debate on the role of economic factors in explaining American fertility rates. Here Easterlin extended the empirical evidence lending support to his theory of family formation as expounded in earlier studies. He again not only found that fertility rates are sensitive to economic conditions, but also that the emergence of the postwar baby boom is fully consistent with his model of family formation.

Easterlin's primary theoretical contribution rests on his hypothesis that the family-size decision is in large part based on a comparison by prospective parents of their actual (or expected) economic situation with that to which they aspire. These aspirations, in turn, are based on the economic conditions prevailing many years earlier in late childhood and in early adulthood.

The postwar baby boom can be explained by a rapid rise in the relative economic conditions of prospective parents—the high earnings in the fifties by comparison with the thirties; the subsequent downturn in birth rates results from a reversal in the trend in relative economic conditions. Because Easterlin interpreted his theory as explaining the process of family-size preference formation, or "taste" formation, he suggested that his model is one which, in contrast to many in the economics literature, explicitly takes into account the possibility of changes in tastes. This should meet with the approval of sociologists and demographers who have long criticized the economist for his preoccupation with models assuming either unchanging tastes, or with models in which tastes are unrelated to other explanatory variables in the analysis.

Given the tests of the theory which Easterlin presented, however, I would interpret his model as being more in the mainstream of economic methodology than he might admit. In particular, he compared measures of total fertility, age-specific fertility, and per cent ever-married with several indices of relative economic status. The dependent and independent variables were found to move together. Moreover, his analysis of these correlated swings, and especially of those cases where deviations in timing and amplitude occurred, skillfully takes into account some of the alternative influences on fertility—the marriage squeeze, the increasing use and efficiency of contraceptives, and so forth.

Note, however, that an interpretation of these empirical comparisons can plausibly rest on the hypothesis of relatively *stable* tastes and parameters; it is the variables in the system that are changing, the indices of relative economic status, and not necessarily the tastes or behavioral parameters. His theory does not, in my mind, necessarily explain *changing* tastes for children over time. Rather, his main theoretical contribution is one of proposing yet another behavioral parameter—the one attached to the relative economic-status variable—which permits us to account for variations in fertility due to swings in the specified independent variable.

What Easterlin has provided is additional parameters and arguments in the demand function, not necessarily a dynamic theory of taste formation. My interpretation of his theory and results is not inconsistent with his assertion that tastes, as influenced by the economic-status variable, are important. This importance derives from the *size* of the relevant parameters. I therefore find his discussion and interpretation of taste formation somewhat subsidiary to his main theoretical contribution.

Focusing on the latter, I would argue that his main theoretical notion is one of proposing a relatively *large* effect of the economic-status variable on the family-size decision by comparison with the influence of this variable on other household decisions. Presumably, changes in the economic-status variable explain not only the desire to have more or fewer children, but also to vary one's consumption of cars, radios, and leisure.

If all items in the household budget were equally sensitive to variations in the relative economic-status variable, then one would not necessarily anticipate marked variations in the number of children due to changes in the household's relative economic position during a period when the long-run pace of per capita income is relatively stable or changing only slowly. At the basis of Easterlin's theory, then, is the hypothesis of an especially large elasticity of family size with respect to the economic-status variable; in my judgment it is this hypothesis which merits highlighting and explaining.

None of the above is a criticism of Easterlin's theory or results, but rather a redirection of attention away from the debate over the existence of stable or variable "tastes"—a debate which results in part from semantic difficulties arising from differences in the definitions of "tastes"—and a direction of attention toward the basic hypothesis which I see as underlying Easterlin's analysis. With this in mind, his work must be judged largely by whether he has been successful in assembling sufficient evidence to attribute significant explanatory power to the economic-status variable in accounting for variations in the fertility rate. Given the limitations of data, Easterlin has provided a reasonable case. He did not assert that the economic-status variable is the only influence on fertility, or even the most important one; indeed, he attributed a notable role to the marriage squeeze and the increased efficiency of contraceptives. Moreover, he has carefully qualified his empirical analysis to take into account several variables omitted from the current study—the costs of children, urbanization rates, female employment opportunities, and so forth.

If a single criticism of his empirical work were to be cited—a limitation which he explicitly recognized—it would be the omission of a formal model which he could analyze with appropriate statistical techniques to appraise the nature and significance of the resultant correlations. Given his concern with the relative importance of alternative influences on fertility, the absence of formal multivariate statistical analysis—and particularly an analysis of variance—has proved to be somewhat constraining. On the other hand, having examined many of Easterlin's previous studies which employ a similar methodology, I can testify that his skill at visual regression analysis is not only subjected to objectivity, but is indeed very refined; this skill is as carefully applied in the present study as in any I have read.

Thus, while minor quibbles over Easterlin's interpretation of specific correlations are possible, the main force of his empirical analysis stands: the family-size decision responds to economic conditions, in general, and to the influence of the household's relative economic position, in particular. However, the precise measurement of the quantitative magnitude of this response must await formal model building and the application of alternative statistical methods.

What the present paper does, then, is to provide substantial new evidence supporting a particular direction for this model building by proposing a specific mechanism by which the economic and demographic variables interact in the family decision-making process. It moreover partially reconciles the existence of the postwar baby boom with the economic theories explaining long-run trends in the American fertility rate. Finally, it provides additional caution to the application of simple projection models used to forecast future trends in American population growth. On all accounts, Easterlin's study has made a notable contribution to the growing literature on the determinants of family life styles and economic behavior.

6

*Work Response
and
Family Composition Changes
in a Negative
Income Tax Experiment:*

PRELIMINARY MID-EXPERIMENT RESULTS

Authors' Note: The research reported in this paper was supported by funds granted to MATHEMATICA, Inc. by the Office of Economic Opportunity pursuant to the Economic Opportunity Act of 1964, and by the Institute for Research on Poverty at the University of Wisconsin. We wish to thank Harold W. Watts for permission to report his mid-experiment results and for his very helpful criticisms. We are especially indebted to Felicity Skidmore for her invaluable editorial assistance. We wish also to thank Craig Winans for his research work and Rita Jurinko for her help.

ARNOLD R. SHORE and ROBERT A. SCOTT

Introduction

The Shore-Scott presentation of "The Effects of a Negative Income Tax Experiment" is a descriptive analysis of mid-experiment results in conventional language. Arnold R. Shore and Robert A. Scott's purposes were

1. To identify possible consequences (a change in work incentive, family stability, and fertility) of a set of experimental treatments.
2. To test for the occurrence of these consequences.

The results of the study can be summarized in a single, complex empirical generalization.

EG17. A guaranteed family income provided by an experimental negative income tax plan produces a slight work disincentive and does not significantly affect family stability or fertility; undesirable effects, where they occur, are most pronounced for families with the lowest guaranteed level under the plan.

This particular empirical generalization should be interpreted at a low level of abstraction compared with most other such generalizations stated thus far. We know too little about the comparative effects of various alternative welfare programs to be able to generalize to a particular class of programs. Indeed, such a circumstance is a major reason why this experiment was conducted—to add a piece to the puzzle concerning the consequences of potential social policies.

Because the questions posed are from a policy perspective, Shore and Scott suggested that little theory guided their research. However, conferees proposed several historical explanations of the mid-experiment results.

The slight disincentive effect on the experimental group reflected by a net decrease in numbers of persons employed and total hours worked (but counteracted by an increase in hourly income) might be explained alternatively as follows:

1. The experimental treatment provides security to enable earners to engage in a longer and more selective job search in order to obtain better paying jobs (Watts).

2. The experimental treatment encourages people to quit low paying jobs and keep higher paying ones (Felson).

A third alternative that has occurred to us might be the following:

3. The experimental treatment encourages greater utilization of the husband as breadwinner, because he can command higher wages.

These interpretations are not incompatible and some combination of the processes suggested may be happening simultaneously. Each interpretation may be viewed as a rational response, but not the kind of economic rational response that a work-incentive hypothesis would anticipate.

The absence of a marked effect on family stability as a result of the experiment may reflect, Shore and Scott suggested, the absence of forces tending to produce a change. On the one hand, fathers are not forced to abandon their families in order to collect payments; on the other, spouses are not forced to stay together to receive them. Furthermore, the length of the experiment may be too short for any family stability effects to emerge.

There is clearly a need for a theoretical formulation that would predict the long-term family stability effects, if any, of a negative income tax plan such as this one. One place to start might be a proposition that asserts the following: an increase in family economic security causes an increase in family stability. (It might also be hypothesized that the causal priority is reversed. Thus, an increase in family stability produces an incentive to increase economic security.) Because Shore and Scott found earned income to be positively related to family stability but transfer payments not related to family stability, one could surmise that earned income is more conducive than transfer payments to economic security. This position is compatible with the Shore-Scott finding that the duration of an earned income crisis (length of time below the poverty level) is inversely related to family stability. An increase in family stability would depend, therefore, on the increase in economic security being a fairly stable increase. In conclusion, it seems highly probable that the experimental treatment provides security to enable a more selective job search, but not the kind of security that helps keep families together.

Reuben Hill and David M. Klein

Work Response and Family Composition Changes in a Negative Income Tax Experiment: Preliminary Mid-Experiment Results

By Arnold R. Shore and Robert A. Scott
With the assistance of Vincent L. O'Brien

This paper reports mid-experiment data on families participating in the New Jersey-Pennsylvania experiment on the negative income tax with respect to work behavior and household stability. Section I provides a brief explanation of the general purpose, design, and current status of the experiment; in Section II we present data through the first year of the experiment on labor supply and earnings; and in Section III, data through the first year and a half of the experiment on family stability.

I. Background of the Experiment

The negative income tax has been proposed as one possible form for a national system of income supplements. The term "negative income tax" is used to denote the fact that the proposed system is different in a fundamental way from the current concept of public assistance, and can in fact dovetail effectively with the current positive tax system. Under a negative income tax system families earning less than a specified amount of money are entitled to receive cash payments. The amount of these payments is determined according to a formula which includes the family's earned income and the number of its members. If a family has no earned income it is eligible to receive a basic payment, the amount of which is dependent on the size of the family. As the family earns, there is a rate (tax rate or "reduction" rate) at which this basic payment is reduced. Such a formula ensures that the net income of the family will increase as more hours are worked and earned income increases. Such a system guarantees uniform payments for all families with the same earnings and the same family size, and is independent of the current welfare concept of "special need."

One of the key problems in assessing the feasibility of any transfer program is estimating its total cost within limits acceptable to policy makers. For a negative income tax program these costs depend largely on what economist call the "labor-supply response" or "labor-supply function." These terms essentially refer to the following question: How much will people change their work and leisure habits when they are guaranteed an annual income? The major rationale of the New Jersey-Pennsylvania Graduated Work Incentive Experiment, funded by the Office of Economic Opportunity, is to obtain data pertinent to this question.

The experiment's central concern with labor supply is reflected in its design [4]. First, the experiment is limited to households in urban industrial areas which include at least one working-age male who is neither a full-time student nor permanently disabled, and at least one other family member. The eligible population is further limited to include only those whose incomes place them in the category of the poor or near poor, by which we mean incomes of less than 1.5 times the official poverty threshold.

The category we have chosen—intact families with at least one working-age male—is an important group in the total population of the poor in our society. From an experimental point of view these are the households most likely to have observable changes in their labor supply, since they include household heads with few income alternatives except employment. At the same time it is important to remember that significant subgroups of the poor are excluded by our criteria. These include unattached males, heads of families who are female, aged heads of families, and the rural poor.

Households meeting our criteria and selected for the sample were assigned either to a "treatment" consisting of one of eight negative income tax plans, or to a control group which is merely being observed while receiving nominal payments for permitting us to interview them periodically. Each tax plan can be described in terms of the relationships between two variables: the tax rate, which is the rate at which earned income is taxed while payments are being made; and the guarantee level, which is the amount of money guaranteed to a family each year if there is no earned income. In our experiment tax rates on earned income range from a low of 30 per cent to a high of 70 per cent, and guarantee levels range from 50 per cent to 125 per cent of the poverty line.

A complicated problem in this or any tax system is how to define the household unit and what to consider as the income of that unit. For a variety of reasons, the decision was made to define an eligible unit (for our experiment) as one consisting of spouse, and any child or stepchild or descendant of any child or stepchild so long as such a person is either living with the head or derives more than half of his support from the head. In addition, any other person who both lives with and derives more than half of his support from the head is included. This definition comes reasonably close to the economic notion of a family unit as well as to the concept of the family unit used by the Bureau of the Census. It should be recognized, however, that it does differ from the positive income tax definition in that the basic unit in this experiment is the family, while in the current personal tax system it is the individual.

Some additional qualifications about family unit and members eligible for payment were required in order for the experiment to be feasible. For example, with the exceptions mentioned below, no new individuals who join the eligible household after initial eligibility has been established are included in our definition of the family unit. These exceptions are children born to an eligible female and any minor child who joins the unit after an initial waiting period of six months. Eligible members of units who join the armed services, leave the country, or are institutionalized by our criteria (in this latter case there are also some exceptions) cease to be considered unit members while in such statuses. Finally, persons marrying an eligible member are not themselves eligible for payment. (We mention these qualifications both for their bearing on the issue of who is considered to be in the experiment and who is not, and also because the definition of the family unit bears directly on the level of benefit calculation through its implications for family unit size and level of income.)

A request to the Internal Revenue Service produced the ruling that benefit payments do not constitute income under the personal income tax laws and are therefore not taxable. This ruling enables us to retain control over the marginal tax rate of each family. (The families are also paid to take the interviews. These were ruled as payments for services rendered, and therefore were taxable.)

One final complication must be explained. When the experiment was being planned, the state of New Jersey did not have an Unemployed Parent provision in any of its welfare programs. We did not, therefore, have to worry about the possibility of welfare payments confusing our observations, since the only significant welfare program was AFDC and we were not concerned with female-headed households. However, in January 1969 New Jersey instituted an AFDC-UP program, the benefit level of which was higher over some income ranges than all our tax plans then in effect.

We therefore introduced one more tax plan which dominates New Jersey welfare levels over all income levels, and we also had to reconsider an earlier decision to ignore competing welfare payments in our sample. After much discussion, we adopted a rule, the substance of which is the following: Although any family in our sample which becomes eligible for AFDC-UP benefits will remain in our sample, during any month for which members elect to receive those public assistance benefits they cannot receive any payments from us. They do remain eligible to return to our plan whenever (and as soon as) welfare payments stop.

With these definitions and criteria in mind, we then proceeded to select sites and families for the experiment. The general decision was made to concentrate on urban areas since a large portion of the working poor are in cities. The Northeast was chosen because of its dense population and proximity to Washington where OEO is located. New Jersey was selected because it is densely populated and has a relatively large poverty population. The decision was made to take samples in Trenton, Paterson, Passaic, Jersey City, and Scranton, Pennsylvania, the latter having been selected in order to achieve ethnic balance in the sample. Short screening interviews were administered to a random sample of households in poverty areas in each city. The purpose was to obtain enough data to determine whether or not a household might be eligible for inclusion in our experiment. In total, some 30,000 screening interviews were administered; just under 10 per cent of those interviewed were deemed eligible for inclusion in the study.

The eligible families were then interviewed a second time. This extensive second interview was designed both to supply a check on the information gathered during the initial interview and also to yield base-line data on the sample families.

From information obtained in both interviews, final eligibility was determined and families were assigned to one of the eight experimental plans or to the control group. Those assigned to the experimental group were then visited and enrolled in the program. In the enrollment interview the plan assigned to the family was explained and the interviewer attempted to obtain agreements from the family to participate. Those who agreed were given their first benefit checks immediately, and subsequent ones are sent every other week. Every fourth week the families are required to report their income for the preceding four-week period. As long as the household reports its monthly income it will continue to receive benefits for a three-year period. Eligibility is not affected if a family moves as long as it remains in the United States and continues to fill in income report forms.

Families whose income is, or rises, above their "breakeven point"—that is, the income level at which the tax rate has finally reduced the basic guarantee to zero—no longer receive benefits. They do, however, remain eligible for future cash payments in the event of subsequent declines in income. In order to maintain contact with these families, we continue to give them a small payment for filling out the required income report forms; we also allow them to file their income reports quarterly until such time as they may again become eligible for benefits.

Each household in both the experimental and control groups is interviewed every three months. These interviews last about an hour and consist of two sections: A core of questions about labor-force activity which is repeated each time; and a second (predominantly noneconomic) section, the contents of which vary from one quarter to another and consist of items relating to a whole range of issues in which there is a policy interest. Included in the second section of quarterly interviews are questions about various aspects of education, work, family life, religion, politics, leisure time, health, community involvement, and general social and political attitudes and values. These twelve quarterly interviews, the screening and pre-enrollment instruments, and a "thirteenth" quarterly which will be given after payments stop comprise the basic longitudinal data for studying economic and noneconomic responses to the experimental treatments.

Co-operation with the quarterly interviews is not a requirement for receiving benefits, and the control group, of course, receives no benefits at all, although members get a small payment each time they are interviewed. As a result, we are not able to keep track of the complete panel of respondents over the three-year period. In addition to interview attrition, some experimental families have failed to fill out income report forms, and a few have even refused payments. (We will comment further on this problem of attrition in the context of presenting data in each of the two subsequent sections.)

Actual field operations began in Trenton in June of 1968. Trenton was selected as a pilot site in which all interview schedules and administrative procedures could be tested before putting them into full-scale operation in the other cities. The Trenton site was phased out in August 1971, Paterson and Passaic were terminated in early 1972, and Jersey City received the last payments in July 1972. Since the decision to include Scranton in our sample was made comparatively late, that city phased out in September 1972.

There are many other details that could be mentioned in describing the experiment. Some of these (including sample size, allocation of families to tax plan, and attrition) will be discussed in the context of presenting our data. Other details not essential to this presentation have been omitted entirely.

The problems of processing and analyzing a body of data as large as this are enormous, and it will be some time before the complete results of the experiment will be available. At the time of writing only preliminary data on aspects of work response and family stability for the full sample through the first year to year and a half of the experiment were available. Any firm conclusions must await more comprehensive analyses of both topics, as well as more data. The materials that follow are not "results" of the experiment as such, since we have no way yet of being sure about what has been happening or is going to happen for the remainder of the three-year experimental period. Bearing these qualifications in mind, we now turn to a presentation of the data available on work response.

II. Work-Effect Response

We have seen that in a negative income tax program transfer payments to families are defined (for a given family size) by the amount of money they receive if they have no earnings, and the tax rate at which this guarantee is reduced as family earnings rise. As long as the tax rate is less than 100 per cent, families can increase the total income they have to spend with each dollar they earn (but not, of course, by as much as that dollar unless the tax rate is zero).

In principle, since a family can get more to spend the more they work —in contrast to most current welfare programs—families whose alternative is welfare may work more if a negative income tax program is instituted. Such an effect can be called an "incentive effect." It is also true, however, that since the family is guaranteed a minimum even if they choose not to work, and since if they choose to work they keep less than the full amount they earn, they may choose to work less than if their alternative were no program at all. Such an effect can be called a "disincentive effect." The extent to which a negative income tax program would produce incentive and disincentive effects on the economic behavior of families has major policy implications for instituting a national program.

The costs of a national income-maintenance program of this type, for example, depend heavily on whether or not primary and secondary earners work more, stop working, or reduce by any significant increment the amount of money they earn. Moreover, if there is a disincentive effect, the earnings lost will be only partially reimbursed in a negative tax program —resulting in a proportionate drop in the amount of money available for household members to spend. Incentive and/or disincentive effects, therefore, provide important clues for identifying basic priorities household members hold with respect to work and nonwork activities. Moreover, the impact of this program on work-force participation will have important implications both for the composition of the labor force in the years to come and for the availability of different types of workers to fill positions in the work force. For all of these reasons, the impact of a negative income tax program on earned income and labor-force participation of a household's primary and secondary earners are key issues for us to consider.

One of the principal investigators in the New Jersey-Pennsylvania experiment, Harold W. Watts, has analyzed data on labor supply and earnings for the entire sample through the first full year of the experiment. The following analysis of work-effort response is based on his report [5].

Watts' report is based upon data obtained from 1,075 families in four of the first five quarterly interviews, one of which had to be the base-line or pre-enrollment interview. The control group consisted of 422 of these families, the remaining 653 being in the experimental group. This sample excluded 138 families originally enrolled in the program—of which 114 failed to complete two or more of the quarterly interviews during the first year; and the remaining 24 families, although administered enough interviews, gave insufficient data on the basic indicators of earnings and work-force participation. Seventy-one of these unusable observations were in the experimental group and 67 in the control group, yielding an attrition rate of 9.8 per cent for experimental families and 13.7 per cent for families in the control group. The characteristics of families who attrited have an important bearing on any interpretations that are made of any of the results of the study; unfortunately, the data needed to compare attriting and nonattriting families are not yet available. This lacuna in the information available provides still another reason for interpreting with extreme caution the data we present.

From these 1,075 families two subgroups were formed for analysis—the "nonwelfare" subgroup and the "husband-wife" families. The nonwelfare families were examined separately in an effort to partial out of the analysis the effect of those changes (mentioned above) in public assistance regulations instituted during the experiment which enabled certain sample families to qualify for welfare.[1] This nonwelfare subgroup consists of families reporting welfare benefits received for at most one quarter during the first year of the experiment excluding the last one. Using this criterion, the original 1,075 families yielded 825 nonwelfare families—501 of which were in the experimental group and 324 in the control group.

The reader should interpret results involving the nonwelfare subgroup with caution. The effect of public-assistance programs on families enrolled in the experiment poses a complex problem which is not easily solved. The analysis of results for the nonwelfare subsample is not a satisfactory means of studying this problem. The utility of this sample lies in the fact that it does provide some confirmation that tendencies observed in the entire sample do not disappear when the welfare group is broken out of it.

The second subgroup Watts created consists of families in which both the husband and wife are present. The husband-wife families were analyzed separately for several reasons: (1) The nuclear family is the most common family unit in our society, making it particularly important to understand the impact of a negative income tax program on the work effort of this large group in planning for a national program; (2) male-headed households are the only major group in the United States that have not traditionally been eligible for public assistance. This means that they have the closest attachment to the labor force and the most (potentially withdrawable) labor; very little is known about their reactions to public assistance. Of the 1,075 families comprising the sample, Watts found that 943 could be classified as "husband-wife" families. Of these, 372 are in the control group and 571 are in the experimental group.

Watts compared experimental and control families on four key indicators of labor supply and earnings: the number of employed persons in the household; the total number of hours worked per week by all employed persons in the household; the combined total of earnings per week for all

240 · *Work Response and Family Composition Changes*

employed persons in the household; and the combined average earnings per hour for all employed persons in the household. For each variable, crude time series analyses were done for experimental and control families (1) in the entire sample of 1,075 families (Table 1), (2) for the nonwelfare subgroup (Table 2), (3) for the subsample of husband-wife families (Table 3), and (4) by experimental plan for the full sample of families (Table 4).[2]

A number of patterns emerge from his analysis. First, in Table 1 we see a marked divergence between control and experimental families with respect to the number of persons employed per family. Control families move steadily in the direction of increasing the average number of employed persons while experimental families show a steady decline over time. This same pattern appears in Table 2, which presents a comparison of experimental and control families in the nonwelfare subgroup. As seen in Table 3, this divergence is not apparent among husbands in the husband-wife subgroup, but is still visible for wives in this group. Finally, when we examine this variable in terms of experimental plans (Table 4) we see that no obvious differences among plans appear.

Second, a similar divergence between experimental and control families occurs with respect to the total hours of work per week among wage

TABLE 1. LABOR SUPPLY AND EARNINGS BY QUARTERLY AND EXPERIMENTAL STATUS

Indicator of Labor Supply and Earnings	Quarter	Experimental Families N=653	Control Families N=422
Number of employed persons per family (mean)	0	1.14	1.08
	1	1.05	1.15
	2	1.09	1.16
	3	1.04	1.16
	4	1.02	1.18
Total hours per week per family (mean)	0	39.8	39.4
	1	36.7	40.8
	2	34.9	37.0
	3	36.9	39.6
	4	35.0	40.3
Total earnings per week per family (mean)	0	$88.84	$87.74
	1	91.81	94.28
	2	88.88	88.90
	3	96.98	96.13
	4	94.03	96.65
Average earnings per hour	0	$2.23	$2.23
	1	2.50	2.31
	2	2.55	2.40
	3	2.63	2.43
	4	2.69	2.40

TABLE 2. LABOR SUPPLY AND EARNINGS BY QUARTERLY AND EXPERIMENTAL STATUS, NONWELFARE SUBGROUP

Indicators of Labor Supply and Earnings	Quarter	Experimental Families N = 501	Control Families N = 324
Number of employed persons per family (mean)	0	1.16	1.10
	1	1.11	1.20
	2	1.16	1.20
	3	1.12	1.24
	4	1.11	1.27
Total hours per week per family (mean)	0	41.2	40.2
	1	39.3	42.5
	2	38.2	39.3
	3	40.6	43.1
	4	39.2	44.7
Total earnings per week per family (mean)	0	$ 92.63	$ 91.92
	1	99.03	100.80
	2	99.35	96.71
	3	108.53	106.50
	4	106.55	108.60
Average earnings per hour	0	$2.25	$2.29
	1	2.52	2.37
	2	2.60	2.46
	3	2.67	2.47
	4	2.72	2.43

earners in each family. Among the full sample of families (Table 1), control families remain fairly constant through the quarterly periods while experimental families show a decline of an average of 4.8 hours of work per week through this period. In Table 2 experimental families in the nonwelfare subgroup also show a decline in hours worked per week (although less sharply), while the control families in this subgroup show a rise from an average of 40.2 hours per week to 44.7 hours per week. Similarly, husbands in control families in the husband-wife subgroup (Table 3) showed a slight decline through the first year of the experiment—from an average of 34.5 hours per week to an average of 33.6 hours per week—while husbands in experimental families in this subgroup showed a much sharper decline—from an average of 33.6 to an average of 31.5 hours per week. The nuclear family wives in the control group showed an increase over the first year from an average of 2.8 hours per week to an average of 4.7 hours per week. Comparable findings for the experimental group showed little change over time. Finally, Table 4 shows there are no obvious differences by experimental plan.

Third, this basic picture with respect to the number of persons em-

TABLE 3. LABOR SUPPLY AND EARNINGS BY QUARTERLY AND EXPERIMENTAL STATUS, HUSBAND-WIFE SUBGROUP

		Primary Wage Earners			
		Husbands		Wives	
Indicators of Labor Supply and Earnings	Quarter	Experimental Families N=571	Control Families N=372	Experimental Families N=571	Control Families N=372
Per cent of persons employed (mean)	0	.89	.90	.15	.10
	1	.87	.85	.13	.15
	2	.90	.88	.12	.14
	3	.89	.90	.12	.17
	4	.86	.88	.14	.16
Total hours per week per head or per spouse (mean)	0	33.6	34.5	4.0	2.8
	1	33.0	33.8	3.4	4.5
	2	31.3	31.3	3.0	3.8
	3	33.9	33.8	3.2	4.7
	4	31.5	33.6	3.9	4.7
Total earnings per week per head or per spouse (mean)	0	$79.69	$81.01	$6.65	$5.39
	1	88.34	82.40	6.79	8.40
	2	84.52	79.57	6.09	7.75
	3	93.87	86.61	6.48	9.46
	4	89.06	86.60	8.04	9.05
Average earnings per hour	0	$2.37	$2.35	$1.66	$1.92
	1	2.68	2.44	2.00	1.87
	2	2.70	2.54	2.03	2.04
	3	2.77	2.56	2.02	2.01
	4	2.83	2.58	2.06	1.93

ployed per family and the total hours of work per week changes when we examine the total weekly earnings per family. Watts found a generally increasing overall trend in earnings per family but no divergence between families in the control and experimental groups.

Finally, since there are more earners per family and more hours worked per week for control than for experimental families, but no divergence in earnings between the two groups, it follows that there must be differences between them with respect to average earnings per hour. Such differences are apparent in Table 1. We see that control and experimental families began with the same average hourly wage, but by the fourth quarter experimental families showed an average income which was nearly $.30 per hour higher than for control families. This same divergence is visible in both the nonwelfare subgroup (Table 2) and the husband-wife subgroup (Table 3). It is also apparent in Table 4 which reports average hourly earnings for families in the various tax plans.

In summary, these crude time series data show that there is a slight dis-

TABLE 4. LABOR SUPPLY AND EARNINGS BY QUARTERLY, EXPERIMENTAL STATUS, AND POVERTY-LEVEL BENEFIT

Indicators of Labor Supply and Earnings	Quarter	Experimental Families				Control Families
		Low Payment Plan N=139	Medium-Low Payment Plan N=224	Medium-High Payment Plan N=162	High Payment N=128	N=442
Number of employed persons per family (mean)	0	1.09	1.14	1.16	1.17	1.08
	1	1.08	1.04	1.07	1.02	1.15
	2	1.06	1.08	1.11	1.09	1.16
	3	.99	1.05	1.08	1.01	1.16
	4	.99	1.03	1.04	1.02	1.18
Total hours per week per family (mean)	0	38.2	39.7	41.1	39.9	39.4
	1	36.5	36.9	36.0	37.5	40.8
	2	33.0	34.3	35.4	37.3	37.0
	3	33.1	38.4	38.5	36.3	39.6
	4	34.4	35.1	35.8	34.5	40.3
Total earnings per week per family (mean)	0	$83.06	$89.27	$91.14	$91.33	$87.74
	1	91.69	92.28	90.47	92.80	94.28
	2	82.72	88.47	87.12	98.76	88.90
	3	90.29	100.43	100.22	94.06	96.13
	4	95.12	92.02	95.70	94.32	96.65
Average earnings per hour	0	$ 2.17	$ 2.25	$ 2.22	$ 2.29	$ 2.23
	1	2.51	2.50	2.51	2.47	2.31
	2	2.51	2.58	2.46	2.65	2.40
	3	2.73	2.62	2.60	2.59	2.43
	4	2.76	2.62	2.67	2.73	2.40

incentive effect in terms of work effort as indexed by average number of employed persons per family, and total hours worked per week per family. However, these divergences in work effort are not so far reflected in income.

Watts then attempted to estimate more precisely the tendencies reflected in changes in mean values for the variables shown in the first four tables. He did this by calculating simple control-experimental differentials which were estimated in "dummy" variable regressions controlling for the pre-enrollment value of the variable in question. He fitted these regressions for the number of employed persons per family, the total hours worked per week per family, and the total earnings for the family aggregates. These regressions were run for the full sample of 1,075 families, and for families in the nonwelfare subgroup. In the case of the subsample of husband-wife families separate regressions were run for the husband, the wife, and other earners.[3]

Table 5 shows the results of Watts' analysis for the 1,075 families in the full sample, for the nonwelfare subgroup, and for the subgroup of husband-wife families. Table 6 shows similar regressions for husband-wife families broken down in terms of wage earners. The data in these tables indicate that there are significant negative differences between experimental and control families in terms of the number of employed persons per family and the number of hours worked per week per family. For the full sample of families, the experimental group is 13.5 per cent below the control group in terms of the number of persons employed per family, and 10.0 per cent below the control group in terms of total hours of work per week per family. For the nonwelfare subgroup, experimental families are about 14 per cent below control families on both variables, and in the husband-wife subgroup experimental subjects are about 12 per cent lower than control subjects on each variable. In all cases these differences are significant at the .01 level.

Differentials in terms of earnings per family are not great. Among all families in the full sample, those in the experimental group are only about 2 per cent below those in the control group in terms of earnings; about 5 per cent below them in the nonwelfare subgroup; and 3.6 per cent below them in the husband-wife subgroup. Finally, the data in Table 5 reveal differences in average hourly earnings among the experimental and control groups. In all cases these differences favor experimental families but none of them reach statistical significance. Thus the computations in Table 5 confirm the tendencies observed in the crude time series data presented in Tables 1 through 4.

Husband-wife families comprise about 88 per cent of the sample (943 of the 1,075 families in Watts' sample). In an attempt to clarify the meaning of differences between experimental and control families on the mea-

TABLE 5. ADJUSTED MEAN ESTIMATES DERIVED FROM REGRESSION ESTIMATES OF EXPERIMENTAL-CONTROL DIFFERENTIALS IN EMPLOYMENT, HOURS, AND EARNINGS

	(1) Number of Persons Employed Per Family	(2) Total Hours Per Week Per Employee	(3) Total Hours Per Week Per Family	(4) Average Earnings Per Hour	(5) Average Earnings Per Family
(A) Total Sample					
(a) Control mean	1.18	33.6	39.7	$ 2.42	$ 96.09
(b) Absolute difference	− .16*	+ 1.3	− 4.0*	+ .22	− 2.02
(c) Experimental mean	1.02	34.9	35.7	2.64	94.07
(d) Percentage difference	−13.5 %	+ 4.0%	−10.1%	+9.1 %	− 2.1 %
(B) Nonwelfare Subgroup					
(a) Control mean	1.29	34.8	44.8	$ 2.43	$108.95
(b) Absolute difference	− .19*	+ .1	− 6.4*	+ .27	− 5.35
(c) Experimental mean	1.10	34.9	38.4	2.70	103.60
(d) Percentage difference	−14.4 %	+ .3%	−14.3%	+11.1 %	− 4.9 %
(C) Husband-Wife Families					
(a) Control mean	1.24	34.4	42.67	$ 2.45	$104.36
(b) Absolute difference	− .15*	+ .1	− 5.02*	+ .22	− 3.76
(c) Experimental mean	1.09	34.5	37.65	2.67	100.60
(d) Percentage difference	−12.2 %	+ .3%	−11.8 %	+9.0 %	− 3.6 %

* Significant at the .01 level.

sures of labor supply and earnings, Watts analyzed earners in these families on the four basic indices of these variables. The results appear in Table 6. The most striking finding in this table is the large difference between experimental and control families in terms of the number of "other earners" employed per family (control families have more) and the number of hours worked by "other earners" per week per family ("other earners" in control group work more). Watts found that the differential in employment for other earners makes up one-half of the total family differential. Just over one-half of the remaining difference is accounted for by the wife.

About two-fifths of the differential between experimental and control group families in hours worked in the husband-wife subgroup is accounted for by the husband's work activity. The most marked differential in hours per worker occurs for "other earners." Also, the minor, statistically non-significant difference in total family earnings in the husband-wife subgroup is composed of a minute positive effect for the husband, offset by roughly equal-sized negative ones for wives and other earners. These offsetting differences imply very similar (7 per cent) positive differences in average hourly earnings for husbands, wives, and other earners. The net increase of 9 per cent for the total family comes about because of the compositional differences whereby the husband's hours or earnings become a larger fraction of the family's total earnings.[4]

Taken in their entirety, the data in Tables 5 and 6 suggest that there are substantial and significant differences between experimental and control families in terms of number of employees per family. In terms of aggregates, the differences between experimental and control families amount to 12–14 per cent. This reduction in employment is partially offset by the fact that experimental families show a slightly higher amount of total hours per week per employee than control families so that the differences between control and experimental families with respect to total hours per week per family favor controls by only about 10–14 per cent. Because of the large differences in average earnings per hour, which favor the experimental families, experimental and control families do not differ markedly (only by 3.6 per cent in favor of control families) on earnings per family.

An inspection of the data in Tables 1 through 4 suggests that most of the changes which occurred took place between the pre-enrollment and the first quarterly observation. This raises the question of whether all of the results Watts has reported come from adjustments which took place during the first quarter of the experiment. To determine if this is the case he ran an additional set of regressions in which he examined the differentials at the first quarter including among the adjustments the value of the same variable at the time of pre-enrollment, and a second to show the differential at the fourth quarter after adjustments had been made for whatever differences already existed at the first quarter [6]. He found that the larg-

TABLE 6. ADJUSTED MEAN ESTIMATES DERIVED FROM REGRESSION ESTIMATES OF EXPERIMENTAL-CONTROL DIFFERENTIALS IN EMPLOYMENT, HOURS, AND EARNINGS, HUSBAND-WIFE SUBGROUP

Earner	(1) Number of Persons Employed Per Family	(2) Total Hours Per Week Per Employee	(3) Total Hours Per Week Per Family	(4) Average Earnings Per Hour	(5) Average Earnings Per Family
(A) Husbands Only					
(a) Control mean	.885	37.9	33.55	$ 2.61	$ 87.52
(b) Absolute difference	− .032	− 1.0	− 2.09	+ .20	+ .75
(c) Experimental mean	.853	36.9	31.46	2.81	88.27
(d) Percentage difference	− 3.6 %	− 2.6%	− 6.2 %	+ 7.7 %	+ .9 %
(B) Wives Only					
(a) Control mean	.176	28.6	5.03	$ 1.92	$ 9.66
(b) Absolute difference	− .044	− .1	− 1.27	+ .14	− 1.93
(c) Experimental mean	.132	28.5	3.76	2.06	7.73
(d) Percentage difference	−25.0 %	− .4%	−25.2 %	+ 7.3 %	−20.0 %
(C) Other Earners					
(a) Control mean	.180	22.7	4.08	$ 1.76	$ 7.17
(b) Absolute difference	− .075 ‡‡	+ .3	− 1.66*	+ .14	− 2.58
(c) Experimental mean	.105	23.0	2.42	1.90	4.59
(d) Percentage difference	−41.7 %	+ 1.3%	−40.7 %	+ 8.0 %	−36.0 %

* Significant at the .05 level.
‡‡ Significant at the .01 level.

est single adjustment indeed occurred during the first quarter, but that equally significant and roughly equal changes also occurred over the period from the first to the fourth quarterly interviews. In neither case were differences in earnings significant. Consequently, the same positive differentials in average hourly earnings are observed over both sets of comparisons.

Two aspects were explored further in order to gain a more complete picture of the differences between families in the experimental and control groups. First is the question of whether lower employment levels for experimental families are caused by a few persons leaving or staying out of the labor force, or by a more pervasive incremental change in behavior on the part of a majority of primary earners. Second, there is the question of how average hourly earnings changed to produce the observed divergences between experimental and control families.

Watts attempted to answer the first question by looking at how many husbands in husband-wife families employed when the experiment first began were found to be employed at each of the subsequent three quarterly interviews. These data were analyzed separately for husbands who were employed at the onset of the experiment and those who were not employed when the study began. Among the former, Watts found no evident tendency for the experimental group to gain "retirement cases" relative to the control group. The excess of "not employeds" appears instead to be spread out over many persons who are out of work for short periods of time. Similarly, the overall reduction among husbands not employed when the study began is not concentrated in a few dropouts.

Watts approached the second question of how the pattern of hourly earnings changed for experimental and control groups by studying the distribution of average hourly earnings for husband-wife families and for the husband and wife separately within such families. To do this he examined, for experimental and control families, how average hourly earnings per family were distributed at pre-enrollment and then again at the time of the fourth quarterly interview, and how each group, classified by hourly earnings at the time of pre-enrollment, was classified at the time of the fourth quarterly interview. These computations were made for the sample of husband-wife families as well as for husbands and wives separately. The data indicate a tendency for average hourly earnings to increase over time for families in both experimental and control groups, and the amount of increase is greater for the experimental group [7]. Watts also examined how the number of hours worked each week by husband and wife was distributed at the time of pre-enrollment and then again at the time of the fourth quarterly interview. The data indicate that the likelihood of gaining or retaining full-time work is much higher for husbands than for wives [8]. Also, less than one-third of the 39 wives employed full time at the time of enrollment were still so employed one year later, even though there was a net increase of 9 full-time working wives.

Part-time work is generally more prevalent among wives than husbands. About half the control husbands who were not working full time at the outset were doing so at the fourth quarter. In the case of experimental households, those working part time when the experiment began are more likely than controls to have moved into full-time employment. The experimental heads who were not employed at all at the beginning are, by contrast, less apt than equivalent controls to move to full-time employment. In the case of wives the numbers are too small to warrant any attempt to interpret the observed transition except to say that over the first year control wives entered employment in substantial numbers while there was a net reduction in employment among experimental wives.

In summary, it is apparent that a differential response is occurring among experimental families as evidenced by the fact that fewer of their members are employed, and there is a reduced total of hours worked by wage earners in their families. These differences are offset by increases in hourly wages which are in turn produced by the complex changes in work-force participation reflected in this analysis. The remainder of the differential is a result of increased earnings on the part of individual earners. The data also show that the lower number of hours worked and the fewer employees per family do not seem to be concentrated in just a few people nor are they primarily due to changes attributable to the head of household.

Watts' findings yielded an unanticipated outcome. From the outset most economists and other social scientists associated with the project had assumed that any disincentive effect would be reflected in all the indicators of labor supply and earnings. Watts suggested one possible explanation for the findings—that perhaps the experimental treatment provides the security to enable earners to get better paying jobs. Members of experimental families may be able to search longer for jobs, a process which would account for at least part of the reduced employment and hours. However, the final answers to these questions await further analysis, particularly of families in both the experimental and control groups who have attrited from the experiment.

There is one final point. Differential responses within the experimental group by tax plan, and differential responses by ethnic group are of central concern in this experiment. However, at the present time it is difficult to provide even a preliminary indication of what has been occurring in this regard. The reason is that a substantial part of the sample of white families came from Scranton, and enrolling was done in this city well after payments had begun in the other cities.

III. Household Stability

There are a number of important reasons to study the relationship of negative tax payments and outcomes of household stability. First, the costs of a negative income tax program will be affected somewhat by the size and continuity of family units since family size is a determinant of how large the negative tax payments will be [1]. Second, the chances of establishing a negative tax program nationally will be reduced if large numbers of households in the experiment break up. In addition to these two program-related issues, there is the important theoretical issue of the relationship between family stability and an assumed cycle of poverty. Data on household stability from the New Jersey-Pennsylvania experiment may indeed help to shed light on the issue.

It does not follow that the reverse is true; namely, that knowledge and perspectives existing in the technical literature on family stability can be used to formulate hypotheses worth testing. In fact, there is no *a priori* reason to believe that a negative income tax program—especially one of only three years' duration—will have any impact on household composition. Rather than project hypotheses about the relationships between negative tax payments and household stability outcomes, we have decided to take a policy perspective and ask the question: *Do* negative tax payments have an impact on household stability? Perhaps answers to this question will enable us to specify hypotheses for testing.

This section begins with a description of overall or net changes in family types over the first 18 months of the experiment, followed by some discussion about the nature of these changes and the effects of attrition on outcomes. Next we examine a subgroup of composition changes—those related to divorce, desertion, and separation [5]—and attempt to relate outcomes of divorce, desertion, and separation to the tax parameters and some basic economic variables. While we look at data that bear on these topics, we must note that the analysis we present is not nearly so well developed as that for work response. The research subject itself is less well defined, and data bearing on the full range of projected plans for analysis of the topic of household stability can not yet be reported.

Household composition changes

Table 7 presents the overall distribution of family types at pre-enrollment and sixth quarterly. At pre-enrollment there were no significant differences between experimental and control families except in the category of "other," there being distinctly more controls classified as "other" than experimentals.[6] Similarly, at sixth quarterly there were no significant differences between experimental and control families by type (even includ-

TABLE 7. FAMILY TYPE AT PRE-ENROLLMENT AND AT SIXTH QUARTERLY INTERVIEW: PERCENTAGES

Family Type	Experimental		Control	
	Pre-Enrollment	Sixth	Pre-Enrollment	Sixth
Nuclear	87.2	76.7	85.4	79.5
Extended (nuclear)	6.0	7.9	5.6	5.2
Female spouse/head with children	2.8	9.4	2.9	7.9
Other	4.0	6.0	6.1	7.4
Column total	100.0	100.0	100.0	100.0
Column (N)	(649)	(649)	(555)	(555)

ing the category of "other family types"). However, among both experimentals and controls there was a significant shift in distribution of family types between pre-enrollment and sixth quarterly.

In both groups there was a significant increase in female-headed families, as measured by a χ^2 test. Since this event occurred for both experimental and control families, there seems to have been little experimental impact on the distribution of family types during the first 18 months of the experiment. And the event itself is not remarkable since families chosen for the experiment were, by design, almost all male-headed at the time of enrollment.

Mean and median family size are two further ways of measuring gross differences, if any, between experimental and control families. In Table 8 we see that family size was not one of the "all other things equal" at pre-

TABLE 8. FAMILY SIZE AT PRE-ENROLLMENT AND SIXTH QUARTERLY INTERVIEW FOR INTACT FAMILIES: ADJUSTED MEANS AND MEDIANS

	Family Size	
Experimental Status	Pre-Enrollment	Sixth Quarterly
Experimental (N=595)		
Mean	6.10	6.17
Standard deviation	2.19	2.24
Median	5.38	5.25
Control (N=488)		
Mean	5.82	5.87
Standard deviation	2.01	2.14
Median	5.11	5.15

enrollment, since there are statistically significant differences between the mean size of experimental and control families. It is not surprising, then, that the difference in mean family size of experimentals and controls is also significantly different at the time of the sixth quarterly. Since, however, no appreciable difference in means for experimentals and controls, respectively, showed up over time, we have no reason to suspect that negative tax payments had an appreciable effect on family size during the first half of the experiment.

Many factors are related to changes in family size—among them the addition of newborn children, the differential attrition of large and small families, and the addition and deletion of adults. Because fertility is a key policy issue we shall restrict our attention here to the relationship of fertility to family size. (The other factors will be examined in future work.)

During the first year of the experiment, of course, we would expect no differences between experimental and control fertility rates, because there would not have been time for any experimental influences to have affected actual births. During the second full year of the experiment, (tabulations were extended through the end of 24 months for this topic alone) the first period in which experimental plans could have had an effect, rates were not significantly different for experimentals and controls. It should be noted here that the adjusted birth rates of both our groups are higher than the national average in 1970 of 8.8 births per one hundred women, 15–44 years of age [3]. This is due to the fact that our sample has a very different ethnic composition from that of the nation as a whole—being much more predominantly black and Spanish than the general population (see Table 9).

Attrition

As mentioned above, our study (in common with most panel studies) has suffered some attrition of families—more in the control group than in

TABLE 9. FIRST AND SECOND YEAR ADJUSTED BIRTH RATES OF FEMALE HEADS AND FEMALE SPOUSES OF ORIGINALLY ENROLLED UNITS: BIRTHS PER ONE HUNDRED FEMALES 15–44 YEARS OLD

Experimental Status	Adjusted Birth Rate	
	First Year	Second Year
Experimental	13.9	11.5
Standard error	(1.3)	(1.3)
Control	15.8	14.0
Standard error	(1.5)	(1.5)

the experimental group. We must, therefore, worry about the effects of this attrition on changes in the distribution of family types, family size, and birth rates. If families attrite differentially with respect to these factors, doubt must be cast on our results. The data are not available at this time to enable us to make any definitive statement on the characteristics of the families who have attrited. We can, however, test what the effects on our data would be on different assumptions regarding the family distribution of the group we have lost.

In Table 10 we present three forms of the distribution of families that have remained unchanged in composition from pre-enrollment through the sixth quarterly. In the first we made no assumptions about attrition; in the second form we assumed that all attritors changed family status; and in the third we assumed that no attritors changed family status.

TABLE 10. FAMILY TYPES WHICH HAVE REMAINED UNCHANGED FROM PRE-ENROLLMENT THROUGH THE SIXTH QUARTERLY INTERVIEW: PERCENTAGES

	Family Type				
Experimental Status	Nuclear	Extended (Nuclear Core)	Female Head With Children	Other	Total
I. No assumptions made about attrition					
Experimental	82.0	43.6	66.7	73.1	78.9
Control	88.0*	45.2	87.5	64.7	84.1*
II. Assume all attritors changed					
Experimental	74.7	33.3	66.7	54.3	70.6
Control	78.1	33.3	82.3	56.4	73.9
III. Assume no attritors changed					
Experimental	83.6	56.8	66.7	80.0	81.1
Control	89.3*	59.5	88.2	69.2	86.1*

* Differences in proportion are statistically significant at $p < .05$.

For purposes of evaluating the effects of various assumptions about attrition, the categories of "nuclear" and "total" are the most useful. Categories of "extended" and "female head with children" have sample sizes that are relatively small, and since the differences between experimentals and controls are not significant when no assumptions are made about the nature of the relationship between attrition and composition changes, it is not possible to note the effects of extreme assumptions on these differences.

If we consider differences between control and experimental groups in the proportion of nuclear families that remained unchanged through the sixth quarterly, they are significant in two instances: (1) if no assumptions are made about attrition, and (2) if it is assumed that no attritors changed family status. If we make the assumption that all attritors changed status, the difference between experimentals and controls is no longer significant. Exactly the same configuration of outcomes holds for the category of "total." If the assumption is made that all attritors changed status, the significant difference between experimental and control groups no longer exists.

Intactness

Our review of household composition utilized a broad and practical notion of change—namely, any change in family composition for whatever reason that resulted in a change in family type. Reasons included hospitalization and institutionalization as well as divorce, desertion, separation, and the comings and goings of various members of the household. This section will distinguish among the reasons for change—in particular divorce, desertion, and separation in contrast to all other reasons.

The impact of income-maintenance programs on family stability is an important policy issue. For the purposes of the following discussion we shall attribute two assumptions to policy makers: (1) it is best that units remain intact or revert to an intact status and (2) it is best that children live in family units headed by both a male and a female. On these assumptions, insofar as a negative income tax program is expected to have an impact, desired outcomes include reduced rates of divorce, desertion, and separation, and thereby a strengthening of the family.

There are various theoretical positions regarding the expected outcomes of a negative income tax program on divorce, desertion, and separation rates. One line of reasoning goes as follows: In the past, fathers have had to leave their family because, when they have been unable to support them economically, welfare laws forced them to leave in order for the family to be eligible for public assistance. A negative income tax program would help to increase family stability by enabling the family to become eligible for transfer payments without forcing the male to leave the household.

Another line of reasoning suggests that household instability may increase as a result of negative taxes: Family members stay together as a family, even in the face of economic insecurity, because they do not perceive available alternatives. Under a program of negative taxes where the transfer payment does not depend on the individual's position in a family,[7] not only male heads but female heads and other eligible adults would be able to leave their family unit without losing their payments altogether.

Household Stability · 255

A reading of the literature on family stability does not yield a set of specific hypotheses convincing enough, in our view, for testing. We shall, therefore, pursue our analysis from the point of view of the two assumptions attributed to policy makers above. Taking those two assumptions, we are led to the view that a negative income tax program will be considered acceptable to policy makers if it can be shown to lower divorce, desertion, and separation rates, or at the very least not significantly increase those rates. In other words, only if rates go up will there be a problem.

However, the reader should be cautioned about the relationship between the relatively greater economic security afforded by negative tax and outcomes of household stability. Many factors operate on outcomes of household stability and income may not be the most important among them. We must be clear that we are interested in the possible effects of increased economic security on outcomes of household stability—we are not assuming that positive outcomes are to be expected.

In tables that follow we show divorce, desertion, and separation together, and refer to them collectively as separation; the data do not yet enable us to separate the three categories. We do expect eventually to distinguish at least between divorce and separation; desertion may remain moot because in some instances spouses are not able to assess whether the separation constitutes a desertion or not.[8]

For quarterlies one through six, we find that although experimentals have a higher rate of separation than controls—namely 8.0 per cent (or 55 out of 689) compared to 6.1 per cent (or 36 out of 592)—that difference is not significant.[9] There were 72 attritors from the experimental group and 77 from the control group. Of these 8 and 7 respectively separated before attriting. If we assume that the separation rate for those who attrited while still intact was the same as that for those who remained in the sample, the overall rates of separation for experimentals and controls become 8.7 per cent and 6.8 per cent—also an insignificant difference. These rates amount to 91 separations altogether—compared to 46 nonseparation cases where household stability was affected by the absence of a spouse from the household for other reasons (including hospitalization, incarceration, and military service).

Table 11 gives separation rates by stratum[10] and plan. The stratum is given because previous economic circumstances can be expected to have a continuing and significant impact on intactness. Experimental plan is given as low, medium, and high[11] because, if we do expect an impact of negative taxes on the rate of separation we might also expect a gradient of outcomes.

We find in Table 11 that there are no significant differences between separated and intact families by stratum. This is the case for experimentals as well as controls. Differences between the distributions of families by ex-

TABLE 11. SEPARATION BY STRATUM: PERCENTAGES

Stratum	Family Status Experimental			Family Status Control		
	Separated	Intact	Row (N)	Separated	Intact	Row (N)
I.	11.3	88.7	(159)	8.7	91.3	(207)
II.	7.2	92.8	(276)	3.7	96.3	(161)
III.	6.7	93.3	(254)	5.4	94.6	(224)

perimental status also are not significant. By experimental plan (Table 12), differentiated according to groupings of low, medium, and high plans, differences are again not significant statistically. However, by guarantee level (Table 13) we do find significant differences and a clear trend as follows: Families on lower plans have higher rates of separation than families on higher plans. By tax rate (Table 14) we find no significant differences. Of the experimental parameters, then, only the guarantee level seems to have a significant and definite pattern of relationship to family stability outcomes during the first half of the experiment.[12]

In addition to the experimental parameters, we are interested in looking at other variables, independent or intervening, that could be related to outcomes. Of these, data relating to ethnicity were examined next and appear

TABLE 12. SEPARATION BY EXPERIMENTAL PLAN: PERCENTAGES

Experimental Plan	Family Status		
	Separated	Intact	Row (N)
Low	9.2	90.8	(153)
Medium	10.6	89.4	(235)
High	5.3	94.7	(301)

TABLE 13. SEPARATION BY EXPERIMENTAL GUARANTEE LEVEL: PERCENTAGES

Experimental Guarantee Level	Family Status		
	Separated	Intact	Row (N)
50	13.6	86.4	(118)
75	8.8	91.2	(284)
100	7.0	93.0	(156)
125	2.3	97.7	(131)

χ^2 significant at $p < .05$.

TABLE 14. SEPARATION BY TAX RATE: PERCENTAGES

Tax Rate	Family Status		
	Separated	Intact	Row (N)
30	9.3	90.7	(140)
50	8.5	91.5	(388)
70	5.6	94.4	(161)

in Table 15. Separation rates are significantly related to ethnicity, in the case of both experimentals and controls: Spanish families have the highest rates, black families have next highest rates, and white families have the lowest rates.

TABLE 15. SEPARATION BY RACE-ETHNIC GROUP: PERCENTAGES

Race-Ethnic Group	Family Status Experimental			Family Status Control		
	Separated	Intact	Row (N)	Separated	Intact	Row (N)
Spanish	13.4	86.6	(209)	8.7	91.3	(195)
Black	7.4	92.6	(257)	5.0	95.0	(198)
White	3.6	96.4	(223)	4.5	95.5	(199)

χ^2 significant at $p < .05$.

Here, too, a word of caution is in order. There is good reason to believe that the variables of stratum, plan, ethnicity, and site are somewhat confounded. Therefore, the results with respect to all those variables must be treated with extreme caution, pending the further statistical analysis necessary before the confounding can be pinpointed.

Time (meaning how long the family has been receiving payments) may well be related to separation. To examine this question we divided the first 18 months of the program into two time periods—the first six months after enrollment and then the rest of the period. Table 16 shows that the overall figures are very similar for experimentals and controls in each

TABLE 16. SEPARATION BY TIME PERIOD: PERCENTAGES

Experimental Status	Time Period		
	I.	II.	Row (N)
Experimental	47.3	52.7	(55)
Control	47.2	52.8	(36)

period—about half the separations took place in each period for each group. Similarly, the proportions of intact and separated units by stratum (as can be seen from Table 17) appear to be very stable from one time period to the next. While we cannot yet say very much about the relationship of duration on the program to separation outcomes, we do want to stress the possible importance of this dimension. We intend to treat the issue in regression analysis form when we have data on the whole sample for the full three years.

TABLE 17. SEPARATION BY STRATUM AND TIME: PERCENTAGES

Stratum (Experimental and Control)	Time Period I.	II.	Row (N)
I.	56.8	43.2	(37)
II.	48.0	52.0	(25)
III.	34.5	65.5	(29)

Income and intactness

The treatment in the negative income tax experiment is an economic treatment. It is, therefore, important to examine possible relationships between family stability and economic variables.

First, we can compare the distribution of families by income to determine if there are differences in income between separated families and families which have not separated. Second, assuming that the source of money is important—that negative tax payments are essentially different from earned income—we can focus on what proportion of a family's total income comes from transfer payments. Third, we can relate income fluctuations to family composition outcomes. Because of the nature of negative income tax accounting, one would expect fluctuations in total income to be reduced somewhat by the presence of negative tax grants in the total.

We examined the distribution of three kinds of income—earned, subsidy (including negative tax payments), and total income—by family status (separated or intact) fog a complete sample of separated families,[13] and for a random (one-tenth) sample of intact families.

For earned income we find that there are more separated families with lower earned income and fewer separated families with higher earned income, and the reverse is generally true for intact families. Although the trend is clear, however, the differences are not great. For transfer payments there is virtually no difference between separated and intact units. Not surprisingly, therefore, there were proportionately more separated families with total incomes below $4,000.

Because the sample sizes in individual cells are small, tests of significance on the distribution of families by earned income, subsidy income, and total income are inappropriate. The observed tendency of separated families to have lower earned income and lower total income than intact families, therefore, must be viewed with caution, pending further analysis.[14]

Source of money

Since negative tax payments are essentially different from earned income, it is possible that not simply the amount of money but the proportion which is unearned may be important in understanding the relationship between a negative tax program and intactness. To look at this question, we divided our sample into three groups—insured, supplemented, and maintained. We define the insured as those who receive 0–9 per cent of their total income from negative income tax and similar transfer programs; the supplemented as those receiving 10–59 per cent of total income from transfers; and the maintained as those receiving 60–100 per cent of total income from such programs. The data showing the per cents of separated and intact families in each of these categories are not statistically significant.

Income fluctuation and household stability

Negative income tax payments help to offset fluctuations in total income from month to month, simply by their nature. As income rises, payments decrease; as income falls, payments rise. Perhaps, however, fluctuations in earned income as distinct from total income may affect outcomes of separation. This reasoning, too, assumes that negative tax payments are viewed by the families as essentially different from earned income. A detailed test of this notion is not now possible but we can begin to consider the problem.

Our data related earned income fluctuations with the Social Security Administration's definition of poverty (updated for the 1969 cost-of-living increase), with a crisis income situation defined as one in which the family's earned income dropped below the poverty level for two or more payment periods.[15] Of those who did not experience an income crisis relatively few were split families; of those who did experience an income crisis, about a third were separated families. The relationship between economic crisis and household stability is statistically significant—the caveats we have emphasized above should be kept in mind.

Summary

A summary of the five topics covered in this section on the relationship of income to household stability is as follows:

1. For earned income, there was some indication that more separated families had lower incomes and fewer had higher incomes than intact families.
2. For unearned income there seemed to be virtually no difference between separated and intact families.
3. For total income, therefore, there was some indication that more separated families had lower incomes and fewer had higher incomes than intact families.
4. No significant relationships were found when income was separated into earned and transfer income.
5. For income fluctuation, there were more instances of economic crisis among separated families than among intact families.

IV. Conclusion

In our discussion of work incentive and work disincentive we focused on four indicators of work response (number of workers, hours worked, wage rate, and total earnings). We presented experimental-control differences for each of these indicators; we presented more specific results in the form of regression coefficients; and we presented both the more and the less specific results for subgroups of the experimental sample.

In our discussion of household stability we approached the topic in a number of ways. We examined change in family for controls and experimental status: by specific family types; by lack of change in family type over time; in relation to experimental status; by ethnicity and time on the program; by income differences; and by fluctuation and adequacy of income. For experimentals only we looked at changes in family type by plan, guarantee level, and tax rate.

In the case of work incentive and disincentive we could test the existence of a direct relationship between the receipt of negative tax monies and the earning of other monies, utilizing relatively few indicators and relating them, in turn, to no more than three subgroups. Utilizing these variables we found a definite relationship between receipt of negative taxes and work response, though the findings differed according to the indicator used. We found that experimental families and controls were not significantly different in terms of their earned income, but that experimental families worked fewer hours than control families.

In the case of household stability we felt there was no presumption of a direct relationship between the receipt of negative tax monies and the occurrence of divorce, desertion, or separation. We started, therefore, with a general policy concern for a possible relationship between the two factors and approached the problem in a number of ways. This approach was taken because since the publication of the Moynihan report [2] policy makers have been wary of the implications for family composition of a welfare program. Though government officials may not share the Moynihan idea of implementing an income-maintenance program to increase the stability of the black family (and by extension other families), they are concerned with the possible effects of income maintenance on family composition.

We found that guarantee level seems to be associated with family separation, but that stratum, plan, and tax rate are not. The other variables found to be significantly related to separation—ethnicity and income fluctuation, to name two—are nontreatment variables. For the most part, then, our general conclusion is one of "no difference"; adverse effects of a negative income tax program on household stability are neither largely nor consistently evident at this point.

It should be apparent that interpretations of the data presented in this paper depend heavily on knowing more about families who have attrited. Because of the unusual nature of this experiment, we assumed at the start that some families would drop out along the way, and a large percentage of attrition was planned for in the original design. Throughout the experiment extensive and costly efforts have been made to keep these families in the study. In spite of these efforts some of them have attrited. From the point of view of interpreting results, the critical fact to determine is the form which attrition has taken in both experimental and control groups. In order to do this we are planning to do a full-scale study of attriting families so as to obtain from them information about labor-force participation, changes in family composition, and other data needed to compare them with families who have not attrited. When the results of this special study become available we will then be able to complete a full analysis of the topics discussed in this paper and supply more definitive interpretations of the data.

Similarly, we also want to stress that the analysis of both topics discussed in this paper can hardly be considered complete. Because the experiment is still ongoing at the time of this writing, much of the data we need to complete our analysis of labor-force participation and changes in family composition either have not yet been collected or, if collected, are not yet available for analysis. Thus, in this paper we are unable to present the results of analysis of many variables that will clearly have to be looked at before we can make any definitive final statements. Factors such as ethnicity, age, site, knowledge level of the experiment, education, general labor-market conditions, opportunity structures for alternative employment and job training, and a host of other issues and questions must be examined in preparation for the final report.

Notes

1. In January 1969 (five months after our pilot site had been enrolled) the state of New Jersey introduced an Unemployed Parent section into their AFDC program. They also made the welfare provisions much more generous. Before that time only female-headed families had been eligible for welfare in New Jersey—meaning that almost all our sample families were excluded by definition.

2. In these first four tables tests of statistical significance are not reported. Data in these tables are presented merely to provide sample experimental-control comparisons on each of the indices of labor supply and earnings. Results of significance tests are reported along with Watts' regression analysis.

3. In interpreting the results of this analysis, two things should be borne in mind. First, the adjusted means for control and experimental families shown in the tables that follow are adjusted in the sense that each one represents the regression value for the variable for a control or experimental family having the same (that is, sample average) values for all of the other variables in the regression. Thus, they are adjusted in such a way that they would be identical to the crude means in a sample that was exactly balanced between control and experimental groups. Second, the entries for hours per employee and earnings per hour have been calculated from the adjusted means in adjacent columns, and from them the absolute and per cent differences have been derived.

4. It should be noted that the principle of sample selection used is partly responsible for the small fraction of employed wives. Families with total incomes over 150 per cent of the poverty line were not eligible for participation in this study and this in turn makes it difficult for two-earner families to get into the experiment in the first place, even though the husband might be a relatively low-wage earner.

5. This is only one of several subgroups eventually to be studied. Others will include children coming into and leaving the household, the extended family, large and small families.

6. The category "other" included at pre-enrollment: married couples without children, males with children, the above types with extended members, and male- or female-headed families without natural children but with extended members present, usually grandchildren.

7. The Rules of Operation for the New Jersey Negative Income Tax Experiment state, "A family head or spouse who leaves the original unit will take with him or her one of the two adult payments initially assigned to that unit." (p. 21)

8. We are not distinguishing between a legal separation and a mutual agreement to live separately for a period of time.

9. Standard errors for these proportions are .98 and .92, respectively. The bases of 689 and 592 were used because these represent the number of families at pre-enrollment who had the possibility of separating (i.e., those intact at the start of the experiment).

10. Stratum is defined as follows:
Stratum I   Permanent income below 100% of poverty level
Stratum II   Permanent income 100–125% of poverty level
Stratum III   Permanent income 125–150% of poverty level

11. The distribution of plans is as follows:

Plan level	Breakeven point in dollars	Guarantee level as a proportion of poverty standard	Tax rate as a proportion of income
Low plans	$3,692	50	50
	3,952	75	70
Medium plans	$5,304	100	70
	5,654	75	50
	6,084	50	30
High plans	$7,384	100	50
	9,204	75	30
	9,204	125	50

12. There is no reason to present cross-tabulations of these variables because within-cell sample sizes are small and standard errors are large. We shall have to utilize more advanced techniques to get at these relationships, even in a preliminary way.

13. All separated families for whom income data were available for six months or more.

14. The interpretation of lack of differences in subsidy monies leads us into a discussion of the allocation model and the relationship of the negative tax experiment to ongoing welfare programs. Both of these topics are beyond the scope of this paper.

15. A payment period is four weeks long. Crises, as we defined them, are generally widespread in our sample.

References

1. Klein, William A., "Familial Relationships and Economic Well-Being: Family Unit Rules for a Negative Income Tax," Institute for Research on Poverty Reprint Series, Reprint 71. For a discussion of family composition and negative tax accounting.

2. Moynihan, Daniel Patrick, *The Negro Family: The Case for National Action*, Office of Policy Planning and Research, United States Department of Labor, March 1965.

3. U.S. Bureau of the Census, *Current Population Reports, Population Estimates and Projections: Estimates of the Population of the United States and Components of Changes: 1950–1971*, Series P-25, No. 465, Washington, D.C.: September 8, 1971, p. 3.

4. Watts, Harold W., "The New Jersey-Pennsylvania Negative Income Tax Experiment," *The American Economic Review*, May 1969.

5. ———, "Mid-Experiment Report on Basic Labor-Supply Response," *Discussion Papers Series*, Madison, Wisconsin: Institute for Research on Poverty, University of Wisconsin, May 1971.

6. *Ibid*. These data are reported in Table 10, p. 21.

7. *Ibid*. These data are reported in Tables 12–14, pp. 24–26.

8. *Ibid*. These data are reported in Tables 15 and 16, pp. 28–29.

7
*Consumerism:
Origin and Research Implications*

Introduction

In this paper Scott Maynes, author of "Consumerism: Origin and Research Implications," undertook the following:

1. To provide an historical explanation for the consumerism social movement.
2. To describe taxonomically the elements of contemporary consumerism.
3. To present a subjective cost modified "rationality model of consumer choice."

With two exceptions—a quality-adjusted price equation purported to aid in the determination of consumer-market effectiveness, and a list of consumer grievances—Maynes utilized conventional language. Of all the conference presentations Maynes' most clearly addressed all three identified types of theoretical enterprise: description, historical explanation, and deductive explanation.

His deductive explanation of consumer choice gives rise to the following empirical generalizations:

EG18. Consumers will make rational purchase decisions if sufficient price-quality information is available and relatively cheap to obtain, and if the consumer is willing to use it.

EG19. The extent of information search is positively associated with the expected gain relative to the cost of the information.

The profit-loss feature of EG19 defines the marginal level of "relatively cheap" in EG18. Maynes readily admitted that his theory of consumer choice is not only insufficiently tested, but also not completely constructed: "The development of a theory of consumer markets incorporating both imperfect information and quality differences constitutes a . . . major challenge." In our discussion of underlying assumptions above, we considered some of the problems that conferees saw in the theoretical position toward which Maynes is tentatively moving.

Because the historical process of emerging consumerism is complex, we have summarized the key relationships among concepts in Chart 1.

CHART 1. MAYNES' MODEL OF EMERGING CONSUMERISM

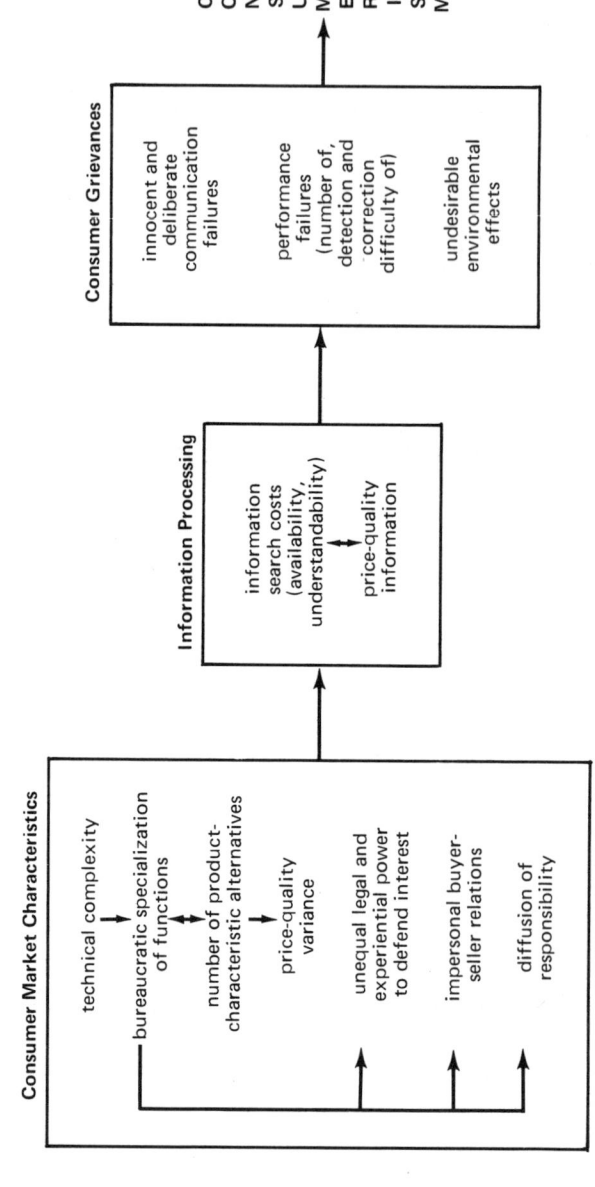

Variables are grouped under three general factors: consumer-market characteristics, information processing, and consumer grievances. The historical route to contemporary consumerism is thought generally to proceed through a causal chain beginning with consumer-market characteristics. Each of the variables, or—more conservatively—most of them, in a block is hypothesized to have a direct effect on the variables in the right-hand adjacent block. Chart 1, therefore, summarizes a number of between-block relationships as well as within-block relationships. For example, Maynes asserted that the more sophisticated the product design (technical complexity), the greater the probability that the product delineated will have some defect and the less likely the consumer will identify and hence avoid the defective specimen (of a good design or a poor design). Information-search costs may be seen here as intervening between technical complexity and the several predicted consequences. High levels of technical complexity make perfect quality-control information too costly for the manufacturer as well as the buyer.

The reader should notice that the above example is presented outside of any special historical context. The model of emerging consumerism, therefore, ought to generalize to any situation where the relevant antecedent conditions exist.[1] Such a deductive explanation and the historical explanation for consumerism in the United States merit further testing and modification.

Reuben Hill and David M. Klein

Note

1. It is also obvious that Chart 1 takes purchase acts and product use for granted. Maynes constructed his explanations of consumerism and consumer choice rather independently, and Chart 1 is intended to reflect the historical development of consumerism. However, if the consumer movement is really a subset of consumer behaviors, then it is probably a consequence of an evaluative response of dissatisfaction. Consumers not only process information in order to make purchase decisions, but also react favorably or unfavorably to the form and content of the information itself.

Consumerism: Origin and Research Implications

By E. Scott Maynes

Among consumers across the land there exists a widely shared feeling of being ill-served by our present production and marketing arrangements and of a need to take corrective actions. Their complaints: poor quality, poor service, dishonored promises, unsafe products, polluting products, deceptive advertising, fraud. To the articulation and dissemination of their views and to the effort to secure corrective measures, we append the label "consumerism." [1]

This paper seeks, in Part I, to trace the economic and historical origins of consumerism and, in Part II, to spell out the implications for research of the growth of consumerism.

I. The Economic Origins of Consumerism

The argument in advance—It may help the reader to present a capsule preview of the argument of this section.

Traditional economic theory suggests—with qualifications, of course—that our present economy should serve up the best quality products at their single, lowest prices. Instead, consumer markets are characterized by the coexistence of high and low prices, high and low quality, high and low price-per-unit-of-quality as well as by dishonored promises, unsafe products, and the like.

Why is it that consumers are so ill-served? [2] The culprit is consumer information. Often consumers are unable to assess quality or to obtain accurate information regarding prices. Sometimes, too, they fail to act upon the relevant information even when they possess it. With its information component in poor repair, the reward-punishment mechanism at the heart of our market economy works badly, giving the results just noted.

The delivery of poor quality, high-priced goods is certainly one of the bases for consumerism. But consumerism is grounded in another manifestation of market failure: the high volume and unsatisfactory resolution of consumer grievances. Consumer grievances include performance failures, misunderstandings between buyer and seller, misrepresentation-deception-fraud, and failure to take account of the environmental effects of products.

It turns out that the technical complexity of products, the impersonality of buyer-seller relations, the difficulty of placing responsibility for consumer complaints, and the dominance of sellers in buyer-seller disputes account for both the high frequency and the unsatisfactory resolution of consumer grievances in 1972.

The Informational Imperfections of Consumer Markets—
Conditions for Effective Functioning of Markets

The consumer's role in a well-functioning market is to identify and reward good performance on the part of sellers. To perform his role effectively, the consumer in turn needs to know the following:

1. What products, brands, sellers exist and where they are available.
2. What characteristics of a product are desirable (product information).
3. The extent to which particular product-brand-seller combinations possess the desired characteristics.
4. Prices of product-brand-seller combinations.

It goes without saying that consumers must not only possess the required information; they must also be willing and able to act on it, all at low cost.

Additional conditions are that there exist numerous alternative brand-seller combinations, and that resources be mobile.

Markets and consumers in 1776

Consider the functioning of retail markets in 1776, notable as the year in which Adam Smith published his *Wealth of Nations,* the first satisfactory analysis of the working of a market economy.

In general, the amount of information required then was much less than now. In the rural, small town markets of that time the identity and location of sellers were common knowledge, available at almost zero cost. What is more, the number of choices to be made was much less than now, due to smaller incomes, access to fewer products, and fewer sellers.

At the same time information was easier to obtain. Products were simple. From common experience people knew what characteristics of products were desirable and the extent to which particular items possessed them. Consider the horse as transportation. No one had any difficulty in understanding how a horse "worked." And, despite a classic literature on horse trading and the people taken in thereby, most people could identify good-performing and poor-performing horses.

The main defect of these local markets was structural: the small size of the market led to local monopolies. Little wonder that this is the defect which economic theory has stressed from that time to this.

Monopoly aside—and this is an important exception—consumers could usually identify and reward good and poor performance by sellers. Under these conditions the reward-punishment system at the heart of a market economy worked well. Through an effective market the presumably selfish motivations of sellers were channeled to a constructive end. Markets tended to be cleared by a single low price.

Markets and consumers today

Two hundred years later the picture has changed drastically. The volume of information which consumers require is now massive. Why? In the first place, consumers have more income to spend. Second, there are more products, brands, and sellers. Third, not only are there more products and brands, but variants of brands have proliferated.[3]

As every car buyer knows, you must decide on body type, "line," transmission, motor size, type of brakes, trim, numerous accessories. The same phenomenon applies, though on a reduced scale, to other products which until recently were single-variant products. Fourth, model changes are becoming more frequent, except (thankfully!) for automobiles.[3] Finally, given urbanization and the automobile, each consumer now has access to more product-brand-seller combinations.

On the other hand the cost of obtaining price and quality information is much greater. Here we properly count as costs not only money outlays devoted to the search for information, but also such subjective though real factors as the utility of activities given up in order to undertake shopping (e.g., the tennis match sacrificed to shopping), and the disutility shopping itself may have for an individual.

As Staffan Linder has so cogently pointed out [9], affluence has brought us more goods, but we are still stuck with the 168-hour week. Interpreted: time is worth more now; hence, the cost of shopping has increased drastically. In addition, the task *per se* of obtaining price-quality information has become more difficult. The accumulated experience of the consumer and his acquaintances, acquired at near-zero cost, no longer enables the consumer to know prices and qualities. Technical complexity accounts in large measure for the extent of consumer ignorance concerning most modern products. This difficulty applies to the ascertaining of prices and the extent to which a brand possesses the desired characteristics as well as knowing what characteristics are desirable. Regarding the latter, we may ask rhetorically: who—before Ralph Nader—had any idea whatsoever of the characteristics of a "safe" automobile?

The widespread dissemination of price and quality information is not *per se* sufficient to assure the effective functioning of markets. Consumers must be willing to act on the information. Everyone knows that new automobile prices are bargainable, but many consumers find bargaining distasteful or lack the essential skills or the supporting information required to bargain effectively. Similarly, even if most consumers were aware of the wide range of prices for a standard package of automobile insurance ($129 to $227 for a "standard" package for an identical driver in Minneapolis),[4] many would not make the effort to search out the lowest priced company.

While the local markets in which consumers deal have deteriorated informationally between 1776 and 1972, they have improved structurally. Due to the automobile, urbanization, and the development of mail-order organizations (especially from 1900 to 1940), the typical consumer today has access to a larger number of product-seller-brand combinations than formerly. Thus, he faces a local monopoly less often. But not all structural developments are favorable. While the consumer typically has access to more local sellers, the number of brands may be smaller, due to economies of scale in both production and selling. The very same economies of scale may, of course, lower the price of products marketed.

The net effect—a judgment, of course—is the coexistence for the same product of high and low prices, good and poor quality, and most important —high and low prices-per-unit-of-quality.

The Matter of Consumer Grievances

The analysis above explains in large part why consumers often fail to obtain the best quality at the lowest price. And the delivery of poor quality, high-priced goods is certainly one of the bases for consumerism. But consumerism is grounded in another manifestation of market failure: the high volume and unsatisfactory resolution of consumer grievances. In this section we shall attempt to account for this phenomenon.[5] We start by enumerating a "catalogue" of consumer grievances.

A catalogue of consumer grievances

The most common consumer grievances may be classified as follows:

Performance failures

1. Goods or service ordered, but not delivered or delivered tardily.
2. Goods or service delivered, but not as specified. For example, a car is delivered minus the power steering with which it had been ordered.
3. Goods fail to perform as might reasonably be expected.
   a. Due to production failure, the particular specimen is defective;

e.g., because a worker on the auto assembly line failed to install a gasket properly, the radiator coolant leaks.
  b. Due to design failure, all specimens suffer same defect; e.g., the design permits water to seep into brakes and hence they operate unreliably during rain.
4. Seller fails to correct production fault or design fault after it is called to his attention.
5. Product is unsafe (an extreme form of 3a or 3b).

Innocent failure of communications

Seller and buyer have different understanding regarding what seller (purchaser) promised with respect to what characteristics the good possesses, price, terms other than price.

Misrepresentation, deception, fraud (clear, deliberate intent to deceive)

1. Seller does not intend to deliver goods or services promised.
2. Seller misrepresents price or other terms.
3. Seller asserts that the product or service has characteristics it lacks.
4. Seller asserts that product is safe, when he has evidence that it is unsafe. (This is what Nader alleged to be the case with General Motors and the Corvair.)

Environmental effects of product not taken into account

Except for the last category, all these classes of complaints existed in 1776, but it is probably true that their number was smaller relatively, and their disposition more satisfactory to consumers than now. Why?

Consumer grievances in 1776

Let us put performance failures aside for the moment and turn our attention to the matter of innocent and not-so-innocent failures of communication.

If, as we argued earlier, consumers in 1776 were in a better position to know price and to assess quality, then it seems plausible that fewer consumer complaints arose. Consumers, we argued, could see through the exaggerations and omissions of sellers. But factors other than those cited earlier probably contributed also to the expectation of fewer communications grievances.

The most important was that, under the conditions of 1776, the buyer was likely to have a personal and long-run relationship with the seller. This prompts the question: how many sellers have the temerity to look a personally known buyer in the eye and then to mislead him deliberately?

And what of the instances where deception and innocent failures in communication did occur? Except for the colorful case of the traveling flimflam man, the placement of responsibility was relatively easy due to the prevalence of small, locally owned, long-lasting retail units whose principal decision makers were likely to be personally known to the buyer.

And if a dispute should arise between buyer and seller, the contest in those days was not likely to be as unequal as it is now. In 1776 it would have been unlikely for a retail organization—even the term sounds alien to 1776—to have a complaint department or a staff (additional alien concepts!) specialized in the handling of complaints. By the same token, the less harried, less affluent consumer of 1776 undoubtedly had more time to invest in the prosecution of his complaint. Not the least of the consumer's levers was the need of the seller—unless he was in fact a monopolist—to maintain his reputation in a small, gossip-prone community where bad news traveled fast.

We are now ready to consider performance failures under conditions of 1776. It is worth repeating: given simpler products, the consumer was better able to detect and avoid performance failures prior to purchase. But even if he should encounter a performance failure, he was in a better position to deal with it.

Being more often a jack-of-all-trades, he could sometimes correct defects himself. If he had to turn to the seller for the correction of a performance failure, conditions were favorable. As noted above, he would have no difficulty in identifying a responsible representative of the seller. In many cases, it was the owner; in most cases, he knew the individual personally. Finally, the seller was often the maker of the goods. If not, either the seller could effectuate a repair himself or he could quickly contact the maker of the goods who was likely to be close at hand.

In sum, in 1776 the relative simplicity of products, the personal relationship between seller and buyer, and the unambiguous placement of responsibility for performance or communication failures contributed to the minimization of consumer grievances and to their satisfactory resolution.

Consumer grievances today

Unfortunately, conditions today are worse in all three respects. And though we are probably unaware of it, the deterioration in all three conditions stems from the increasing complexity of products. But first we will deal with the immediate consequences of complex products.

The technical complexity of modern products by itself is enough to assure a larger number of consumer grievances under the performance failure count. Simply put, the more parts or the more sophisticated the design, the greater the probability that a product will be delivered to market with some defect. By the same reasoning, the more complex the product, either in technical design or number of parts, the less likely it is that the consumer will identify and hence avoid either a defective specimen (of a good design) or a poor design.

Not only is the technical complexity of products likely to increase the number of consumer complaints, it also is likely to affect adversely the correction of complaints. In the first place, it is now less likely that the buyer can correct the faults himself.

Second, it becomes less likely that the retailer—now unlikely to be the maker of the product—can correct the defect, short of replacing the product. (Live there many owners of 35 mm. cameras who have not, at some time, had their cameras returned to the factory for difficult repairs?)

Finally, the large number of parts in modern products coupled with the larger number of products available produces an inventory organization problem of massive dimensions. (Sears, for example, maintains 500,000 "inventory units" for some 65,000 merchandise items.[6]) Only a large and necessarily bureaucratic organization can administer the large inventories characteristic of modern retail establishments. And the size and complexity of this inventory assures numerous delays in identifying, locating, and retrieving the correct part to effect a particular repair.

Product complexity also affects the incidence of complaints arising from innocent and not-so-innocent failures of communication. Since there is more to tell regarding the characteristics of the product, the probability of an innocent failure in communication is greater. And, unfortunately, the same inability of consumers to assess quality enhances the opportunities for deception and fraud.

The retail outlet of 1972

Product complexity is not the only factor giving rise to more consumer grievances and their less satisfactory resolution. A large part of the problem must be chalked up to the vastly changed character of retailing in 1972. Given (1) the mobility which the automobile confers, (2) economies of scale in advertising, financing, and procurement, (3) time economies of scale to consumers in shopping in a single location, (4) the risk insurance feature of multi-establishment enterprises, it follows that today's retail outlet is likely to have the following characteristics:

1. It is large in terms of personnel, financial resources, and—except for specialized outlets—the number of products, brands, and product variants offered.
2. It is *not* locally owned, but is part of a multi-estabishment organization, and perhaps of a multi-establishment, multi-industry organization.
3. It is *not* the maker of the goods it sells.

4. Its handling of various functions is performed by specialists in advertising, complaints, credit granting, etc.

The consequences for the consumer are unfortunate. First, he is unlikely to deal with persons he knows either by name or by sight. Thus, the personal factor which in 1776 minimized the number of consumer grievances and facilitated their resolution will usually be missing in 1972.

In the second place, when a grievance arises, the consumer complainant is likely to encounter difficulties in placing responsibility for the grievance. Why so? The first part of the answer is that the consumer is now dealing with very large organizations, subject to all the infirmities to which bureaucracies fall prey—excessive rule-following, the protective avoidance of responsibility, and the ambiguous division of responsibility. Since these large organizations contain many "parts" and are often themselves parts of even larger organizations, the opportunities for buckpassing are considerable.

Finally, since the retailer is no longer the manufacturer of the product, there arise problems as to the allocation of responsibility between the retailer and the manufacturer. As many car buyers have discovered to their chagrin, auto dealers and manufacturers tend to have conflicting understandings of their respective responsibilities under new car warranties.

With impersonal buyer-seller relations and an ambiguous placement of responsibility, little wonder that more grievances occur and that the probability of satisfactory resolution of grievances is less than it was two centuries ago.

On the communications front the use of the mass media for advertising assures that there will exist no personal relationship between seller and buyer which might inhibit the tendency to dissimulate.

A final, undesirable feature of buyer-seller relations today is that when the consumer seeks correction of a grievance, the contest between the two parties is now vastly unequal. This inequality is explained largely by differences in the nature of the seller's interest in a consumer complaint and the buyer's interest in the same complaint. The seller has a deep, abiding, and highly focused interest in the products he sells and any complaints they generate. By contrast, the complaining consumer has a transient interest in his complaint which could tomorrow be replaced by a different complaint arising from another of the thousands of purchases he makes in a year.

Consider now the capacity of each party to defend his interest. The seller is a specialist in complaints affecting his products. He has accumulated immense experience in handling complaints and defending himself against them. Dealing with many complaints (often of a similar character), he can hire specialized talents at "wholesale" rates (reflecting economies of scale) and develop standardized procedures for dealing with them. His financial resources are enormous as compared with the buyer's. Finally, reflecting the ascendancy of merchants in our society, the laws of contract have usually been drawn to protect sellers and hence tend to make the consumer's right to "his day in court" an imaginary right, not a realistic one [7] [15].

By unhappy contrast, the consumer's capacity to further his complaint is limited indeed. First of all, he is an amateur confronting a professional. Second, the inconvenience and time costs of achieving redress are often large as compared with the money value of the grievance. Third, if legal action is necessary to achieve redress, then it is highly likely that the legal costs will exceed the financial worth of the complaint. Remember that experienced lawyers charge from $40 to $100 an hour and that even the simplest case will involve interview time with the complainant, time to draft a complaint, time to research the law, time to ascertain and confirm the facts, time to track down and interview witnesses, and finally time to try the case. It follows that there are few cases indeed where the consumer complainant would get off for less than $500 to $1,000 of legal fees. Philip Schrag concluded: "The barriers that the legal system has erected to consumer litigation go a long way toward explaining the relative unconcern of merchants and manufacturers about truthful selling and the quality of their products" [15, p. 6].

To all of these disabilities there is one major offsetting factor: the interest of most sellers in retaining the consumer complainant, and those he may influence, as possible future customers. Against this must be balanced the cost of correcting the consumer complaint. If the type of complaint is infrequent or the cost of correction small, then it clearly pays the seller to provide redress politely and willingly. If, however, the cost of correction is large or the complaint applies to a large number of consumers, some conscious of the wrong and others unconscious of it, the seller may feel his interests best served by correcting the complaint for only the most competent and most persistent complainants. In so acting, he would hope that, due to consumer ignorance, his organization's standing with others would not be adversely affected. This explanation is consistent with the routine manner in which automobile manufacturers and distributors have sometimes sought to notify car purchasers of the need to replace defective parts.

To the extent that unequal relations between buyers and sellers prevent the satisfactory resolution of consumer grievances, it must be written down as a cause of consumerism.

Unsafe products—Product safety, arising from failures either in production or in design, deserves our special attention. With the generally simpler products of 1776, the common experience and common sense of consumers usually enabled them to detect and to avoid, or to correct, unsafe products. To the extent that this assumption was true, the cost of design failures was borne by producer-sellers.

As products have become increasingly complex, the ability of the consumer to detect unsafe products has decreased until it must be near-zero for many classes of products. Unable to identify unsafe or badly designed products, many consumers will purchase them. And unfortunately these consumers will bear the costs of the defective design in the form of bodily or property injury, or uneconomic performance on the part of the product. And what recourse does the consumer-victim have? The answer—until recently—has been, "None!" Legal doctrines, conceived in an era when consumers could be assumed capable of identifying seriously defective products, held that makers and sellers were not liable for harmful effects derived from their products [18]. It turned out that for many sellers, it was less costly to market a potentially unsafe product than to incur possible heavy costs in further testing, redesign, or postponement of the introduction date.

So it is hardly surprising that in recent years many unsafe products have found their way to market. And it is equally unsurprising that the marketing of unsafe products has given a strong impetus to consumerism and to strong demands that the rules be changed so as to reduce the probability of unsafe products being put on sale.

Environmental effects—Though economists—Pigou, Kapp, and Coase, for example [12, 8, 4]—have long been aware that the production and consumption activities of one set of people could have adverse (or beneficent) effects on others, environmentalism only became a popular "cause" in the mid-sixties. It is a cause which extends far beyond consumerism. However, it should be catalogued here because, as anyone who has attended a consumer movement meeting can attest, complaints against sellers who fail to take account of environmental effects in designing and selling products are shared by all who identify themselves as consumerists.

A chronology of consumerism

As we have seen, the spelling out of the economic origins of consumerism is a difficult task because of the complex, amorphous nature of the case. Not so the historic growth of consumer concerns. This is graphically mirrored in the circulation growth of *Consumer Reports,* the consumer movement's most enduring institution:

1936	3,000
1937	40,000
1942	80,000
1947	175,000
1952	480,000
1957	780,000
1962	800,000
1967	1,100,000
1972	2,200,000

To flesh out the growth of consumerism and to underline in a different way the growth of consumerism, it is perhaps useful to set down a chronology of consumerism.

1927 Stuart Chase and Frederick J. Schlink published *Your Money's Worth* [3].

1929 F. J. Schlink started Consumers Research, Inc., the first consumer product-testing organization, publisher of *Consumer Bulletin*.

1934 Two New Deal agencies, NRA and AAA, established "Consumer Counsels" to represent the consumer interest.

1936 Consumers Union, publisher of *Consumer Reports,* was formed from a breakoff of staff members and supporters from Consumers Research.

1955 Office of Consumer Counsel was established in New York State.

1957 Consumers Association was formed in Great Britain to publish *Which?*

1960 International Organization of Consumers Unions (IOCU) was formed. By 1970 IOCU included 56 organizations from 32 different nations.

1962 President Kennedy's Special Consumer Message enunciated the four rights of consumers: to be safe, to be informed, to choose, to be heard.

1964 President Johnson appointed a Special Adviser on Consumer Affairs.

1965 *Unsafe At Any Speed* was published by Ralph Nader.

1968 Consumer Federation of America (CFA) was formed to co-ordinate the activities of 189 local consumer organizations.

1969 Truth-in-Lending Bill was passed by Congress.

1970 President Nixon announced that all government product test information will be made public.

1972 Consumer Interests Foundation (CIF) was established by Con-

sumers Union to undertake pro-consumer research other than product tests of interest to individual consumers.
1973? Department of the Consumer was established in the Federal government.

II. Research Implications: A Sampler of Possible Pro-consumer Research

Economists, home economists, market researchers, sociologists, and others have contributed in full measure to research about consumers, as Robert Ferber's review of the consumer behavior literature attests: (See page 29). By unhappy contrast, relatively little research has dealt with either the causes of consumerism or consumerism's "causes." It is the thesis of this section that social scientists owe an undischarged debt to consumers, and further that the repayment of this debt will turn out to be both fruitful and satisfying. In this section I shall present a sampler of potential pro-consumer research proposals.

Documentation of the imperfection of consumer markets

It was argued in Part I that consumer markets work very badly.[2] Instead of being served the best possible product at a single lowest price, consumer markets are characterized by wide variations in prices, quality, and, most importantly, price-per-unit-of-quality. To amplify the last point: quality differences emphatically do not compensate for differences in prices. The foremost reason for this failure of markets is the inability and sometimes the unwillingness of consumers to obtain and to act on relevant price-quality information.

But the illustrative evidence and argumentation of the previous section will fail to convince many. What is greatly needed is careful documentation of the imperfections of consumer markets. Specifically, we need to ascertain for a representative set of consumer goods just how much variation exists in local markets with respect to price, quality, and price-per-unit-of-quality. If convincing evidence is obtained of substantial variations on these variables, then we may properly conclude that markets are operating badly and turn our attention to further diagnosis and to consideration of corrective actions.

There are two compelling reasons for undertaking such a study. In the first place, numerous groups in the economy—professional economists, politicians, civil servants—are unaware of the imperfections of consumer markets and need to be convinced that markets do perform badly (if in fact they do). Second, such a study would reveal to intelligent consumers the substantial payoffs in terms of lower prices and higher qualities which are to be had in response to effective searches.

A study of the imperfections of markets poses some intriguing conceptual problems. For what set of product-seller-brand combinations is it meaningful to measure price and quality variations? We propose to answer this question by defining a *product* as "the set of goods for a given range of outlay which is believed in the consumer's mind to serve the same general purpose." Thus, "intermediate station wagons," "35 mm. cameras under $100," and "gourmet restaurants" might constitute recognizable and plausible product categories. Presumably different specimens within a product class would have rather similar characteristics. The concept is subjective.

The concept of *market* is more difficult. Rational shopping procedures imply that a consumer should continue to search for information as long as the expected gain from a search exceeds the expected cost of that search. But costs will properly include such subjective matters as the individual consumer's distaste for shopping and the utility of alternative activities he gave up in order to shop, e.g., an afternoon of sailing. And the expected gain will be dependent upon his perception, correct or incorrect, of variations in price and quality.

The concept of *consumer market* which we propose is "the set of sellers the consumer would consider if he had perfect knowledge regarding sellers, prices, and qualities." This definition permits the boundaries of a market to be narrowed as a result of high search costs, but not because of ignorance of price, quality, or the existence of sellers. Note that this definition, too, is subjective. Note, however, that the extent of the market is limited by net payoffs from the search, not spatially. It could include mail-order sellers, for example.

We come finally to the *pièce de résistance,* the definition of quality. We define the *quality* of a specimen (a product-brand-seller combination) as "the extent to which the specimen possesses the characteristics which a consumer desires." We take "characteristics" to be an elementary term. Durability, beauty, safety might be examples of characteristics. Essentially, quality, as we conceive it, is a weighted average of characteristics where the weights and judgments regarding the degree to which the specimen possesses a given characteristic are subjective.

Formally, Q_{ijk}, the quality score assigned by the ith individual to the kth specimen of the jth product, is defined as follows:

$$Q_{ijk} = \sum_{\lambda=1}^{n} (W_{ij\lambda} \cdot Ch_{ijk\lambda})$$

where

Ch = a scale with values from 0 to 1.0 denoting the extent to which a specimen possesses a given characteristic.

$Ch_{ijk\lambda}$ = the rating by the ith consumer on the λth characteristic of the kth specimen of the jth product.

$W_{ij\lambda}$ = the weight (relative importance) assigned by the ith consumer to the λth characteristic of the jth product. (Note that the weights for a given characteristic are the same for all specimens of a given product; that is, $W_{ij1\lambda} = W_{ij2\lambda} = W_{ijm\lambda}$ where there are specimens 1 through m.)

For convenience, weights will be set so that

$$\sum_{\lambda=1}^{n} W_{ij\lambda} = 1.0$$

If P_{ijk} is the money price reported for the kth specimen of the jth product by the ith consumer, then we arrive at the quality-adjusted price, P*:

$$P^*_{ijk} = \frac{P_{ijk}}{Q_{ijk}}$$

If "excessive" variation is observed in P^*_j, the quality-adjusted price for a product as reported by all consumers in a market, then we will conclude that a particular market is working badly.

The thoughtful reader will note at once that some variation will arise in P^*_j because of differences in tastes. That is, some consumers will prize characteristics which others disdain. A difficult problem is to determine at what point variation in P^*_j is so "excessive" as to justify the conclusion that a market is working badly.

That measurements of variations in P_j, Q_j, and P^*_j are feasible is suggested by the following estimates for mattresses, food blenders, wool carpeting, and automobile insurance obtained for subareas of Minneapolis by four students of home economics in 1970.[8]

	P_{ij}	Variation in Q_{ij}	P^*_{ij}
Mattresses	$89 to $279	.72 to 1.0	$104 to $278
Food Blenders	$15 to $50	.60 to 1.0	$18 to $56
Wool Carpeting	$10.20 to $20.95 (per yd)	.45 to 1.0	$12.00 to $42.11
Automobile Insurance	$124 to $227	.50 to 1.0	$198 to $348

One qualitative footnote to these estimates: when questioned, all four students expressed the opinion that (1) others undertaking the same investigation would arrive at highly similar results, and (2) that if they were to repeat their own investigation a second time, the results would be relatively unchanged.

An Information- and Quality-Explicit Theory of Consumer Markets

The development of a theory of consumer markets incorporating both imperfect information and quality differences constitutes a second major challenge. A "good" theory incorporates the chief elements of reality, and no more. If the analysis of Part I is approximately correct, then theories which fail to take account of imperfect consumer information as well as differences in product quality will mislead rather than illuminate. Thus the challenge here is for economists to improve the body of economic theory and thus our understanding of the economic system.

An additional reason for suggesting the development of an information-explicit and quality-explicit theory of markets is that theory tends to organize the efforts of the economics profession. For example, the existence of a theory of markets focusing on structural defects as the source of market failures has given rise to the field of industrial organization. Within this field the efforts of a large body of economists are channeled towards the elaboration of theory in this area and also towards the development and evaluation of appropriate public policies.

On the other hand, the activities of Consumers Union in producing and distributing information on product quality have failed to obtain direct support from the economics profession. The same is true of "consumerism" more generally. In my judgment, the incorporation of imperfect information and quality differences into the theory of consumer markets would do much to change this.

A survey of consumer grievances

No matter how important imperfect consumer information is in accounting for market failures, what energizes consumer activists most is the high volume and unsatisfactory resolution of consumer grievances—those instances where individual consumers feel themselves wronged by particular actions or nonactions of sellers.

The rising tide of consumerism is a matter of interest, and sometimes concern, to politicians, civil servants, businessmen, consumerists themselves, and students of consumer behavior. It follows, as a derived relationship, that these groups should be greatly interested in the "facts" of consumer grievances. Perhaps surprisingly, no one has yet made a systematic effort to collect the facts on consumer grievances.[9]

To collect the facts on consumer grievances, what is needed is a "Survey of Consumer Grievances," to be undertaken on a recurring basis. Such a survey might collect data of the following kind with respect to the major classes of consumer grievances: relative frequencies, the nature of the grievance, dollar estimates of damages, subjective importance to consumers, actions taken by consumers in seeking redress, disposition of the grievance, the consumer's satisfaction (or dissatisfaction) with the disposition of the grievance, the time and money invested by the consumer in seeking redress.

Obviously consumer grievances should not be accepted at face value. The design of such a study should provide for the collection of information on the same grievance from both consumer and seller. This would enable the investigators to identify "genuine" (confirmed) grievances, bogus grievances (where the investigators conclude that the consumer was *not* wronged), and disputed grievances (those alleged grievances which cannot be placed in either of the foregoing classes with confidence).

Earlier research suggests that the poor, blacks, and ghetto dwellers experience more frequent and more serious (relatively) grievances [7]. The sample design, data collection techniques, and field arrangements of any SCG should be designed so that the consumer grievances of these groups will be well measured.

To students of family or consumer behavior it is perhaps not untoward to suggest that an SCG might be a suitable successor to the Surveys of Consumer Finances.[10]

The effectiveness of consumer search procedures

When the intelligent consumer asks the consumer economist, "How much should I shop?" the standard answer derived from the economist's model of utility maximization is likely to be: "Shop (search) as long as the expected gain from the next search exceeds the expected cost of that search." This response of course is a nonanswer, leading to the further questions: "How do I know what the expected gain will be?" "On what does it depend?" "What do you mean by the 'cost' of the search?" [11] Easy questions first. The costs of the search might include direct, objective costs (e.g., the operating costs of the car on a particular shopping expedition); direct, subjective costs (e.g., the dollar equivalent of the disutility of shopping with a car full of children); the indirect, objective costs (income foregone in order to undertake shopping); indirect, subjective costs (the dollar equivalent of the activity in which the consumer might otherwise have engaged; e.g., reading, a picnic, tennis). The sum of these comprises the cost of the search.

The answer to the first two questions is complex, and necessarily qualified. Perhaps the most convincing and illuminating answer would be to cite the results of studies which carefully simulated sequential searches under realistic conditions. Such a study would serve two purposes: (1) it would exhibit the size of consumer gains (payoffs); (2) it would test the rationality model of consumer choice.

For discussion purposes it is perhaps useful to consider a simulation study of automobile insurance purchases I conducted several years ago. The study population consisted of 64 students who either owned an automobile themselves (55 per cent) or whose parents owned an auto (45 per cent). The students were asked to price a standard package of automobile insurance, approaching sellers in the order they would normally use. If they wanted, students could price additional coverages, but they were required to obtain a separate estimate for the standard package. After each price quotation—and prior to obtaining another quotation—students were asked to state whether, under real life conditions, they would "buy now" or "search further." Each student was asked to obtain three price quotations.

The study obtained estimates of gross payoffs; i.e., the reduction in price, if any, obtained from each search. The study was defective in that the gross payoff was not adjusted to take account of possible differences in quality. Nor did the study collect estimates of search costs. It was assumed that "consumers" of the study could judge for themselves whether the payoffs obtained would exceed their own likely search costs.

Some salient results from the study were as follows:

1. The study uncovered evidence of a wide range of prices. The mean of the price range (the highest price minus the lowest of the three obtained) was $60, to be compared with a mean price of $180. Bear in mind that all the price quotations were for cars to be driven by a person under 25. On the other hand, bear in mind that the price quotations were obtained by persons already possessing insurance who were seeking the lowest possible prices.
2. Consumers appeared to know when to "search further" and when to "buy now" on the basis of bids on hand.
   a. The probability of obtaining a lower bid was .47 for those who decided to search further as compared with .25 for those who decided to buy now.
   b. However, the average gain—the amount by which the search actually reduced the price for those who chose to search further or would have reduced the price for those who chose to buy now was about the same for both groups, about $31 on the average.
3. Consumers appeared to be knowledgeable about their own capacity to decide effectively. Those who labeled themselves high on a scale with respect to their competence as consumers tended to have obtained their lowest bid on the first search more frequently (61 per cent) as compared with those who labeled themselves as less competent (27 per cent).

All in all, the data from this study suggest that these university students, and perhaps all consumers, are capable of using a rational search framework effectively in making a major purchase.

A single study, too sketchily summarized to permit an adequate appraisal of its quality, can be no more than suggestive. What I do urge is that studies such as this are a proper focus for a pro-consumer research program. Their results should ultimately enable consumer economists to provide intelligent consumers with well-supported advice regarding the effectiveness of alternative consumer-purchase procedures.

The efficiency of regulation

Scratch a consumerist and, chances are, you will discover an economic interventionalist—one whose almost automatic response to a class of chronic consumer grievances is to propose government regulation.

It is my suggestion that the application of disciplined thinking and research to the question of appropriate remedial policies for consumer grievances would have high payoffs for consumers in general.

Let us consider government regulation. There are at least two steps in utilizing government regulation as a remedy: (1) the specification of the appropriate rules or corrective actions; (2) the allocation of resources sufficient to assure that the corrective rules or actions are enforced with some acceptable level of probability. Let us call the first the "appropriateness" problem and the second the "efficiency" problem. We will discuss each in turn.

The key question in the appropriateness problem is whether the proposed corrective rules or actions will achieve the desired end. As an example, consider ghetto dwellers' access to short-run consumer credit. Numerous studies suggest that the poor in general are charged higher finance charges or have their loan applications rejected at a higher rate than the nonpoor [16, 17]. As a remedy, most people in the consumer movement would probably support legislation establishing a maximum legal finance rate. Existing legislation in many states already includes such limits. The leading variants of the Uniform Consumer Credit Code also include a limitation of this sort. Enforcement problems aside, would such an enactment achieve its intended end? I believe not, on the grounds of the following simple argument.

Common experience and common sense suggest that lending to the poor is a high-cost proposition—the "bad loan" rate will be higher than for other groups and if loans to the poor are to be profitable to the lender, he must be able to cover his bad loans by charging a higher over-all finance rate. If the legally allowable finance rate is not high enough on the average to enable him to recover his costs, he will not make this type of loan. Hence, rather than enabling the poor to obtain credit at a reasonable rate, legal loan limits at too low a rate (how low?) will cut off credit to the poor —at least from legitimate lenders.

Recent, empirical evidence relevant to this cutoff phenomenon comes from the regulation of revolving credit in Minnesota. When a court decision reduced the allowable finance charge on revolving credit from 18 per cent to 12 per cent—an obviously desirable end—BankAmericard in Minnesota stopped accepting new applications, evidently on the grounds that the new permissible rate was not profitable [14].

The discussion above is too cursory, probably, to be convincing. It is offered as an example of the proposition that the "obvious" corrective measure may not yield the desired objective. What is needed is careful study of alternative means.

Until the appropriateness problem is solved for a particular policy matter, the efficiency problem remains irrelevant. If the analysis of the previous example is correct—and I do not assert that the case was in fact made—no amount of resources devoted to enforcing a maximum allowable finance charge will attain the desired end.

But suppose the appropriateness problem is successfully solved, then the efficiency problem must be faced: what amount of resources is required to see that the corrective rules or actions are enforced with some acceptable level of probability?

I have canvassed practitioners and literatures of several social sciences in search of a compact set of principles relating to the efficiency problem. Finding none—perhaps due to an insufficient or inefficient searching—I propose the following set of propositions for critical review.[12] In general, government regulation will be more efficient when

1. *The number of units to be regulated is smaller*—Suppose, for example, one wanted as a matter of public policy to dampen the noise output of snowmobiles. One alternative, adopted by a number of communities, is to enact a local ordinance prohibiting noise emissions above the critical limit. For this approach to be effective, the actions of millions of snowmobile owners must be monitored and, in many cases, corrected by hundreds of communities. A more efficient alternative approach would be to impose a decibel limit by regulation or by tax on the relatively small number (one hundred?) of snowmobile manufacturers.

2. *The number of actions to be monitored is smaller*—It is more efficient for the Price Board and the Wage Board to monitor the prices and wages of a small number of important industries and firms than to perform the same task for all producers.

3. *The action being regulated is conceptually simple*—It will be easier, and hence more efficient, for an agency to verify the installation of a given set of safety features in new automobiles than to insure that public utilities are charging prices which yield a reasonable rate of return on investment.

(The latter question has given rise to an entire profession, complete with university courses, professional association, and journal.)

4. *The agency is smaller*—When regulatory agencies become large, we would expect them to suffer from all the classical defects of bureaucracies.

5. *The agency is younger*—Like people, government agencies appear to exhibit with the passing of time both the favorable and the unfavorable effects of aging.

6. *The agency is independently and adequately financed*—Suppose that a state tax department were authorized to hire additional personnel up to the point where the expected additional revenues of the last employee hired just equaled his salary. Suppose further that the department's budget represented a first claim on tax revenues. We could then say that this department was independently and adequately financed. Under such conditions one would expect a much more vigorous and equitable enforcement of tax laws. Agencies whose budgets are dependent upon legislative appropriation are vulnerable to "starvation through underappropriation." A standard second line of defense for opponents of particular regulations or agencies is to reduce the agency's budgets so that it lacks the resources to perform its assignment effectively.

7. *The agency is armed with meaningful enforcement levers*—For example, a $5,000 fine to a giant corporation is not a meaningful lever. By contrast, the requirement that ITT Continental Baking Company dedicate 25 per cent of its advertising budget over a six-month period to the dissemination of the message that its product "Profile Bread is *not* effective in [attaining] weight reduction," is a meaningful lever.[13]

The above list, probably incomplete and perhaps defective, is submitted as exemplifying the type of propositions which would help consumerists and others in forming judgments regarding the desirability and form of government regulation in particular instances.

The Consumption Function from the Consumer's Viewpoint

It was argued earlier that economists have a responsibility to assist consumers in making better choices at a level of abstraction and reality which is useful to them.

As an example, consider the consumption function. Vast efforts have been expended by economists seeking to develop and test theories explaining how consumers do in fact divide their income between consumption and saving. But turn the question around and you have a subject which is almost untouched: what fraction of its income should a family save, year in and year out? Specify that the household wishes to save for (1) the children's college education and (2) retirement income, and, with careful specification, you have a researchable problem. The pro-consumer viewpoint produces a new and interesting question. If the results are successfully communicated on a wide scale, they should prove helpful to consumers.

A second example concerns life insurance. It is an interesting socioeconomic question to ask whether families purchase enough (or too much) life insurance to provide the level of after-death income which the husband-wife really want for survivors. If they fail to do so, they suffer from a life insurance "deficit." A research problem on which I have already conducted a pilot study [11] is to ascertain the size, distribution, and determinants of the life insurance deficits of American households.

A "Truth Tax" to Finance a "Consumer Information Corporation"

Research on behalf of consumers can also involve the development and refinement of policies and institutions designed to improve the functioning of markets from the viewpoint of consumers. The proposal for a "Consumer Information Corporation" (CIC) is an example.

In 1970, according to estimates made by Professor Ivan Ross of the University of Minnesota, businesses devoted $67 billion to informing and persuading consumers. It was distributed as follows:

Advertising	$21 billion
Sales promotion, including direct mailings	7
Personal selling (the information and persuasion efforts of all sales personnel)	36
Public relations	3
Total	$67 billion

By contrast, consumer organizations spent but $13 million for the same purposes.[14]

The business expenditures on consumer information and persuasion were financed by what is, in essence, a 10.9 per cent "sales tax" on consumer spending. That is, prices on the $616 billion of aggregate consumption expenditures were set high enough to enable the businesses involved to recover the $67 billion they expended on consumer information.

Is this arrangement, sanctioned by long usage, in the best interest of consumers? I think not. We know, both from vivid personal experience and from *a priori* argument based on the self-interest of sellers, that the price-quality information provided by businesses is biased by exaggeration or omission. Nonetheless, business-provided price-quality information might be acceptable if we could be reasonably sure that consumers could "see through" the distortions and omissions. Unfortunately, they cannot, due to the technical complexity of products and other factors cited in earlier sections of this paper.

For consumers to obtain accurate price-quality information, it follows that some information-providing resources should be shifted from business to consumer control. How might this be achieved? Perhaps by levying a tax—a "Truth Tax" if you will—on business-promotion expenses (the four categories listed above) and transferring the proceeds to a consumer-controlled Consumer Information Corporation (CIC).[15]

Such a corporation might in the near future (1) conduct product tests, (2) collect data on consumer satisfaction with providers of services (plumbers, lawyers, doctors, automobile repair agencies), (3) use the mass media as well as the printed word to disseminate such information, (4) append comparative rating labels to products marketed. In the more distant future, CIC might investigate new technologies for performing its role; for example, the use of cable television or the telephone to provide consumers with two-way access to computer information "banks."

* * *

The foregoing represent examples of pro-consumer research. It is my hope that they will inspire our several professions to undertake more research from this viewpoint.

Notes

1. Colston Warne, President of Consumers Union, spoke succinctly of efforts to develop a "national consumer consciousness." [19] Presumably this represents his definition of consumerism.

Virginia Knauer, President Nixon's Special Adviser on Consumer Affairs, offered a more detailed definition.

"Consumerism is nothing more and nothing less than a challenge to business to live up to its full potential—to give consumers what is promised, to be honest, to give people a product that will work, and that is reasonably safe, to respond effectively to legitimate complaints, to provide information concerning the relevant quality characteristics of a product, to take into consideration the ecological and environmental ramifications of a company decision, and to return to the basic principle upon which so much of our nation's business was structured—'satisfaction guaranteed, or your money back.'" From a speech by Mrs. Knauer in Indianapolis on January 14, 1972.

Finally, Aaker and Day [1] defined consumerism as "the organized efforts of consumers seeking redress, restitution, and remedy for dissatisfaction they may have accumulated in the acquisition of their standard of living."

2. Lest the reader be misled, let me state at the outset that this paper does not essay a comprehensive assessment of the effectiveness of markets. Instead, it focuses on those aspects of market failure which, in the author's judgment, account for the rise of consumerism.

3. These points were suggested to me by John Hancs, Director of Marketing Information for Consumers Union.

4. Data were obtained by Letha Phelan, a graduate student in Home Economics at the University of Minnesota from a set of seven insurance companies thought to

include both low- and high-priced companies. When the data were deflated roughly to take account of quality, the range increased somewhat from $198 to $348.

5. We will usually use the term *grievance* rather than *complaint*. In our usage *grievances* are instances of consumer dissatisfaction, whether communicated to other persons or not. We reserve the term *complaint* to those grievances where the dissatisfaction has been communicated to someone else.

6. Source: *Sears 1969 Annual Report,* p. 10, and letter from William P. Zabler, National Manager of Service for Sears, dated December 6, 1971.

7. For two graphic examples of consumers' difficulties in using the law to seek redress, consider [17, 16].

8. The students were Susan Clausen, Patricia Gangelhoff, Letha Phelan, and Ruth M. Sargent.

9. In 1971 Consumers Union collected some information regarding consumer complaints in its Annual Questionnaire. About 55 per cent of respondents reported making a complaint. Of those reporting complaints, about 41 per cent were satisfied with the disposition as against 59 per cent who were dissatisfied. (The 14 per cent who did not answer the satisfaction question are excluded.)

The CU data, though helpful, are of limited use since subscribers to *Consumer Reports* differ greatly from the average American consumer and respondents to CU's Annual Questionnaire differ from nonrespondents.

10. Though only a relatively small number of close friends knew of it, the venerable Survey of Consumer Finances (SCF), for 24 years a fixture in the research establishment, has passed away. More accurately, the *1971 Survey of Consumer Finances* will be the last of the annual reports updating series on consumer income, durables spending, debt, liquid assets, etc. Henceforth, it is expected that comparable data will be collected and published on a bi-annual or tri-annual basis.

The Survey Research Center will continue the quarterly series of surveys on which its Index of Consumer Sentiment is based.

It might be an apt turn of events if the late SCF were to be succeeded by SCG, the Survey of Consumer Grievances. The Survey Research Center which conducted SCF for so many years is admirably equipped to undertake an SCG. A continuance of the SCF basic data series, via an SCG, would be a welcome by-product for the research community.

11. For an analysis showing the consumer how to locate payoffs from the search, see [10].

12. For the reader interested, however, in a searching review of government procedures for evaluating alternative socioeconomic policies, see Alice Rivlin's little book [13].

13. At about the time this statement was written, it was proved wrong, a victim of the "appropriateness" problem. More specifically, the author failed to take account of two factors: (1) the psychological principle cited by Gwen Bymers that individuals do not differentiate carefully between negative and positive messages, and (2) the ingenuity of advertising copywriters in perverting a negative message.

This is the negative advertising message televised on behalf of Profile Bread:

"I'm Julia Meade for *Profile* bread. And like all mothers I'm concerned about nutrition and balanced meals. So, I'd like to clear up any misunderstandings you may have about *Profile* bread from its advertising or even its name. Does *Profile* have fewer calories than other breads? No, *Profile* has about the same per ounce as other breads. To be exact *Profile* has about seven fewer calories per slice. That's because it's sliced thinner. But eating *Profile* will not cause you to lose weight. A reduction of seven calories is insignificant. It's total calories and balanced nutrition that counts. And *Profile* can help you achieve a balanced meal. Because it provides protein and B vitamins as well as other nutrients.

"How does my family feel about *Profile?* My children love *Profile* sandwiches. My husband likes *Profile* toast. And I prefer *Profile* to any other bread. At our house delicious taste makes *Profile* a family affair." Quoted in *Consumer Reports,* February, 1972, p. 64.

Consumer Reports quoted an official of ITT Continental as stating that this advertisement "has not proved detrimental" to the company.

14. As noted in the text, I am indebted to Professor Ivan Ross for this estimate of business expenditures for consumer information purposes. Sources and assumptions were as follows:
   a. Advertising—21 billion. From S. Banks, R. Reisman, and C. Y. Yang, *Advertising Age*, June 7, 1971, p. 27.
   b. Sales promotion—$7 billion. From A. W. Frey and J. C. Halterman, *Advertising*, ed. 4 New York: Ronald Press, 1970, p. 40.
   c. Personal selling—$36 billion. There exists no satisfactory estimate of expenditures on personal selling. However, Brink and Kelley are quoted in Boyd and Levy as asserting the existence of a 3-to-1 or 4-to-1 relationship between expenditures for personal selling vs. advertising. Splitting the difference and applying the 3½-to-1 ratio in 1970, we estimate total personal selling expenditures at $72.8 billion. Assuming arbitrarily that one-half of the efforts of sales personnel are devoted to informing and persuading, we arrive at the $36 billion estimate (½ × $72.8 billion). Cf. Harper W. Boyd, Jr. and Sidney J. Levy, *Promotion: A Behavioral View*, Englewood Cliffs, N.J.: Prentice-Hall, 1970, p. 10.
   d. Public relations—$3 billion. The estimate for public relations expenditures is even cruder than those for other components. Ross accepted a forecast by Kalman Druck (*Business Week*, July 2, 1960, p. 42) that public relations expenditures, estimated at $2 billion in 1960, would be $6 billion in 1969. He assumed, again arbitrarily, that one-half of public relations expenditures activities are directed toward consumers.
   e. Aggregate personal consumption expenditures—$616 billion. From *Survey of Current Business*, July, 1971.

15. It turns out that a strikingly similar proposal was made twelve years ago by a British economist, W. M. Corden. Cf. Max Corden, *A Tax on Advertising*, Fabian Research Pamphlet 222, London: The Fabian Society, 1961. Corden proposed to tax only advertising expenditures while we propose to tax a much broader base, the sum of business expenditures devoted to informing and persuading consumers.

References

1. Aaker, David A., and George S. Day, "A Guide to Consumerism," *Journal of Marketing*, October 1970.

2. Buskirk, Richard H., and James T. Rothe, "Consumerism, an Interpretation," *Journal of Marketing*, October 1970.

3. Chase, Stuart, and Frederick J. Schlink, *Your Money's Worth*, New York: Macmillan, 1927.

4. Coase, Ronald H., "The Problem of Social Cost," *Journal of Law and Economics*, October 1960.

5. Hermann, Robert O., "Consumerism: Its Goals, Organizations and Future," *Journal of Marketing*, October 1970.

6. Holton, Richard H., "Business and Government," *Daedalus*, Winter, 1969.

7. Kaplovitz, David, *The Poor Pay More*, New York: The Free Press, 1963.

8. Kapp, K. W., *The Social Costs of Private Enterprise*, Cambridge: Harvard University Press, 1950.

9. Linder, Staffan B., *The Harried Leisure Class*, New York: Columbia University Press, 1970.

10. Maynes, E. Scott, "The Payoff for Intelligent Consumer Decision-Making," *Journal of Home Economics*, February 1969.

11. ———, and Loren V. Geistfeld, "The Life Insurance Deficit of American Families: A Pilot Study," manuscript submitted, 1972.

12. Pigou, A. C., *The Economics of Welfare*, ed. 2, New York: Saint Martin's, 1960 [1931].

13. Rivlin, Alice M., *Systematic Thinking for Social Action*, Washington: The Brookings Institution, 1971.

14. Ross, Irwin, "The Credit Card's Painful Coming-of-Age," *Fortune*, October 1971.

15. Schrag, Philip G., "Consumer Rights," *Columbia Forum*, Summer, 1970.

16. ———, "Bleak House 1968: A Report on Consumer Test Litigation," *New York University Law Review*, March 1969.

17. "Translating Sympathy for Deceived Consumers into Effective Programs for Protection," *University of Pennsylvania Law Review*, January 1966.

18. Vanderwicken, Peter, "Toward the Socialization of Injury," *Fortune*, November 1971.

19. Warne, Colston E., "The Impact of Consumerism on the Market," *The San Diego Law Review*, February 1971.

Consumerism: Origin and Research Implications
A Response

By Gwen J. Bymers

Professor Scott Maynes has written a wide-ranging paper. In the introductory section he either nodded to or touched most of the bases of an introductory course in consumer problems. The research implications section is aptly named a sampler of proconsumer research because in this section he identified several substantive researchable questions. It is just this ability to blend an understanding of the broad dimensions of the consumer field with the insights of the research scholar that makes Scott Maynes one of its leaders.

The paper provides us with his definition of consumerism, its history, a rundown on the current market environment, with all its imperfections. It contains a section on the information gap, on grievances and problems associated with their resolution, on product safety, and on environmental concerns. Among the research suggestions, we have price-per-unit-of-quality, both marginal and total cost of consumer-market search, an attempt to make operational a definition of quality, and a suggestion for a survey of grievances. In the area of regulation he raised the dual issue of appropriateness and efficiency; regarding the consumption function—that aspect of consumer economics that economists are apt to know best, at least at the macro level—he has introduced a micro concept that most of us who have worked with consumer problems at the family level have intentionally shied away from as a matter of principle. Last, and far from least important, he tackled the question of delivery of consumer information and even suggested one method of making the present institution of advertising more effective in this role.

It is obvious that I cannot discuss all these concepts; therefore, I have been selective in the issues that I am going to raise. I deliberately chose a few points on which I hold a somewhat different position than Maynes does. This selection factor may exaggerate the negative. I do not mean it that way because *in toto* I agree on most of the points he made. We are in a period of rising consumer concern. The information gap is a key barrier to effective reduction of consumer problems; we need to teach people to be more efficient customers; intervention should not be viewed as a panacea, without explicit study of its appropriateness and efficiency; and, somehow, the institution of advertising has to be made to serve the interest of those of us who pay for it.

With that as my introduction, let me get on with the first point I should like to discuss—Maynes' definition of *consumerism*—which focuses on the failures of the market, the widely shared feeling among consumers of being ill-served, and the need to take corrective action. "To the articulation and dissemination of their views and to the efforts to secure corrective measures, we append the label consumerism." I find I need a different definition of consumerism. This may be because it is a term I have avoided for years. I have only recently succumbed to the power of the journalists and decided that if the word was here I had better learn to live with it.

My definition of consumerism goes like this: Consumerism is a term that connotes the rising level of public awareness of problems and issues that affect consumer well-being, both in the private market and in the public sector of the economy. The key words are *rising awareness, issues, consumers, private market,* and *public sector.* I think this definition encompasses all of Maynes' problems, but it also leaves room to consider successes, as well as failures. These, too, are in the domain of the consumer interest and should be encompassed in the definition of consumerism.

This definition grows out of a hypothesis as yet untested. The rising level of concern about consumer issues is a product of two successes—one a production and marketing success and the other an educational accomplishment. The first success placed a large proportion of the American public in command of more discretionary purchasing power than they ever expected to control when growing up. The second is less obvious but only a little less pervasive—the gradual accumulation of a rising level of education among the population.

These two successes—the expanded purchasing experience (both the good and the bad) plus the increased years in formal schooling—augmented by the consciousness-raising activities of such institutions as Consumers Union and Ralph Nader and the addition of a generation of high school and college Home Economics teachers and the County Extension Service, even though many of their efforts have been derided as too feeble, combine to create a climate conducive to consumerism. It has not been a planned co-operative venture; indeed the activities of these groups have not always been in harmony. Nonetheless, there is emerging in a sizable portion of the population a rising level of expectations about their rights and responsibilities in the market. I doubt that this could have occurred if we had not increased the average level of education in the entire population by approximately 3.5 years between 1940 and 1970.

Professor Theodore Schultz alerted us some years ago to the role of investment in human capital as the key explanatory variable in productive improvement [9]. The rising level of consumer awareness, *consumerism*, may be a concomitant development that we have been a little slower to recognize.

This approach to consumerism has another advantage; it has helped explain a riddle that has been bothersome for some time. Why was the consumer movement so markedly unsuccessful at earlier periods in our history? There were obvious problems faced by the consumer in the marketplace (I do not agree that somehow the earlier economy served consumers better than it does today). There were even some early attempts to organize nationally to solve problems. Both in the early 1900s and in the 1930s there were efforts in the consumer direction; a modest amount of consumer-oriented legislation was passed; a few organizations were born but only one really survived.

My previous explanations were economic and somewhat cynical. In neither 1906, nor in 1936, could we as a nation afford to cope with consumer problems. Subsistence production still had priority for too many of us; and furthermore, the political structure provided token legislation aimed at the most flagrant abuses, often taking the steam out of the critics. By the 1960s the situation had changed (despite our well-documented levels of poverty): the bulk of our population had discretionary income. Today we can enter into more purchasing experiences, and we have increased our intellectual capacity to reflect upon our environment, to raise issues, and to ask questions.

My definition of consumerism is broad enough to include the questions that have been framed by the Welfare Rights Organization and by student groups. Both are raising consumer-oriented questions regarding services or products generated in the public sector, be it a welfare service or a college curriculum that is at issue. A portion of the consumer concern of the 1970s is likely to be an allocation question. How much of our national product is being directed through the public sector? In what form will this occur? These are policy-level questions that consumerists will have to face in the 1970s if a responsible job is to be done in this area.

Enough on consumerism. I hope I have made the point that consumer issues are broader than the poor performance of the market sector. I want to continue on another point. This one reflects a disappointment on my part. Professor Maynes stated in connection with the varying-prices-per-equivalent-quality discussion "that consumers are unable or *unwilling* to obtain the relevant price-quality information and are unable or *unwilling* to act upon the information they possess." The italics are mine. When I read this, I anticipated that in the research implications section there would be some mention of research aimed at explaining this continued unwillingness of consumers to behave the way we professors think they should. That is: identify need, search the market, compare price and product characteristics, read the independent consumer testing and rating agency reports, put all this down in an orderly fashion, add preference vectors for particular characteristics and come up with a "best buy for me" solution. Instead, most of Professor Maynes' suggestions focused on the unable part of the statement; the unwillingness was not tackled directly.

Maynes is convinced, as I am, that the market is capable of serving us better than it does and that there are substantial payoffs for the individual consumer who will engage in careful shopping. An interesting thing about this is that, if we succeed in teaching consumers to be better shoppers, the entire performance of the market should improve. Once that happens there will be a decided reduction in any payoff that one can expect to earn by spending time on comparative shopping! A nice thought—one measure of success for the buymanship school of consumer educators may be how soon they put themselves out of business!

The model suggested by Maynes to define quality of a multifaceted product for an individual consumer is an interesting and attractive exercise for present-day economists or students who are trained to put their ideas into a mathematical form (see page 282). For many items purchased by the average household, the class of product can be identified and the salient characteristics defined, and some individuals may be able to establish the relative importance of each characteristic so that a set of appropriate weights can be determined. Most careful shoppers, whether they are inclined to think mathematically or not, actually behave in somewhat the fashion Professor Maynes described. They make trade-offs when trying to select a product.

Take a dress, for example—fashion, durability, ease of care, color, and fit, are characteristics one expects to find in some combination in a garment. In all likelihood, one trades off durability and ease of care for higher ratings on the other three. The market responds. In my experience it is easier today to find fashion and fit than it is to find a quality fabric. Ease of care has moved up fast at the expense of durability and that elusive something we used to call "hand-made" in the garment business.

A group of young professors and researchers at the Cornell School of Business and Public Administration have been experimenting with simulated buying exercises. The purpose of their approach has been market-oriented, but it is not unrelated to the type of exercise Professor Maynes used. The Hughes [4] experiment was designed to answer four questions: (1) Are computer-controlled experiments a viable means for studying consumer behavior? (2) Do subjects behave realistically during such an experiment? (3) Can information in a simulation induce changes in subjective probability? (4) Can changes in attitudes be induced and measured with computer-controlled simulation? The answers were affirmative for questions 1, 3, and 4. For question 2, the answer was uncertain, but like Professor Maynes' subjects, 73 per cent felt they had behaved realistically. Only 10 per cent thought they had not. The rest were not sure.

The interesting thing about this experiment is that it allowed for the impact of personal (friends' and neighbors') experience as well as test data from Consumers Union and dealer input as the subject pursued the game over time. It began with present brand preferences (3 out of a possible 70) and current probability of purchasing a new car within the next six months. In the course of the experiment all subjects increased the probability of replacing their present car. Furthermore, 66 per cent altered the rankings of their probabilities of buying specific brands. The experiment was designed with a subtle bias toward switching. This was an experiment: it cannot be generalized to all buying behavior; but it does have promise in another direction which would be much closer to Professor Maynes' pro-consumer research.

The cost of the search for most prospective buyers both in direct cost of visiting several sellers, seeking out necessary information, to say nothing of the indirect costs (ranging from what you did not do with the time involved to the frustrations generated), all conspire to make consumers unwilling to engage in careful shopping behavior. Perhaps we will some day program a computer on which current prices, characteristics, and brand information on given classes of products can be stored. The prospective buyer could then assign his own weights to the set of characteristics he deems important within the constraint that the sum of these must equal one. This information could be plugged in and a quality adjusted price (P_j^*) would emerge for an initial selection of preferred items. Of course, this service could be made available at a price. Many careful shoppers would be willing to pay for it. I understand that the hardware is already available to make such a service possible. The trick has been to get the cost of a pass through the computer down to a reasonable figure.

Before I go any further, I would like to add a caveat—one that I think is related to explaining the general unwillingness of a sizable section of the public to act on the information it now possesses, let alone engaging in the esoteric mathematics and gyrations of the computer to obtain more. It is a subjective reaction, not an objective one. People hesitate to use what they do not understand.

This failure to use what we do not understand accounts in great measure for the reluctance to make use of the technical information available every month in *Consumer Reports* on a dozen or more durable items. My colleagues at Cornell, V. R. Rao and David Hughes, wrote an interesting paper on this topic [7]. They suggested that the Consumers Union rating scheme be reduced to a three dimensional model, substituting (1) technical complexity, (2) performance, and (3) user convenience for the several specific attributes now being tested. Scales would have to be developed for these three dimensions, but this could be accomplished and the information reported in a manner to enable a consumer to incorporate his prior knowledge of a product class and/or additional sources of information that might have appeared in the market since the Consumers Union tests. The consumer should also be able to apply his own preference or weights to these three characteristics.

As it is currently released, product information is so detailed as to make cross-product comparison by price on selected sets of attributes difficult. Furthermore, less information appears on products that fall in the "not acceptable" range. This precludes the interested consumer from examining the Consumers Union evaluation critically [8].

Having attempted to work my way through the Rao-Hughes model, I am not at all sure I will find their approach easier to use than I do the current Consumers Union reports, but I do think they are on an interesting track. As a consumer, I could make more sense out of concepts such as complexity, performance, and user convenience than I can out of vertical tracking force, alkalinity, displacement, or axle ratio.

In line with my theory that people are willing to lay out money for products they do not understand before they will engage in the ego-deflating exercise of gaining information they cannot process prior to making the purchase, there is another angle. Our bad experiences in the market have not cost us enough. Individual consumers are not penalized enough for sloppy shopping habits.

In spite of the spate of statistics that consumer advocates give us about the costs of the failures in the market, for the individual the market has performed tolerably well. When a consumer does get a "lemon" it may become a grievance for which he seeks redress, but it is more likely charged off to experience, in some cases not even discussed. It may emerge as a sore point for a short period of time but seldom remains salient for very long. Furthermore, the reaction is most likely against the manufacturer or seller for providing a bum product (which may well have been done) and seldom motivates the consumer to engage in more careful shopping practices before making the next purchase.

As a consumer educator, I keep hammering on the need to register product or service complaints with retailers and with the manufacturers. They have a right to know when something is unsatisfactory, and we have a responsibility to provide the information. There is scarcely a person in consumer education who has not wished from time to time that he really knew the extent of consumer dissatisfaction. I have some sympathy for the suggested Survey of Consumer Grievances suggestion (see page 284). There is always the suspicion that we are dealing with only the tip of the iceberg. Press releases and general statements of consumer dissatisfaction can be pretty sweeping.

In this connection there have been several small studies, mostly on appliances, made over time and the experience of the Major Appliance Consumer Action Panel (MACAP) is informative. In the more general complaint area, the joint committees that have been formed among federal, state, and local law enforcement and consumer groups in several major cities should begin to provide some clues to the real dimensions of the consumer complaint situation [3]. The committees operate with an executive secretary and keep a record of total complaints received by subject, type, and business operation involved. The information thus collected should form a sizable data bank on the general topic of consumer grievances. Certainly we need to recognize that many dissatisfied customers will not make their complaints official. However, if we are willing to apply the same standard to consumer dissatisfaction as we do to consumer demand—that is, to be counted as a consumer want an object must be translated into a purchase decision that makes a cash register ring—then to be counted as a consumer dissatisfaction a complaint must have been salient enough to be reported somewhere. The increase in public awareness and the presence of local consumer action offices make reporting a possible assumption.

In the 1950s, when millions of homes were being equipped with washers, dryers, and dishwashers for the first time, the repair and service call business flourished. *Time* magazine and other popular media ran extensive news stories on rising consumer dissatisfaction. During these years and into the early 1960s the many students who investigated consumer satisfactions or dissatisfactions with purchases found a lower level of dissatisfaction than they had anticipated. One appliance study in an upstate New York community that involved 60 homemakers and 305 small appliances ranging in age from one to over twenty years, found only 12 per cent had ever been repaired; 2 per cent needed repair, and 84 per cent needed no repair [10].

In another study [6] dealing with larger appliances, information was gathered from 206 homemakers living in villages, small towns, and farms, and owning 739 large appliances. This study investigated the amount of service needed, service resources utilized, difficulties encountered, and a rating on the service agency on such items as know-how, courtesy, pride in work, and leave-the-work-place-clean. Even here, where 43 per cent of the items required service at least once, a figure that I thought was rather high, the homemakers were not dissatisfied and they gave the service or repairman high marks on his performance. Service calls were frequently related to installation problems, inappropriate electrical wiring, or plumbing problems; perhaps the homemakers honestly did not judge this to be the fault of the equipment manufacturer.

One student recently analyzed a random selection of consumer correspondence received by a large food manufacturing firm [2]. The firm followed the policy of logging every piece of correspondence and filing either the letter or a manifest in a chronological manner. These were kept for approximately one year. This made it possible to select on a purely random basis a sample of all the mail received over a period of several months. She analyzed each piece of correspondence according to content. Whenever a problem was involved, she related it to an appropriate function in the company. The letter was also rated as to its tone and its effectiveness as communication. Much to her surprise, less than half of the total correspondence had to do with complaints of any kind, and even in connection with these only about half again could be classified as unfavorable or angry in tone. Perhaps one of the findings most useful to the field of consumer education is that only about one letter out of ten contained enough information to be really helpful to the manufacturer without his having to follow up to obtain such obvious clues as where or when the item was purchased or for how much.

One study did turn up a finding that I regard as troublesome [1]. In the early 1960s one of our students investigated consumer relations programs and the post-purchase communication to the dealers and manufacturers. The study focused on the channel of distribution and its operation in receiving and transmitting consumer complaints and other communications. An unexpectedly low frequency of consumer response was noted; retailers reported less than did manufacturers. One must either presume that homemakers are more prone to communicate with manufacturers than with retailers if they have a complaint, or that what filters through the service desk to top management of the retail institution is limited. One is tempted to guess the latter is the case.

The most recent attempt of industry to cope with the consumer grievance problem is the experience of the Major Appliance Consumer Action Panel [1] established by the Association of Home Appliance Manufacturers and the Gas Appliance Manufacturers Association, the trade associations in the electrical and gas home appliance field, and ARF, the American Retail Federation.

The panel has no enforcement powers, but as of November 1, 1971, out of more than 3500 complaints that reached its office, 262 came back to MACAP for review between June 1970 and November 1971. Out of this group, 57 per cent had been resolved to the mutual satisfaction of both parties; 20 per cent were found to be unjustified; 9 per cent are pending; 7 per cent are unresolved because the customer is not satisfied; 2 per cent unresolved because the manufacturer would not accept the recommendation; and 5 per cent had to be ruled out of MACAP jurisdiction. For example, the case may be in the courts and then MACAP pulls back [5].

The MACAP experiment, if extended to other product lines, may prove one of the more effective approaches to the consumer grievance question and the eventual improvement of the market. It has not proceeded without mishap, but as routines have been developed and systems established for handling the paper work, and as panel members have become familiar with the appliance industry and the nature of consumer problems that occur, they are developing a kind of expertise that produces mutually acceptable results.

On the theoretical front most of us in consumer work will agree with Professor Maynes that the development of a theory of consumer markets that incorporates imperfect information and quality differentiation into a workable model will be a giant step forward. In addition to its possible intellectual value, such a development has practical import. Several policy issues currently before state and federal legislative bodies involve both regulatory and advocacy proceedings. In either case, those charged with considering the proposed legislation and those charged with implementing it will be benefited if such an economic analysis can be provided.

The last point I would like to make has to do with Maynes' suggestion that we research how a family should allocate its income. I question this, unless it is framed very carefully in terms of desired goals. The single most frequent question asked those who teach family financial management goes something like this: "How much should my wife spend on food or clothes?" or "How much should we save?" I always counter with, "What are your savings goals? Where do you want to be when? How many children are you planning to educate? What kind of income earning capacity does the wife have?" We need to improve the tool kits that are available for families in the area of spending and saving; but I think if we prize the need for teaching individuals to arrive at their own decisions, we must be very careful to avoid saying how much a family should spend or save.

Perhaps the most crucial challenge facing professionals in the consumer field is how to arrive at a set of workable solutions to the real problems of product safety, inadequate product performance, and poor communication in the market without creating a monstrous bureaucracy with a host of new problems for everybody concerned. This is what I think Professor Maynes was alluding to when he spoke of the dual problems of appropriateness and efficiency in relation to regulation.

It will be a pity if having reached the highest level of living in human history and having the capacity to provide a higher level of education than we ever thought possible, we create so many problems in the production and distribution of goods and services that we have to opt for less freedom in the market and a more costly distribution system. This could not be regarded as progress under my definition of consumerism.

Note

1. MACAP is a panel consisting of eight independent members who represent a broad range of expertise in the fields of education, counseling, research, design,

home management, finance, communications, and law. Its assignment is to serve as an investigatory panel on any complaint that has not been resolved at an earlier stage. It has received considerable publicity since its inauguration in 1970. Complaints may come to it directly from individuals who have been unable to obtain satisfaction on particular issues involving a malfunctioning appliance, poor service, or similar failures. One can also reach MACAP through the Office of Consumer Affairs in the White House or through any other consumer representative or office. When a complaint is received at the Chicago address of MACAP, the plan is to send it immediately to the appropriate trade association for investigation or resolution. MACAP follows up within two weeks if not informed of a solution. If the individual and the company involved cannot reach an agreement on an adjustment, the MACAP panel reviews the case and makes its recommendations.

References

1. Averitte, Marlene D., "Consumer Relations Programs and Post Purchase Communication to Dealers and Manufacturers of Selected Kitchen Appliances," master of science thesis, Cornell University, 1963.

2. Brousseau, Mary Catherine, "An Investigation of the Content of Consumer Correspondence in the Food Processing Industry," master of science thesis, Cornell University, 1970.

3. Federal Trade Commission, *Consumer Alert*, 1, No. 9, October 1971.

4. Hughes, G. David, and Philippe A. Naert, "A Computer Controlled Experiment in Consumer Behavior," mimeographed report of a project later reported in several articles.

5. MACAP report, Appendix A of the December 1971 meeting, and a conversation with Dr. Mary Purchase, member of the panel.

6. Miller, Helen G., "Servicing Major Household Appliances," master of science thesis, Cornell University, 1958.

7. Rao, V. R., and G. David Hughes, "A Search for Models of Consumers Union's Brand Evaluation: A Multi-Dimensional Approach," Proceedings of the 2nd Annual Conference of the Association for Consumer Research, College Park, Maryland, September 1971.

8. *Ibid.*, pp. 172–173.

9. Schultz, Theodore W., "Investment in Human Capital," *American Economic Review*, LI, March 1961, 1–17.

10. Woodard, Janice E., "The Extent and Nature of Repair of Household Electrical Appliances," master of science thesis, Cornell University, 1956.

8

Consumer Financial Management and Financial Institution Response –

A TWO-DECADE PERSPECTIVE

Author's note: The extensive professional assistance of Bernard Clyman, William Gobbo, Yul Rhee and Mrs. Rita Scholze (all members of The Equitable's economics staff) is gratefully acknowledged. All errors remain the author's responsibility.

FRANCIS H. SCHOTT

Introduction

In his paper "Consumer Financial Management and Financial Institution Response—A Two-Decade Perspective," Francis H. Schott's theory-relevant purposes can be viewed as both descriptive and historical explanations which

1. Describe and explain recent historical changes in consumer financial management behavior.
2. Describe and explain the recent historical changes in the structure and performance of various financial institutions.

Schott used the conventional mode of expression to develop his analysis. Empirical generalizations that can be adduced from the Schott paper are stated as follows:

EG20. Increasing education levels, disposable income, and financial management experience have increased the consumer's financial sophistication and his investment and disintermediation of financial assets in response to investment performance.

EG21. Financial institutions have responded to the competitive climate created by an increased consumer financial asset orientation with differential growth rates partly contingent on the variation in government regulations.

EG22. The discrepancy between long-run expectations and current investment performance, in part, causes consumer financial asset management decisions (Puckett).

EG20 is rather straight-forward and reflects Schott's basic thesis: that consumers over the last twenty years have become more active and discretionary, more return-conscious as well as safety-conscious, in their allocation of net worth increases. While not emphasizing the historical antecedents of the rising level of real income, Schott mentioned technological advances and improved productivity as logical possibilities.

In his attempt to demonstrate that increased sophistication is a diffuse phenomenon, Schott indicated that "the distribution of total income by percentiles of income groups has shown very little change over the past two decades." We wonder how this evidence can be reconciled with the Segal-Felson evidence that relative deprivation in income has increased over roughly the same period. Schott himself recognized that "the larger depositor and the owner of a life insurance policy of greater cash value are more likely to have the knowledge and ability to disintermediate." The implication to draw from this confusing situation, Juster noted in effect, is that aggregate analysis may conceal group differences in the applicability of EG20.

The interrelationship between consumer financial management and the actions of financial institutions is a very complex matter. EG21, therefore, residualizes a number of important considerations. Schott preferred to see consumers exhibiting a "revealed preference" for delegating asset management to financial institutions and otherwise making enlightened use of their services, thereby creating new opportunities for those institutions. But such opportunities are also limited by legal constraints which vary from institution to institution and from time to time, as Schott illustrated. Other factors which Schott considered to exert minor influence are the promotional strategies of financial institutions and their locational convenience. Schott's data led him to conclude that the major variables accounting for the utilization of various types of financial institutions are "disintermediation incentive" (relative rates of return), the inflationary condition of the economy and, especially, disposable income levels.

In his special treatment of the depressed competitive state of the life insurance institution, Schott generated an intriguing hypothesis: "the financial returns from life insurance savings are either insufficient or insufficiently understood to compete with the clear and explicit rates of return available on alternative forms of savings." This hypothesis implies, among other things, that information costs to determine investment–savings payoffs must be "reasonable" in order for the consumer to engage in a particular asset management behavior. Confusing information is costly, even for the sophisticated consumer. We have here, it appears, a special case of the more general information processing dynamic discussed in other contexts by Ferber, Maynes, and several other discussants.

EG22, derived from Puckett's formal discussion, deserves close examination. Schott had suggested that the improved performance of the investment market during the last twenty years increased the consumer's confidence and, in turn, shifted the saving-spending balance further in the direction of various forms of saving. Puckett explored this general idea in some detail. His line of reasoning may be summarized using a series of situation-specific propositions derived from his comments.

1. A progressive increase in economic expectations from 1950 to 1965 produced an improvement in the financial position of families.

2. The extinction of the Depression Psychology produced increased consumer confidence from 1950 to 1965 which, in turn, improved the performance of the investment market.
3. During the 1950s, realized investment return rates exceeded expected investment return rates, producing windfall wealth.
4. Windfall wealth in the 1950s produced an increase in the incentive to save and invest.
5. A decrease in the performance of equity investments from 1965 to 1970 produced disintermediation in favor of more secure savings and investments.

Proposition 1 is a general statement encompassing the chain of events asserted to have taken place in propositions 2 through 4. These latter propositions express the reciprocal feed-back effects between the dispositional constructs, expectation and confidence, and the economic variable, investment performance. Proposition 5 reflects the profit-loss orientation that Puckett shares with Schott and is only implied by proposition 1 if one assumes that maximization of economic utility is expected as well as desired by consumers.

The interaction of dispositions with economic performance is further recognized if one asks the question, "How else is pessimism extinguished except by learning about or experiencing real performance increases?" In other words, the causal priority of variables in the scheme abstracted from Puckett is not satisfactorily disentangled. Schott moved outside economic variables to education level, for example, in order to locate exogenous inputs to consumer sophistication. One might propose other exogenous inputs to account for sources of change in consumer expectations and investment market performance, respectively. Perhaps part of the answer lies in the conceptual distinction between expectations and confidence.

More theory building along these lines is clearly called for and is certainly within the present capabilities of the social sciences. We do not think we have expected too much of Puckett's short discussion, for it can be a valuable source for generating new ideas.

As a closing comment, we wish to call attention to a particular feature of proposition 1 and EG22 above. In discussing relativity concepts in Section 1, we identified the discrepancy between expectations and performance in the investment market as "relative performance." Puckett viewed the recent historical manifestation of this notion as a case of expectations lagging behind performance. Long-term trends, however, might show that for certain periods, expectations exceed performance. Worthy of further exploration are the psychological consequences of discrepancies in either direction, as well as their "natural" limits or self-correcting tendencies. A cognitive dissonance theory might be as useful a tool for deductive explanation here as it has been speculated to be in other contexts during the conference, although at this point we will leave to others the task of constructing such an explanation.

Reuben Hill and David M. Klein

Consumer Financial Management and Financial Institution Response – A Two-Decade Perspective

By Francis H. Schott

I. Introduction

The consumer as a financial factor has been relegated to a subordinate role in the literature on aggregate economic activity. In both Keynesian and monetarist economics, the consumer is largely passive, responding to income changes caused by exogenous factors. In Keynesian economics, these factors are largely fiscal policy and business investment; in monetary economics they consist chiefly of one or the other of various measures of aggregate liquidity.

Both schools of thought have been giving some attention to the "linkage mechanisms" that connect the respective suspected primary causes with their resultant responses in household behavior by studying portfolio and wealth effects of changing economic circumstances upon the consumer. It is clear, however, that both theories start out with a heavy ideological handicap vis-à-vis an eclectic approach to the direction of causation in aggregate consumer behavior.

Empirical verification of any and all of the "linkages" through which fiscal and/or monetary policy is supposed to influence consumer behavior continues to be sharply complicated by data difficulties. Theoretical and practical deficiencies abound in the figures on consumer savings and financial assets and on liability management derived from either the national income or flow-of-funds accounts. Furthermore, it has also been virtually impossible to reconstruct aggregate savings data from the limited cross-section studies of consumer financial behavior available from microeconomic data.

Meanwhile, the problem of explaining consumer financial management is an increasingly nagging one. It became abundantly clear in the late 1960s that the individual (or family unit) exercises considerable discretion and increasing acumen in financial management. These developments will be better documented once the reader has perused the review of aggregate consumer finance in Section II of this paper and studied the major economic factors shaping changing consumer reactions presented in Section

III. But to anticipate briefly and summarize baldly, it may be stated that there have been two important contributing factors in changing relatively passive consumer attitudes into increasingly active personal financial management. First, the interacting forces of increased education levels, real incomes, and financial assets of the general public; and second, the associated greater recognition given to financial rates of return, which has been sharply accentuated by the growing need for inflation protection during the late 1960s.

The consequences of these developments present problems not only for aggregate economic analysis and fiscal and monetary policy, but also for financial institutions. It is this latter aspect of progressively more sophisticated public attitudes towards consumer financial management that will be the focus of Sections IV and V. The facts that can be derived from an analysis of differential growth rates and from the consumer attitudes implicit in these growth trends are worthy of review and can perhaps be exploited as indicative of future trends, as attempted in Section VI.

II. The Consumer's Financial Position, 1951–70

1. Assets, liabilities, and net worth

Our review of major developments in consumer finance will begin with a summary of broad trends in aggregate consumer financial assets, liabilities, and net worth over the past two decades. In this first step, we shall minimize hypotheses and assumptions and shall let the data speak for themselves.[1]

Important work in this area was done by A. Marshall Puckett and Joel I. Brest in an article on "The Financial Position of the Consumer," which appeared in early 1966 [1]. The authors undertook an appraisal of the gross and net financial position of the consumer sector by grouping major classes of consumer assets and liabilities as recorded in the Federal Reserve flow-of-funds accounts and striking a balance between the two for the years 1952 and 1964. The deflator problem was attacked by relating both assets and liabilities to personal outlays (basically personal consumption and interest payments) in percentage terms.

Certain shortcomings of this approach were freely acknowledged. None of these is more disturbing than the massive aggregation involved in just identifying and terming the "consumer sector" of the economy. Apart from the inclusion of certain private nonprofit institutions (principally foundations) in the "consumer sector," there is an unhappy failure to distinguish wealth or income groups by even the crudest of criteria.

As a first step in adjusting for this shortcoming, Puckett and Brest defined the net financial position of consumers in two different ways. They distinguished between total assets and liabilities and "widely held" assets and liabilities in measuring the gross and net financial position of the consumer sector. Total assets included the categories of bonds, stocks, and (ownership of) mortgages. "Widely held" assets included only "liquid" assets such as demand and savings deposits and United States Savings Bonds, plus life insurance and pension fund reserves. In the first case, assets were netted out against all liabilities—consumer installment debt, mortgage debt, and a catch-all category of "all other"; in the second case, the "all other" category of liabilities was omitted in the netting out. The broader measure was all-inclusive but the narrower measure was said to be a better rough approximation of the financial position of the typical consumer.

No major improvements in this approach to the consumer sector's total financial position have been presented in the intervening years, although sections of a recent paper by Mahlon R. Straszheim hold promise in terms of a more refined econometric approach [11]. Meanwhile, there follows a summary updating of the broad trends in the consumer's financial position over the last two decades.

A. *Absence of sharp swings in consumer's net financial position*— Disregarding all but the broadest trends apparent in the two panels of Chart 1, one cannot help but be struck by the remarkable degree of stability shown by either measure of the consumer's net financial position relative to his outlays. While it is perfectly apparent that there are noteworthy trends in either measure which should be explored, the total variations over the span of nearly two full decades are not of major magnitude. If one were to strike a simple arithmetic average of the end-of-year figures recorded in Chart 1, the maximum deviations from that average in any one year would be within ±20.5 per cent in the case of Measure 1 of the consumer's financial position, and within ±7.5 per cent in the case of Measure 2. Moreover, a first glance at Chart 2—which gives the main components of the two measures arithmetically averaged for the three most recent five-year periods—also suggests considerable stability in the composition of the main asset and liability groupings adding up to the net worth measures.

It is, of course, observations of this type—along with the relative stability of the savings rate as recorded in either the national income or the flow-of-funds accounts—which encourage the proponents of a "passive" consumer. In some basic sense, the consumer in the aggregate has in fact managed his financial assets and liabilities in a reasonably stable manner. Nevertheless, as I hope to show, some probing in these figures for the evolutionary changes will prove rewarding.

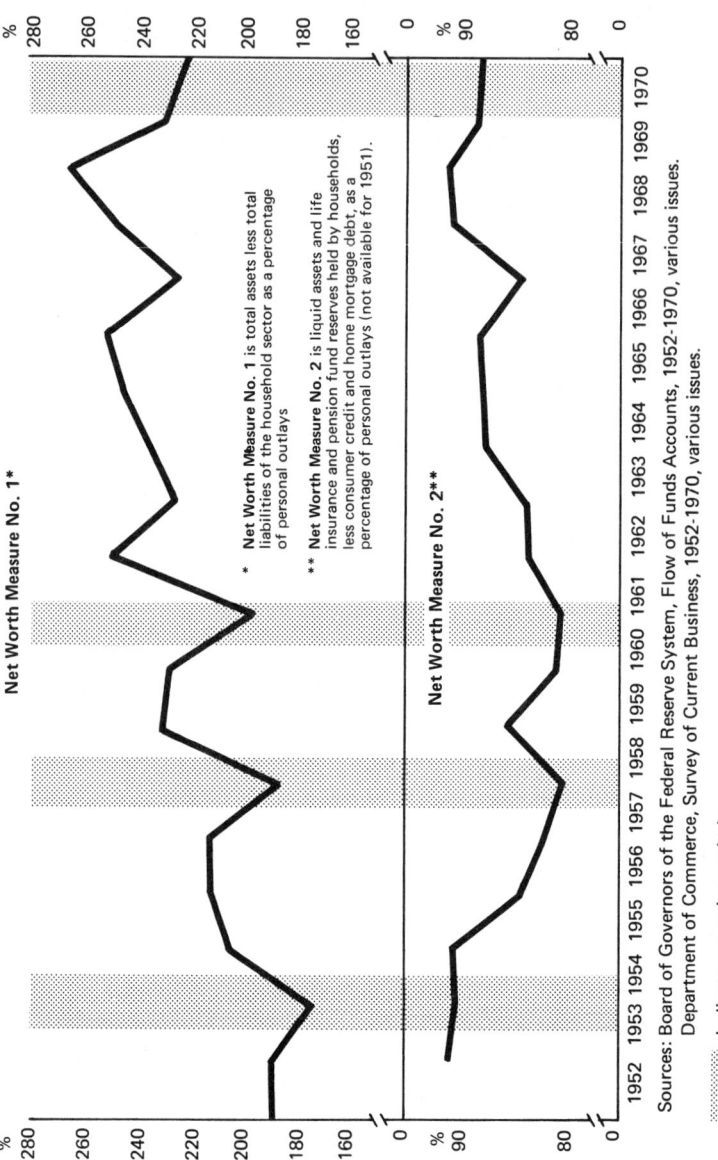

CHART 1. TWO MEASURES OF CONSUMERS' NET WORTH, 1951-70
(Based on Year-end Levels)

* **Net Worth Measure No. 1** is total assets less total liabilities of the household sector as a percentage of personal outlays.
** **Net Worth Measure No. 2** is liquid assets and life insurance and pension fund reserves held by households, less consumer credit and home mortgage debt, as a percentage of personal outlays (not available for 1951).

Sources: Board of Governors of the Federal Reserve System, Flow of Funds Accounts, 1952-1970, various issues. Department of Commerce, Survey of Current Business, 1952-1970, various issues.

Indicates recession periods.

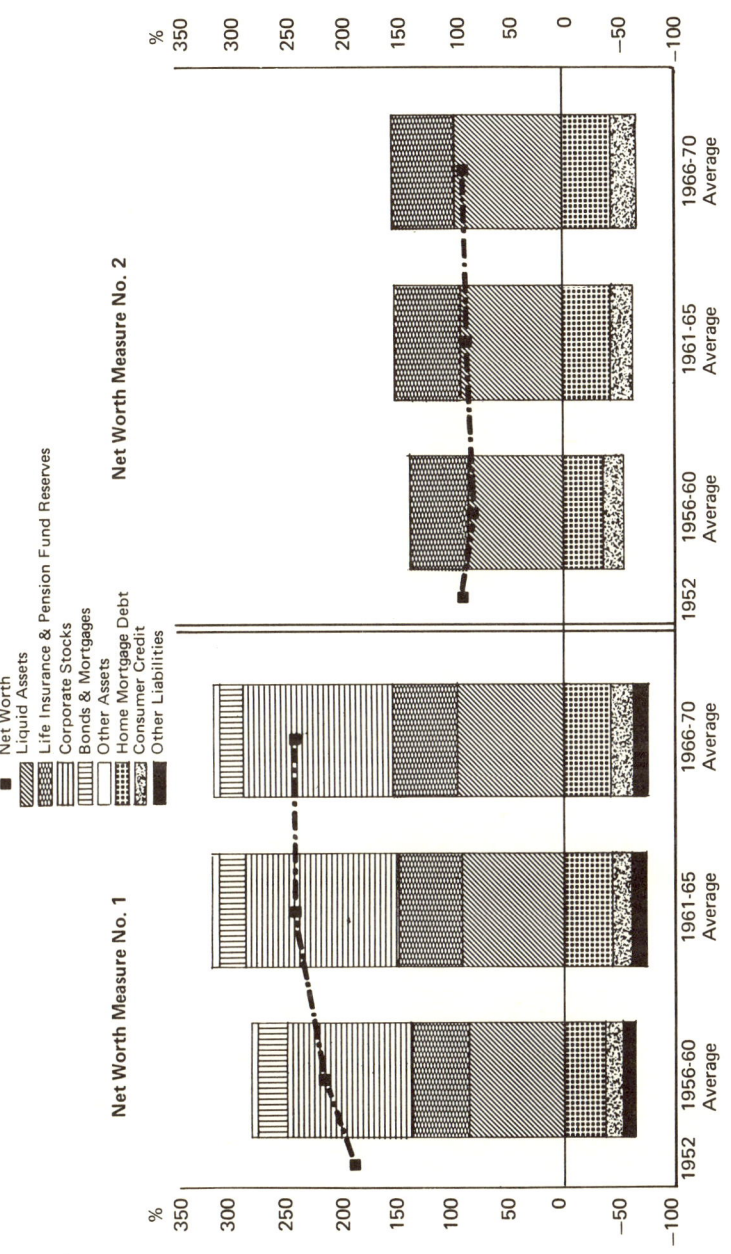

B. *Upward trend in total net worth*—The most noteworthy trend apparent in Chart 1 is the statistically significant upward movement in total consumer net worth virtually throughout the past two decades (Measure 1).[2] This trend, which was already observed by Puckett and Brest in their comparison of the years 1952 and 1964, is no more and no less than one of the logical consequences of real economic growth—i.e., the accumulation of wealth. It is not inconsequential to note, however, that at any given growth rate of total wealth, its accumulation could in theory have taken place exclusively within either the corporate or the government sector of an economy, or some combination of the two.[3] In actual fact the consumer has been gaining in net financial wealth and consequently requires more financial expertise, either personal or institutional.

C. *Cyclical sensitivity of aggregate net worth measures*—It is immediately apparent from Chart 1 that both measures of consumer net worth are sensitive to the business cycle, particularly the more comprehensive of the two (Measure 1). The upward trend of that measure typically is interrupted during business recessions, and more so than the measure allowing only for liquid assets and insurance and pension reserves in consumer assets. It should be carefully noted—although no adjustment will be attempted here—that broad comparisons over the past two decades undoubtedly suffer from a differential strictly related to the incidence of an expansionary phase in the early 1950s and of a recession at the end (1970) of the observations. (The uptrend in aggregate net worth is probably underestimated by the choice of 1970 as the end point.)

The greater volatility and cyclical responsiveness of Measure 1 results largely from the inclusion of common stocks in that measure of consumer assets. More broadly applicable to both measures, however, is the notion that advances in consumer net worth have depended heavily on economic growth. The prevalence of basically satisfactory employment and income conditions may be accepted as a *sine qua non* of rising consumer wealth.

D. *The aggregate net worth figures versus "typical consumer" figures*—It is clearly apparent from Chart 1 that net worth trends for the "typical consumer" (Measure 2) materially diverge from the larger aggregates of Measure 1. By the narrower definition, consumer net worth is essentially trendless for the past two decades as a whole, but does show a statistically significant downtrend in the 1950s, largely offset by a likewise significant uptrend during the 1960s.

Dealing with a point-to-point comparison of the year-ends 1952 and 1964, Puckett and Brest observed a slight deterioration of Measure 2 as against a substantial advance in Measure 1. They went on to suggest cautiously that neither measure was wholly adequate and then proceeded to draw guarded conclusions giving in effect equal weight to the two measures. If one were to proceed on this basis again, the preceding statements might not have to be substantially modified. Measure 2 at the end of 1970 was again below its early-1950s level, although it had approximated that level in the late 1960s.

The problem is, however, that the distinction between the "typical" and "atypical" consumer becomes blurred over a twenty-year period. In particular, questions such as whether a typical consumer does or does not have the type of asset and liabilities included in Measure 1 but not in Measure 2 cannot be solved by definition. These questions are intimately linked to the distribution of wealth. Thus, if the percentage of individuals and families owning stocks and bonds can be shown to have risen significantly over the past two decades—as against a situation in which a constant percentage held larger and larger amounts—the term typical consumer does not have an identical meaning throughout the measurement period. Since it will be shown that such a shift has in fact occurred, Measure 2 is a subaggregate of dubious meaning, even though the intent of the distinction is as reasonable now as it was when originally formulated.

2. Changes in consumer financial management

We shall now seek to supplement the broad picture of a gradually more affluent consumer just portrayed with some evidence regarding the increased diversification of personal portfolios and rising sophistication in their management. It should be noted from the start that this evidence is neither dramatic nor wholly conclusive. All shifts in this direction—as have been those in aggregate net worth—have been moderate, and not necessarily uniform throughout the past two decades.

A. *Rising ratio of financial to nonfinancial wealth*—One of the most intriguing developments of the past two decades has been a rising trend of financial versus nonfinancial asset accumulation. The measurement of this trend is subject to severe problems since the stock of nonfinancial wealth (equity in homes, real estate, durable goods) is far harder to evaluate in current terms than is the stock of financial assets. For this reason, the existence of the hypothesized trend was measured by calculating the ratio of household financial savings to the sum of financial and physical net investment flows, as shown in Table 1. The ratio was found to be rising for 1951–70 as a whole; and statistical tests (based on yearly data) showed the trend to be accelerating during the 1960s as against the 1950s.

The interpretation of this trend is very much open to question. Tentatively, it may be suggested that at rising levels of real income and wealth there is a satiation effect in terms of physical assets and therefore a turn

TABLE 1. NET FINANCIAL INVESTMENT
BY HOUSEHOLDS AS A PER CENT OF
TOTAL HOUSEHOLD SAVINGS
(Arithmetic Averages of Four Five-Year Periods)

Five-Year Period	Net Financial Investment As a Per Cent of Total Saving
1951–1955	28.1%
1956–1960	35.4
1961–1965	42.5
1966–1970	53.6

Note: Net financial investment of households equals their increase in financial assets less the increase in liabilities. Total household savings includes net physical investment of households (i.e., net equity in and increased debt on owner-occupied homes, consumer durables, and nonprofit plant and equipment), in addition to net financial investment.

Source: Board of Governors of the Federal Reserve System, *Flow-of-Funds Accounts*, various issues.

toward financial assets as an alternative outlet for additional savings. Such an explanation would be far more satisfactory if it could also be shown that the rate of return on financial assets versus an imputed rate of return on nonfinancial assets had also risen. Such a demonstration is virtually impossible. It will have to suffice to note that enlarged financial versus nonfinancial saving offers increased opportunities for both the saver and the financial institutions dealing with him.

B. *Rising ratio of earning assets to nonearning assets*—Measured on either a flow or stock basis, there is a trend over the past two decades as a whole in the direction of a gain for earning assets vis-à-vis nonearning assets. In other words, demand deposits and currency have declined somewhat in relative importance in the consumer portfolio. The most logical explanation of the uptrend in the fifties is the rising opportunity cost of holding nonearning assets during a period of rising interest rates on all types of savings accounts and market instruments. As Chart 3 shows, however, this trend virtually spent its force during the 1950s while the 1960s considered separately are essentially trendless.

On the other hand, it is interesting to note that the cash/GNP ratio for the economy as a whole has continued to decline in the 1960s. Thus, the consumer, while reacting to rising interest rates, has apparently not been able to do so to the same extent in the sixties as has business [4].

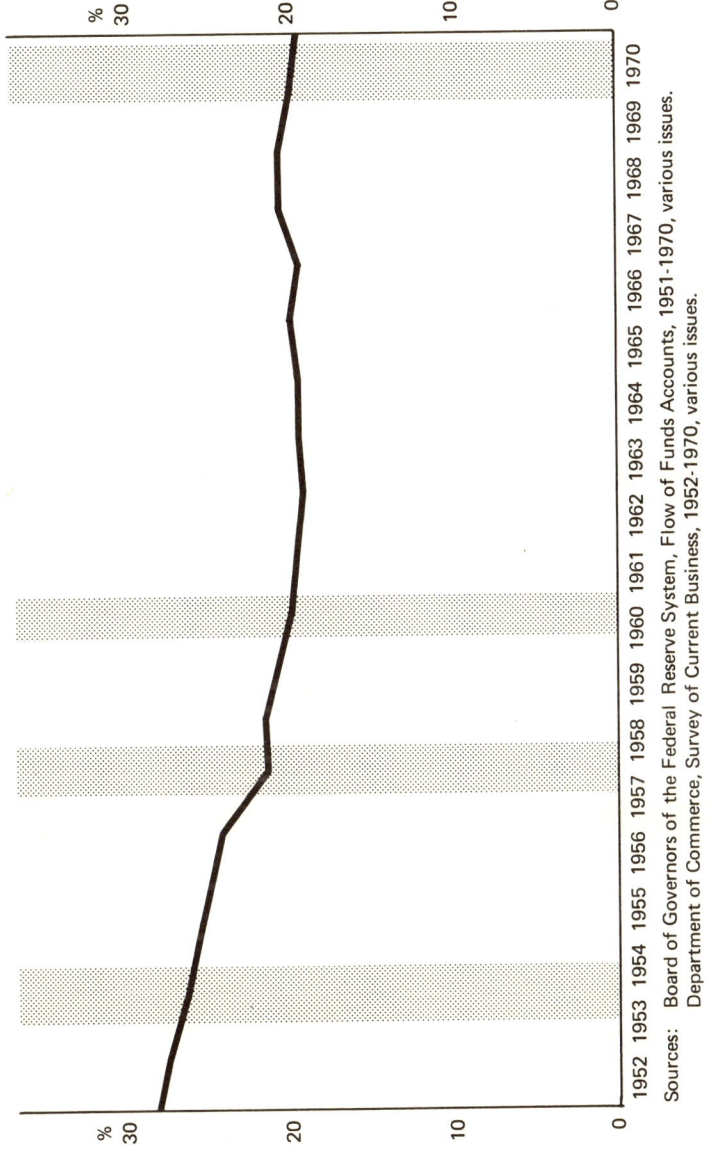

CHART 3. DEMAND DEPOSITS PLUS CURRENCY HELD BY HOUSEHOLDS
AS A PERCENTAGE OF PERSONAL OUTLAYS, 1951-70
(Based on Year-end Levels)

Sources: Board of Governors of the Federal Reserve System, Flow of Funds Accounts, 1951-1970, various issues. Department of Commerce, Survey of Current Business, 1952-1970, various issues.

Indicates recession periods.

C. *Uptrend and leveling-off in savings accounts holdings*—Up to the mid-1960s, the steady gain in savings accounts (of all types and at all institutions combined) could have been considered the major counterpart to the relative decline in nonearning assets that occurred during the 1950s. In fact, Chart 4 shows this strong uptrend to be no more than leveling off in the late 1960s.[4]

The notion that such accounts became the logical alternative to an improved recognition of the cost of holding cash is reinforced by the simultaneous continuous decline in low-yielding United States Savings Bond holdings relative to personal outlays (not shown in the chart). Increased awareness of interest rates was being transmitted to the United States public by the financial institutions most directly linked to the consumer, and a thoroughly rational response to relative interest-rate incentives was being obtained.[5]

D. *The resurgence of interest-bearing securities in the late 1960s*—Prior to the early 1960s, there was a modest but steady upward trend in household assets in the form of bonds and mortgages relative to personal outlays. As Chart 5 shows, this upward trend could be related primarily to a gradual gain in state and local government bond holdings of the household sector. It was a virtually universal assumption that holdings of such securities were heavily concentrated in the highest income groups, where exemption from income tax of interest from such securities tended to raise after-tax yields to above those obtainable from savings accounts.

The chart also shows, however, that following several years of modest declines there was a resurgence of consumer holdings of interest-bearing securities in the late 1960s—this time taking the form of very rapid increases, relative to personal outlays, in corporate bonds and United States agency securities. "Disintermediation" (See Section V) in all likelihood accounts for a substantial part of this phenomenon. In sum and substance, the consumer whose appetite for interest-earning assets had been whetted by both increased ability to hold such assets and rising interest rates, focused more squarely yet on the best rates obtainable, even if doing so involved going outside the range of the traditional intermediary institutions.

E. *The trend toward equity ownership*—No other major trend has been as pronounced and important in raising the net worth of the household sector as the increase in the value of that sector's corporate stock holding (see Chart 6). Without the existence of this increase, household net worth would be essentially trendless since 1955. Furthermore, corporate stock (at market value) has remained by far the single largest component of the financial assets of the household sector.

Yet the very existence of this trend has at times been questioned on the

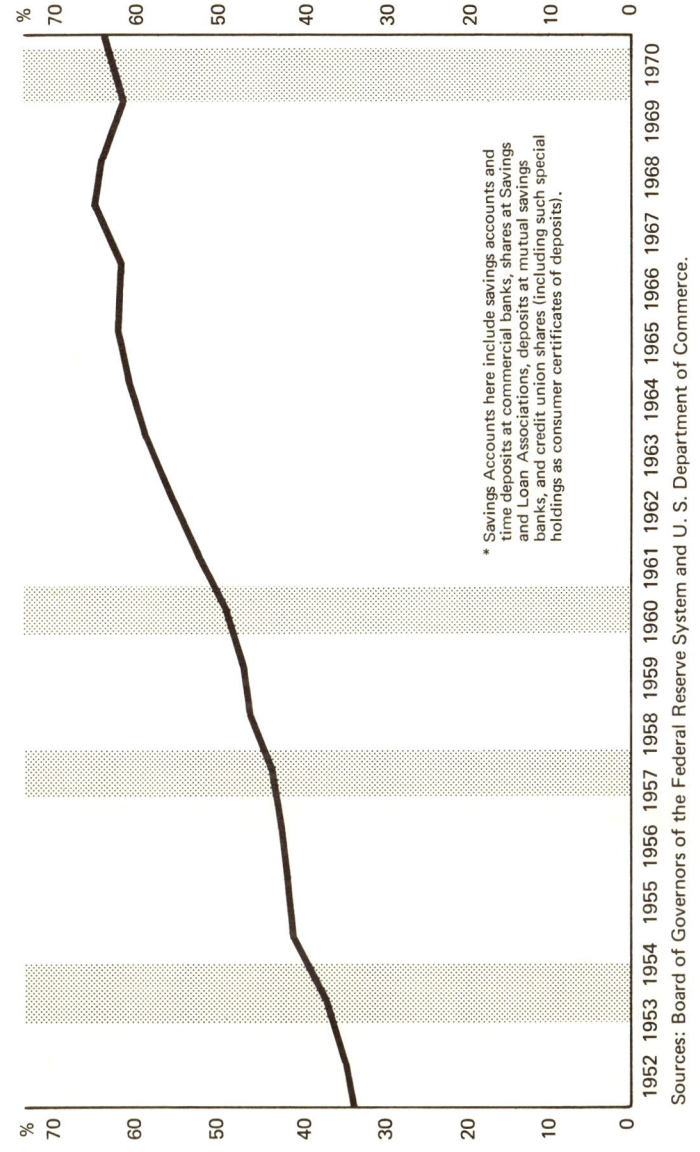

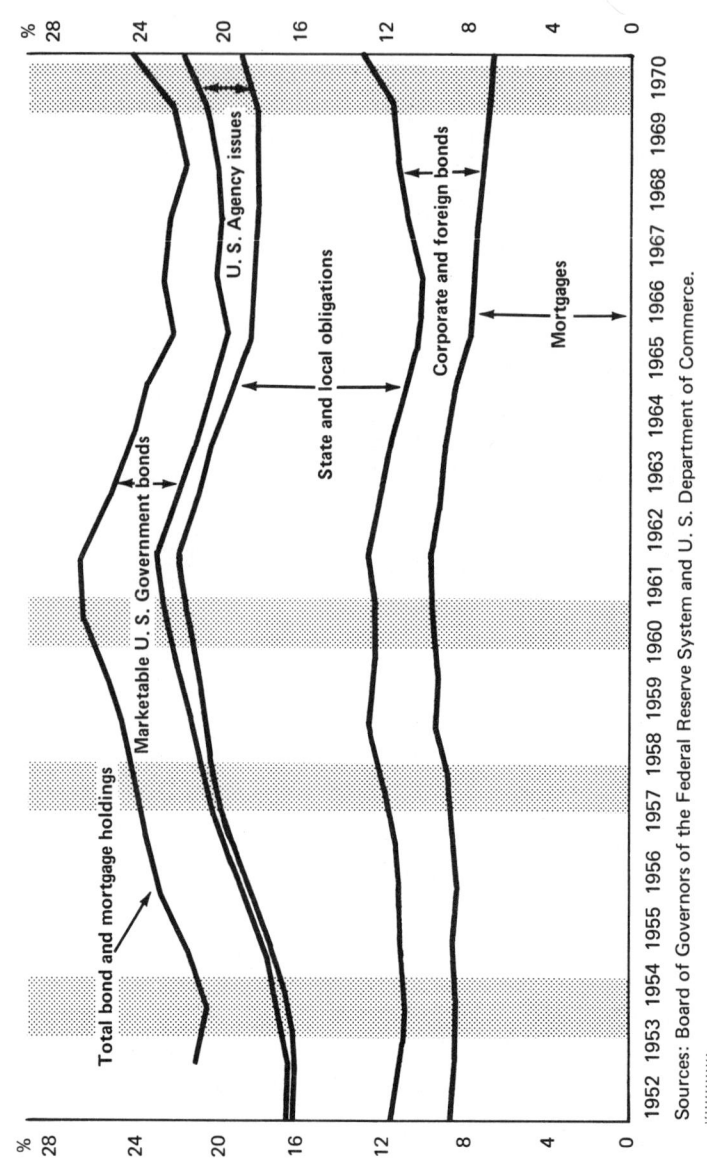

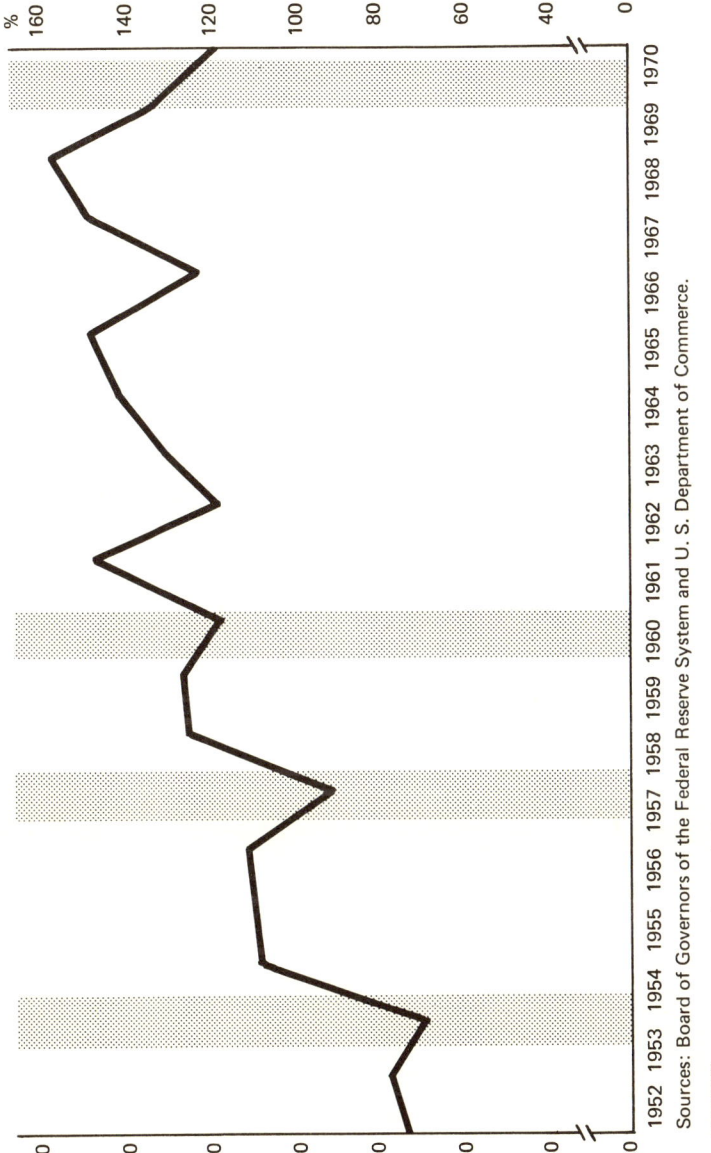

basis of two sets of data—one, the flow-of-funds data showing net disinvestment by the household sector in common stock for substantial parts of the past two decades, in amounts sufficient to suggest net disinvestment for the period as a whole. (This is the case even if the net inflow into investment company shares over this period is considered part of the assets of the household sector.) The second, although of course interrelated, set of data pointing in the direction opposite to the trend described above is the well-publicized increase in the institutional share both of the value of stock exchange-listed shares and in the volume of transactions on these exchanges.[6]

It had of course been recognized throughout this questioning that the trend toward enlarged values of equity holdings in the household sector and strengthened net worth because of that trend might be compatible with an increased institutional share of total equity holdings if increased equity values (a stock concept) more than offset the individual net disinvestment (a flow concept). Thus, this disinvestment—and the very gradual decline in the individual ownership share of total outstanding equities from over 90 per cent to about 80 per cent during the 1951-70 period (as measured in the flow-of-funds accounts)—were generally accepted as factual. Nevertheless, the picture of the household sector as a net seller of stocks presented something of a contrast to the documentable notion that stock ownership was in fact spreading among individuals by either criterion of percentage of families or percentile of income groups owning stocks (see Section II-4).

Recent new evidence, collected by the National Bureau of Economic Research (NBER) in connection with the SEC's *Institutional Investors Study* throws additional light on the matter. Basically, the NBER found the institutional share of aggregate stock ownership to be higher than that recorded in the flow-of-funds accounts, but also essentially trendless since the mid-1950s through 1968 at just over 25 per cent of total equities outstanding, after trending only slightly upwards in the early 1950s [12]. The level of the discrepancy of institutional stock ownership between the NBER and the flow-of-funds figures is in all likelihood primarily explicable by the statistical "impurities" of the household sector in the Federal Reserve data (as noted, nonprofit institutions are included). The constancy of the institutional (and by implication, of the household) share in stock ownership in the new data vis-à-vis the net individual disinvestment recorded in the Federal Reserve data, on the other hand, is traced by the NBER to the incompleteness of Federal Reserve (and corresponding SEC) data on total stock outstanding.

In essence, the traditional data—relying almost by necessity primarily upon reports relating to major stock-exchange listed securities—sharply overestimate the trend toward institutional stock ownership since the growing equities investment of institutions (partly because of legal requirements) has been heavily concentrated upon such "listed securities." Thus, household disinvestment in stocks—to the extent it has actually occurred—is shown to have been concentrated upon what is essentially the stock of major corporations, while the household-sector value of other corporation stocks has risen in a roughly offsetting fashion. An additional important factor in explaining the constancy of the relative household-institutional shares of common stock holdings (at current values) is that household-owned shares have experienced greater price appreciation, on average, than have institutionally held stocks [3].

There remains the objection that the "passive" accumulation of additional net worth through a roughly unchanged consumer share in total outstanding equities that are rising in aggregate value is not the equivalent of a trend, which might be understood to imply "aggressive" net acquisition in a flow sense (such as is the case, e.g., in the reported net gain in savings accounts relative to personal outlays throughout the 1950s and into the mid-1960s). The objection is reasonable but unconvincing since portfolio decisions "to hold" must be judged to be the economic equivalent to positive decisions not to invest in alternatives—if not necessarily over short periods, certainly over periods as long as two decades.

F. *The rising trend of contractual savings*—Before leveling off in the mid-1960s, there occurred a statistically significant upward trend in the level of contractual savings—life insurance and pension fund reserve combined—relative to personal outlays. As Chart 7 shows, however, this aggregate trend is composed of widely divergent tendencies in the two major components. There was a substantial decline in life insurance reserves relative to personal outlays, which was more than offset by a major rise in pension fund reserves.

It should be noted at once that an interpretation of this over-all trend and of its components is fraught with difficulties. Very broadly, it is unquestionably true that a significant part of rising household wealth has been devoted to the provision of increased security against the contingencies of old age. Furthermore, the divergence of the components of this series is in all likelihood not coincidental. A relative decline in the use of individual life insurance as a savings instrument vis-à-vis savings through pension funds for similar purposes occurred. Some key statistics on the growth of pension funds of all types include the following—total coverage increased from 16.7 million (27 per cent of the work force) at the end of 1951 to 46.2 million (57 per cent of the work force) at the end of 1969; and total pension fund assets, administered by all types of institutions, have grown from $24 billion at the end of 1950 to $205 billion at the end of 1970—a compound annual growth rate of almost 12 per cent.[7]

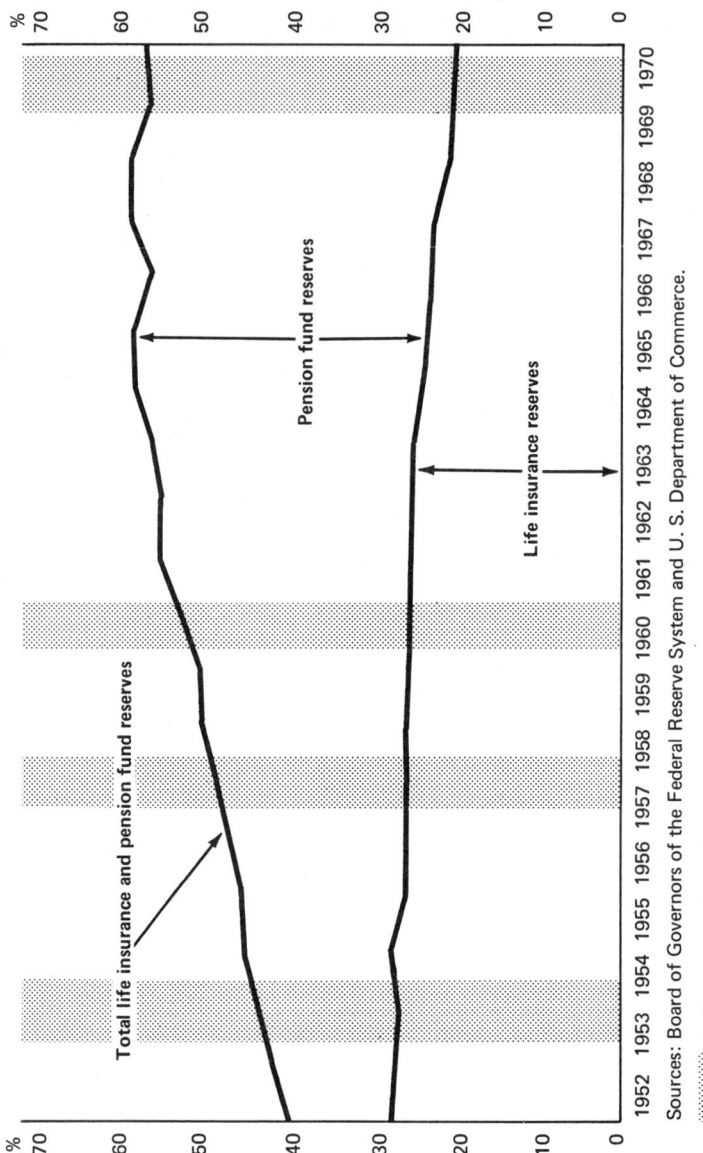

On the other hand, the specialized definitions of "reserves" as representing the household sector accumulation of financial assets through life insurance and pension funds should not be confused with the over-all role either one of these institutions plays in total household financial management. For example, the distinction drawn in the chart leaves unanswered the question of the role the life insurance industry itself has played in the growth and administration of pension plans. All pension fund reserves are included in that category, whether or not administered by life insurance companies. Thus, the decline in life insurance reserves relative to personal outlays refers only to individual and group life insurance. (See Section IV for elaboration on the relative role in total pension fund administration of different types of institutions.)

It may also be well to refer even at this early stage to one of the implications of the dual role of the life insurance industry as a provider of protection along with its savings-generating function. There is strong evidence that the industry has held its own in terms of family protection. The ratio of life insurance premium receipts to disposable personal income has held roughly stable, and life insurance outstanding per family relative to disposable personal income has increased substantially.[8] Basically, the "protection-oriented" share of the premium dollar, which is nonreserve-creating, has risen relative to the "savings-oriented" share of the premium dollar. (I hope to have clarified the above distinctions in another article; see [9].) More concretely, individual term insurance and term group insurance have gained relative to individual whole-life insurance. The slow growth of the life insurance "savings dollar" (in absolute terms) will be further explored in Section IV.

Notwithstanding these considerations, it is important to realize that the growth of pension fund reserves relative to insurance reserves is somewhat of a countertrend to the increased direct consumer responsibility for personal financial management. The use of the term "countertrend" might be disputed on two grounds. One is that the push toward increased pension benefits itself reflects employee (i.e., consumer) decisions. Granting this point, however, does not change the fact of a "revealed preference" for delegation to institutional management of the potential equivalent of self-administration of corresponding financial assets. The second objection, valid as far as it goes, is that to the extent pension plans have voluntary contributory features, personal financial management is in fact involved in the accumulation of pension fund reserves. It is also true, however, that noncontributory pension plans have grown relative to contributory plans and that employee contributions as a percentage of the annual flow into private pension plans have declined significantly over the past two decades.[9]

G. *A note on consumer liabilities*—The focus of this paper is on rising consumer net worth and financial asset management and their consequences. The main point with respect to consumer liabilities therefore has to be that they have not risen sufficiently to offset the rise in aggregate net worth. The following sketchy observations will have to suffice.

The grand total of consumer liabilities relative to personal outlays has continued to increase throughout the 1950s and into the mid-1960s but has since leveled off (see Chart 2). Three important trends stand out. One is that mortgage debt (in the relative sense as here measured) has shown the first sustained postwar decline in the late 1960s, reflecting no doubt in part difficulties in mortgage availability and the associated trend toward multiple-dwelling and mobile-home living. A second item worthy of note is that even consumer installment credit, which grew especially quickly in the late fifties and early sixties, has been leveling off in recent years, most likely reflecting the uncertainties of the post-Vietnam period and the recession of 1969–70. A third important fact is that other liabilities—although small compared to mortgage and installment debt—have in the aggregate risen sharply in the 1960s. Among these other liabilities, the increase in net policy loans at life insurance companies has figured prominently and will be further discussed in Section V.

3. Evolution of the consumer's financial position
   —A summary review

The composite picture emerging from the preceding two subsections is that of a consumer who has been gradually accumulating additional net worth over the span of the last two decades. There are occasional setbacks during recessions because of declines in asset values and because the further accumulation of liabilities relative to outlays has persisted until the mid-1960s and used to be substantially insensitive to cycles. Nevertheless, there is a considerable net gain.

In this net worth accumulation, the consumer is slowly beginning to emphasize financial assets as against physical assets. He is learning to minimize nonearning as against earning assets. He is raising his savings account balance relative to his outlays. He has participated fully in the over-all rise of equity values over the period by roughly maintaining his traditionally dominant share of equity ownership. He appears to be taking an increased interest in corporate and government agency debt securities in the course of sharply rising interest rates on such securities toward the end of the 1960s. Simultaneously, he is increasing his death protection while obtaining a rising share of this protection through group insurance. Leaving aside Social Security as a subject beyond the scope of this paper, he is providing better for his old age mainly through improved group pension benefits and his other financial asset gains while the relative importance of life insurance savings has declined.

It is a question of semantics whether these changes can be further summarized by referring to a gradually more sophisticated consumer. To this observer, the growth of financial portfolios and the evidence of increasing discretionary exercise of widening options justifies use of the term.

4. Selected additional evidence from microeconomic studies

A. *The distribution of increased wealth*—There is no more intriguing a question than that of decomposing the aggregate trends described so far. In particular, an answer should be sought to the possible challenge that the sum total of the evolution of consumer financial management or of its subsidiary trends—however characterized—is not a mass phenomenon, but rather applicable only to, say, the upper 10 per cent of the population in terms of wealth. In that case, the increase in aggregate net worth in the household sector would carry the strong implication of an increasing concentration of wealth at the upper end. To some extent, even such a finding actually would not vitiate the thrust of the preceding sections—the upper 10 per cent of the population has increased in number with the population itself (by about 5 million to over 20 million, given a total population rise of 52 million to 205 million over the past two decades) [14]. Hence, the number of people with financial sophistication and the need for financial institution response to their requirements would have increased anyway, especially given their (presumed) increased share in net worth.

In actual fact, such a situation is unlikely to have developed. It is far more likely that the increase in aggregate net worth of the household sector has been spread sufficiently widely among the population to make it virtually certain that a larger percentage of families is now handling and managing financial assets of some kind. There is no consistent set of cross-section analyses of wealth by income group, 1951–70, to prove the point.[10] But there is ample secondary evidence to support the contention.

For one, all cross-sectional studies actually available point in the direction of a close association between education, income, and net worth. The average education level and real family income level have risen substantially and virtually without interruption over the past two decades [15]. Furthermore, the distribution of total income by percentiles of income groups has shown very little change over the past two decades [16]. Hence, there is a strong probability that a considerable percentage of families have crossed the border line where their current dollar income—representing, as it did, not only higher nominal but also higher real wages—encouraged the acquisition of financial assets and management skills. However, the questions of the share of the population and of income groups thus participating at the beginning and end of the time period is not thereby answered, in spite of the strong presumption these data establish.

B. *The 1970 Michigan survey*—As already noted, Puckett and Brest in their "first approximation" approach in 1966 in effect passed on the question of net worth distribution over time by distinguishing among consumers by type of asset held rather than by percentages of consumers holding different types of assets.

It is clear enough, however, that one of their distinctions between a typical and atypical consumer—the absence or possession of securities (other than government savings bonds)—can reasonably be considered one of the tipping points toward a "more sophisticated" consumer. This test, and others that suggest themselves from the aggregate figures, can be shown to be easily passed with the aid of figures such as the following from the latest published Michigan Survey:

TABLE 2. PER CENT OF FAMILIES HOLDING SELECTED FINANCIAL ASSETS
(Annual Figures from Surveys Early in the Year)

	1951	1960	1963	1968	1969	1970
Savings accounts	47	55	56	64	62	65
Certificates of deposit	N.A.	N.A.	N.A.	4.5	4.9	7.7
Checking accounts	44	60	62	71	72	75
Bonds[a]	43	32	26	26	26	28
Stocks[b]	9	17	20	23	23	26
Number of family units (in millions)	46.3	53.5	56.2	61.2	62.5	63.7

[a] In 1968 and before, only government savings bonds were included.
[b] Includes mutual fund (investment company) share holdings.

Source: G. Katona, L. Mandell, and J. Schmiedeskamp, *1970 Survey of Consumer Finances,* University of Michigan, 1971, p. 98.

Table 2 shows a consistent upward trend in the proportion of families holding selected financial assets. Referring to common stocks alone, the table shows an approximate doubling of the proportion of families owning stocks during the 1950s and a further considerable advance during the 1960s. Unfortunately, the data on bond holdings as recorded in Table 2 will have to be disregarded in terms of the securities-possession test since these data are dominated by the well-known liquidation of government savings bonds over the postwar period. (A consistent series including only corporate and marketable government securities by proportion of families owning them is not available.)

On the other hand, the table is helpful in testing the consistency of additional ones of the observed aggregate trends with the notion that higher aggregate net worth relative to total personal outlays has led to at least a roughly proportional spread of financial sophistication among consumers. Thus, the sharp rise in the proportion of families owning both savings and checking accounts over the past two decades can hardly be considered anything other than an advance in mass financial management skills once the notion is abandoned that families not owning such assets are as typical as those that do. In fact, in the early 1950s ownership of either type of account was still a minority phenomenon. It did not rise to what reasonably might be considered typical (a substantial majority) until roughly the mid-1960s, as shown in the table. Thus, there is a strong suggestion that advances in consumer financial education and management fully consistent with aggregate trends previously described are a continuing, evolutionary, broad-based phenomenon.

C. *The spread of stock ownership*—Because of the importance of the rise in equity values to the increase in aggregate net worth and its obvious relevance to progress in financial discernment, the question of the spread of stock ownership will be pursued two steps further. First, we shall summarize the cross-section data on stock ownership by percentage of families reporting such ownership from various studies besides the Michigan Survey (see Table 3).

In spite of disturbing discrepancies in the figures where available for identical years, it is clear that the trend of the figures is unequivocally upward. Thus, while stock ownership remains confined to a rising minority of families, the data strongly support the presumption from the aggregates that rising household net worth has been accompanied by a substantial broadening of financial portfolios among the population at large.

The presumption could be further supported if one could in fact show that over the last two decades financial net worth has been strengthened in each percentile of the income distribution. The data to support this contention are not available. However, a careful examination utilizing University of Michigan stock ownership data and Census Bureau income distribution data, 1959 versus 1969, suggests a much stronger rise in the probability of family stock ownership at the median family income than for the population at large; this result again strongly supports the presumption that increased financial net worth and the attributes associated with it have spread among income groups at least proportionately to the rise in aggregate net worth.[11]

Additional statistical evidence bearing on the question, but related to the interest rate responsiveness of financial asset holders, will be taken up later. Meanwhile, it may be claimed that income distribution and cross-

TABLE 3. PER CENT OF FAMILIES OR POPULATION REPORTING CORPORATE STOCK OWNERSHIP ACCORDING TO VARIOUS SURVEYS OF FAMILY FINANCES

	University of Michigan (1) (Per cent of Families)	New York Stock Exchange (2) (Per cent of Population)	Federal Reserve Board (3) (Per cent of Families)
1951	9	4.2	
1956		5.2	
1959	17	7.1	
1960	17		
1962	16	9.2	16
1963	20		18
1964	19		
1965		10.4	
1966	24		
1967	23		
1968	23		
1969	23		
1970	26	15.1	

(1) Source: Annual volumes of *Survey of Consumer Finances*, Survey Research Center, University of Michigan. Includes both publicly traded and privately held stocks. Ownership includes direct ownership and ownership through mutual funds and investment clubs. Figures from latest annual volumes are used for revised percentages of earlier years.

(2) Source: *Shareownership–1970 Census of Shareowners*, New York Stock Exchanges. The census includes shares of all publicly held United States corporations.

(3) Source: *Survey of Financial Characteristics of Consumers* (published in August 1966) and *Survey of Changes in Family Finances* (published in November 1968), Board of Governors of the Federal Reserve System. Includes publicly traded stock which consists of common and preferred stock in corporations, other than closely held corporations, shares in mutual funds and other investment clubs, plus net credit balances at security dealers.

(4) Note: The Office of Economic Opportunity (OEO) sponsored two annual surveys of family finances for 1966 and 1967, with significant oversampling of lower-income classes. They are entitled "Survey of Economic Opportunity," and the University of Wisconsin is the custodian of the tapes. There is no comprehensive tabulation of the OEO statistics at this time, and the author was unable to obtain specific data on the percentages of families owning corporate stocks in 1966 and 1967.

The Consumer's Financial Position, 1951–70 · 333

sectional wealth data are, at a minimum, consistent with what common sense suggests. Rising net worth and financial assets in the course of broadly based real income gains have increased the financial sophistication of the hypothetical "average consumer."

5. Per capita wealth

In response to a question raised at the Williamsburg Conference, additional data were compiled, *on a per capita basis,* of the dollar amount of both the broad and narrow net worth measures of the consumer sector (as defined in Section II, 1-A). In addition both per capita net worth measures were deflated by the consumer price index (1967 = 100) to arrive at "real" per capita net worth measures (or purchasing power of net worth per capita). The period of analysis was again year-end 1952 to year-end 1970, as in the paper.

The basic figures are:

	1952	1970
Population (average for calendar year) in millions	157.5	204.8
Broad Net Worth (Measure 1), year-end, in billions of current dollars	415.8	1,404.9
Narrow Net Worth (Measure 2), year-end, in billions of current dollars	203.6	558.6
Consumer Price Index Yearly average (1967 = 100)	79.6	116.3

Sources: United States Department of Labor; Department of Commerce (Census Bureau); Federal Reserve Flow-of-Funds Accounts.

The first step taken was to see whether the measures showed any difference between year-end 1952 and year-end 1970 on a point-to-point basis. The results were as follows: (1) Current dollar broad and narrow per capita net worth measures increased 160 per cent and 111 per cent, respectively; and (2) in deflated terms, the two measures showed gains of 78 per cent and 44 per cent, respectively.

The presence of a statistically significant uptrend over the period has also been established. Current dollar broad and narrow per capita net worth measures have risen on average $255 per annum and $80 per annum, respectively. The analogous "real" per capita measures have risen $181 per annum and $48 per annum, respectively. (The test consists of a linear regression relating the per capita net worth measures to time. It was determined that the b-coefficients were significantly different from zero.)

I believe that these figures are conclusive as far as they go. The originally used deflator (personal outlays) is in fact a rough-and-ready approximation of the effects of both population growth and inflation on the household net worth figures. Anyone claiming that household financial net worth has not risen over the past two decades will have to prove the above figures incorrect.

It may be granted that any and all deflators are open to some argument. Obviously, these computations still leave wealth distribution out of account. Also, nothing has been done on a per-family-unit basis. There would be quite a major problem of interpreting the results if a significant change in average family-unit size had occurred over the period.

III. Economic Milestones Influencing Developments In Consumer Financial Management

In the course of the preceding pages, there have been occasional references to certain ingredients shaping developments in consumer financial behavior—primarily to the broad-based rising level of real incomes, over the past two decades, traceable in turn to improved productivity stemming from both technological and educational advances. Other major influences have had a significant bearing on changing consumer financial behavior as well as on financial institution response. The following highly selective listing is intended only to highlight some of those additional influences. A more thorough evaluation would undoubtedly involve political, sociological, and demographic factors. The listing may be considered as an economist's broad-brush contribution to an inventory of factors explanatory of the evolution of consumer financial management.

1. Employment and the threat of unemployment

Attitudinal surveys of consumer financial behavior invariably and rightfully focus on the question of employment and the threat (and occasional actuality) of unemployment as an important factor in individual consumer finance. Twenty-five years have passed since the Full Employment Act of 1946. Innumerable words have been written—and many official deeds performed—in furthering the cause of full employment. Much has been accomplished to alleviate the consequences of unemployment when it does occur.

Nevertheless, the state of the job market—and not only unemployment as such—of necessity continues to be one of the important factors in consumer finance. Apart from a few euphoric years in the early and mid-1960s, one may safely assume that job uncertainties are still one of the "facts of life" for much of the public at large. There have been four "recognized" recessions in the past two decades (1953-54, 1957-58, 1960-61, 1969-70). Their total duration is only 3½ years out of twenty. Perhaps more important, however, if "full employment" is defined as implying an unemployment rate averaging no more than 4½ per cent of the labor force, there have been no less than ten out of the past twenty years (1951-70) when the standard was not achieved. Even if the definition is raised to 5 per cent as the borderline, there are still eight years when performance fell short of the standard.[12]

Apart from any implications derived from observed declines in aggregate net worth during recessions, the major influence of continuing job insecurity has probably been one of inducing conservatism in consumer financial management. A number of the observed trends in the direction of "venturesomeness"—such as the increase in liabilities relative to personal outlays and the spread of stock ownership—may well have been attenuated by job insecurities. On the other hand, the rise in savings accounts relative to personal outlays may well have been accentuated by "rainy day" considerations with respect to jobs.

2. The long-term uptrend of interest rates
   And heightened interest rate sensitivity

There has been no systematic exploration so far, nor can there be within the framework of this paper, of the effect upon consumer financial behavior of the sustained upward trend in the general interest rate level over the past two decades. Section V will, to be sure, attempt to measure the interest-rate responsiveness of consumer savings from the viewpoint of its effect on selected groups of financial institutions. However, since the measurement will be confined to short periods of virtually pathological conditions in the interest rate markets, it will lack the historical breadth an analysis of the question actually should have.

Such a review, however brief, should begin with the following facts. Beginning in the early 1950s and to an ever-increasing extent in the late 1960s, the United States consumer has been subjected to the experience of rising interest rates and large-scale attempts to educate him to the relevance of such rates in personal financial management. Table 4—in which the 40-year sweep of financial history from the original source has been deliberately left intact—will help recall that during the 1930s and 1940s interest rates ranging across the spectrum of savings and long-term market instruments were declining, eventually reaching levels so low as to be virtually meaningless as an alternative to cash or as a competitive device among different consumer savings outlets.

This situation began to change in the early 1950s. Technically speaking, the change dates from the Treasury-Federal Reserve Accord of 1951

TABLE 4. AVERAGE ANNUAL YIELD ON SELECTED TYPES OF INVESTMENTS 1930–1970

Year	Savings Accounts in Savings Associations	Savings Deposits in Mutual Savings Banks	Time and Savings Deposits in Commercial Banks	United States Government Bonds	State and Local Bonds	Corporate (Aaa) Bonds
1930	5.3%	4.5%	3.9%	3.3%	4.1%	4.6%
1931	5.1	4.4	3.8	3.3	4.0	4.6
1932	4.1	4.0	3.4	3.7	4.6	5.0
1933	3.4	3.4	3.4	3.3	4.7	4.5
1934	3.5	3.1	3.0	3.1	4.0	4.0
1935	3.1	2.7	2.6	2.8	3.4	3.6
1936	3.2	2.5	2.0	2.6	3.1	3.2
1937	3.5	2.4	1.8	2.7	3.1	3.3
1938	3.5	2.3	1.7	2.6	2.9	3.2
1939	3.4	2.2	1.6	2.4	2.8	3.0
1940	3.3	2.0	1.3	2.2	2.5	2.8
1941	3.1	1.9	1.3	2.0	2.0	2.8
1942	3.0	1.9	1.1	2.5	2.2	2.8
1943	2.9	1.9	0.9	2.5	1.9	2.7
1944	2.8	1.8	0.9	2.5	1.7	2.7
1945	2.5	1.7	0.8	2.4	1.5	2.6
1946	2.2	1.7	0.8	2.2	1.5	2.5
1947	2.3	1.6	0.9	2.2	1.8	2.6
1948	2.3	1.7	0.9	2.4	2.3	2.8
1949	2.4	1.8	0.9	2.3	2.2	2.7
1950	2.5	1.9	0.9	2.3	1.9	2.6
1951	2.6	2.0	1.1	2.6	2.0	2.9
1952	2.7	2.3	1.2	2.7	2.2	3.0
1953	2.8	2.4	1.2	2.9	2.8	3.2
1954	2.9	2.5	1.3	2.6	2.5	2.9

under which the Federal Reserve gradually reclaimed monetary policy flexibility [13]. This new freedom gradually created room for maneuver among competitive institutions, generating a general upward push on consumer savings rates, which was in turn reinforced by the Federal Reserve's awareness of and action toward reducing the excess liquidity in the economy left over from World War II. By the early 1960s—years of essential interest rate stability—the general level of interest rates had roughly doubled vis-à-vis the early 1950s. (A careful perusal of Table 4 will also show that very substantial differences in the degree of the advance among different types of savings outlets had occurred.)

The general history of the late 1960s is of course that of another substantial advance of all interest rates, but with special emphasis upon the rise of rates on market instruments while depository-rate advances lagged.

Year	Savings Accounts in Savings Associations	Savings Deposits in Mutual Savings Banks	Time and Savings Deposits in Commercial Banks	United States Government Bonds	State and Local Bonds	Corporate (Aaa) Bonds
1955	2.9	2.6	1.4	2.8	2.6	3.1
1956	3.0	2.8	1.6	3.1	2.9	3.4
1957	3.3	2.9	2.1	3.5	3.6	3.9
1958	3.38	3.07	2.21	3.43	3.36	3.79
1959	3.53	3.19	2.36	4.07	3.74	4.38
1960	3.86	3.47	2.56	4.01	3.69	4.41
1961	3.90	3.55	2.71	3.90	3.60	4.35
1962	4.08	3.85	3.18	3.95	3.30	4.33
1963	4.17	3.96	3.31	4.00	3.28	4.26
1964	4.19	4.06	3.42	4.15	3.28	4.40
1965	4.23	4.11	3.69	4.21	3.34	4.49
1966	4.45	4.45	4.04	4.66	3.90	5.13
1967	4.67	4.74	4.24	4.85	3.99	5.51
1968	4.68	4.76	4.48	5.25	4.48	6.18
1969	4.80	4.85	4.87	6.10	5.73	7.03
1970*	5.09	5.03	4.92	6.59	6.42	8.04

* Preliminary.

Sources: Savings and loan associations: effective rate of interest, i.e., interest distributed relative to average savings balance, based on data of members of Federal Home Loan Bank System; mutual savings banks: "per deposit" rate reported by National Association of Mutual Savings Banks; commercial banks: effective interest rate, based on data of Federal Reserve Board and Federal Deposit Insurance Corporation; bond yields: Moody's Investors Service.

Source: United States Savings & Loan League, *Savings and Loan Fact Book, 1971*, Chicago: 1971, p. 17.

In the face of a near "interest-rate war" among competing depositary institutions, the federal government intervened through a law in September 1966, which in effect has provided a common although flexible and somewhat differentiated umbrella for depositary institution savings rates ever since [2].

It should be reasonably clear, even in the absence of conclusive evidence, that these developments have had major influences on consumer finance. They may have contributed to the trend toward earning versus nonearning assets. They may have contributed greatly to the shaping of the consumer's portfolio in his build-up of net worth, including the continued growth of depositary savings as a major consumer savings outlet. Most important, they appear to have induced a consumer interest-rate consciousness and responsiveness beyond anything previously witnessed in United States financial history.

3. The performance of equities

A third major factor shaping consumer attitudes has been the relatively good performance of equities over the period as a whole. It is by now well known that the 1950s marked the emergence of equities from the shadows of the Great Depression. Along with satisfactory corporate earnings records, there grew a recognition that these earnings themselves appeared to be more predictable and reliable than had previously been believed. Thus, the investor—including of course institutional investors—began to be willing to pay increasing multiples of current earnings for equities and the resultant upward shift in P/E ratios added to investment results that in turn inspired further consumer confidence. Needless to say, the interaction of consumer affluence and financial institution response was at least as close in this case as it was in that of rising interest rates.

Table 5 is as fair a representation of equity performance of a broad-based average as may be possible to present in a rock-bottom summary. It enables the reader to verify from any beginning period to any end period of his choosing the performance of equities over the past two decades, while also gaining an impression of the increasing P/E ratios that were a feature of equity performance until the early 1960s. (An example for reading Table 5: An investor placing funds in the "Standard & Poor's 500 stocks" in the "initial year" 1957 would by the "final year" 1967 have realized a compound annual rate of return of 12.9 per cent.) It should be reasonably clear that equity performance, aside from its contribution to increased aggregate net worth, has almost certainly for substantial periods enhanced the attractiveness of financial versus nonfinancial saving and, along with the rise in interest rates, has been partly responsible for the rising ratio of earning to nonearning assets.

At the same time, there have been a sufficient number of unsatisfactory periods, including most emphatically the late 1960s, to prevent the gradual move into equities from becoming an outright rush. Thus, the uncertainties of equity performance have attenuated portfolio diversification in this direction and may well have played a role in the renewed upsurge in recent years in consumer interest in high-yielding fixed-interest instruments.

4. Inflation

There is no other subject in consumer finance in which potential importance and absence of factual knowledge contrast as glaringly as in the case of inflation. It would appear obvious that recurrent bouts with inflation—concentrated in the immediate post-World War II period, the post-Korean-outbreak period, the mid-1950s, and the late 1960s—must have had major effects on consumer financial behavior. Yet, there is neither a com-

TABLE 5. RATES OF RETURN ON INVESTMENT IN STANDARD AND POOR'S
COMPOSITE STOCK PRICE INDEX (500 STOCKS WITH QUARTERLY
REINVESTMENT OF DIVIDENDS
(Per Cent Per Annum Compounded)

INITIAL YEAR

Year-End P/E Ratio		(7.6)	(9.8)	(10.3)	(10.1)	(12.1)	(12.5)	(13.9)	(12.5)	(17.0)	(18.8)	(19.0)	(18.8)	(20.7)	(15.9)	(17.8)	(18.7)	(17.6)	(14.7)	(17.4)	(17.5)	(16.6)	(17.2)
Final Year	Asset Value (Index Round)	1950	1951	1952	1953	1954	1955	1956	1957	1958	1959	1960	1961	1962	1963	1964	1965	1966	1967	1968	1969	1970
1950	100																						
1951	125	25.0																					
1952	148	21.8	18.6																				
1953	146	13.6	8.3	−1.2																			
1954	224	22.3	21.4	22.9	52.8																		
1955	295	24.2	23.9	25.8	41.9	31.7																	
1956	315	21.1	20.3	20.7	29.0	18.6	6.7																
1957	280	15.9	14.4	13.6	17.6	7.8	−2.5	−10.9															
1958	403	19.0	18.2	18.1	22.4	15.8	10.9	13.1	43.6														
1959	451	18.2	17.4	17.2	20.6	15.0	11.2	12.7	26.8	12.0													
1960	453	16.3	15.4	15.0	17.5	12.5	9.0	9.5	17.3	6.1	0.4												
1961	575	17.2	16.5	16.3	18.6	14.4	11.8	12.8	19.7	12.6	12.9	27.0											
1962	524	14.8	13.9	13.5	15.2	11.2	8.6	8.9	13.3	6.8	5.2	7.6	−8.8										
1963	644	15.4	14.6	14.3	16.0	12.5	10.3	10.8	14.9	9.8	9.3	12.5	5.8	22.8									
1964	750	15.5	14.8	14.5	16.0	12.9	10.9	11.5	15.1	10.9	10.7	13.4	9.3	19.6	16.5								
1965	844	15.3	14.6	14.3	15.7	12.8	11.1	11.6	14.8	11.1	11.0	13.3	10.1	17.2	14.5	12.5							
1966	758	13.5	12.8	12.4	13.5	10.7	9.0	9.2	11.7	8.2	7.7	9.0	5.7	9.7	5.6	0.5	−10.1						
1967	941	14.1	13.4	13.1	14.2	11.7	10.5	10.5	12.9	9.9	9.6	11.0	8.6	12.4	9.9	7.8	5.6	24.1					
1968	1045	13.9	13.3	13.0	14.0	11.6	10.2	10.5	12.7	10.0	9.8	11.0	8.9	12.2	10.2	8.6	7.4	17.4	11.1				
1969	956	12.6	12.0	11.6	12.4	10.2	8.8	8.9	10.8	8.2	7.8	8.7	6.6	9.0	6.8	5.0	3.2	8.0	0.8	−8.5			
1970	994	12.2	11.5	11.2	11.9	9.8	8.4	8.6	10.2	7.8	7.5	8.2	6.3	8.3	6.4	4.8	3.3	7.0	1.8	−2.5	4.0		

Source: *Standard and Poor's Trade and Securities Statistics, Security Price Index Record*, 1970 Edition and October 1971 supplement.

Notes:

1. Basic assumption: an initial investment (at the indicized dollar asset value) is made on the last trading day of any year. Changes in these "asset values" directly reflect percentage changes in the Standard and Poor's 500 Index, plus the quarterly reinvestment of (tax-free) dividends, pro-rated to indicized asset values.

2. "Asset values" are for the last day of each calendar year, but the "portfolio" was valued quarterly (before annual consolidation) in order to allow for quarterly reinvestment of dividends.

3. Price-earnings ratio equals Standard and Poor's 500 Index for the last trading day of each calendar year, divided by earnings for the fourth quarter, seasonally adjusted and annualized.

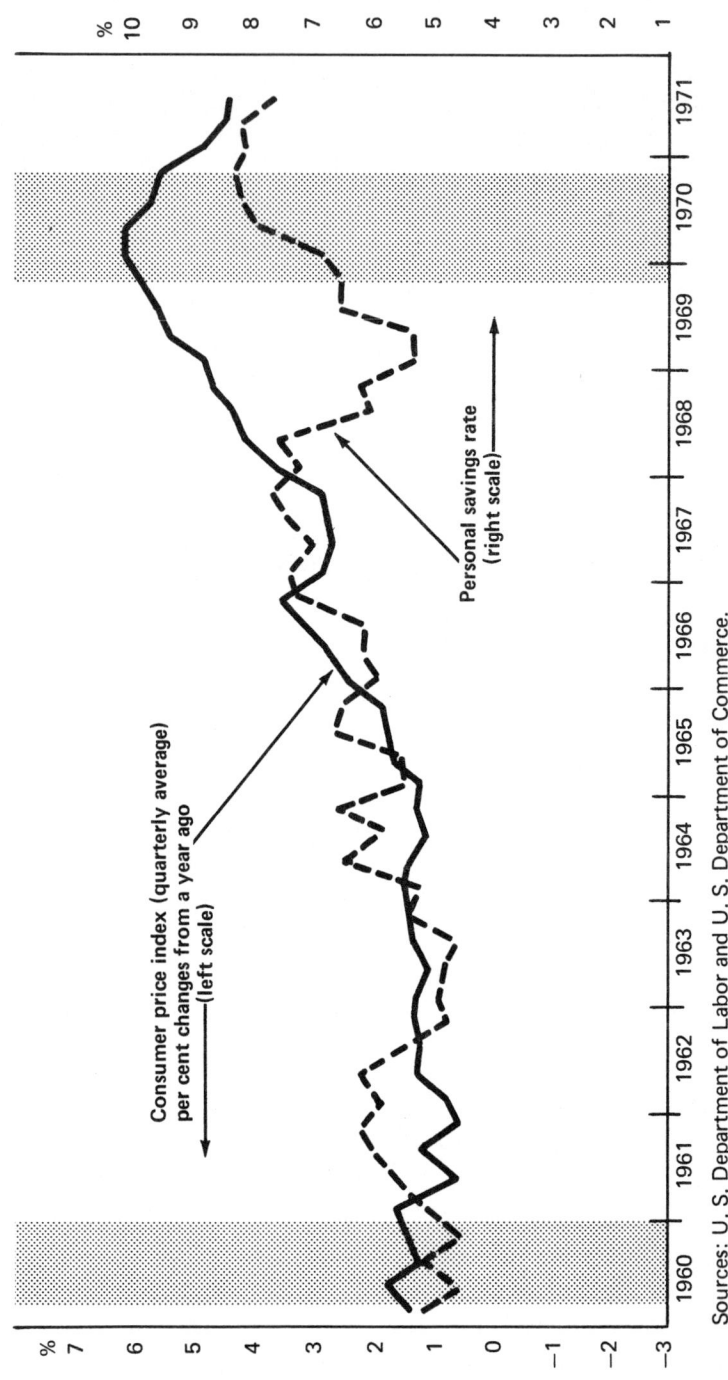

CHART 8. INFLATION AND THE SAVINGS RATE

Sources: U. S. Department of Labor and U. S. Department of Commerce.

Indicates recession periods.

prehensive theory nor empirical testing that would justify even summary reporting.

Perhaps the single most important reason for this state of affairs is that, despite its pervasive effects, inflation of the United States variety cannot be shown to have presumptively unequivocal influences that "should" make the consumer change his behavior adaptively. The issue is most clearly visualized if United States style inflation rates (actual or expected) of 2 per cent–5 per cent are compared with 25 per cent–50 per cent inflation rates, or outright hyperinflation, as has frequently occurred abroad. Abstracting from income redistribution effects—and without denying their very real importance upon the distribution of wealth—experience here and abroad shows that financial systems as such can withstand moderate as against very strong inflationary strains.

Possibly the key question in the context of this paper is why inflation has not so far seriously impaired the gradual accumulation in consumer net worth and the over-all growth of the financial institutions that interact with the household sector in managing consumer financial assets. This question in turn raises that of the relationship between the rate of savings, which is the basis for increased net worth, and the rate of inflation.

Observed savings rate behavior has exhibited remarkable over-all stability over the past two decades, but it has shown fluctuations with consumer price rate changes of the following type. As the rate of increase in prices (expressed in year-to-year percentage variations) rises, the savings rate declines, while stabilization or decline of the inflation rate thus measured coincides with increases in the savings rate. Chart 8 shows this relationship clearly. For example, the savings rate declined to an unusually low level in the early phase of the acceleration of the inflation after the Vietnam escalation in 1965, but it has been unusually high recently as the inflation rate has begun to stabilize.

This phenomenon is fully consistent with the notion—although far from being proof—that gradually increasing net worth relative to outlays is not only a "fall-out" result of real income growth but also a basic household sector objective in income allocation. The initial reaction to accelerated inflation tends to be maintenance of real consumption and a decline in savings. As soon as any relief from inflation is obtained, however—and even if it is no more than a stabilized inflation rate at a higher level than before the acceleration—consumption is cut in favor of savings. It should be understood that the "sacrifice" is facilitated by the secular growth of real incomes so that the cut may not involve an actual decline in real consumption. It should be further added that the entire process, if it is indeed a partial explanation of actual events, has fortunately not been subjected to the possibly insurmountable test of inflation accelerations beyond a few years at a time.[13]

Besides this highly tentative explanation of the key linkage needed to reconcile the facts of inflation and rising consumer wealth, there are subsidiary facets of the consequences of inflation for consumer finance that are worth special mention. One of these is the effect of inflation on nominal as against real rates of interest, which has been well established through recent research [18]. In essence, expected inflation tends to be discounted in market rates of interest. This fact is again of direct relevance not only in explaining the rise of interest rates, but also in explaining continued consumer interest in fixed-interest savings instruments of various types during periods of pronounced inflation such as the recent past.

Most other subsidiary facets of the question remain in the category of unexplored territory, although at times popular mythology has no doubt had potent effects on consumer financial behavior. Thus, the "inflation hedge" faith in common stocks no doubt came close to self-fulfilling prophecy before the denouement of the late 1960s, in spite of the fact that the theoretical case for the proposition has always been open to question.[14] Another such proposition—although one probably far more widely accepted in business circles than it ever was in the household sector—is that a rise in indebtedness is virtually bound to "pay off" during inflation.

5. Summary

The balance of major external economic forces operating on the household sector of the United States economy has been to generate a climate of tempered optimism in consumer financial behavior. In effect, the facts of moderate but widespread net worth advances and financial management skills have been a rational response to an environment in which jobs have been available—but not always easily obtained; where savings nest eggs have had excellent reasons for being started—provided rates paid held some promise of return in real terms; where the performance of equities and rising real income have permitted some risk-taking—but where the existence of that risk has been sufficiently real to serve as a cautionary reminder; and where inflation has frequently forced unpleasant choices between consumption and savings in the pursuit of some moderately advancing standard of "desired" wealth.

IV. Financial Institution Response in Broad Perspective

It is not the purpose of this paper to write a financial-institution history of the past two decades.[15] Rather, the focus here should be on a few selected key points of institutional interaction with a clientele that has gradually become more educated and sophisticated. The next several sections will aim at isolating certain problems—some unresolved—that have made their appearance and have had to be dealt with by the institutions. Nevertheless, such an examination should not be launched without a minimum survey of general institutional developments from the viewpoint of their interrelations with consumer finance.

1. Increasing opportunities for financial institutions

Perhaps the single most important observation one might venture is that the combination of increased consumer net worth, greater orientation toward acquisition of financial assets, and heightened awareness of financial returns has meant enlarged opportunity in a more competitive climate for financial institutions taken as a group. A first glance at the data in Table 6-A and 6-B, for example, shows that the aggregate growth rate of the assets of all major institutions holding consumer financial assets has been 7.6 per cent over the last two decades (measured on either one of two equally relevant bases). This is a growth rate well in excess of money GNP over this period (6.3 per cent) and in excess of the rise in personal disposable income (6.2 per cent). Small percentage point differences of the magnitude

TABLE 6A. COMPOUND ANNUAL RATES OF GROWTH OF FINANCIAL ASSETS AT VARIOUS FINANCIAL INSTITUTIONS
(End-of-Year Values) [1]

Asset Growth Rate:	1950–1970	1950–1960	1960–1970
at: Commercial Banks	6.3%	4.3%	8.2%
Mutual Savings Banks	6.5	6.1	6.9
Savings and Loan Associations	12.4	15.5	9.5
Total at Depositary Institutions	7.2	6.1	8.4
at: Life Insurance Companies*	6.0	6.4	5.7
Noninsured Pension Funds	14.9	19.0	10.9
State and Local Government Retirement Funds	13.0	14.6	11.4
Open-End Investment Companies	14.3	17.8	10.8
Credit Unions	15.3	18.7	11.9
Total at Other Financial Institutions	8.9	9.6	8.2
Grand Total	7.6	7.2	8.3

* Includes life insurance-administered noninsured pension funds.
[1] Asset values at end of year reflect effects of equity price changes.
Sources: See Table 6B.

TABLE 6B. COMPOUND ANNUAL RATES OF GROWTH
OF FINANCIAL ASSETS AT VARIOUS
FINANCIAL INSTITUTIONS
(Flows Cumulated on the 1950 Asset Value Base) [1]

Asset Growth Rate:	1950–1970	1950–1960	1960–1970	1950–1955	1955–1960	1960–1965	1965–1970
at: Commercial Banks	6.3%	4.3%	8.3%	4.6%	4.0%	8.4%	8.1%
Mutual Savings Banks	6.5	6.2	6.8	7.0	5.4	7.5	6.2
Savings and Loan Associations	12.5	15.5	9.5	17.3	13.7	12.7	6.5
Total at Depositary Institutions	7.2	6.1	8.4	6.3	5.8	9.3	7.5
at: Life Insurance Companies*	5.9	6.2	5.5	6.8	5.6	5.7	5.4
Noninsured Pension Funds	13.7	17.2	10.4	19.0	15.4	11.3	9.4
State and Local Government Retirement Funds	12.9	14.6	11.2	16.7	12.7	11.0	11.4
Open-End Investment Companies	11.4	12.8	10.1	11.2	14.5	10.0	10.1
Credit Unions	15.3	18.7	12.0	21.7	15.8	13.2	10.8
Total at Other Financial Institutions	8.3	8.8	7.7	9.2	8.5	7.9	7.6
Grand Total	7.6	7.0	8.2	7.2	6.7	8.8	7.6

* Includes flows into life insurance-administered noninsured pension funds.

[1] Flow computations are designed to eliminate the effect of equity price changes for 1951–70.

Sources: *Flow-of-Funds Accounts, 1945–1968*, Board of Governors of the Federal Reserve System, March 1970.

Flow-of-Funds Accounts: Financial Assets and Liabilities Outstanding, 1959–1970, Board of Governors of the Federal Reserve System, May 1971.

Flow-of-Funds, 2nd Quarter, 1971, Preliminary, Board of Governors of the Federal Reserve System, August 1971.

indicated have of course major effects when cumulated over a twenty-year period.

It should be acknowledged that such comparisons suffer from certain deficiencies, a few of which should be mentioned. One is that the asset growth rate of financial institutions is a reflection of an impure mixture of business and consumer financial asset growth. Thus, one is unable to distinguish categorically between the respective effects on financial institutions of business and consumer net worth gains. Looking through the list of institutions included in the tabulation, the problem is clearly most serious in the case of commercial banks where the distinction between assets (or liabilities) ascribable to the business versus the household sector becomes too blurred to be meaningful short of a major investigatory effort. As it happens, however, the growth rate of commercial banks has fallen short of that of the tabulated institutions as a group, which is suggestive although not conclusive in proving that the basic point made in the previous paragraph would stand up under closer examination.

A second and perhaps more fundamental objection relates to the direction of causation in the linkage between increased financial asset orientation in household saving and what is here called "opportunities" for financial institutions. It should be clear that the linkage mechanism adopted in the descriptive tone of this paper runs from the consumer to the financial institutions. It shares this approach with the following phrasing from the SEC *Institutional Investor Study:* "Households have substituted corporate for proprietors equity, have shifted into short-term claims, and have exhibited a preference for intermediated rather than direct holdings of long-term assets (which include equities)." [16]

This reasoning is open to the "Galbraithian" counterargument that the chain of causation has run from institutional promotion of financial asset acquisition as an outlet for rising consumer net worth to the consumer himself—i.e., a denial of consumer sovereignty.[17] One need not be a sociologist or market research analyst to recognize the merits of this argument. All that is necessary is to grant that massive advertising and promotion has indeed gone into consumer education by many of the financial institution groups covered in the tabulation. But it would appear hopeless to say more than that there is indeed a two-way causation here that is impossible to disentangle. It will be shown later, however, that the facts of disintermediation in recent years prove beyond reasonable doubt that "sensitization" of the consumer to financial rates of return—even if originated by institutions—leaves the consumer with a far from negligible power over individual portfolio decisions even vis-à-vis all institutions as a group.

Besides this somewhat philosophical point, there is the further—and considerably more pointed—objection that certain financial asset gains, such as those represented by the growth in popularity of pension and retirement funds, should be viewed as a trend toward collectively enforced savings rather than a "preference for intermediated claims." I have sought to deal with this objection in Section II-2F, without being able to deny a substantial element of validity in it.

2. Differential growth rates among financial institutions

It is tempting to equate the differential growth rates of financial institutions shown in Table 6-A and 6-B with the relative degree of responsiveness to the new consumer. Any such temptation should be resisted unless this ambition is curbed by careful recognition of the many other factors playing a role in differential growth of types of financial institutions. The single most important such factor is in all likelihood government regulation. Others will be mentioned. However, it is precisely because government regulation is typically emphasized by industrial, government, and academic specialists and dominates public discussion that it is tempting to speculate briefly on the interrelationships that may exist between the differential growth rates as recorded and the developments in consumer finance as here described. Regulatory factors cannot be neglected, nor perhaps even deemphasized; but they can be supplemented.

The main distinction between the two parts of Table 6 is that in part A the effect of price changes in equity holdings directly affects the reported growth rates, whereas in part B an effort has been made to eliminate this effect by cumulating current net flows into the respective institutions on the 1950 base. The difference is insignificant in the case of depository institutions (once commercial bank-administered, noninsured pension funds have been grouped separately, as they are and should be). The difference is substantial between the depository institutions and the other institutions, and it is the more substantial the more equity-oriented in their investment policies the other institutions were or became in the course of the period.

Picking and choosing among the many observations one might make on the data in Table 6, perhaps the first and most obvious is that aside from credit unions (which remain a minor factor in the aggregates) the fastest growth rates have been recorded by the equity-oriented institutions such as noninsured pension funds. (This remains true even if measured on a flow basis.)

Perhaps as interesting as this point is that the depository institutions staged a comeback in the 1960s. Whereas their growth rate, on a flow basis, fell far short of that of the nondepository intermediaries during the 1950s, the situation was reversed during the 1960s. It is worthwhile considering whether the sustained uptrend in consumer interest rates paid by the depository institutions, combined with the gradual deterioration in equity performance during the latter sixties, may not have contributed substantially to this reversal. The trend fits the picture of an increasingly return-conscious, but still safety-conscious, consumer that has previously emerged.

This broad explanation is strengthened considerably if one examines the relative growth performance among the depository institutions. As Table 6 shows, the savings and loan associations achieved roughly triple the growth rate of commercial banks and mutual savings banks during the 1950s, but less than double that rate during the 1960s and 1970. Furthermore, there was a progressive equalization of growth rates during the 1960s if the past decade is further subdivided into halves. These facts should be judged against the background and data on interest rates (Table 4) supplied in Section III-2.

During the entire decade of the 1950s and into the early 1960s, the savings and loan associations enjoyed a very significant advantage over the other depositary institutions in the average rate paid on savings accounts. This differential coincided with the period when interest rates for the first time since the 1930s were becoming a factor of measurable importance in the relative attractiveness of various institutions vying for consumer savings.

Let it be granted that locational convenience has been and will remain a leading factor in attracting savings deposits; let it be granted that savings and loan associations enjoyed an advantage in this regard as the suburbs grew, while commercial banks and mutual savings banks were hamstrung through branching regulations; let it also be acknowledged that maximum rates payable to depositors under the authority of different regulators and additional regulatory factors (such as minimum liquidity rules), as well as tax laws, all played a part in these developments. Granting all of this, there remains an element of varying institutional responsiveness to the more return-conscious yet safety-conscious consumer in helping to explain the relative performance. Commercial banks, it can be argued, did not discover that broadening segment of the public until the early and middle sixties when the large banks first began to compete seriously for consumer savings, while smaller banks began to realize that locational advantages in obtaining such deposits could be more than offset by excessively adverse interest-rate differentials [5].

3. Special problems affecting life insurance

A. *The slow rate of growth*—It is clear from Table 6 that the life insurance industry has had the lowest growth rate over the past two decades among the institutions included in the survey, whether measured on an asset market valuation basis or on a flow basis. The industry did outperform the depositary institutions during the 1950s. (The rapid growth of the savings and loan associations, starting from a very low base, was more than offset by the slow growth of the commercial banks and the mutual savings banks.) However, during the 1960s and for the past two decades as a whole, the industry fell behind all other institutions in its growth.

These facts have of course been noted before and extensively discussed. Two principal villains have been singled out—regulatory factors and inflation. Both of them are too important to be dismissed after mere mention. Before beginning this sketchy review, however, it should once again be noted (as was done in Section II-2F) that the orientation of this paper dictates formulation of the industry's performance as an accumulator of household net worth. The emphasis in measurement and evaluation is on the role of the industry as a savings intermediary—directly for the individual (whole life insurance and annuity reserves), or indirectly (pension fund and group annuity reserves). The industry's role in protection as such, as well as its role as a service industry in the economy as a whole, is disregarded. In effect, this orientation precludes a "balanced view" of the industry's importance or growth performance. The bias could be largely remedied if one also were to discuss the relative role and growth of the industry in total life insurance protection, and in GNP and employment. This is outside the scope of this paper.

B. *Regulation*—The regulatory factors inhibiting the life insurance industry's growth as a savings intermediary over the past two decades have been superbly summarized in Chapter VI of the *Summary Volume* of the SEC's *Institutional Investor Study*. In effect, the industry was handicapped during the period of the rediscovery and exceptional performance of equities (1950–65) by severe portfolio and tax restrictions upon its entry into common stocks as either an investment medium for general account, or in any direct linkage with insurance for insurance-related products, or in the funding of noninsured pension plans. In addition, regulatory restraints prevented rising interest rates on current general account fixed-debt investments from being translated into corresponding advances in investment returns to corporate pension clients, who were the forerunners and *de facto* representatives of the return-conscious consumer. The industry in its capacity as a savings intermediary was thus doubly affected—first, by the trend toward collective rather than individual saving for retirement; second, by its inability to compete on equal regulatory terms with non-life insurance funding agents in the investment of the collective savings thus generated.

The gradual removal of many of these barriers occupied much of the late 1950s and early 1960s, but has now reached the point where the SEC study could conclude on the pension fund side that "insurers generally feel that they have regained a competitive position." [18] The matter is far from settled on the individual side, where variable (equity-funded) annuities can be considered no more than a beginning in dealing with the new consumer. The industry's entry in force into the mutual fund field in the late 1960s and the current active interest in variable life insurance are other facets of an ongoing evolution and adaptation to new consumer demands that have frequently been slowed by regulatory factors.

C. *Inflation and life insurance*—Inflation as a factor inhibiting the growth of individual savings through life insurance reserves has to be evaluated with the utmost caution. Assuming that the savings rate itself has not clearly been adversely affected by inflation (as argued in Section III-4), the question remains whether inflation has had an adverse reallocation effect on the particular form of savings represented by cash values in life insurance policies. The logical case for the proposition is strong, especially in view of the fact that life insurance is the longest term savings contract an individual makes, so that the potential erosion of the purchasing power of his savings is more severe than, say, in the case of savings deposits. Yet, the cumulative effect of inflation on savings deposits—if maintained rather than withdrawn and spent—is identical with that of the erosion upon savings through life insurance; and the aggregate growth rate of savings deposits at depositary institutions speeded up rather than slowed down until the late 1960s.

The most refined econometric study of the subject led its author to the conclusion that in the period studied "price expectations had no discernible effect on saving through life insurance . . . ," but he also allowed that "one may speculate that even a 'creeping' inflation may have potential cumulative effects that take time to influence the slow process of social learning" [8]. The final qualifying phrase was no doubt conditioned by the time period of the data examined (1946–64) versus the date of appearance of the study (1969)! Valid as it may be, the point was again sharply disputed when argued (with an attempt at documentation) by me on a recent occasion [10].

D. *Additional observations*—The evidence presented so far, together with the tests reported in Section V, suggests a simple hypothesis worthy of further exploration in seeking to explain the declining share of life insurance in individual savings. It is that the financial returns from life insurance savings are either insufficient or insufficiently understood to compete with the clear and explicit rates of return available on alternative forms of savings. It is difficult in the extreme to sort out the cost of protection from the return on the savings dollar in the total benefits obtainable from a level-premium whole life insurance contract. Precisely because of this difficulty, cash value calculations do not answer the question of the rate of return. Explicit rates paid by life insurance companies—such as those on dividends or death benefits left on deposit—have typically lagged behind rates on savings deposits and fixed-debt securities.

This explanation has the merit of a unifying principle underlying a trend that is adverse to individual life insurance savings vis-à-vis both equity-oriented intermediaries and depositary intermediaries. It may in fact also help explain the "revealed preference" for collective (group) savings for retirement to which repeated reference has been made. Such plans, whether or not funded through life insurance companies, are in fact administered within the framework of explicit and competitive rates of return that encompass both equity and fixed-debt investment performance. It is

V. Disintermediation as a Test of Consumer Response to Financial Incentives

1. Statement of the problem

Disintermediation is a shorthand financial-market term describing a process in which households withdraw from financial intermediaries financial savings previously held there and apply the proceeds to the direct purchase of other types of financial claims (typically marketable securities). The origin of the term is somewhat shrouded, but its popularization and widespread understanding is without doubt related to the financial events of 1966.

In that year, the Federal Reserve made a short-lived but forceful attempt to halt through strong monetary restraint the inflation developing in the wake of the Vietnam escalation. While market rates of interest were rising rapidly, depositary institutions were at first seeking to follow suit, but were severely handicapped—at least in the case of the savings and loan associations and mutual savings banks—by the slow turnover of existing portfolios at interest rates largely reflecting pre-Vietnam home mortgage rate levels. Their ability to enter into mortgage commitments virtually collapsed.

Commercial banks with more liquid portfolios at shorter maturities, on the other hand, were better able to attempt to maintain their lending capability. They were bidding vigorously at rising rates not only for high-denomination Certificates of Deposit (CDs)—up to that time largely held by corporations in amounts of $100,000 and above—but also increasingly so for consumer savings deposits and for consumer CDs (whose minimum denominations were being scaled down progressively). As previously noted (Section III-2), this "interest rate war" was more or less terminated by the imposition of unified supervisory regulation dating from 1966—but it is precisely at that point at which an "ornery" public began to prove that rising market rates of interest combined with regulated deposit interest rate ceilings could lead to disintermediation. Neither financial intermediaries nor their regulators could in fact take the consumer sector for granted in seeking to direct the allocation of financial savings. The response to "interest arbitrage incentives" was immediate and strong.

The years 1967 and 1968 provided an interlude of sorts. Market rates of interest were dropping or reasonably stable, and various minor adjustments in the deposit rate ceilings were being made. However, the phenomenon recurred with a vengeance during the monetary restraint period of 1969–early 1970. It then subsided once more later in 1970, following a substantial upgrading of depositary ceiling rates (around the turn of 1969–70) and the decline in market rates of interest after mid-1970.

The problem as stated so far has focused on household allocation of financial asset acquisition as between depositary institutions and market instruments. This would be a valid view only if public discretion in financial asset acquisition were confined to these choices. This is emphatically not the case for individual savings through life insurance. The cash value of life insurance policies is the equivalent of a savings deposit withdrawable upon demand. Life insurance policy loans have in fact proved to be as much of a target for disintermediation as have savings deposits in any of the depositary institutions (more precise statements and statistical measurements will follow shortly).

The issue just raised is more debatable in the case of the other nondepositary intermediaries. Pension fund reserves and the rate of net inflow into such funds are largely outside the ultimate beneficiaries' control and can therefore be safely neglected in analyzing disintermediation. Open-end investment companies (mutual funds) occupy a somewhat indeterminate position. In strict logic, the financial-return-conscious saver might consider mutual funds (or equities in general) eligible for the alternative placement of his funds as much as fixed-interest securities if rate spreads between equities and depositary rates develop. In practice, however, such a neutral view is unrealistic. The objections are both theoretical and practical. On the theoretical side, it is reasonable to assume the elasticity of substitution to be higher among various fixed-rate assets themselves than between fixed-rate assets as a group vis-à-vis equities. On the practical side, it would be next to impossible to compare expected rates of return on equities with actually obtainable rates of return on fixed-interest assets.

2. Measurement

A. *Crude approach*—The measurement problem of disintermediation will be approached in two stages. The first one is for the easily or already convinced; the second one for the statistician. Chart 9 presents quarterly observations, 1965–70, of the percentage of household net financial asset acquisition (exclusive of equities) through the media of savings deposits at all depositary institutions, plus individual life insurance reserves less policy loans, vis-à-vis a reasonably representative open-market rate.[19] The remainder of household financial asset acquisition as defined consists basically of fixed-interest securities, such as federal, state, and local notes and bonds, corporate paper and bonds, and mortgages.

It is immediately obvious that there is a fair degree of negative correlation—the higher the interest rate, the less the percentage of net financial asset acquisition through the savings media just enumerated; the lower the interest rate, the higher the percentage so allocated.

Table 7 is an even cruder approximation. The yearly figures for the same variables (more so than the quarterly figures in Chart 9) have the major disadvantage of mixing up high interest rate periods (and their consequences) with calendar periods. Nevertheless, they should be sufficient to show that 1966 and 1969 are known in financial circles as "the years of disintermediation"—and why.

TABLE 7. ALLOCATION OF HOUSEHOLD SAVINGS AND INTEREST RATES
(Annually, 1965–1970)

Year	Household Savings at Selected Institutions as a Per Cent of Net Financial Asset Acquisition*	Average Annual Yield on Prime Commercial Paper (4–6 months)
1965	55.7%	4.38%
1966	44.1	5.55
1967	57.5	5.10
1968	43.8	5.90
1969	26.4	7.83
1970	47.5	7.72

* Household savings at selected institutions equals households' net flow of funds into commercial banks, savings and loan associations, mutual savings banks, and credit unions (inclusive of special accounts such as consumer certificates of deposit), plus net increase in life insurance reserves at life companies less net increase in policy loans. (For reasons explained in the text, net financial asset acquisition as defined excludes flows into investment company shares and other corporate shares.)

Sources: Board of Governors of the Federal Reserve System, *Flow-of-Funds Accounts* and *Federal Reserve Bulletin*.

B. *Statistical tests*—Disintermediation has drawn increasing interest among statisticians. A recent issue of the *Journal of Finance* [6], for example, devoted three articles to the subject. They dealt with selected facets of the problem as it has affected savings and loan associations, mutual savings banks, and life insurance companies, respectively.

In the paper on policy loans at life insurance companies, I presented evidence [6], based on extensive multiple regression studies, which shows that for the period 1965–mid-1970 open market interest rates have the strongest explanatory power in the association of variations in the net increase in policy loans at life insurance companies with various economic

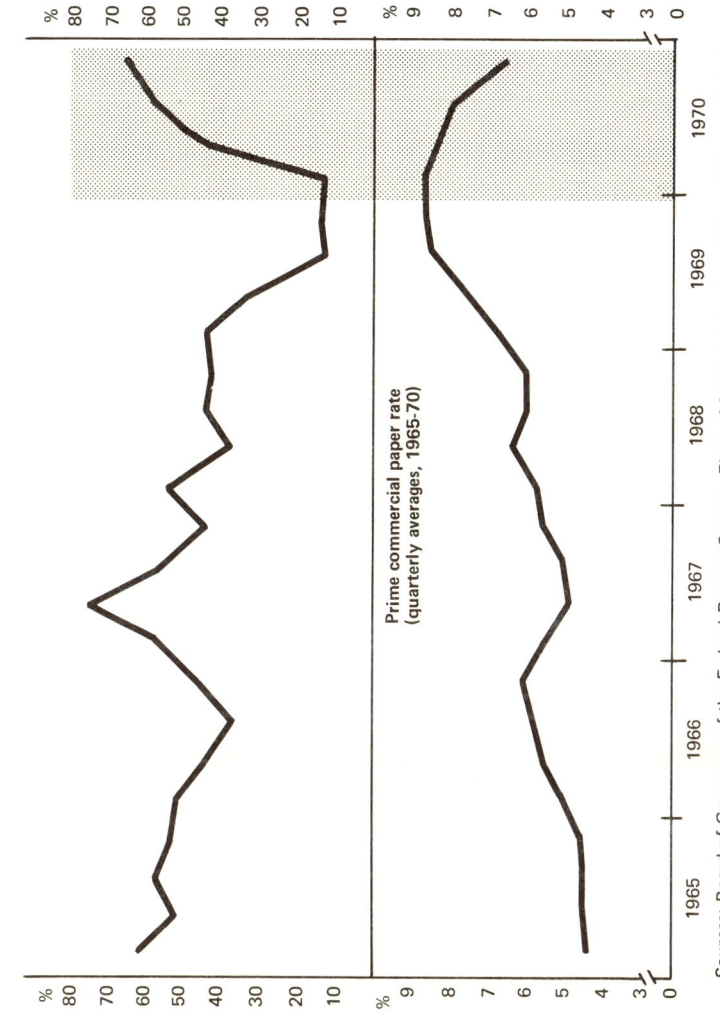

CHART 9. ALLOCATION OF HOUSEHOLD SAVINGS AND INTEREST RATES
Household Savings at Selected Institutions as a Percentage of Net Financial Asset Acquisition (Exclusive of Equities), Quarterly 1965-70

Sources: Board of Governors of the Federal Reserve System, Flow-of-funds Accounts and Federal Reserve Bulletin.

Indicates recession period.

and financial factors. For the purpose of the present paper, these studies have been broadened to include, into a conceptually unified framework, flows of savings into each one of the three main depositary institutions, along with the flow of savings into life insurance reserves less policy loans.[20] It has been attempted to find the main explanatory variables of these flows tabulated quarterly, for 1965–70.

The hypothesis can be succinctly stated as follows. The flow of the particular forms of savings as defined—which should be carefully distinguished from total savings—is at least partly associated with one or more of the following economic and financial variables: (1) the difference between open market rates and the institutions' own rate; (2) disposable personal income; and (3) price changes. Variable (1) represents the disintermediation incentive. Its expected coefficient is negative. Variable (2) can be considered either an explanation or a constraint since current income provides both the basis and limits for savings flows as defined. Its expected coefficient is positive. Variable (3) represents the notion that inflation discourages low-interest-rate savings, regardless of its effect on total savings. The expected coefficient is therefore negative.

Table 8 presents, in a radically abbreviated form, results from extensive stepwise multiple regression experimentation in which the variables were entered in the order given.[21] The results are all compatible with the composite hypothesis. The coefficients have the expected signs and generally pass the t-test for significance at the 95 per cent confidence level. The relative importance of the variables in the equation is obtained by the ranking of the beta coefficients. Taken jointly, the variables explain 70–80 per cent of the observed variations in savings flows as defined.

It should be noted, however, that the interest rate variable was clearly dominant only in the case of life insurance flows where it explained over 80 per cent of the observed variations. Taken alone, it explained only about 40 per cent of the variations in commercial bank savings flows and less than 20 per cent in the cases of the savings and loan associations and the mutual savings banks. In the latter two cases (and possibly also in that of the commercial banks), income effects predominated while the price effect ranked third in all cases.

These results virtually invite considerable speculation and further experimentation, but the following summary will have to suffice for the present purpose. The postulated disintermediation effect is fully compatible with observed variations in savings flows at all four types of institutions studied. It is the single most important factor only in the case of life insurance companies and—as far as the tests have gone—is secondary only to income effects at the depositary institutions.[22]

TABLE 8. FUNCTIONAL RELATIONSHIPS BETWEEN NET
FLOW OF SAVINGS INTO SELECTED INTERMEDIARIES
AND VARIOUS FINANCIAL AND
ECONOMIC VARIABLES
(Quarterly, 1965–1970)

Regression Equation				Cumulative R^2's	Standard Error of Estimate	Durbin-Watson Statistic
A. Flow of Savings into Commercial Banks						
CBFF = −23.28 − 6.92CBNO1 + .09GYD − 5.78CP3*				.332		
t-ratios:	(−6.05)	(5.12)	(−1.82)	.676		
Beta Coefficients:	(−1.15)	(1.13)	(−0.38)	.722	$3.55 bil.	1.80
B. Flow of Savings into Savings and Loan Associations						
SLFF = −26.98 − 3.76SLNO1 + .08GYD − 5.68CP3				.164		
t-ratios:	(−5.86)	(7.11)	(−2.95)	.663		
Beta Coefficients:	(−1.12)	(1.47)	(−0.58)	.765	$2.11 bil.	1.69
C. Flow of Savings into Mutual Savings Banks						
MSFF = −8.38 − 1.40MSNO1 + .03GYD − 1.65CP3				.173		
t-ratios:	(−7.14)	(7.91)	(−2.77)	.732		
Beta Coefficients:	(−1.20)	(1.48)	(−0.49)	.807	$0.66 bil.	2.05
D. Flow of Savings into Life Insurance Companies						
LIFF = −.07 − .56LINO1 + .01GYD − .32CP12*				.819		
t-ratios:	(−4.32)	(2.90)	(−1.50)	.878		
Beta Coefficients:	(−1.03)	(0.87)	(−0.66)	.890	$0.27 bil.	1.76

* These particular t-ratios are not significant (5 per cent confidence level). Equations for flows into commercial banks and life companies which do not take into account price changes show even greater interest sensitivity of flows to these institutions.

DEFINITIONS:
  CBFF: Net flow of savings into commercial banks
  CBNO1: Yield on prime commercial paper (4–6 months) less commercial banks' own rate (Table 4, column 3)
  SLFF: Net flow of savings into savings and loan associations
  SLNO1: Yield on prime commercial paper (4–6 months) less savings and loan associations' own rate (Table 4, column 1)
  MSFF: Net flow of savings into mutual savings banks
  MSNO1: Yield on prime commercial paper (4–6 months) less mutual savings banks' own rate (Table 4, column 2)
  LIFF: Net increase in life insurance reserves at life companies less net increase in policy loans
  LINO1: Yield on prime commercial paper (4–6 months) less 5 per cent, the most common interest rate charged on policy loans
  GYD: Disposable personal income
  CP3: Percentage change in the consumer price index over *one quarter*
  CP12: Percentage change in the consumer price index over *one year*

Sources: Board of Governors of the Federal Reserve System; United States Department of Commerce; United States Department of Labor; and annual fact books of the trade associations listed in Note 15.

3. Institutional response

It is interesting and enlightening to observe that over the years 1966–70 there has been a progressive disenchantment of regulators and regulated institutions with depositary institution ceiling rates. The debate over ceiling-rate influence on the effectiveness of aggregate monetary policy is a morass.[23] The effectiveness of the ceilings in protecting the residential mortgage market in terms of availability of funds and interest charged on mortgages has been increasingly questioned, in good part because the federally sponsored agencies assisting mortgage-granting depositary institutions have obviously drawn some part of their funds raised in the public markets from the proceeds of disintermediation.[24] The equity argument is at long last being brought out into the open—the larger depositor and the large life insurance cash value owner are more likely to have the knowledge and ability to disintermediate [7].

The depositary institutions, partly under the prodding of the regulatory authorities, have not always resisted upward revisions of the rate ceilings and refinements in these ceilings rationally relating them to economic criteria acceptable to the new consumer. Thus, rates are now typically scaled upward by amount and maturity of deposit. As a result—and again illustrating interest-rate responsiveness—the higher-yielding certificates and special accounts (versus passbook savings) rose to over 40 per cent of total savings and loan associations deposits by the end of 1970, as against under 12 per cent in October 1966 [17].

Basically, the disintermediation problem remains unsolved. It *is* a problem even if viewed strictly from the consumer (as distinct from the institutional or regulatory) side since inequities among income groups are clearly involved, as noted above. Naturally, the problem might be decisively eased if 1966–70 turned out to be a temporary extreme in the alternation of high-interest rate and low-interest rate cycles that have characterized United States financial history.

VI. Concluding Observations.

The cumulative effect of this paper, in spite of data inadequacies and precautionary and tempering notes, has no doubt been that of a reasonably defensible case strongly pleaded. It may therefore be well to emphasize once more that it is not claimed that the past two decades have witnessed the conversion of the United States householder from ignoramus to financial sharp-shooter. All that is claimed is that gradual changes in this direction, speeded up by the severe inflation of the late 1960s, have taken place. Neither the beginning point nor the end point rates the crass terms just used. Financial institution adaptation has proceeded accordingly, but perhaps somewhat more slowly than the consumer has learned, partly because public policy on financial institution regulation is lagging behind the need of the times—as is the case in other areas of life in the United States.

Nevertheless, the question inevitably arises—where will it all end? Without firm conviction, I am inclined to the view that the trends described will continue in the same direction and at about the same pace for some years to come. The underlying factors of rising education and real incomes that have propelled the consumer in the direction of greater financial sophistication are simply too strong to make a halt, let alone a reversal, very plausible.

Given this assumption, the question of the one-stop financial institution is likely to acquire still more prominence than it has had so far. Increased net worth and rational portfolio allocation choices have led the United States consumer in the direction of emphasizing financial asset acquisition and diversification within his own portfolio. A clearly possible institutional response would be to offer him all the financial services he needs under one roof. The innumerable conglomeration and diversification moves towards invasion of the other institutions' territory actually made or currently advocated by each historically distinct type of institution are signs pointing in this direction. The drive runs head-on into cherished traditions on both the institutional and public policy side.

An intermediate solution is of course the broadening of product lines traditionally associated with each type of institution so as to amplify consumer portfolio choices within each institution to the virtual equivalent of a full spectrum of services. Offerings of consumer CDs by depositary institutions at rates equivalent to open market instruments (after allowance for differential risk and maturity features) is typical of this approach. Variable annuities and variable life insurance (which is currently moving beyond the discussion stage) are other such examples since they facilitate the placement of savings through life insurance into equities rather than into fixed-debt instruments. Precisely because of the evolutionary pace of consumer financial management, such an approach will probably suffice to keep intact for quite some time the images associated with different types of institutions without impairing their gradual conversion into all-purpose financial establishments serving the broad-spectrum yet individualized demands of an increasingly affluent household sector.

A totally different scenario might of course be drawn. Suppose that over the next few decades economic growth and rising financial affluence are radically downgraded by individuals and by society as national objectives —be it for ecological or sociological reasons, or for reasons not yet perceived. In that case, the early 1970s might be the zenith of the trends discussed in this paper. To this observer, the probability of such a reversal appears small but not totally beyond reasonable argument.

Notes

1. The main source of macroeconomic data on financial operations of the household sector is the Federal Reserve Board's quarterly and annual *Flow of Funds Accounts* series, published since 1950. The major source of microeconomic data is the University of Michigan's annual *Survey of Consumer Finances*, published annually since 1960 by the University of Michigan Press.

As regards basic background, the reader is referred to numerous studies in income and wealth published by many authors under the auspices of The National Bureau of Economic Research (NBER) by the Columbia and Princeton University presses. Possibly the most significant contributions are those of Professor R. W. Goldsmith —*A Study of Savings in the U.S.*, Princeton (for the NBER): 1956; and *The National Wealth of the United States in the Postwar Period*, Princeton (for the NBER): 1962.

2. All references to a "statistically significant trend" as applied to time series are based on the value of the "t" ratio at the 95 per cent confidence limit. The test measures whether or not the "b" coefficient is significantly different from zero (at the stated confidence limit) and therefore correlated with time.

3. In a socialist state, the accumulation of wealth in the household sector might be considered ruled out by definition.

4. The main reason for the leveling off is disintermediation, explained and discussed in Section V. In addition, it should be noted even at this early stage that there is a strong likelihood of an underestimate of actual total consumer savings account holdings in 1969 and 1970. (The Flow-of-Funds Accounts are plagued by difficulties in distinguishing between business and consumer Certificates of Deposit at commercial banks.)

5. Unfortunately, the interest rate comparisons of Table 4 (Section III-2) do not contain United States Savings Bond rates. A sample comparison for the year 1965 shows that savings and loan associations and mutual savings banks were then paying around 4⅛ per cent–4¼ per cent on savings deposits that were in most cases in effect withdrawable upon demand, whereas United States Savings Bonds, even if held for five years, would yield only 3.69 per cent (*Annual Reports of the U.S. Secretary of the Treasury*).

6. New York Stock Exchange (NYSE) data (*1969 New York Stock Exchange Public Transactions Study*, published by the Exchange, 1970) show that institutional holdings of NYSE-listed stocks rose from about 19 per cent to about 25 per cent of the total between 1951 and 1969, while the institutional share in total transactions increased from roughly 30 per cent to about 56 per cent over the two decades.

7. In this broad aggregate, the persons covered under pension plans are defined to include those who are currently receiving pensions as well as those who are not yet receiving pensions. Number of persons covered and total pension assets are for all private plans and government-administered pension plans (at all levels of government) other than Social Security (OASDI). The broad compilation rests upon data from the Institute of Life Insurance; the Social Security Administration; the United States Department of Labor; the Railroad Retirement Board; and the Securities and Exchange Commission. It is not strictly comparable with the data given in Table 6 and discussed in Section IV.

8. Life insurance premium and annuity considerations receipts have been approximately 4 per cent of disposable personal income throughout the past two decades. The amount of life insurance per family was $4,600 in 1950, compared with per-family disposable personal income of $4,100 for the same year; by 1970, life insur-

ance per family had risen to $20,900, compared with per-family disposable income of $10,200. (*Life Insurance Fact Book,* 1971, p. 25 and p. 59.)

9. Employer contributions to private pension and deferred profit sharing plans amounted to $1.8 billion, or 84 per cent, of the total contributions in 1950. By 1969, employer contributions had risen to $11.1 billion, or 90 per cent, of total contributions. (Social Security Administration, *Social Security Bulletin,* April 1971, p. 27.)

10. This lack is one of the widely recognized but uncorrected deficiencies complicating analysis of the evolution of United States household financial management.

11. The rise in the statistical probability of a median-income family's stock ownership over time can be compared with the rise in that probability for all families. The *Michigan Survey* cross-sectional data on stock ownership by income group for seven selected years, 1959–70, in each case include income groups encompassing (although overlapping) the median family income for that year (from Census Bureau data). Using linear interpolation, it can be shown that, whereas the probability of stock ownership in general rose from 17 per cent of all families in 1959 to 26 per cent in early 1970 (a 53 per cent increase), the corresponding rise at the median income level was from 13 per cent to 24 per cent (an 85 per cent increase). The assumption of linear distribution of stock ownership within and among the "Michigan income groups" is admittedly open to serious statistical objections.

12. Computed from United States Department of Labor, Bureau of Labor Statistics, *Employment and Earnings* (monthly), various issues.

13. There is "considerable insensitivity of saving to gradual but prolonged declines in the purchasing power of money . . . so long as inflation is kept in bounds . . ." R. W. Goldsmith, *op. cit.* (*A Study of Savings in the U.S.* I, p. 22).

14. Among the theoretical points made in this controversy, reference may be made to just one. "Neither United States depreciation tax policy nor traditional accounting procedures permit adjustment for changes in the cost of capital goods . . . Owners of capital, especially equity capital, have been relatively quiescent as regards the purchasing power of capital recovery allowances." (Tax Foundation, *Depreciation Allowances: Federal Tax Policy and Some Economic Aspects,* New York: Tax Foundation, 1970, p. 38.) On the more practical side, it has been noted time and again that the positive correlation between stock market prices and the rate of inflation is weak at best. In fact, a recent econometric study measuring a number of explanatory variables vis-à-vis stock market prices showed the inflation rate to be negatively correlated with equity prices in a multiple regression taking into account also changes in the real money stock and the level of expected real corporate earnings. (Anticipated inflation was measured through the level of nominal interest rates.) See Michael W. Keran, "Expectations, Money and the Stock Market," *Monthly Review* 53, January 1971, Federal Reserve Bank of St. Louis, pp. 16–31.

15. The *Summary Volume* of the *SEC Institutional Investors Study* can serve this purpose very well as long as its special orientation (the equities market) is kept in mind. However, it should also be noted that, quite aside from individual quotes, trade association and official sources have been a valuable input throughout this paper—especially the annual *Life Insurance Fact Book* (Institute of Life Insurance); *National Fact Book* (National Association of Mutual Savings Banks); *Savings and Loan Fact Book* (United States Savings and Loan League); *Annual Report,* Board of Governors of the Federal Reserve System; *Annual Report,* Federal Reserve Bank of New York; and *Economic Report of the President* and *Annual Report of the Council of Economic Advisers.*

16. *Summary Volume, ibid.,* p. 10.

17. At the risk of caricaturizing, Galbraith may be summed up on this point as claiming that the large corporation itself creates the demand for its product. J. K. Galbraith, *The New Industrial State,* Boston: Houghton Mifflin, 1967.

18. *SEC Institutional Investors Study, Summary Volume, op. cit.,* p. 43.

19. The prime commercial paper rate, 4–6 months, serves for the moment as simply one of many highly variable open-market rates, but it will later be shown to be the statistically most significant one in the generality of the cases examined.

20. It should be noted in particular that in the present exercise the life insurance flow is measured in terms of increases in policy reserves less policy loan increases in order to work with a concept as closely comparable as possible to net savings flows into depositary institutions. (In the *Journal of Finance* paper just cited [6], such comparability was not the aim and therefore the net increase in policy loans alone was analyzed vis-à-vis outside variables.) An attempt was made to strengthen the comparability further by deducting passbook loans (and similar devices) from net inflows into the depositary intermediaries, but it was quickly determined (a) that consistent series for each type of depositary institution would not be available; and (b) that, where available, the data suggest increases in passbook loans amounting to no more than two per cent of the net inflow even during "disintermediation years."

21. The interested reader is invited to write the author for more extensive tables on the statistical results. There are many issues in model specification, including for example the question of levels versus changes in the variables, that should be pursued further.

22. I shall permit myself the following bit of speculation on the relatively higher sensitivity to interest rates of life insurance savings less policy loans as against net inflows at depositary institutions. Interest rates on the *positive* side of the flow into life insurance reserves are, as already noted, difficult to calculate. This "invisibility" works against reserve-creating types of insurance at a time when consumer interest rates of depositary institutions have risen, albeit slowly, and are being heavily promoted. On the *negative* side of the flow, the bulk of policy loans at life insurance companies has been and is being made at a constant (5 per cent) rate, whereas interest rates on passbook loans at depositary institutions have risen at least parallel to deposit rates.

23. Here is a summary by one leading theorist of the contribution to the question by two other leading theorists, James Tobin ("Deposit Interest Ceilings as a Monetary Control") and Milton Friedman ("Controls on Interest Rates Paid by Banks") —"Tobin argues that the aggregative effects of changes in the ceiling rate are small, whereas Friedman emphasizes the uncertainty of these results."—Karl Brunner, "Two Major Issues in Recent Monetary Policy—A Symposium," *Journal of Money, Credit and Banking* 2, No. 1, February 1970, pp. 1–2.

24. This is the thrust of the article cited by Kwon and Thornton [6] who for this reason term "inefficient" housing assistance operations of the Federal Home Loan Banks.

References

(*Additional References may be found in the Notes.*)

1. Federal Reserve Bank of New York, *Monthly Review* 48, No. 1, January 1966, pp. 12–18.

2. Federal Reserve System. For background and description, see Board of Governors *Annual Report 1966,* pp. 28–29, and Federal Reserve Bank of New York, *Monthly Review* 48, No. 10, October 1966, p. 221.

3. Freund, William C., "Will Institutional Demands Outrun the Supply of Common Stocks in the '70s?" *Financial Analysts Journal,* July–August 1971, pp. 37–43. These data problems are well explained (and identical conclusions reached).

4. Garvy, George, and Martin R. Blyn, *The Velocity of Money,* New York: Federal Reserve Bank of New York, 1969. Actually, the statements imply hypotheses on "sectoral" velocities that would be difficult to prove (see p. 58 of Garvy and Blyn for a description of the problem and for references). On the other hand, Garvy and Blyn appear to have no serious doubts that the continuing rise of income velocity in the 1960s prevailed throughout the economy, including the consumer sector (see especially Chapter 6, pp. 76–77).

5. Kardouche, G. K., "The Competition for Savings: Determinants of Deposits at Commercial Banks, Mutual Savings Banks, and Savings and Loan Associations," *Studies in Business Economics, No. 107*, New York: The National Industrial Conference Board, 1969. The statements are substantially consistent with the econometric evidence presented by Kardouche.

6. Kwon, Jene K., and R. M. Thornton, "An Evaluation of the Competitive Effect of FHLB Open Market Operations on Savings Inflows at Savings and Loan Associations," pp. 699–712; Neil B. Murphy, "The Demand for New York State Mutual Savings Bank Deposits: 1960–1969," pp. 713–718; and Francis H. Schott, "Disintermediation Through Policy Loans at Life Insurance Companies," pp. 719–729; all in the *Journal of Finance* 26, No. 3, June 1971.

7. Lindsay, Robert, *The Economics of Interest Rate Ceilings*, New York: New York University Institute of Finance, Nos. 68–69, December 1970, argues the case most forcefully.

8. Neumann, Seev, "Inflation and Saving Through Life Insurance," *The Journal of Risk and Insurance* 36, No. 5, December 1969, pp. 567–582.

9. Schott, Francis H., "Life Insurers, Variable Annuities and Mutual Funds: A Critical Study-Comment," *The Journal of Risk and Insurance* 38, No. 3, September 1971, pp. 463–486. I hope to have clarified the above distinctions in this article.

10. ———, "Monetary Policy and Life Insurance Companies—Panel on the Impact of Monetary Policy on Financial Institutions: Gurley–Shaw Revisited," *1970 Proceedings,* Washington, D.C.: Business and Economic Statistics Section, American Statistical Association, 1971, pp. 335–341; and the "Comment" by Eli Shapiro, *ibid.*, pp. 354–356.

11. Securities and Exchange Commission, "The Demand for Corporate Stock in the Postwar Period," Chapter 5, pp. 201–49, in *Institutional Investor Study Report of the Securities and Exchange Commission, Supplementary Volume I,* consisting of a report of the National Bureau of Economic Research, Washington, D.C.: Government Printing Office, 1971. This volume and the *Summary Volume* of the SEC *Institutional Investory Study* have been important sources throughout this paper. Naturally, the general focus of the SEC study is more on institutions and their equity holdings and trading than on household financial management.

12. Securities and Exchange Commission. The most relevant table is No. 3–31, p. 144, on *SEC Supplementary Volume I*, as cited in reference [11].

13. Sproul, Allan. The best description of the episode and its immediate aftermath is in Sproul's "The 'Acord'—A Landmark in the First Fifty Years of the Federal Reserve System," *Monthly Review* 46, November 1964, Federal Reserve Bank of New York, pp. 227–236. The more lasting consequences of course have to be traced elsewhere (see general bibliographical list in Note 15).

14. United States Department of Commerce, Bureau of the Census, *Current Population Reports,* Series P-25, No. 464, August 19, 1971.

15. United States Department of Commerce, Bureau of the Census, *Current Population Reports,* various issues for relevant data, including those showing the linkage between average educational attainment and average income.

16. United States Department of Commerce, Bureau of the Census, *Current Population Reports,* Series P-60, No. 8, October 1971, p. 28, for a table demonstrating the point strikingly.

17. United States Savings and Loan League, *Savings and Loan Fact Book, 1971,* p. 66.

18. Yohe, William P., and Denis S. Karnosky, "Interest Rates and Price Level Changes, 1952–69," Federal Reserve Bank of St. Louis, *Review*, 51, No. 12, December 1969, pp. 18–36; and William E. Gibson, "Price Expectations Effects on Interest Rates," *The Journal of Finance*, 25, No. 1, March 1970, pp. 19–34.

Consumer Financial Management and Financial Institution Response — A Two-Decade Perspective

A Response

By A. Marshall Puckett

Frank Schott has unquestionably done a very thorough job of analyzing aggregate trends in the postwar financial position of the household sector. I concur in his analytical approach; share his concerns about the data inadequacies, especially at the micro level; and, for the most part, agree with his broader conclusions. Households have indeed become more sophisticated over the past two decades and are increasingly exerting an independent and dynamic influence on the course of the economy and on its financial institutions and markets.

In this regard, it is striking how frequently of late the business forecasts of economists have begun to carry a hedge to the general effect that "the final outcome will, however, depend upon what the consumer decides to do," and how less frequently reference is made to the old demons of the business cycle—inventory investment and capital spending. One almost gets the impression from reading some of these forecasts that the line of causality in business cycle thinking has been about totally reversed.

That is, whereas previously business spending for plant and inventory was assumed to be the principal cyclical element in the economy that reacted back on the income and spending of consumers, now the spending decisions of consumers seem to be taken as the independent variable reacting on the income and spending of businesses. I think it fair to say, then, that a good many economists besides myself would probably agree with Dr. Schott that the consumer has increasingly become more dynamic—and hence less predictable—in his approach to decisions about spending, saving, and investing. And, in becoming so, he has injected a major new uncertainty into the management of our national economic and financial affairs that is not easy to contend with.

But my purpose here is not simply to place a blessing on Dr. Schott's analysis and conclusions. While I cannot accuse him of any important error of commission, I do think he has made one of omission that leaves his analysis and explanation of postwar household financial developments seriously incomplete. What he failed to take account of was the profound change in economic expectations during the period, and of the direct consequences of that change for the economic and financial position of households and for the climate in which their decisions were being made. This, I might note parenthetically, is a criticism which I think could also with fairness be leveled at several other papers on family decision making presented at this conference.

To illustrate how changing economic expectations can have a direct influence on the financial position of households, let me draw your attention to the remarkable average profitability of stock market investments over the period from 1950 through 1965. In that 15-year span, common stocks in the Standard and Poor's 500 stock index yielded investors a compound annual rate of return of fully 15.3 per cent, and that at a time when alternative investments in corporate bonds were yielding in a range of from only 3 per cent to 4¼ per cent. Also, I might further note that the long-run average rate of return in the stock market has been about 10 per cent per annum, again far below the 1950–65 performance. The reason for this outsized rate of stock market return in the 1950–65 period was, as I am sure many of you are aware, due to rapid share price appreciation that flowed from improving confidence in the stock market and which gave rise to huge capital gains income.

Now, the point I would like to make is that, in all likelihood, the performance of the stock market in the decade and a half ending in 1965 created vast amounts of *unexpected* wealth for those fortunate enough to have been equity investors during the period. In the stock market, unlike the markets for fixed-income securities, there is a sharp distinction to be made between the expected—or *ex ante* rate of return—over a particular holding period, and the realized—or *ex post* rate of return. Now, the very size of the return of stock ownership in the 1950–65 period by itself suggests strongly that the *ex post* rate of return almost surely exceeded the *ex ante* rate of return, with the excess taking the form of capital gains that were windfall additions to the huge stock market component of household wealth.

I would now like to speculate a little about the actual magnitude of the extent to which the realized accretion of stock market values may have exceeded the expected, and to consider some of the implications thereof for the household behavior that Frank Schott has so meticulously detailed. Permit me to set aside for the moment the underlying reason for this stock market performance. I will, however, return to that matter shortly, since its economic significance extends far beyond the rise of stock prices that it engendered.

As a first approximation, let us assume—plausibly I would argue—that the expected or *ex ante* rate of return prevailing in the stock market over the 1950–65 period was no more than the historical average of about 10 per cent, implying that fully five percentage points of the actual *ex post* yield was of a windfall nature. What does that mean in terms of dollars? (Actually, cross-section work this writer and some others have done would strongly suggest that the *ex ante* rate of return during the period was consistently less than 10 per cent.)

The market value of household's holdings of common stock rose steadily from $133 billion in 1950 to $665 billion in 1965; thus the base to which the assumed 5 per cent applies is huge. To simplify my point, let me concentrate on the magnitudes involved around the middle of the period. The value of common stock holdings of households in 1958, for instance, averaged about $320 billion; thus, a 5 per cent windfall gain thereon would come to some $16 billion. To put that sum in perspective, such a windfall gain would also have equalled 5 per cent of total personal disposable income in 1958. That is, a 5 per cent windfall gain on household common stock investments around the time of 1958 would have produced an increment in household wealth almost as large as that achieved that year through consumers' conscious decisions to save out of current income. Creation of windfall wealth on such a scale must, therefore, have had a significant impact on the incentive to save out of income in the 1950–65 period, and also on the choice consumers made in the allocation of that saved income among investment alternatives.

Before proceeding, I am fully aware that common stock ownership is confined to a relatively narrow percentage of total households. However, these households are unquestionably far more important in the aggregate statistics on income, consumption, saving, and investment that their mere numbers would suggest. In this connection, I might note that wealth held in the form of common stock alone has in recent years approached half of the household sector's total financial wealth.

Now, I may have stretched your indulgence a bit by simply asking you to accept the notion that the stock market generated huge amounts of windfall wealth in the 1950–65 period without offering any detailed explanation at the outset as to why this should be so. Frank Schott touched upon the explanation in alluding to the fact that the economy in the period was moving out of the shadows of the Great Depression. As recently as 1950, fears of the recurrence of a deep depression seemed almost unanimous. This was reflected in highly depressed stock prices relative to earnings and dividends, and just as strikingly in massive price discounts on lower quality corporate bonds subject to default in a depressed economy.

However, that depression psychology faded markedly as the 1950s wore on, and by the end of the decade investors seemed to have almost entirely discounted the possibility of another 1930s episode. Indeed, by the early 1960s the stock market had attained a price level that could be explained on rational grounds only by the presence of expectations among investors of long-run economic prosperity accompanied, perhaps, by only occasional and minor interruptions. For instance, for the Standard and Poor's 500 stock index, the ratio of the level of stock prices to the current dividend income from those stocks was by 1965 twice as high as it had been in 1950.

In 1965, moreover, the current dividend yield on common stocks was down to only about 3¼ per cent versus yields of over 4 per cent available on high grade corporate bonds. Clearly it would have made no sense for an investor to buy or hold more risky common stock at such a low relative yield unless he expected that dividend payment to grow over the future, and quite rapidly so. This is not the place to enter into an exercise in the mathematics of share price determination, but it is relatively easy to show arithmetically that a 3¼ per cent current dividend yield is reasonable only if one is expecting that dividend—and the profits that must be earned to pay it—to grow at a rate consistent with a roughly 4 per cent pace of *real* economic expansion. Thus, it appears rather unambiguous, from a reading of the stock market at least, that expectations about the prospective health of the economy changed from deep pessimism and doubt as recently as 1950 to almost full confidence and optimism by the 1960s.

This progressive change in economic expectations may have been the outstanding development of the 1950s, and not only from the standpoint of what it meant for sky-rocketing stock prices and correspondingly for household wealth. Long-run expectations about the economic future are, I would assert, a key variable in all major income and portfolio decisions. It was Frank Schott's failure to consider adequately the role of such changing expectations in shaping the saving and investing decisions of households that is my basic criticism of his paper.

Let me offer only one example of how I think consideration of changing expectations would lead me to alter some of Dr. Schott's conclusions. Dr. Schott attributed the decline in holdings of currency and demand deposits as largely due to rising yields on alternative forms of liquid investments. I would argue more was involved than that. The huge holdings of money—and especially of currency—by households in the 1950s was probably due in good measure to deep fears of another economic and financial collapse. Consequently, as those fears were reduced in the 1950s, households released these defensive balances in favor of other more profitable investments.

Finally, let me conclude by discussing some current puzzlements about household economic and financial behavior. Up to now, I have talked only about the 1950–65 episode. Now let me focus on the period from 1965 to date. As Frank Schott has pointed out, these six years have been a period of unusually high saving out of income by consumers as a group and one that has seen some far-reaching changes in the aggressiveness with which household portfolios are managed.

Now, let me see if I can again go back to the stock market for a plausible explanation. I noted earlier that Frank Schott's data indicated a 15.3 per cent rate of return in the stock market from 1950 through 1965. It also, however, indicated a rate of return of only 3.3 per cent from 1965 through 1970. Thus, equity investment has in recent years failed to add to household wealth to any appreciable degree, in great contrast to the earlier years. Perhaps, then, what we have seen in the aggregate consumer and household statistics in recent years is the reflection of an attempt by the stock-owning segment of the population to make up for the poor performance of the equity sector of their portfolio, both by saving more out of current income and aggressively seeking high yielding fixed-income investments such as bonds. Certainly this is not an implausible hypothesis, though we lack the data to verify it.

One last speculation: Much ink has been spilled in recent years trying to explain the exceptionally high savings rate of consumers that has been developing since 1966. In discussions of the current saving behavior, reference is almost always made to the remarkable constancy of the saving rate in the pre-Vietnam years (around an average of about 6 per cent of personal disposable income). Because the rate remained so closely around that figure for so long a time, economists have come to define it as the "normal" rate and, hence, to term the more recent levels of 8 per cent or more as abnormal. However, my earlier remarks about the windfall stock market wealth being created in the 1950–65 period—wealth which lowered the amount of saving out of income needed to achieve any particular wealth objective—lead me to have considerable skepticism that the 6 per cent average saving rate for that period was, in fact, normal.

9
*Toward a Research Agenda
and
Theoretical Synthesis*

Toward a Research Agenda and Theoretical Synthesis

By Reuben Hill and David M. Klein

In this concluding section we derive from each of the presentations and discussions suggestions for future research. We draw primarily from the rapporteurs' notes and the transcripts of exchanges from the floor to render visible those research ideas not explicitly suggested in the foregoing sections. Finally, we attempt a theoretical synthesis of the papers and discussions (formal and informal) produced for the Williamsburg Conference.

Research Implications

Family decision making

The interdisciplinary review by Ferber drew the most cross fire at the conference because every disciplinarian was sure his own area had been shortchanged in coverage and misinterpreted conceptually. Some of the comments of participants which are listed below include statements of their dissatisfaction as well as research ideas which need further attention:

> Although there is much about family economic decisions in Ferber's review, one major area seems to have been neglected which is of growing interest to economists and sociologists; namely, the analysis of time use among family members, as reflected both by decisions about participation in the labor force on the part of various family members and by the way in which "non-marketable time" is used within the family. The latter is of special interest in assessing the time spent in the parental training of preschool children.
>
> Another suggestion relates to the importance of longer term expectational considerations in the explanation of present behavior. While family units generally do not have carefully quantified lifetime plans, most probably do have general notions about the future path of relevant economic and other variables which have, or may have, a pronounced influence on present actions. For example, a doctor or lawyer newly established in practice will have very different behavior patterns than an unskilled blue-collar worker of comparable age, primarily because of what must be very different expecta-

tions about the path of future income. Similarly, family units with wives of markedly different levels of educational attainment may well make different types of economic decisions because the potential contribution to family income is known to be, on the average, quite different. The point is that longer-term expectations, however vaguely or dimly perceived, influence present actions. (Juster)

I found Ferber's focus on decision-making roles played by various family members a very interesting and potentially fruitful focus. I did not, however, find any evidence presented about whether it makes any difference how these roles are allocated within the family. I would like to have seen some evidence pointing up the implications of different role-playing allocations, and different budgeting procedures for the economic behavior and well-being of families. Furthermore, if it could be shown that such "within family arrangements" do make a difference, we should seek to know more about the determinants of family role allocation, family budgeting, and planning arrangements. (Orcutt)

Decision making involves the use of power to make effective policy in an encounter. What are the sources of power?
1. Economic: who brings in the income?
2. Information: who has the expertise?
3. Personality: dominance in interpersonal relations.
4. Specially defined role expectations: who has the legitimate authority to make the decision?

The interplay of these sources within the family provides the dynamic for understanding change in allocation of power which Ferber's model lacks. (Nayar, by rapporteur Hermalin)

The Ferber framework is too market-oriented, interactions between families and their environment being seen in terms of economic-exchange relations. What we need is a study of the unconditional intra-family transfers which amount to several billion dollars annually in this country. A comparison of exchange-type and transfer-type financial decisions would be fruitful. (Pfaff, by rapporteur Hermalin)

What is needed is an approach to structure family decision making in terms of philanthropy rather than power. Why do people contribute more to the family than they take out? Why do they withdraw these contributions? The high rates of family dissolution currently suggest that the distinction between transfers inside the family versus those outside the family deserve more attention. (Morgan, by rapporteur Hermalin)

These comments point up the multi-dimensionality of consumer behavior, particularly in the thorny area of family decision making. Families as decision-making groups might be compared with other natural groups in our society and with ad hoc artificially contrived groups in their decision-making effectiveness. Comparing families with other decision-making groups we may discover that they are more frequently engaging in playful, impulsive, irreversible, and de facto decisions in which there is more "doing before thinking and discussing" than "planning before doing."

Karl Weick [18] has suggested that families are handicapped in many ways as problem-solving and decision-making groups:

1. Decision making is usually undertaken in the evening when members are tired and at their worst.
2. There is a masking of expert power to maintain legitimacy of the decision maker.
3. Access to the full range of information needed to make good decisions is blocked in families because there is a tendency to concentrate information, expertise, authority, and concern for quality control in one person.
4. Family decision making on a new problem tends to be undertaken amidst distractions and competes with other unfinished business and unsolved problems.
5. There is a tendency for families to concentrate less on identifying and defining the problem than on considering the acceptability of solutions.
6. Because goal-less dissatisfaction rather than goal-oriented dissatisfaction characterizes the discontent in natural groups with developmental histories of so-called normal troubles, families as a prototype of such natural groups make less use of negative feed-back to channel dissatisfaction into changed problem-solving procedures.

A number of conference participants touched on the issues of accessibility of information within and outside the family, the cost of inertia involved in searching for more information, and the issue of utilizing this information to improve the quality of family decision making.[1] Weick's characterization of families as masking expertise to maintain legitimacy and of rendering information less accessible within the family by concentrating it in one person begs research attention. Donald Granbois' review of family decision studies told us that information handling has been undertaken without reference to the particular decision stages in which information is pertinent, specifying primarily the extent of information seeking, the mix of sources consulted, and the relative importance of each type of source [6]. It would appear from his review that scanty attention has been paid even to the descriptive questions of how and to what extent feed-back of information from past experience influences family decisions, who evaluates the family experience, who "stores" the information for future use, and who draws on this information storage when the need arises. These are straightforward mapping tasks which must precede more sophisticated explanatory research.

Using information to solve problems has been given even less attention, although this was a major focus of the 1958 Consumer Behavior Conference [5]. Research directed specifically at the decision-making structure exhibited by families indicates that the responsibility for purchase decisions may be divided among family members to reduce the chances of conflict.

Some of the phases of decision making can be better studied in laboratory or field experimental settings than by questionnaire or porch interviews. The University of Minnesota Family Problem Solving research team is one of the few committed to utilizing laboratory games for studying the utilization of information in problem solutions. The research undertaken by this team has the virtue of testing out its propositions within different social classes and in contrasting societies [17].

In examining the several microresearches highlighted in Ferber's encyclopedic review it is apparent that much more attention has been given in the past decade to family behavior at the level of planning, choosing between products, and deciding whether to spend or save, than on plan fulfillment on the one hand, or on satisfactions derived from outcomes of the decision process on the other hand.[2] Moreover, there appears to have been almost no attention to the impacts of dissatisfaction or satisfaction on future consumption patterns, which would enable us to see to what extent families utilize negative feed-back to profit from unpleasant experiences.

One study [9] not covered in Ferber's presentation to the conference partially rectifies both of these deficits and should be noted briefly before spelling out the directions that further research might take on these matters. The study was undertaken by a University of Minnesota team in Minneapolis-St. Paul, Minnesota, with an area probability sample of more than 300 intergenerationally linked families three generations in depth.

The study design called for four interviews distributed over a twelve-month period, every three months with the wife, and one joint interview with both spouses present. Retrospective histories were undertaken on a number of family behaviors for each of the three generations back to the beginning of the marriage to provide the historical background for comparable information obtained in panel form forward in time over a year's period. Data were collected at each interview about plans to make a change in several crucial areas of economic and social behavior. The decision process followed in choosing to act or to postpone acting on the plan (what Granbois has termed "aborting the plan") [6, p. 49] was recorded for every plan and for every unplanned action. Satisfaction-with-outcome scores were constructed from answers to two questions for every action undertaken, whether planned or unplanned:

1. If you could start over again would you make the same decision (with respect to a given plan)?
2. If you could turn the item purchased back or push a button and be back (in your old residence, for example), would you do it?

The correlates of consumership (percentage of plans fulfilled and percentage of preplanned actions) and the correlates of satisfaction with outcome were pursued in some depth based on several hundred observations over a twelve-month period. Consumership is explained best by high rationality in decision making (based on a Guttman scale of rationality), high educational and occupational level of spouses, flexibility of family organization, adequacy of spousal communication, and a history of leading one's generation in economic achievements over the life span. These findings were consistent with *a priori* hypotheses deduced from family-development theory.

In contrast, the alleged payoff of consumership—namely, satisfaction with the outcome of decisions made—provided many surprises.[3] Between two-thirds and three-fourths of the families in all three generations of the Minnesota study were affirmative about most of their decisions and most of the actions taken. Regrets and recriminations were not widespread. Such high frequency of unqualified affirmation may carry heavy components of self-justification for many of the actions evaluated. The indicator may be telling more about the distribution of the propensity to rationalize past actions than it does about the actual gratifications experienced in the consumption process.

The consumership expression which best predicts satisfaction with actions during the year is the "rationality of decision making" score, an operationalization of the economist's concept of "rationality" which has usually been treated as an assumption in economic studies of consumption behavior

The findings about the interrelations between high preplanning of actions and satisfaction, however, are not in line with consumption theory. Instead of the expected positive relationship, preplanning of actions is negatively related with consumer satisfaction for all three generations. Not only do those families which carry their plans into action most frequently appear to be dissatisfied with the outcome of their decision, but families which have been most frequently impulsive in making residence moves or purchases without prior plans congregate in the high satisfaction categories. Do we have in the negative interplay of the behavioral variable of high preplanning of actions and the attitudinal variable of satisfaction, suggestions of reaction formation? The more planful, the higher the standards of performance demanded and, therefore, the more critical of the results; the more impulsive, the more halo effects are observed in evaluating the results [4] [13].

Further research on the correlates of satisfaction with outcome of decisions is badly needed to verify the theoretically puzzling findings from the Minnesota study. Note the many reversals of direction from the theoretically expected with respect to the correlates of satisfaction:

1. The more active, needful, risk-taking, youngest generation was especially prone to dissatisfaction.
2. Longer duration of marriage, advanced education, white-collar occupations, and higher social class are all indicators of alignment with established institutions and are also predictive of favorable evaluation of the consumption process.
3. Satisfaction is firmly predicted by a syndrome of largely restrictive

family organization variables: wife at home, low social participation, strict observance of traditional sex role, and equalitarian decision-making patterns. With the exception of the last named, these are all traditional familistic patterns.

Satisfaction with consumption outcomes, in sum, seems to be part of a conformity syndrome of familism with close intergenerational linkages at one level, and of integration into the model setting educated and middle classes at another level. Dissatisfaction with outcomes may reflect some alienation and nonconformity. It begins as a deviant pattern expressed most frequently by socially marginal marriages of short duration, by families of flexible organization manned by gainfully employed socially active wives and upward mobile husbands whose alignment as yet with the establishment appears tenuous. These characterizations begin to suggest that improvements in consumership in the early phases of the consumption process may be promoted as much by a critical stance with respect to the actions taken as by an affirming stance. Clearly the phases of consumption are interdependent rather than linked in determinant-consequence chains. To specify the quality of feed-back that would be most likely to stimulate improved consumership will require further study using some of the findings of the Minnesota study as the basis of hypotheses to be tested.

Class life-styles, values, and subjective welfare

We have grouped together the suggestions for future research generated by the discussions from two horizon-breaking sessions (Strumpel-Pfaff and Segal-Felson-Douvan) because they tend to share a common scope (economic behaviors of households, values and satisfactions and their interrelations by social and economic categories), and to a limited extent a common vocabulary of concepts and constructs. There is also some clustering of the discomforts expressed by the critics of these papers with respect to both methodology and substance (failure to recognize intergenerational differences and variability over the family life cycle).

The contributions of these sessions are twofold: they have challenged the precepts and assumptions of one or more of the disciplines at the conference about what may be safely treated as constants when aggregating across categories but must be seen as variables when studied micro-analytically; and they have raised questions about the power of some of our most favored economic and social class categories for differentiating households on material style of life and generalized satisfaction.

Strumpel's choice of subjective welfare as a dependent variable to be explained drew many comments about better ways to make the construct operational in future research. Was Strumpel's solution, the evaluation of one's standard of living, one's job and education, and one's reactions to recent and possible future financial changes termed economic satisfaction, the optimum solution?

> On the matter of satisfactions, what puzzles me is the meaning of satisfaction for economic behavior. . . . I know people who will be dissatisfied no matter what they earn. They simply have that sort of personality. And I think before we get a meaningful measure of satisfaction for economic behavior we have to segregate out these personality aspects from the aspects that would measure economic behavior. But then even if we do, what does satisfaction actually measure? We know from experiments in social psychology that in many plants the people who are dissatisfied actually produce the most, and if this is really so on a wide scale, and if we want to increase productivity, maybe the best thing is to make everybody dissatisfied. . . . Before we interpret satisfaction, even if we do have a meaningful measure, we must have some idea of the relation of satisfaction to economic behavior. (Ferber)

> I wish to mention one crucial and still unsolved problem by giving my own emphasis to Strumpel's discussion. It is possible to obtain data on people's satisfactions and dissatisfactions, for instance, with their income, their standard of living, their job, and their savings. But the meaning of these data is far from clear. Does my being satisfied mean that I do not want more, will not strive for advancement or betterment, but try to preserve what I have? And does my being dissatisfied mean that I strive for improvement, or that I am frustrated and resigned to not having more? . . . A combination of measures of satisfaction with data on values, goals, aspirations, and expectations is called for. (Katona, in a commentary prepared for the conference)

> People often start out aspiring to something and engaging in behavior to realize it and then discover they do not want it and they are not satisfied with it. Behavior becomes a means of finding out what you want rather than achieving what you want. (Foote)

Although Strumpel recognized the desirability of continuing his research on the correlates of "subjective welfare" with a sample that draws on a greater spectrum of the family life cycle and acknowledged the desirability of obtaining time series data, many of the suggestions for improving on the research design seized upon these two deficits. Strumpel's sample, it may be remembered, is made up of married men with small children, employed, in their most productive years, and with a history of income increases.

> One of the external factors affecting families' economic behavior is a shortening time span between the age men enter the job market and the age when they retire. Both generation and stage in the family life cycle affect values and behavior in the economic area. Will the sample Strumpel drew of married men with young children reduce their goals as their children mature, as he implies? With a shorter time span within which to achieve their economic goals than their parents had, will they not be less satisfied rather than more satisfied? Only longitudinal data and intergenerational comparisons can answer these questions. (Adapted from comments by Aldous)

> The cross-section survey results reported by Strumpel are interesting primarily because of the clever combination of economic, social, and psychological indicators in the cross-section sample and the diligence and ingenuity of the statistical evaluation. The main difficulty is that a single cross-section survey does not indicate trends nor permit operational conclusions about likely actions—individual or group—on the basis of the opinions expressed. . . . Strumpel might well make a major contribution to our understanding if he followed his respondents over three- or five-year intervals and analyzed the results with his ingenious techniques. (Schott)

Turning to the research ideas generated by the second session on social stratification and family economic behavior, there are good reasons to undertake some of the same specifications in the future for the variables of this study that were recommended for the Strumpel research; namely, specification by stages of the family life cycle and by generation.

Segal and Felson were ingenious in what is essentially a static analysis of concomitant variations in a number of significant indicators of economic position, social status, class identification, and material consumption. They made a distinct contribution in identifying an increasing convergence toward a middle majority in material style of life and in social class identification by occupational categories. Due to the economic affluence of blue-collar families, both upward mobility through education and geographical mobility to the suburbs, as well as possession of status durables, have been increasingly open, making the traditional indicators of social status (occupational rank and educational level) less useful as social class differentiators. The authors' prediction, that status cultures will nevertheless persist via values shared in reference groups and through manipulation of the credit market (with upper class families investing in the future and blue-collar groups investing in the present, making for future life-style gaps), is a provocative prognostication that will require time series data to be verified.

From our standpoint as family sociologists the formulation is unnecessarily static with respect to generational and developmental issues for which the data would appear to be accessible. An early analysis should specify the impacts on material consumption of the age composition of the family, the size of the family, the number of earners, and so on. Would not age at marriage, duration of marriage, years in the labor force, lifetime income as well as income that can be anticipated before retirement, enable the researchers to specify the life-cycle stage as a differentiating category better, which in turn would be better than current income for predicting the family's material style of life?

A substantially different set of research suggestions was provided by Douvan, a psychologist serving as critic and discussant of the Segal-Felson paper. Douvan pointed up the strategies which a social psychologist would be likely to pursue with the dependent variables of satisfaction (from the Strumpel session) and material style of life or material consumption in the

Segal-Felson research. To give meaning to consumption behavior the psychologist would turn away from the beguiling simplicity of money expenditures to seek a more primitive pattern grouping of variables such as honor or self-esteem which would enable him to see the several routes individuals follow to achieve honor. Douvan saw the need for numerous internal criteria by which the individual would judge his success rather than a simple universalistic external scale of success such as is represented by the scholastic grading system or the occupational ranks of social status categories. Self-esteem can come from several comparisons unique to the individual when internal criteria are used.

As soon as one gets to an external and unidimensional system, where everyone is comparable on the same scale, then almost by definition it becomes comparative or relative. That is, there is always someone who is higher on any particular scale and to the extent that we make it always external we increase possibilities for dissatisfaction, because the resources are limited and one is constantly making comparisons. This is dramatized in the managerial group of the Strumpel study, the group which is holding the most external criterion of success of any of the occupational categories in his sample. Here one has the highest propensity for dissatisfaction and apparently no possibility for the resolution of that dissatisfaction; that is, again, no matter how high the income there is, there is always the possibility of more. No matter how high the material success is, there is always the posibility for more.

Douvan saw an altogether healthier route to self-esteem and honor, and with it a style of life that would bring greater satisfaction, from maximizing the size of one's position set. Maximizing of internal criteria is a product of the intersection of roles. That is, to the extent a person plays a number of different roles and is forced into a number of different experiences and is required to integrate them, we can expect to find the development of a greater awareness of internal criteria. Douvan offered a hypothesis which needs to be tested, that mobility or any kind of marginality in the society, even status inconsistency, should lead to the articulation of a clearer set of internal criteria so long as the marginality is not too extreme and the status inconsistency is not too great.

In sum, the confrontation of the disciplines of sociology and economics with psychology in these two sessions on life-styles and economic behavior has generated a host of research ideas in the general area of economic socialization that as yet have been given relatively little attention.

Economic determinants of family size

The potentialities of the subject matter treated by Easterlin are enormous. The planners of the conference first gave the title "Family Fertility and Economic Behavior" to this session but in a second draft of the work assignments the title appeared as "Economic Determinants of Family Size" and as the program went to the printer it was given the promissory title of "A New Look at the Recent Fertility Swing" only to be revised as finally presented, "Relative Economic Status and the American Fertility Swing." The final title is less descriptive than its predecessors and communicates a more limited scope, but it comes closer to suggesting the underlying theory of the author's ultimate presentation.

As family sociologists we would have been particularly challenged by the first topic, "Family Fertility and Economic Behavior," since the negative consequences of early childbearing, and large family size, are very apparent in the poverty linkages of leaving school early, entering dead-end jobs, and instability of employment. The negative feed-back of early childbearing, rapid childbearing, and eventual large family size on the incapacity to control one's future is dramatically portrayed in the University of Minnesota consumership study with a three generation sample [1, 9]. It is our contention that a better case can be made for family fertility decisions as *determinants* of family economic behavior than vice versa. Further research is required, however, to disentangle what is cause and what is effect in the interplay between family fertility and family economic behavior.

If we turn the topic around as it appears in the second title suggested for this session, "The Economic Determinants of Family Size," the issues become considerably more controversial. A number of economists, including Professor Easterlin, offer evidence of a positive relationship between the affluence of the economy and the nation's fertility rate. Still other economists extend these generalizations which have always been based on aggregate data to advance a theory that individual families form their family-size preferences and even control their completed family size in line with their economic resources. Most social demographers and virtually all family sociologists, on the other hand, see these relationships in reverse, pointing to the differential fertility rate in industrializing societies where income and occupational rank are inversely related to family size. (Perhaps due to a lag in the effective use of fertility control methods.) Indeed, it is only when "planned families" are examined that income tends to relate positively to family size. In general, those families with the most modest resources who are experiencing the most overcrowding are least likely to have used birth control, even though they had more pressures of progeny on resources than families with fewer children. In Puerto Rico, none of the "economic pressure theories" for accounting for families reaching a threshold for taking action on family size could be verified using cross-sectional survey methods, because of the inability of the respondent to reproduce the sense of pressure after it had been removed through effective family planning. We ended up in the Puerto Rican study affirming the adage, "The rich get richer and the poor get children" [17, p. 463].

It is against this backdrop of differences among the disciplines about the direction of the relationship between economic behavior and fertility behavior that the discussions of the Easterlin-Kelley session and the research ideas generated can be rendered intelligible. Like Douvan, Easterlin advanced the importance of "economic socialization" for accounting for the way people form their desires in childhood and adolescence in the parental family for a certain style of reproductive and economic behavior. He saw the fertility behavior of the current cohort of childbearing couples as a function of their parents' economic achievements almost a generation earlier. This is the base line from which the couples of the current generation perceive their own relative affluence or deprivation, and from which they formulate family-size goals and act upon them. Both Easterlin and Kelley treated this sense of relative economic advantage as the basis for "the family-size decision" which lies behind the contemporary marital fertility rates.

The research response of a family sociologist to this provocative thesis would be to undertake a carefully designed microsurvey of childbearing couples and of their parents of different durations of marriage to ascertain what the actual circumstances were in which the current childbearing generation was socialized. Data would be collected about the perceptions of the childbearing generation concerning their economic prospects relative to the base line established by their parents at the points in time when this generation's tastes were allegedly formed. The interrelationship of such economic prospects with age at marriage and timing of the first birth and the crystallization of family-size preferences would be examined to test the Easterlin thesis with intergenerationally linked couples. Needless to say, since he is an economic demographer, with a preference for manipulating secondary aggregate data, this is not what Easterlin did. Moreover, in the thoughtful statement of new research needed to further validate his thesis, he made no suggestions for microstudies of couples with the parents who socialized them to assess on a one-to-one basis whether the relationships which he so ingeniously imputed are actually found in flesh-and-blood cases.

Impacts of guaranteeing income stability
on family intactness and work performance

The novelty of the New Jersey-Pennsylvania field experiment for consumer researchers, combined with the candor of the reporters in presenting tentative mid-experiment findings, generated a host of comments which defy summarization. Many focused on the shortcomings of the experimental design and its execution (Sheldon) but the majority related to the experimental results, especially to possible explanations for the modest increments of change in the output variables among experimental families compared with the controls. From these reactions we can infer some suggestions for needed research either by this research team later in their research program or by others in future field and laboratory experiments.

Felson has noted a number of assumptions which are implicit in the hypotheses of the field experiment as reported. Several of the participants turned these assumptions into research questions.

1. To what extent do men pursue material gain? Do they seek to maximize material gain or merely seek a satisfactory amount of gain? If the latter, is it not possible that a guaranteed income may undermine work incentive, since labor is sufficiently undesirable that men who desire material gain may not work if the rewards offered do not offset the undesirability of work?

2. To what extent do men pursue material gain with full knowledge? The poor may be ignorant about opportunities available or about the relative benefits of various economic strategies, and this lack of information may impede decisions. To what extent did the experimenters explain the realities of the negative income tax plan to the subjects?

3. To what extent do men pursue material gain in the short run with the short run in mind? Morgan and Moss in the discussion suggested that men take the long run into account when planning for the short run. Thus, an experiment ought to guarantee the plan for twenty years in order to see what effect such a guarantee will have on present behavior. Why give up a job in a tight market in exchange for a program not likely to last longer than three years? Morgan also suggested that men may behave according to the law of inertia requiring time to adjust to any new policy. Felson added that the time period of the experiment does not allow people the interpersonal communication to learn how to abuse the rules of the system and work them to their advantage.

4. Does work incentive actually lead to more work being done? Ideally this experiment should have been made during a period of prosperity or of rising expectations to maximize the impacts of a guaranteed income. It is actually occurring at a time of relative economic stagnation, which means that work incentives will not necessarily lead to employment or overtime. There may be much more work incentive than can be translated into work performance. The fact that reported work is not a good indicator of incentive to work may attenuate the correlation between the latter and the experimental treatment. Strumpel suggested in this connection that work participation of the poor and the near poor may be governed by rules that apparently affect the participation of the aged in the labor force, and suggested that the poor and the aged can be fruitfully compared in the same framework. Their incentive to work may be attenuated by the increase in types of guaranteed income from transfer payments, pensions, capital in-

come, and saving. These types of transfer payments have increased, while the amount of work by the aged has decreased over the last several years.

Two concluding comments stem from attempts to explain the modest impacts of the program on work participation and family stability:

> To pass the legislation necessary for income maintenance programs, lawmakers not only must be convinced that such programs do not discourage labor-force participation among recipients, but they also have to see that they have some positive payoffs. For this reason the present findings of essentially "no difference" between control and experimental groups beg for further investigation to determine why there is not a difference favoring the recipients. One area to examine would be their social networks. If recipients' networks are composed of persons in less favorable financial straits, reference group theory suggests that the recipients may already be performing up to their aspiration level. Their failure to do better than the controls would therefore result from a lack of associates whose economic superiority would encourage greater striving. (Aldous)
>
> The data indicate that earners per family and hours per employed individual tend to decline for experimental families relative to control families as the duration of the experiment increases from one to four quarters, while earnings per hour for employed workers tend to rise in experimental families relative to control families. Much of the experimental-control differential appears to be concentrated in the behavior of supplementary earners rather than of the main earner in the family. The calculated data are based on employment, hours, and earnings of all experimental families in the sample, not on only those families in which labor-force participation was the same over the experimental period. Thus, it is not clear whether the relatively rapid growth of earnings per hour among experimental families is the typical relationship, or whether it results simply from the fact that relatively unproductive and part-time workers among experimental families tend to drop out of the labor force. If the latter, the income guarantee has only resulted in shifting weights so that later experimental periods are more heavily influenced by the earnings of workers who have always been more productive and more highly paid.
>
> On the question of attrition, it seems important to find out what has happened to the earnings of families who left the panel. This is especially so for families in the experimental panel, where being attrited takes the form of passing up an opportunity to continue receiving a substantial guarantee. One might speculate that two kinds of families would tend to be attrited from the experimental panel: on the one hand, there are families whose financial situation and internal organization are so chaotic that they simply tend to disintegrate as family units whether or not they are provided with a financial subsidy via the experimental program; on the other hand, some of the attrited families in the experimental panel ought to be families for whom the program no longer has any financial meaning because their earnings have risen far enough to make them ineligible for continued assistance. The first type of families would be found among both the experimental and the control panel, and presumably account for some fraction of the attrition in each case. But the second type of family would not necessarily be attrited out of the control panel, hence one would expect the comparisons with attrited families included to show even more favorable results for the experimental versus con-

trol group because the experimental panel has lost more of its financially most successful families. Thus for proper evaluation of what the income guarantee has done to work incentives and to the financial viability of low-income families, analysis of records for attrited families seems crucial. (Juster)

An area of research which could be generated from these experimental data would be the analysis of deviant family types searching for the patterning and distribution of responses that are masked by the exclusive attention to averages and significant differences. Were there families of educationally deprived backgrounds and poor credit risks that nevertheless responded positively to the guaranteed income payments precisely as was intended by the policy and that showed marked improvement over their pre-experimental history in both labor-force participation and in increased family stability? What other patterns appear to be associated with such behavior? What happened to their counterparts among the control group? What was the patterning of families that defeated the program by turning it into a shelter from the necessity to work? How is unearned income perceived and balanced against earned income by these two deviant types of families?

There are also possibilities of designing laboratory experiments where game rules and contexts could be manipulated to follow through on the puzzling findings from this field experiment. Moreoever the costs for carefully designed laboratory experiments with families are much lower than the quasi-natural experiments designed to test policy issues in the field, although the findings from the latter are more generalizable to national programs.

Proconsumer research

The session on consumerism presented a number of research ideas which appear in the paper and critique by Maynes and Bymers respectively and deserve careful reading. The Maynes stance was refreshingly interventionist. He has played the twin roles of social critic and diagnostician in his description of the complex protective system developed by producers and distributors to insulate them from dissatisfied customers. Judging the functionality of the competitive market from the perspective of the consumer–namely, that it should provide high-quality products at low prices–he reported a series of failures to perform and the presence of a number of mechanisms that operate to nullify feed-back from aggrieved customers. It is precisely at the point where seller and consumer intersect that Maynes found the major deficits, the adequacy of information flowing to the consumer about the product and the openness of channels of feed-back for grievances to the producer. The majority of the research ideas generated in the discussion related to the pressing issue of the adequacy and cost of consumer information.

There is the problem of generating too much information for the consumer to handle. And we are doing this at a time when the value of time is increasing. I wonder if it does not become economically irrational to shop rationally—at least for inexpensive goods—as opposed to what making two or three wrong decisions would cost you? (Segal)

Most of the people who concern themselves with consumerism or consumer protection are basically concerned about suboptimal decisions made by low-income families. But I suggest that the real benefits of much actual consumerism really go mainly to relatively high-income households. A classic case in point is probably Consumers Union, the earliest, best-known, and one of the most socially conscious of the consumer-oriented groups. Yet the subscribers to *Consumer Reports* are an upper-middle to high-income, well-educated group. The products rated in *Consumer Reports* are dominated by those with relatively high-income elasticities, bought mainly by high-income families. Regardless of intent, I suggest that the real impact of Consumers Union has been in improving the ability of high-income families to make rational consumption decisions, and that there has been virtually no impact on the low-income families about whom they are primarily concerned.

This result should not be surprising. It follows from the simple proposition that ability to use the kind of information provided by *Consumers Reports* is a function of educational attainment. And most of the research on efficiency level of the information processor is a major explanation for differential efficiency. (Juster)

On Juster's point, above, about the possible negative results of the consumerism movement, Hermalin argued that his work in family planning showed that low-income families do accept information and act on it when they have access and the means to implement it. This suggests a need for more research on the diffusion of consumer information to ascertain to what extent it is differentially accepted and utilized by class. (Hermalin, paraphrased by Kingsley)

Consumer information is a broader problem than just reducing the cost of the search for facts. For one thing, there is in almost every purchasing decision a problem of investment in background information and skills which may well pay off only if it can be amortized over a number of similar or related future decisions. Where we make only one or two decisions in a lifetime, the information search must pay off immediately in that decision (buying a house). Where repeated purchases are involved, better market information pays off many times, as in auto repairs or selection of a dentist. (Morgan)

The sentiment is that all you have to do for a perfect market and perfect competition, with perfect consumers, is provide perfect information, and the more the better. But going back to psychological research—you reach a point of sensory overload per unit of time; a point where too much information is dysfunctional and dissatisfying. It's not a matter of *how much* information can we give the consumer but *what kind* and *in what order*.

My own research interest is in the notion of quality. Inasmuch as this varies from one person to another (I may want performance in a car, my wife may want styling), does not this approach make it impossible to arrive at a general definition of quality which can be applied across all consumers? Moreover, if quality is subjective, what implications does this have for organizations like Consumers Union that attempt to assess general objective quality? There is a distinction I am trying to get at here between objective quality and perceived quality. The literature shows that the two are not necessarily in perfect correspondence. (Jacoby)

Two other research needs were suggested from an exchange between Bymers and Maynes. Bymers responded to Maynes description of the somewhat idyllic way the market operated in an earlier period in our history by saying it was not working terribly well in the Depression when she was growing up. May we suggest that there might be some return from an economic historian reconstructing the economy of colonial America to discover if, under conditions of simplicity and personal contacts, the economic theory underlying the market economy ever worked to assure buyers lower prices and higher quality. The family historians who have reported on this period in New England are failing to confirm many of the most cherished notions asserted in more impressionistic writings about the large size of families, high age at marriage, the high infant and maternal mortality rates, and the low incidence of love marriages in Colonial America [4, 7]. There may be surprises ahead as well about the functionality of the colonial economy for consumers when economic historians have completed similarly rigorous research. An alternative to historical research, to be sure, would be a comparative study of the phenomenon in several preindustrial contemporary societies where the conditions of simplicity and personal contacts are present. Is the consumer less likely to be exploited and more likely to get his money's worth than in the complex American economy?

A suggestion was made by Morgan that an infant industry is emerging to provide low-cost up-to-date market information to the consumer through vending machines, linked via computers to data banks. This seems a bit fanciful in view of the uncertainty about the extent to which consumers may be expected to utilize such information. Is there not a need for laboratory simulation studies to test both the ability and willingness of consumers to utilize information in making purchase decisions when the time, energy, and intellectual costs are reduced to a minimum? The issue of information overload could be built-in as one of the variables to be assessed.

Consumer management of savings and wealth

In his introductory remarks opening the concluding session of the conference, Schott warned that he was asking the conferees to take a gigantic intellectual leap into the world of macroeconomic analysis, although he hoped they would also decide that his paper was about consumers, about households, and about family life-styles. The facet of consumer behavior to which macroaggregate data can contribute significantly is the management of savings and wealth by consumers. This behavior is analyzed largely on the aggregate level because microdata are often poor but also because there could be a cross-check on research from microdata with the findings from aggregate information kept by financial institutions. Schott arrayed aggregate data to demonstrate that there is a mass phenomenon underway of increased household net worth, shifts in types of asset holdings favoring the accumulation of assets capable of generating higher investment yields, and increased discretionary personal financial mamagement among widening options. His message is that slowly but surely better informed and more refined consumer financial asset management is being introduced into the nation's economic, financial, and family-life systems and that this is a force to be reckoned with by all concerned—particularly government and financial institutions.

The majority of the research suggestions stimulated by the discussion of the Schott-Puckett exchanges centered on the theme of "rising consumer sophistication in financial management" inferred by Schott from his aggregate data. Puckett, the chief discussant, offered an alternative interpretation to the sophistication thesis which we will not repeat here because it can be read in full detail in the critique of Schott's paper. Needless to say, Puckett's inputs added fuel to the general discussion. Is it possible to confirm these interpretations from microlevel studies?

Katona, in a brief comment written for the conference, urged caution, indicating that a number of studies at the University of Michigan Survey Research Center question this characterization of consumer sophistication, even for college-educated respondents: (a) buying and selling stocks occurs despite minimal information about the stock market, based almost entirely on superficial advice from friends and brokers; (b) savings transfers from low to higher interest are not great even when publicized widely, although, to be sure, new savings go to high interest locations, and (c) there appears to be little evidence that consumers save more in bad times than good times.

On the question of increasing efficiency of portfolio management, Juster pointed to marked differences in portfolio performance at different income and education levels. The 15 per cent return of stock investments, as described by Puckett, is distributed unequally across the population of households, and until there is some idea of its actual distribution it is impossible to conclude from aggregate data what the impact is on households in general. Juster suggested that what is needed is research using customer files at brokerage houses as data sources to get at the question of the variance of the stock market performance for various customer groups. His concluding comments are quotable:

> There is not a single study that I know which is able to give the distribution of rates of return among individuals for particular kinds of portfolios. There are lots of studies of random portfolio selection guided by particular decision rules or rates of return specified over different time periods, but none in which real individuals are observed making real investment decisions. (Juster)

Burke saw a real need to interrelate micro- and macroanalytic research more closely on these issues and phrased three questions for future research:

1. What is the relationship of changes in savings and investment behavior to the different stages of the family life cycle?
2. What is the relationship of aggregate savings and investment data to changes in the demographic make-up of the population over the past twenty years?
3. Should not studies of financial investments be set in the broader perspective of total investment in human and material capital, including housing and durable goods?

Hermalin noted that more can be done with such concepts as fads, diffusion, goal attainment, and thresholds in the study of financial behavior. Such concepts could be applied fruitfully to study the rate of spread of stock market investing.

In closing this discussion we would like to call attention to advantages of a three-generation research design to elicit microdata that might affirm at the level of families Schott's provocative speculation from aggregate data that consumers are becoming increasingly sophisticated in their participation in the financial markets. By examining the changing content of the financial portfolio for each of three generations of the same family line over the duration of the marriage, class variations can be ascertained, variations in savings and investment behavior by stage of the life cycle can be elicited, and the phenomenon of upgrading and increasing sophistication of consumers by generation can be tested.

New Areas of Research Demanding Attention: A Recapitulation

In recapitulating this discussion of needed research, we present the major new research ideas and questions which seem to us salient enough to require early funding.

Family decision making

1. Analysis of time as a commodity in its own right justifies early attention, i.e. nonmarketable time, and the role it plays in family consumption and decision making.
2. Analysis of rules governing intra-family transfers and inter-kin transfers compared with market-oriented exchanges is needed.
3. Study of family decision making in terms of philanthropy within the family is needed to redress the overemphasis on studies of family power, the allocation of control over who gets what.
4. A comparison of families as problem-solving groups with such ad hoc groups as planning committees in their decision-making effectiveness should be given early priority.
5. Descriptive mapping is needed of how and to what extent information feed-back from past experience influences family decisions, who evaluates the family's experiences, who stores the information for future use, and who draws on this information when the need arises.
6. Analysis of the correlates of satisfaction with outcomes of decisions reached and actions taken by family units offers a test of some economic truisms.

Class life-styles, values, and subjective welfare

1. How does subjective welfare affect work incentives and productivity at the microlevel of individuals and families as against the aggregate level of occupational and income categories?
2. How does economic satisfaction affect leisure patterns?
3. How do individuals estimate future economic satisfaction without knowing what reality factors will be operating in the future?
4. What are the sources of variability in economic satisfaction due to developmental changes of the family life cycle and historical-generational inputs?
5. What patterns of socialization in childhood determine the economic styles of consumption of young adults?
6. What are the consequences in economic satisfaction and self-esteem of employing internal criteria versus external criteria of success?

Economic determinants of family size

1. Longitudinal research conforming to the rigors of experimental design is needed to disentangle what is cause and what is effect in the interplay between family fertility and family economic behavior.
2. To test the thesis that economic socialization in childhood accounts

for family-size preferences among young adults, a microsurvey of childbearing couples and of their parents is indicated to ascertain the impacts of different economic experiences in childhood on the timing of marriage and childbearing.

3. Record linkage checks are necessary to insure that economic data from one set of records and fertility data from a second set reflect the behavior of the same people over time.

4. It would be timely to make a comparison of the yield in theory testing of *postdicting* by use of historical data on fertility trends as against verification by *predicting* in confirming the economic determinants of fertility.

5. How does the relative size of cohorts vis-à-vis the economic opportunities available affect their relative economic status and their subsequent fertility? Is the "rippling effect" of baby booms and baby strikes paralleled twenty years later by lower and higher per capita economic opportunities which would enter into the subjective definition of relative economic status?

Guaranteeing income stability, work performance, and family composition changes

1. A field experiment that compares families with long-run versus short-run guarantees of minimum income is needed to discover whether families take the long run into account when planning for the short run.

2. The New Jersey-Pennsylvania field experiment should be repeated during a period of rising expectations and relative prosperity to test fully the impacts of guaranteed income on work performance.

3. A field experiment which checked aspiration levels of experimental and control group families against the norms of their reference groups would reduce some of the variability in testing the hypothesis that guaranteed income increases work incentives and work performance.

4. A follow-up analysis of the deviant family types from the reported field experiment would offer new insights into the reasons for such modest impacts of guaranteed income on family work performance and family solidarity.

5. A laboratory experiment with families where game rules and employment contexts could be manipulated would offer opportunity to check out the differential perceptions of earned and unearned income, single versus multiple earners, and different levels of knowledge of the labor market as these operate to raise or lower work incentives and the decisions to disemploy, to change jobs, or to shift from part-time to full-time employment.

Proconsumer research

1. Under what conditions do consumers utilize or fail to use available information rationally in arriving at buying decisions?
2. A study utilizing simulation searches for information is needed to test ability and willingness to utilize information in purchasing decisions which, by reducing the cost of searching, increases the likelihood of use (i.e. installing fact banks in supermarkets).
3. What categories of the population engage in optimal information search outside the family before making large ticket decisions?
4. A comprehensive survey of consumer grievances is needed which also taps sellers' attitudes in order to identify genuine versus bogus grievances.
5. A policy-oriented research is needed to develop appropriate and efficient remedial policies for grievances, including legal constraints of policies designed to protect sellers.
6. Historical or comparative research is needed on markets under conditions of simplicity and personal contacts to discover if the economic theory underlying market economics ever worked to assure buyers quality at low prices.

Consumer management of savings and wealth

1. What is the variance of stock market performance for investors of different socioeconomic categories? (Use as source of data customer files at brokerage houses.)
2. What is the distribution of rates of return for particular kinds of portfolios among real individuals making real investment decisions?
3. What is the relationship of changes in savings and investment behavior to the different stages of the family life cycle and/or to generational differences?
4. What is the relationship of aggregate savings and investment data to changes in the demographic composition of the population over time?
5. How do financial investments over time compare with investments in human and material capital including housing, durable goods, and upgrading the competence of the labor force through education?
6. To what extent is stock market investing as a novel practice for most categories of the population subject to the same principles of cultural diffusion and adoption as new farming practices, contraceptives, or new food practices?
7. To what extent are the relationships between values and attitudes of consumers and their savings, investing, and credit utilization, generalizable across countries with market economies?

8. Is the phenomenon of rising consumer sophistication verifiable by generational changes in diversification of investments, retirement provisions, protective and life insurance programs, and multiple investment of liquid assets?

9. Is life insurance disfavored as a form of savings because its payoff formula is noncompetitive or because it is hard to understand?

10. To what extent do experiences with moderate crises such as recessions create behavioral tendencies with respect to investing that endure beyond the crisis itself?

Toward a Theoretical Synthesis

The theoretical developments and some of the suggestions for needed research generated by the Williamsburg Conference can be integrated in a number of ways. Among them are: (a) making generalizations about the structural characteristics of the formulations in terms of theoretical enterprise and mode of expression, (b) arraying the presentations by independent and dependent variables employed, (c) abstracting higher-order propositions from the common elements in the various empirical generalizations, and (d) constructing a comprehensive conceptual model or competing models. In this section we will employ each of these integration strategies in turn.

The theoretical formulations developed for the symposium focus on description and historical explanation using conventional language. There were few attempts at linking basic underlying assumptions to time- and space-bound hypotheses in a deductive, causal system. Likewise, formal modes of expression received limited attention. Several of the presentations appear to be derived from exploratory or unfinished research projects and practical concerns. Whether or not desirable, it is at least typical in the social sciences that such efforts are not guided by fully developed theories.

Another way to link the presentations theoretically is to group them around determinants and consequences. Chart 1 shows one way this can be accomplished. Since alternative variables are often used as indicators of similar concepts, we have condensed the number of categories by remaining at fairly abstract levels of conceptualization. It can be observed from Chart 1 that, for the most part, there is agreement about the basic causal priorities involved. Exceptions occur for the treatment of specific consumer decisions and behaviors (spending, saving, and management of financial assets). This suggests that the insights of Ferber, Maynes, and Schott in these areas might be fruitfully linked by several chain propositions. Such a conclusion would not necessarily be appropriate if the Segal-Felson dependent variable also coincided with any of the independent variables that the above three authors employ. In that case, reciprocal causation might be indicated.

CHART 1. AN ARRAY OF SHARED CONCEPTS BY CAUSAL PRIORITY

Construct	Ferber	Strumpel	Segal-Felson	Easterlin	Shore-Scott	Maynes	Schott
External economic, social, and political events	I	I		I	I	I	I/D
Dispositions (attitudes, goals, values, expectations, aspirations, etc.)	I	I	I	I		I	
Reference groups	I	I	I				
Resources	I	I	I	I	I	I	I
Information processing	I					I	I
Family structure (roles, stability, etc.).	I				D		
Spending and saving decisions	D		I			D	
Financial asset management	D		I				D
Fertility	D				D	D	
Work incentive and productivity		D			D		
Economic life style		D	D				
Satisfaction	D	D		D		D	

I = independent variable, D = dependent variable

We can assume for the present analysis that empty cells in Chart 1 indicate tacit agreement about causal priorities.

Another exception occurs for family structure variables. This case, however, clearly does not indicate disagreement over causal priority since role allocation (Ferber) is conceptually quite different from family stability (Shore-Scott). Most family sociologists would agree that roles play an important part in determining family stability, mediated by some social interaction and intrapsychic behavior. Again, reciprocal causation is not implied.

Schott's use of the activity of financial institutions as a dependent variable offers an interesting counterpoint. His presentation, more than the others, emphasizes the systemic quality of "the family in transaction with its environment." Not only are family economic behaviors conditioned in part by external events, but they also have consequences for "the system." This suggests a reciprocal causation mechanism, even though the points of entry of the external environment (such as technology increasing education opportunities) into family behavior may not be the same as the points of exit (such as financial institution response to increased consciousness of return). Such family-to-environment feed-back processes, it should be granted, are more or less implied in each of the other presentations as well.

Several other comments are warranted at this point. First, the only major concepts included in Chart 1 are those used directly in more than one presentation. Thus, such theoretically interesting concepts as money management (Ferber) are not listed.

Second, some crucial feed-back processes suggested by conferees have been deleted in Chart 1, most notably the effects of changes in satisfaction on goals and accomplishment (Strumpel), and the effect of fertility experience on attitudes and expectations (Easterlin). These ommissions are somewhat arbitrary, inasmuch as cause-effect relationships observed depend on the timing of the observation. We rationalize the omissions on the ground that satisfaction and fertility are the ultimate dependent variables for Strumpel and Easterlin, respectively.

Third, the range of variables within each conceptual category in Chart 1 is broad enough so that the internal causal linkages and the independent effects of each variable are obscured. For example, external events were taken during the conference to include such phenomena as technological development, governmental regulations and policy, messages of the mass media, the development of large-scale bureaucratic organizations, and the economic climate of the country. Goals range from conservative to risky on a continuum of "certainty of outcome"; from hedonistic to altruistic; from lifelong to ephemeral; and so forth. Certainly the specific values of each of these variables make a difference for a family's economic choices.

This problem of multidimensionality is especially acute with respect to the concept, "resources." This concept was explicitly or implicitly used in every major presentation, but with a wide range of indicators. A partial listing would include time, "human capital" (social skills), past experience, information, education, sophistication, income, occupational status, socio-economic status, convenience, youth, self-confidence, occupational skills, social power, action opportunities, relative accomplishment (when high), relative deprivation (when favorable), and relative economic status (when high). There seem to be infinite possibilities for elaborating such a list. Anything might be considered a resource as long as it produces, directly or indirectly, desired outcomes. Noting this, we recognize how much resources are bound up with dispositions. Whether children are a resource or a liability depends on parental attitudes, values, and goals.

The apparent fact that some people do not learn much from past experiences in the consumer market (Bivens) suggests the importance of personality variables in consumer grievance formation. Obtaining resources is not always easy, and families may be unwilling (information costs) or unable (youth) to purchase them. Relativity concepts such as relative accomplishment are notable attempts to demonstrate that objective resources are contingent on dispositions.[5]

As a final example of a multidimensional concept in Chart 1, we draw attention to "information processing." We introduced the term earlier in conjunction with Maynes' historical explanation of consumerism, but aspects of it were indirectly employed by other conferees as well. Essentially, information processing is seen as a step in rational decision making. Among the features of this process that have received discussion are:

1. Amount (curvilinearly related to rationality of decision and satisfaction with it)—Ferber, Maynes, Jacoby, Segal
2. Quality (truth-falsity, clarity-obscurity)—Maynes, Schott
3. Cost of search (objective and subjective)—Ferber, Maynes
4. Order of acquiring elements—Juster
5. Family communication networks—Ferber
6. External sources (reference groups)—Ferber, Maynes

This list suggests to us a dualistic characteristic of information-processing that is of vital importance; namely, that it is a cognitive process and at the same time a social interaction or group process. Further examination of the parallels and discrepencies between these two characteristics is called for. If a cognitive model is insufficient to explain the interactional component of decision making (and vice versa), then the consequences of reductionism for an adequate theory of family consumption may be devastating.

Another potentially useful strategy for theory integration is induction from empirical generalizations.

EG11, 16, and 22 directly incorporate three of the relativity concepts which were discussed earlier, while EG 15 implies the Segal-Felson notion of "relative deprivation." This latter concept appears to be less central to its formulators' arguments than the other three are to theirs. Although the subjective nature of these concepts is not evenly exploited by the authors, it is difficult to escape the conclusion that they are cognitions. This is clearly the intention of Strumpel with "relative accomplishment" and Puckett with "relative performance." It is less clearly the intention of Easterlin with "relative economic status," although our earlier discussion of his underlying assumptions and causal model showed how it might be so considered. The crux of our position has been that fathers' and sons' labor-market experiences are not relative *in vacuo,* but rather perceived and given motivational relevance by the sons themselves. "Relative deprivation" is least clearly a dispositional construct. One does not have to be conscious of income differences in order to allocate resources. Segal and Felson did not argue directly either for or against deliberate maintenance of status culture differentiation. Nevertheless, they emphasized "class identification" in terms of "perceptions of . . . position in the stratification system" or "class consciousness" and its causal role in credit behavior. If "relative deprivation" were extended beyond discrepancies in affluence to encompass discrepancies in social status and reference-group values, this relativity concept could more reasonably be viewed as a disposition.

With this possible exception noted, we can inductively derive the following proposition (symbolized "DP" for "derived proposition"):

DP1. Evaluation of outcomes is a function of the comparison between dispositions and perceived situation.

Such a notion would seem to be a pervasive feature of social behavior[6] [8].

EG7 and 19 contain the common elements expressed in the full statement of EG19: "The extent of information search is positively associated with the expected gain relative to the cost of the information." In addition, when we discussed EG21 we noted Schott's suggestion that differential financial institution performance may be in part caused by the differential information costs associated with determining return rates. This set of generalizations focuses on the rational decision process repeatedly alluded to throughout the conference and in this book. At the interpersonal level this orientation appears to be compatible with cybernetic systems theory, exchange theory, and game theory. Thus, families may be viewed as engaging in nonzero-sum games of strategy that involve mixed motives and require co-ordination or bargaining to arrive at mutually satisfying outcomes [14]. This approach, with its emphasis on reciprocity, may be applicable to intrafamily relationships as well as the transactions between the group and its economic environment.

EG13, 14, 16, and 22 appear to share two assumptions which may be stated as derived propositions.

DP2. Discrepancies between dispositions and perceived situations are negatively evaluated; the greater the discrepancy, the more negative the evaluation.

DP3. Congruity between dispositions and perceived situations is a fundamental equilibrium maintenance process of organic and social systems; action is taken by those systems to maintain or restore congruity.

Examples of congruity maintenance activity are goal reduction, increased productivity, pressures for a fairer distribution of rewards, adjustment of fertility attitudes and expectations, and adjustment of expectations about investment market performance.

DP2 and 3 not only fit nicely with DP1, but are also consistent with social systems theory and various expressions of consistency theory in social psychology [7] [3, 10, 15].

We have suggested earlier that Strumpel specified fairly well the antecedent conditions necessary to predict which route to congruity is taken (EG13 and 14), but that Easterlin (EG16) and Puckett (EG22) were less helpful in this regard. Bivens commenting on Strumpel, mentioned that "discrepancy-tolerance threshold" is another important variable beyond simply the magnitude of the discrepancy. This should lend caution to the interpretation of DP2 and 3. It should also be emphasized that without the more complex mixed-motive conceptualization of strategy, the congruity principle will probably not work well for family or other social systems unless "goal consensus" is assumed. For this reason alone, it is crucial that a theory of family consumption take account of intra-family dynamics.

The remainder of the empirical generalizations can be viewed as mapping out the resources relevant to family consumption alternatives and additional inputs to evaluative responses. The reader can review them to test this perspective. Possible exceptions are EG15 and 21, which may be too bound to historical context to permit inclusion in a deductive explanation.

Our final attempt at theory integration will be the construction of a master conceptual model that, if done properly, should reflect all of the insights gained by the earlier attempts at integration. The rich discussion of poignant suggestions for reinterpreting findings, which we have attempted to capture earlier, might portend competing models. However, we have chosen to concentrate on commonalities at this point in the theory-building process [8] [9, 12].

More specifically, we have elected to couch family consumption in terms of a general systems theory conceptualization. Chart 2 is a diagrammatic representation of this conceptual model. The model focuses on the family as the behaving unit and traces the causal path of information and energy flows from family system inputs to family system outputs. Labels outside each block represent general processes while the labels within blocks represent, for the most part, constructs expressed about family consumption during the conference or developed in this section. Our tentative belief is that similar processes occur for noneconomic family behavior.

Personality and environmental systems are taken to be the exogenous factors with which the family interacts. The environment includes both the physical and sociocultural environment. This latter aspect of the environment as well as the personality systems of family members may be hypothetically taken to be structured isomorphically with the family system;

CHART 2. SOCIAL SYSTEMS MODEL APPLIED TO FAMILY CONSUMPTION

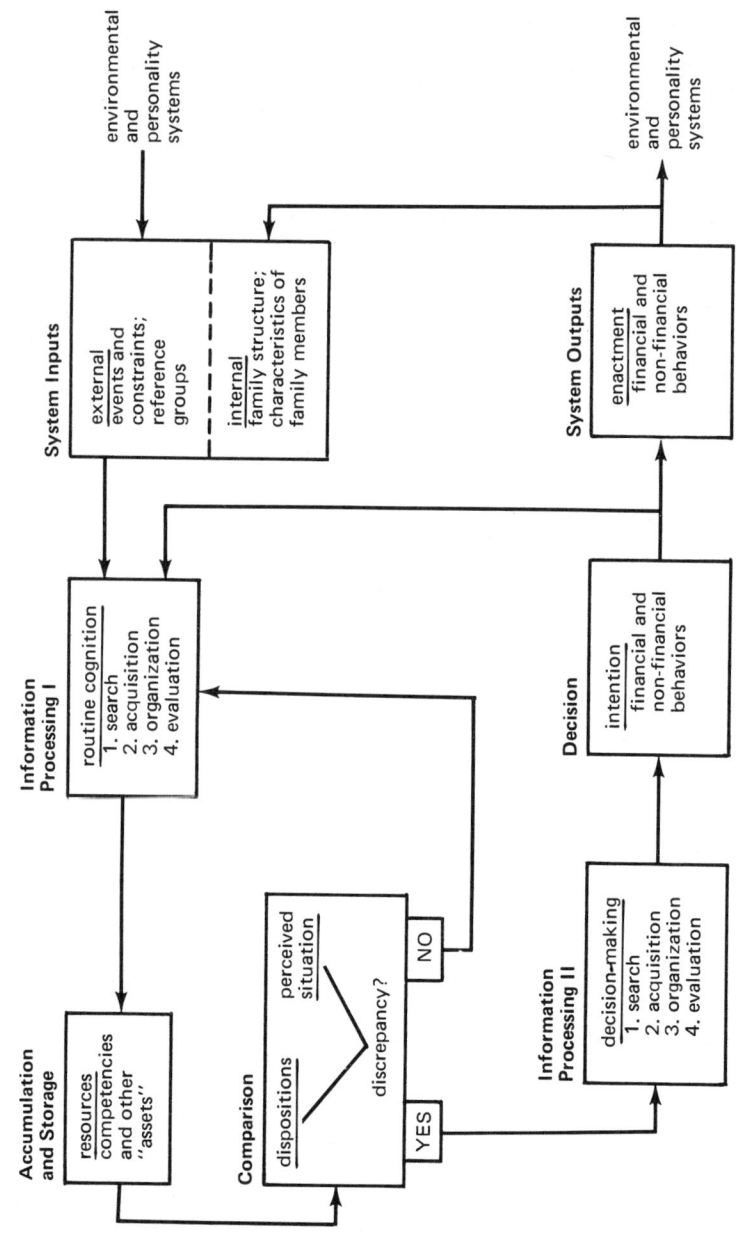

that is, information flows are likely to be subject to the same general patterns and processes.

Family "System Inputs" are specified to represent the selective exposure of families to exogenous elements or to place boundaries on the "life space" of families. External and internal inputs are differentiated to show that family behavior has consequences for the family system itself. This perspective helps avoid the unreasonable conclusion that families are wholly passive reactors to the environment in which they are placed. The personality systems of members can be said to influence the characteristics of family members, and thus to provide internal inputs. The term exogenous, therefore, refers to elements not operating at the level of the family. Since the family system is in some sense a "unity of interacting personalities," personality variables are exogenous but not external. Specific family system inputs have been considered earlier and will not be further detailed except to point out that they include such phenomena as governmental regulations, inflation, friendship ties, exposure to the mass media, the life cycle stage of the family, family size, and the psychological traits of members.

Chart 2 differentiates two information-processing steps. The first, called "Information Processing I," refers to rule-bound, routinized handling of system inputs. In order to make sense out of the stimulus material to which it is exposed, the family searches or scans its life space for relevant data, acquires these data largely through interpersonal communication channels, organizes the data by coding or transforming them with a developed symbolic repertoire, and evaluates the data via standards of adequacy or worth. Insufficient information reinitiates a search for information and the information-processing cycle continues. It should be noted that the criteria by which to evaluate information can be considered to derive from dispositions in the "Comparison" block, to be discussed later, which provide additional inputs to Information Processing I.

This systems framework suggests that processed information creates a reservoir for information conceptualized here as "Accumulation and Storage" in the form of resources. (The variety of phenomena that can be considered resources has already been explored.) Essentially, resources serve as action potentials that may produce consumer behavior if the prevailing conditions are favorable. Just as Information Processing I is not free of direction by dispositions, neither are resources. A family's assets and liabilities, both economic and personality, are defined during the evaluation of information.

In order for resources to guide future family behavior, they must be sorted and subjected to a comparison process labelled here "Comparison." This step is essentially a series of questions which monitor the relationships between group dispositions (goals, values, aspirations, etc.) and the perceived situtation (accomplishment, status, performance levels, etc.). Following DP1 through 3 above, congruity between these elements within some tolerance range is considered to be a steady state which the system seeks to maintain. Because the elements utilized in the comparison are hypothetically subject to modification by system inputs, the equilibrium worked for is a dynamic or moving equilibrium. It is not assumed, for example, that goals are constant or that they are composed of a fixed ratio of material and nonmaterial aspirations.

It is important to recognize several other features of Comparison. First, since congruity is itself desirable, it is properly considered a fundamental disposition. Second, while the comparison process is strictly cognitive for personality systems, it is contingent on social interaction in family or other group systems. Dispositional consensus of family members as well as shared perceptions of situations are explicit assumptions of this approach. When the values of individual family members are discordant, they must be negotiated through the interaction of personality systems. Third, situations perceived by the group may refer to memories of past experience, current contingencies, or expectations of future conditions. It should be clear that in no case are these situations purely objective or realistic. Perceptual filters inject different sorts and degrees of bias, according to the rationality of earlier information processing.

Comparison not only incorporates a choice point, discrepancy or no discrepancy, but also the relativity and satisfaction or welfare notions that have thus far been so compelling. Following DP2, discrepancies generate dissatisfaction states while congruities generate satisfaction states. Some dissatisfactions may be cognitively dissonant while others are dispositionally dissonant. In the former case attitudes are inconsistent with each other, and in the latter case attitudes are inconsistent with reality perceptions. When a family arrives at the "no significant discrepancy" point, it returns to routine information processing. On the other hand, when a significant discrepancy is identified, the family system may be said to experience tension that requires a special decision-making sequence to resolve the discrepancy.

During Information Processing II, the family may search for new information or utilize resources already stored which Comparison has shown to be relevant. The basic structure of Information Processing II may be viewed as equivalent to the structure of Information Processing I, although the form and content of the information in the two steps may be different. The "planfulness" of families may be viewed in terms of the intensity and thoroughness of information processing.

Once information has been processed for decisions, the decision or decisions are made. In the realm of family consumption such decisions involve intentions to buy or sell, transfer unconditionally to a family member, save or invest, and establish or restructure money management responsibilities, as well as decisions about the internal dimensions of these intentions. Nonfinancial decisions include plans regarding family size, time allocation for work and leisure, job changes for husband or wife, residence changes, and educational choices. In addition, nonfinancial decisions include decisions to alter dispositions.

"Decision" is differentiated from "System Output" because intentions are not always predictive of enactments. The feed-back loop from Decision to Information Processing I serves as a validity check. Potential enactments may be reprocessed in light of new, intervening inputs and subjected to a test comparison in order to determine the probability that outputs will achieve desired results.

The consequences of generating System Outputs are manifold. When a family acts on exogenous systems, it provides them with vital inputs utilized in their own information and energy-flow functions. Family System Outputs also have more direct consequences for the structure of the family itself. Investment intermediation and childbearing affect the characteristics of a family and, eventually, its resource pool. System Outputs also serve as data sources for a definitive comparison." Either by reflexively interpreting its own behavior or by incorporating the results of behavioral exchanges with exogenous systems, or both, the family generates new information about dispositions and the perceived situation. Prolonged periods of time in, or repeated entry into, segments of the decision-making sequence probably reflect crisis situations. Symptoms of such crises might include an inexorably fast rate of novel system inputs, a faulty information-processing sequence, or unsuccessful trial-and-error outputs operating at marginal predictability levels.

The systems model of family consumption sketched here has several features of more general sociocultural systems. The family may be characterized as an *open system*. It exchanges information and energy with other systems including the internal personality systems of members and is, therefore, not simply at the mercy of external forces. It engages in *information processing* in order to transform and interpret the data with which it works.

The family also engages in *maintenance of dynamic equilibrium*. Congruity between dispositions and perceived situations is the fundamentally steady state. The family is *morphogenic;* it is adaptive to the environmental and personality systems with which it interacts. The family demonstrates the principle of *equifinality;* there are alternative routes to keep it steady. The family generates feed-back; much of its behavior is viewed as cycles of events so that the products it exports to the environment furnish the sources of energy and information for the repetition of the cycle of activities. Some of this feed-back is negative feed-back, information or energy designed to resolve or correct discrepancies between dispositions and perceived situations. The family is *negentropic;* in order to counteract natural tendencies to deteriorate through disorganization, aging, and death, it attempts to import more energy than it can expend by accumulating and storing reserve resources at a level that will insure a comfortable margin of operation.

A systems-theory perspective offers certain advantages over other accounting models. It is truly interdisciplinary in scope and can incorporate the usual vested interests of economists, psychologists, and sociologists alike. In addition, systems theory can serve as a framework for the deductive explanation of diverse phenomena. Although we have inductively extrapolated various insights from the Williamsburg Conference into this abstract formulation, it is not obvious that the particular systems model we have constructed can adequately account for all of these insights. The reader may wish to test one or more of the preceding sections in the systems-model form to see if large or small modifications in Chart 2 and its interpretation are warranted.

Several caveats are in order that might temper one's enthusiasm about the desirability of systems thinking at this point. First, the conceptual apparatus of systems theory is not well institutionalized into the lexicon of the social sciences. Certain systems concepts may as yet be insufficiently defined and bounded in ways that are intersubjectively certifiable. Second, and largely because of the problem just stated, it is not always clear how the theoretical relationships among systems concepts can be translated into testable hypotheses. For example, is the direct feed-back from Decision to Information Processing I an invariantly used path and, if not, what effects on the efficiency of family-consumption behavior for goal attainment might occur when this path is underutilized? Third, the systems model is inherently more complex than the unidirectional or recursive causal chain models that our research methodologies are most adequately developed to handle. The data-analysis technology for dynamic models has only recently begun to receive extended treatment in sociology [2, Chapter 4, ff.].

In conclusion, the synthesis suggests several high priority requirements for an emerging theory of family consumption:

1. Mapping out the appropriate variables with taxonomies and other techniques of conceptual clarification.
2. Explicitly stating basic underlying assumptions, theoretical as well as methodological.
3. Assessing the empirical support for the major research propositions and generalizations of a higher order.
4. Building deductive theory by integrating the research findings of several disciplines and by constructing abstract models from which testable hypotheses can be derived.

Such efforts will not be easy and may run counter to some of our most cherished principles. Without them, however, it is unlikely that our knowledge of family economic behavior will ever transcend much beyond the fragments of our personal experiences.

Notes

1. There was a particularly lively discussion following the Maynes' paper of the inadequacies in communicating information from seller to buyer to which we will return later in this section.

2. Studies of preplanned versus unplanned purchases to ascertain the properties of products most likely to be planned continued to have salience during the decade of the Ferber review. The degree of deliberation in buying is shown to vary positively with the "size of the ticket," the meaning and importance to the buyer, and inversely with the urgency of his wants. Much of what has been termed "impulse buying" turns out on examination to be deferred purchasing in which the customer has waited to get what he wants until the circumstance is right. What does appear to be lagging in the research reviewed by Ferber are explanatory studies identifying the family determinants of preplanning actions and other expressions of consumership.

3. James Morgan in commenting on the Minnesota findings suggested that expressions of satisfaction with decisions made may be generated through diverse channels which should be specified before drawing firm conclusions about the correlates of satisfaction. He noted a marked tendency among respondents in his own studies, once the decision has been made, to rationalize it as the only possible and reasonable decision to have made.

4. Two consumption psychologists, Howard and Sheth, [13] theorized that there is a negative relation between level of aspiration (expected satisfaction) and actual satisfaction. The higher the expected satisfaction from a purchase the greater the discrepancy between actual and expected satisfaction, contemplation of consumption of a good being more rewarding than the returns from the consumption of the good itself (see pp. 147–148). If it can be established that consumers who preplan their purchases, as against those who do not, have higher expectations of satisfaction, then the former would experience more frequent dissatisfaction than consumers who did not preplan. This is precisely what the Minnesota study found to be the case.

5. This situation suggests other limitations of Chart 1 as a formalization device. The effects of the independent variables and the dependent variables on each other are not portrayed. Neither are interaction effects considered. Using regression techniques within individual studies is, of course, one way to deal with these problems, and the conferees who used them are to be commended. When one attempts to integrate several sets of research findings, however, it becomes difficult to avoid the epigram: "Everything is related to everything else."

6. For an excellent conceptual clarification, a detailed review of the literature on relative deprivation theory drawn from several disciplines, and a political science application, see [8], especially pp. 22–58.

7. Treatment of the issues involved in social systems theory, its application to family phenomena, and of consistency theories, respectively, may be found in Walter Buckley, *Sociology and Modern Systems Theory,* Englewood Cliffs, N.J.: Prentice-Hall, 1967; Reuben Hill, "Modern Systems Theory and the Family: A Confrontation," *Social Science Information* 10 No. 5, 1971: pp. 7–26; Paul F. Secord and Carl W. Backman, *Social Psychology,* New York: McGraw-Hill, 1964, pp. 108–124.

8. Much of the credit for this approach should be extended to Ferber who, in the beginning session, sensitized us to the need for an integrated model of family consumption. Previous model building has usually taken the individual consumer as the behaving unit. For example, see Morgan's model in [9, p. 3], and the Nicosia, Engel, and Howard-Sheth models in [12, pp. 1–4].

References

1. Aldous, Joan, and Reuben Hill, "Strategies for Breaking the Poverty Cycle," *Social Work*, 14 July 1969, pp. 3–12.
2. Blalock, Hubert M., Jr., *Theory Construction*, Englewood Cliffs, New Jersey: Prentice-Hall, 1969.
3. Buckley, Walter, *Sociology and Modern Systems Theory*, Englewood Cliffs, New Jersey: Prentice-Hall, 1967.
4. Demos, John, *A Little Commonwealth: Family Life in Plymouth Colony*, New York: Oxford University Press, 1970.
5. Foote, Nelson N., *Household Decision Making: Consumer Behavior 4*, New York: New York University Press, 1961.
6. Granbois, Donald H., "The Role of Communication in the Family Decision Making Process," in Stephan A. Greyser, ed., *Toward Scientific Marketing*, Chicago: American Marketing Association, 1964.
7. Greven, Phillip T., *Four Generations: Population, Land, and Family in Colonial Andover, Massachusetts*, Ithaca, N.Y.: Cornell University Press, 1970.
8. Gurr, Ted Robert, *Why Men Rebel*, Princeton: Princeton University Press, 1970.
9. Hill, Reuben, *Family Development in Three Generations*, Cambridge, Mass.: Schenkman, 1970.
10. ———, "Modern Systems Theory and the Family: A Confrontation," *Social Science Information* 10 No. 5, 1971, pp. 7–26.
11. ———, J. Mayone Stycos, and Kurt Back, *The Family and Population Control*, Chapel Hill, N.C.: The University of North Carolina Press, 1959.
12. Holloway, Robert J., et al., *Consumer Behavior: Contemporary Research in Action*, New York: Houghton Mifflin, 1969.
13. Howard, John A., and Jagdish N. Sheth, *The Theory of Buyer Behavior*, New York: John Wiley and Sons, 1969.
14. Schelling, Thomas C., *The Strategy of Conflict*, Cambridge, Mass.: Harvard University Press, 1960. For detailed treatment of strategic games.
15. Secord, Paul F., and Carl W. Backman, *Social Psychology*, New York: McGraw-Hill, 1964.
16. Straus, Murray A., "Measuring Families," in Harold T. Christensen, ed., *Handbook of Marriage and the Family*, Chicago: Rand McNally, 1964, pp. 335–400.
17. ———, and Irving Tallman, "SIMFAM: A Technique for Observational Measurement and Experimental Study of Families," in Joan Aldous, et al., *Family Problem Solving*, Chicago: Dryden Press, 1971.
18. Weick, Karl E., "Group Processes, Family Processes, and Problem Solving," in Joan Aldous, et al., eds., *Family Problem Solving*, Chicago: Dryden Press, 1971.

List of Attendance
The Williamsburg Conference
January 1972

Joan Aldous

Associate Professor of Sociology and Family Studies
University of Minnesota
Minneapolis, Minnesota

Milton Amsel

Director, Press and Editorial Services
Institute of Life Insurance
New York, New York

Elinor A. Anderson

Family Economics-Management
Kansas State University
Manhattan, Kansas

Gemma C. Baker

Market Research
The Travelers Insurance Company
Hartford, Connecticut

Elaine N. Barnes

Family Economics-Management
University of Alberta
Alberta, Canada

Ruth E. Berry

Department of Family Studies
University of Manitoba
Manitoba, Canada

Gordon E. Bivens

Professor of Family Economics
University of Missouri
Columbia, Missouri

Murray Teigh Bloom

Reader's Digest
Pleasantville
New York

Zahava D. Blum

Department of Sociology
Johns Hopkins University
Baltimore, Maryland

Aadje C. Boelmans-Kleinjan

Sociologist, Department of Home Economics
Agricultural University
Wageningen, Holland

Jean S. Bowers

Department of Economics
Ohio State University
Columbus, Ohio

Carlfred B. Broderick

Department of Sociology and Anthropology
University of Southern California
Los Angeles, California

List of Attendance

Kathleen H. Brown

Family Studies Department
University of Guelph
Ontario, Canada

Marguerite C. Burk

Economist, U.S. Department of Agriculture
Federal Center Building
Hyattsville, Maryland

Gwen Bymers

Professor and Chairman, Department of Consumer Economics and Public Policy
Cornell University
Ithaca, New York

Glen G. Cain

Department of Economics
University of Wisconsin
Madison, Wisconsin

Charlotte V. Churaman

College of Home Economics
University of Maryland
College Park, Maryland

Leslie A. Cole

Director, Educational Division
Canadian Life Insurance Association
Toronto, Ontario, Canada

Karen E. Craig

Family Economics-Management
Southern Illinois University
Carbondale, Illinois

Elizabeth W. Crandall

Family Economics-Management
University of Rhode Island
Kingston, Rhode Island

Hilda Dailey

Family Economics-Management
Virginia Polytechnic Institute
Blacksburg, Virginia

Ruth Deacon

School of Home Economics
Ohio State University
Columbus, Ohio

Patty Sue Dingle

Family Service of St. Paul
St. Paul, Minnesota

Elizabeth Douvan

Department of Psychology
University of Michigan
Ann Arbor, Michigan

Donna Beth Downer

Family Economics-Management
University of Tennessee
Martin, Tennessee

Robert A. Driscoll

Program Director, Information Services
Institute of Life Insurance
New York, New York

Marilyn Dunsing

Department of Home Economics
University of Illinois
Urbana, Illinois

Richard A. Easterlin

The Wharton School
University of Pennsylvania
Philadelphia, Pennsylvania

Harold Edrich

Director, Research Services
Institute of Life Insurance
New York, New York

Kay P. Edwards

School of Home Economics
University of North Carolina
Greensboro, North Carolina

Ozzie L. Edwards

Department of Sociology
University of Michigan
Ann Arbor, Michigan

Marcus Felson

Center for Research on Social Organization
University of Michigan
Ann Arbor, Michigan

Robert Ferber

Survey Research Laboratory
University of Illinois
Urbana, Illinois

Nelson N. Foote

Chairman, Department of Sociology
Hunter College
New York, New York

Wallace C. Fulton

Second Vice President
The Equitable Life Assurance Society of the United States
New York, New York

Martha L. Garrison

Department of Family and Community Development
University of Maryland
College Park, Maryland

K. Edwin Graham

Program Director, Commission on Church Family Financial Planning
Washington, D.C.

Thomas A. Graves, Jr.

President
College of William and Mary
Williamsburg, Virginia

Harold W. Guthrie

The Urban Institute
Washington, D.C.

Lois J. Guthrie

Assistant Professor of Family Economics
Montclair State College
Upper Montclair, New Jersey

Jeanne L. Hafstrom

Assistant Professor of Family Economics
University of Illinois
Urbana, Illinois

Florence T. Hall

School of Home Economics
University of Washington
Seattle, Washington

James R. Hanson

General Mills, Inc.
Minneapolis, Minnesota

Carolyn Hauswald

Pikes Peak Family Counseling and Mental Health Center
Colorado Springs, Colorado

James T. Heimbach

Social Psychologist
Nationwide Insurance Company
Columbus, Ohio

Sandra A. Helmick

Family Economics-Management
University of Missouri
Columbia, Missouri

List of Attendance

Albert I. Hermalin

Associate Professor of Sociology and Research Associate
The Population Studies Center
University of Michigan
Ann Arbor, Michigan

Mary W. Hicks

Social Psychologist
Virginia Polytechnic Institute
Blacksburg, Virginia

Reuben Hill

Professor of Sociology and Research Program Director
Family Study Center
University of Minnesota
Minneapolis, Minnesota

Jacob Jacoby

Associate Professor
Department of Psychology
Purdue University
Lafayette, Indiana

Kathleen Jeary

Department of Family Social Science
University of Minnesota
St. Paul, Minnesota

Bernadine Johnson

Family Economics-Management
Texas Woman's University
Denton, Texas

Thomas A. Johnson

Director, Special Projects
Institute for Motivational Research
Croton-on-Hudson, New York

F. Thomas Juster

Vice President-Research
National Bureau of Economic Research, Inc.
New York, New York

Suzanne Keller

Professor of Sociology
Princeton University
Princeton, New Jersey

Allen C. Kelley

Department of Economics
University of Wisconsin
Madison, Wisconsin

R. Wayne Kernodle

Professor of Sociology
College of William and Mary
Williamsburg, Virginia

James C. Kimberly

Program Director for Sociology
National Science Foundation
Washington, D.C.

William E. Kingsley

Vice President
Institute of Life Insurance
New York, New York

Josephine H. Lawyer

Extension Service
U.S. Department of Agriculture
Washington, D.C.

Robert Lindsay

Executive Director
State of New York Council of Economic Advisers
New York, New York

Margaret I. Liston

Professor, Consumer Economics and Management
Iowa State University
Ames, Iowa

List of Attendance · 409

Sarah L. Manning

Department of Home Management and Family Economics
Purdue University
Lafayette, Indiana

Esther A. Martin

Family Economics-Management
Virginia Polytechnic Institute
Blacksburg, Virginia

E. Scott Maynes

Professor of Economics
University of Minnesota
Minneapolis, Minnesota

Sue Morfit

Brooklyn Bureau of Community Service
285 Schermerhorn Street
Brooklyn, New York

James N. Morgan

Program Director and Professor of Economics
Survey Research Center
University of Michigan
Ann Arbor, Michigan

Milton Moss

Assistant Director
Office of Management and Budget
Washington, D.C.

N. Parry Nayar

Market Research
Connecticut General Life Insurance Company
Hartford, Connecticut

Blake T. Newton, Jr.

President
Institute of Life Insurance
New York, New York

Robert C. Nuckols

Consumer Psychology
Life Insurance Agency Management Association
Hartford, Connecticut

Ronald L. Nuttall

Social Psychologist
Institute of Human Sciences
Boston College
Chestnut Hill, Massachusetts

Edith Nyman

College of Family Life
Utah State University
Logan, Utah

Guy H. Orcutt

Institute of Social Science
Yale University
New Haven, Connecticut

Eleanor M. Pao

U.S. Department of Agriculture
Hyattsville, Maryland

Beatrice Paolucci

Professor and Acting Chairman
Department of Family Ecology
Michigan State University
East Lansing, Michigan

Martin Pfaff

Department of Economics
Wayne State University
Detroit, Michigan

Gladys K. Phelan

Child Development and Family Relationships
Colorado State University
Fort Collins, Colorado

List of Attendance

Martha A. Plonk

School of Home Economics
Oregon State University
Corvallis, Oregon

Daniel O. Price

Department of Sociology
University of Texas
Austin, Texas

A. Marshall Puckett

Assistant Vice President
Research and Statistics Function
Federal Reserve Bank of New York
New York, New York

Barbara B. Reagan

Professor of Economics
Southern Methodist University
Dallas, Texas

Helen M. Reed

College of Home Economics
University of Tennessee
Knoxville, Tennessee

Olin C. Robison

Dean of the Faculty
Bowdoin College
Brunswick, Maine

Hyman Rodman

Senior Research Associate
Merrill-Palmer Institute
Detroit, Michigan

Gilbert Rutman

Social Sciences Division
Southern Illinois University
Edwardsville, Illinois

Norman B. Ryder

Woodrow Wilson School of Public
 and International Affairs
Princeton University
Princeton, New Jersey

Francis H. Schott

Vice President and Economist
The Equitable Life Assurance Society of
 the United States
New York, New York

Robert A. Scott

Associate Professor
Department of Sociology
Princeton University
Princeton, New Jersey

David R. Segal

Department of Sociology
University of Michigan
Ann Arbor, Michigan

Eleanor Bernert Sheldon

President
Social Science Research Council
New York, New York

Arnold R. Shore

Research Coordinator
Urban Opinion Surveys
Princeton University
Princeton, New Jersey

George S. Siudy, Jr.

Secretary for Stewardship Education
United Church of Christ
Philadelphia, Pennsylvania

Felicity M. Skidmore

Mathematica, Inc.
Washington, D.C.

Josephine H. Staab

Family Economics-Management
University of Wisconsin
Madison, Wisconsin

Kathryn Stafford

School of Home Economics
Louisiana State University
Baton Rouge, Louisiana

Murray A. Straus

Professor of Sociology
University of New Hampshire
Durham, New Hampshire

Burkhard Strumpel

Associate Professor of Economics
Survey Research Center, Institute
 for Social Research
University of Michigan
Ann Arbor, Michigan

Janet E. Swayne

Department of Home Economics
Northern Illinois University
DeKalb, Illinois

Donald L. Taylor

Professor of Sociology
Southern Illinois University
Edwardsville, Illinois

Helen M. Thal

Director, Education Services
Institute of Life Insurance
New York, New York

Judy Van Name

College of Home Economics
University of Delaware
Newark, Delaware

Florence S. Walker

College of Home Economics
University of Nebraska
Lincoln, Nebraska

Phyllis A. Wallace

Vice President for Research
Metropolitan Applied Research Center, Inc.
New York, New York

Kal Waller

Consumer Credit Counseling Service
Cleveland, Ohio

Mary Watson

Institute for Sociotherapy
New York, New York

Harold W. Watts

Cowles Foundation for Research in Economics
Yale University
New Haven, Connecticut

Paul Webbink

Scarsdale, New York

Louise A. Young

Family Economics-Management
University of Wisconsin
Madison, Wisconsin

Index

Akers, D. S., 211
Aldous, Joan, 15, 377
Altruistic principle of goal-striving, 19
Appliances, major, 301-302
Assets, consumer, 312-17
    earning and nonearning, 318
    families holding, 330
    family management of, 34
    rates of growth of, 343, 344
Assumption, problem of, 15-20
Atkinson, John W., 71
Automobile buying, 46
Ayres, E. Daniel, 140

Ball, Duane E., 166
Banks (*see* Financial institutions)
Barton, S. G., 42
Bell, G. D., 49
Berey, L. A., 47
Bharadwaj, L., 39
Birth rates, 171-73, 193, 195
    in fertility study, 208
    in negative income tax experiment, 252
    See also Fertility
Bivens, Gordon, 11, 395, 397
Black workers, blue-collar, 112
    satisfaction, values, goals of, 97-104
    values of, 134, 136
    See also Race
Blake, Judith, 206, 213
Blood, R., 37
Blue-collar workers, economic satisfactions of, 110-12
    values of, 134-36
    See also Occupation
Bonds, 322, 330
Bott, E., 41
Boulding, Kenneth E., 13
Brand choice, 46-47
Brest, Joel I., 312, 316, 330
Britton, V., 38
Brown, George, 46, 47
Bumpass, Larry, 206, 207

Burke, Marguerite, 19, 388
Bymers, Gwen, 8, 11, 14, 16, 384, 386
    on consumerism, 295-303

Cahalan, Don, 43
Cateora, R. R., 53
Catholic women in fertility study, 188-90
Ceiling rates, 350, 351, 356
Certificates of Deposit (CDs), 330, 350
Checking accounts, 330, 331
Children, attitudes toward numbers of, 205-15
    in fertility study, 179, 180
    in spending decisions, 42, 47-48
    teenagers, role of, in saving, 53
Class, consumer index by, 158
    consumption and, 159-61
    future research on, 376-78
    identification with, subjective convergence of, 147-48
        distribution of, 153
        multiple classification analysis of, 154
    Marx on, 143
    occupational, 144
    social, analysis of identification with, 156
    See also Socioeconomic status
Clerical workers, satisfactions of, 107-109
Cohort fertility analysis, 205
Communication between disciplines, 6-20
Condran, Gretchen A., 166
Consumer(s), behavior of, 7-11
    finances of 1951-70, 312-34
        See also Financial management
    grievances of, 273-76, 284-85
    markets of, early, 271-75
        imperfection of, 281-83
        information- and quality-explicit theory of, 284
        today, 272-73
    proconsumer research and, 384-86
    response of, to financial incentives, 350-56

413

Consumer(s) *(continued)*
 views consumption function, 289-90
 See also Decision making, family
Consumer Information Corporation, 290-91
Consumer Price Index, 214
Consumer Reports, 279, 299, 385
Consumer search procedures, 285-87
Consumerism, chronology of, 279-81
 definitions of, 8, 296
 government regulation in, 287-89
 origin and research implications, 267-295
  response to, 295-304
 research in, 281-91
 retail outlets in, 276-79
Consumers Union, 280, 284, 296, 299, 300, 385, 386
Consumption, family, examining, 8-9
 material, multiple classification analysis of, 155
 in status attribute, 148
 welfare and, 12-14
Consumption function viewed by consumer, 289-90
Consumption index, 156-58
Contraception, 186-91
Converse, P. D., 42, 43, 47
Coombs, Clyde H., 207
Coulson, J. S., 47
Cox, D. F., 49
Crawford, C. M., 42, 43, 47
Crow, J. H., 50
Curtin, Richard T., 64, 69

Data, collecting, 150-54
Davis, H. L., 43, 44, 47
Decision making, family, as to brand, 46-47
 economic behavior and, 25-61
 framework for, 30-34
 research implications of, 371-76
 See also Financial decisions
Demby, Emanuel H., 161
Demographic groups, goals in life within, 89
 new job and, 90
 satisfactions by, 79-85
Depositary institutions, 350-51, 356
Dewey, John, 15
Disintermediation, 350-56
Divorce, 255
Douvan, Elizabeth, 8, 11, 19, 21, 140, 378-79, 381
Due, J. M., 35
Duesenberry, James, 48, 74

Duncan Index of Socioeconomic Status, 152, 157

Easterlin, Richard, 7, 9, 16, 17, 73, 379-81, 393-95, 397
 on relative economic status and American fertility swing, 167-223
 response to, 224-27
Economic aspects
 of consumer financial management, 308-309, 311, 334-42
 expectations, and family finances, 364-67
 of family size, 379-81
 period fertility rates and, 212-13
 social stratification and, 140-64
Economic status and fertility, 167-227
 since late fifties, 182-91
 response on, 224-27
 since thirties, 192-97, 215
Education, in fertility study, 176, 179, 180
 satisfaction and, 77, 83-85
Employment, consumer and, 334-35
 in fertility study, 176, 177, 193-196
 in negative income tax experiment, 245, 247
 part-time, 249
Environment, chart on individual adaptation to, 129
Environmentalism, 279
Equities, 320, 338
Erbring, Lutz, 64
Expectancy orientation, 133

Family, composition of, and negative income tax, 250-59
 consumption in research agenda in, 371-92
 systems model of, 397-402
 theoretical synthesis for, 392-403
 across disciplines, 6-7
 economic behavior of, and social stratification, 141-64
 intact, 381-84
 separation in, 254-58
 size of, attitudes on, 205-15
  economic determinants of, 379-81
  in negative income tax experiment, 251
 See also Fertility
 stability of, in negative income tax experiment, 250-59
 as unit of study, 4
 See also Decision making
Farley, J. U., 49
Fate control, 99-100, 118

Felson, Marcus, 9, 12, 14, 17, 19, 231, 308, 378, 382, 392, 393, 395, 396
  on social stratification and family economic behavior, 141-64
Ferber, Robert, 7, 9, 12, 13, 16, 18, 21, 44, 51, 52, 56, 281, 371, 372, 374, 393-95
  on family decision making and economic behavior, 25-61
Fertility, 7, 167-227, 379-81
Fertility differentials, 178-80
Fertility patterns, 168, 171-74
Fertility rates, period and completed, and family size, 205-15
Financial behavior index, analysis of, 157
Financial decisions, family, 30-38
  modified framework, 54-57
Financial incentives, consumer response to, 350-56
Financial institutions, response to financial management,
  consumer, 342-50
  savings and, 355-56
Financial management, consumer, 307-67
  economic milestones affecting, 334-42
  financial institutions response to, 342-50
  between 1951-70, 312-34
Financial planning, 34-36, 375
  See also Rationality
Financial transaction index, 151
Freedman, Ronald, 206, 207
Freeman, R. C., 35
Fults, A. C., 53

Gibbs, M., 48
Gibson, Campbell, 166
Glick, Paul C., 166
Goals, life, 89, 97, 114-116
Goldberg, David, 206, 207
Government regulation (*see* Regulation)
Grabill, Wilson H., 166
Granbois, Donald H., 42, 45, 373, 374
Growth rates, among financial institutions, 343-47
  of life insurance, 347-50
Gurin, Gerald, 64, 71, 99
Gurin, Patricia, 71, 99

Hamilton, Richard F., 147
Hedonistic principle, 18
  of goal-striving
Hermalin, Albert, 20, 140, 372, 385
Hill, Reuben, 36, 38, 51
  on research agenda and theoretical synthesis, 371-404

Hodge, Robert W., 140, 147
Honey, R. R., 34, 38, 41
Hotchkiss, A. S., 38
Households, financial investments of, 318-27
  stability of, 250-59
Hughes, G. David, 298-300
Husband(s), in fertility study, 174, 175
  employment of, 177, 179
  income of, 178, 183-85
  in saving, 52
  wives and, in financial decisions, 36-43
Husband-wife families in negative income tax experiment, 239, 242, 244-48

Impulse purchases, 44-46
Income, consumer index by, 158
  convergence of, 145-47
  family intactness and, 258, 259
  fertility and, 178, 183-85
  guaranteed family, 231, 233, 234
  satisfaction with, 75, 76, 79-82
Income stability, guaranteed, 381-84
Income tax, negative, and work response, 231-63
Index construction, 150-54
Inflation, 350
  consumer and, 338, 340-42
  life insurance and, 348-49
Information, role of, in decision making, 49-50
Inglehart, Ronald, 160
Inkeles, A., 136
Institute of Life Insurance, 4
Interdisciplinary aspects of social science, 3-7, 20-21
Interest rates, 335-37, 350-54
Interviewing and sampling, 115-22
Investment management, 51

Jacoby, Jacob, 16, 386, 395
Jaffe, L. J., 43
Job, choosing new, 90
  satisfaction with, 77, 83-85
Juster, Thomas, 14, 19, 45, 308, 372, 384, 385, 387, 388, 395

Katona, George, 18, 44, 50, 51, 64, 70, 71, 140, 387
Katz, Elihur, 48
Kelley, Allen C., 381
  responds on fertility, 224-27
Keynes, John Maynard, 50, 311
Klein, David M., on research agenda and theoretical synthesis, 371-404
Knoke, David, 140, 147

Komarovsky, Mirra, 41
Kuehn, A. A., 46
Kyrk, Hazel, 34, 38

Labor force, 152
  American, 144-46
  class and, 158
  in fertility study, 176, 177, 194-96, 202
  See also Workers
Labor supply in negative income tax experiment, 240-43
Lazarsfeld, P. F., 48
Lewin, Kurt, 48
Liabilities, consumer, 312-17, 328
Life-cycle relationships, 183, 192
Life insurance, 325-27, 347-50
Life style, fertility and, 181
  future research on, 376-79
  values, subjective welfare and, 65-138
Linder, Staffan, 272
Lipset, Seymour M., 151

McClelland, David C., 71
Management, economic satisfactions of, 107-109
  See also Financial management
Marital roles in spending, 41-44
Markets (*see* Consumer, markets of)
Marriage, in fertility study, 172-86, 189-91
  patterns of, 197-205
  See also Husband; Marriage; Wife
Marriage squeeze, 201, 205, 215-16
Marx, Karl, 143, 149, 152, 159
Maynes, Scott, 7-9, 14, 16-19, 21, 384-86, 392-94
  on consumerism, 267-91
  response to, 295-303
Men, in fertility study, 199-202, 204
Michigan survey of 1970, 330-31
Miller, Herman P., 166
Money management, 32, 38-41
Morgan, James, 4, 12, 14, 17, 19, 71, 372, 382, 385, 386
Morris, Richard T., 151
Mortgage holdings, 322
Moss, Milton, 17, 382
Mott, P., 40, 42, 43, 52
Mueller, Eva, 44
Multiple Classification Analysis (MCA), 154, 155
Munn, Mark, 47
Murphy, Raymond J., 151

Nader, Ralph, 269, 274, 280
National Bureau of Economic Research (NBER), 324

Nayar, Perry, 16, 372
Net worth, 312-17, 333
New Jersey, negative income tax experiment in, 233-37
Newman, J. W., 45
Nicosia, F. N., 51, 52, 56

O'Brien, Vincent L., 233
Oberly, J. A., 50
Occupation, of black workers, 100, 101
  classes of, convergence of, 144-45
  consumer index by, 158
  in fertility study, 177
  organization men, satisfactions of, 107-109
  professionals, satisfactions of, 104-107
  satisfaction, economic, by, 75-77
  values and, 91, 95, 96, 132-34
  See also Blue-collar workers
Office of Economic Opportunity, 234, 235
Orcutt, Guy, 9, 12, 25, 372
Organization men, satisfactions of, 107-109

Paolucci, Beatrice, 19
Parnes, Herbert S., 216
Patriarchal system, 39
Pennsylvania, negative income tax experiment in, 233, 236
Pension funds, 325-27
Pfaff, Martin, 12, 13, 19, 65, 68, 372
  on economic life-styles, values, and subjective welfare, 126-38
Phelan, G. K., 53
Phelan, J. M., 50
Pill, contraceptive, 186-91
Planning, financial, 34-36, 375
  See also Rationality
Pollay, R. W., 47
Population problem, 210-11
Poverty, 243, 259
Pratt, R. W., Jr., 45
Proconsumer research, 384-86
Product safety, 278-79
Professional affiliations of conferees, 5-7
Professionals, economic satisfactions of, 104-107
Puckett, Marshall, 18, 66, 307-309, 312, 316, 330, 387, 395, 397
  on consumer financial management and financial institution response, 363-67
Purchases, impulse, 44-46
  See also Spending

Questionnaire on values, 118-22

Race, fate control and, 100
  satisfactions by, 75-77
  separation and, 257
  See also Black workers; White workers
Rao, V. R., 299, 300
Rationality, 15-20
Rayburn, M. B., 35, 47
Reciprocity principle in goal-striving, 18
Reference groups, role of, in family decision making, 48-49
Regression coefficients, 156, 157
Regulation, government, in consumer affairs, 287-89
  of life insurance industry, 348
Relativity, of social placement, 11-12
Religion, in fertility study, 188-90
Reproduction, 7
  See also Fertility
Research implications, 371-92
Retail outlets, 276-79
Rippel, Betty A., 166
Rodman, Hy, 19
Rokeach, Milton, 87
Rokkan, Stein, 151
Ross, Ivan, 290
Ruef, R. R., 50
Ryder, Norman, 11, 16, 187-90, 211, 214

Sampling and interviewing, 115-22
Satisfaction, economic, 71-87, 97, 374-77
  for black workers, 102, 103
  of blue-collar workers, 110-12
  of professionals, 105-107
  socioeconomic status and, 134-37
Savings, contractual, 325-27
  family decisions on, 33-34
  family goals in, 50-53
  flow of, and economic variables, 355
  interest rates and, 352-54
  management of, 386-88
  spending decisions and, 31-34
Savings accounts, 320, 321, 330, 331
Savings and loan associations, 347
Savings rate and inflation, 340
Schomaker, P. K., 36, 37, 48
Schott, Francis, 8, 9, 17-19, 378, 386-88, 392, 393, 395, 396
  on financial management and financial institutions, 307-62
  response to, 363-67
Schrag, Philip, 278
Schultz, Theodore, 296
Schvaneveldt, J. D., 53
Schwartz, M. Susan, 64, 69
Scott, Robert, 9, 13, 14, 16-18, 393
  on negative income tax, 231-63
Securities, interest-bearing, 320

Securities and Exchange Commission (SEC), 348
Segal, David R., 9, 19, 20, 307-308, 378, 385, 392, 393, 395, 396
  on social stratification and family economic behavior, 141-64
Senft, H., 43
Separation, marriage, 254-58
Sharp, H., 40, 42, 43, 52
Sheldon, Eleanor, 19, 140, 381
Sheth, Jagdish, 6
Shore, Arnold, 9, 13, 14, 16-18, 393
  on negative income tax, 231-63
Siegel, J. S., 211
Siegel, Paul M., 140, 147
Silk, Alvin, 47
Simon, Herbert, 36
Smith, Adam, 271
Smith, W. M., Jr., 35, 41
Social aspects, in analyzing consumer behavior, 11
  of life-styles, values, and subjective welfare, 112-15
  of social change, 69-70
Social status, analyzing, 11
  consumption and, 148
  See also Socioeconomic status
Social stratification and family economic behavior, 140-64
Social systems model for consumption, 398
Socioeconomic status, Duncan Index of, 152
  economic satisfaction and, 135, 137
  See also Class; Social status
Spending, 31-34, 41-50
Staelin, R., 45
Standard of living, satisfaction with, 75, 76, 79-82
Status (see Socioeconomic status)
Stern, H., 46
Stock, corporate, 323-25, 330-33, 339, 364-67
Straszheim, Mahlon R., 313
Straus, Murray, 68
Strumpel, Burkhard, 9, 11, 13, 18, 21, 65-69, 376, 378, 382, 393-95, 397
  on economic life-styles, values, and subjective welfare, 65-125
  response to, 126-38
Sweezy, Alan, 197
Systems model for family consumption, 397-402

Taeuber, Conrad, 166
Teenagers, saving by, 53
Theoretical synthesis, 392-403

Thorp, R. C., 37
Time in consumer behavior, 9-10
Townsend, Peter, 39
Treiman, Donald J., 147
Truth Tax, 290-91
Tucker, Charles W., 147

Udell, J. G., 45, 49
Unemployment, 193-96, 203, 204, 334-35

Value factors, methods of studying, 116-17, 132
Values, 69-71, 87-97
 questionnaire on, 118-22
 Strumpel on, 65-125
  response to, 126-38
Van Syckle, Carla, 47

Watts, Harold W., 230, 231, 238, 242, 244, 246, 248, 249
Wealth, consumer management of, 386-88
 distribution of increased, 329-30
 financial and nonfinancial, 317-18
 per capita, 333-34
Weber, Max, 143, 148-52
Weick, Karl, 372, 373
Welfare, defining concept of, 12-14
 relative, 129, 130
 subjective, 65
  future research on, 376-79
  Strumpel on, 65-125
   response to, 126-38
Welfare programs, 235, 238, 239
Wells, H. L., 35, 39

West, C. J., 45
Westoff, Charles F., 187-89
White workers, blue-collar, 110-12
Whyte, W. H., Jr., 48
Wilensky, Harold L., 147
Wilkening, E. A., 37-39
Williamsburg Conference, 3, 6, 392
Wives, fertility of, 172-75
 husbands and, in financial decisions, 36-43
 saving and, 52
 See also Husband-wife families
Wolfe, D. M., 37
Wolgast, E. G., 41-43, 52
Women, attitudes toward number of children of, 205-15
 education of, in fertility study, 176, 179, 180
 employment of, in fertility study, 176, 177
 in fertility study, 172-79
 20-24 years old, 182-200
 See also Marriage patterns
Women's Liberation Movement, 215
Work performance, guaranteed income and, 381-84
 negative income tax and, 237-49
Workers, class consciousness of, 147
 Marx on, 143
 See also Class; Labor force; Occupation

Young, M., 39

Zunich, M., 53

DATE DUE

GAYLORD   PRINTED IN U.S.A.